INDIA
A Financial Sector for the Twenty-first Century

INDIA
A Financial Sector for the Twenty-first Century

Editors

JAMES A. HANSON

SANJAY KATHURIA

THE WORLD BANK

OXFORD
UNIVERSITY PRESS

OXFORD
UNIVERSITY PRESS

YMCA Library Building, Jai Singh Road, New Delhi 110001

Oxford University Press is a department of the University of Oxford. It furthers the
University's objective of excellence in research, scholarship, and education
by publishing worldwide in

Oxford   New York

Athens   Auckland   Bangkok   Bogota   Buenos Aires   Calcutta
Cape Town   Chennai   Dar es Salaam   Delhi   Florence   Hong Kong   Istanbul
Karachi   Kuala Lumpur   Madrid   Melbourne   Mexico City   Mumbai
Nairobi   Paris   Sao Paolo   Singapore   Taipei   Tokyo   Toronto   Warsaw

with associated companies in   Berlin   Ibadan

Oxford is a registered trade mark of Oxford University Press
in the UK and in certain other countries

Published in India
By Oxford University Press, New Delhi

ISBN 0 19 564904 4

Typeset in Times New Roman
by Urvashi Press, Meerut 250001
Printed in India at Rashtriya Printers, Delhi 110032
Published by Manzar Khan, Oxford University Press
YMCA Library Building, Jai Singh Road, New Delhi 110 001

For Peggy, Kamna, Matt and Kunal

Acknowledgements

This book emerged from the papers presented at a conference, India: A Financial Sector for the Twenty-first Century, held in Goa (India) in December 1997. The conference was organized and sponsored by the World Bank and co-sponsored by the Indira Gandhi Institute of Development Research (IGIDR, Mumbai) and USAID's Financial Institutions Reform and Expansion (FIRE) project. We would like to thank our colleagues Lata Ganesh, Anjali Bhardwaj and Farah Zahir for their dedicated effort in managing and organizing the conference in a very professional manner.

Later, Harpinder Oberai and Priya Mathur did an admirable job in helping to put the papers together for publication, including editing, typing up loose ends, and corresponding with the authors. In this, they were ably assisted by Rita Soni.

We would like to thank all the participants for contributing to the success of the conference, and the authors for contributing thought-provoking papers and cooperating so readily with us. Finally, we would like to thank Ajay Shah (IGIDR) and W. Dennis Grubb (FIRE Project) for their many contributions to the conference's success.

5 July, 1999   JAMES A. HANSON
                                                SANJAY KATHURIA

Contents

Tables

Figures

Contributors

JAMES A. HANSON is Economic Advisor, Poverty Reduction and Economic Management, World Bank.

SANJAY KATHURIA is Senior Economist, Poverty Reduction and Economic Management, World Bank.

MONTEK S. AHLUWALIA is Member, Planning Commission, Government of India.

S.S. TARAPORE is Former Deputy Governor, Reserve Bank of India.

JAYATI SARKAR is Assistant Professor, Indira Gandhi Institute of Development Research, Mumbai.

S. VENKITARAMANAN is Former Governor, Reserve Bank of India.

MATHEW JOSEPH is Deputy General Manager, Economic Research Division, Industrial Credit and Investment Corporation of India, ICICI Ltd.

RUPA R. NITSURE is Assistant Vice-President, Economic Research Division, ICICI Ltd.

MADAN SUBNAVIS is Deputy Manager, Economic Research Division, ICICI Ltd.

AJAY SHAH is Assistant Professor, Indira Gandhi Institute of Development Research, Mumbai.

SUSAN THOMAS is Assistant Professor, Indira Gandhi Institute of Development Research, Mumbai.

P. JAYENDRA NAYAK is Executive Ttustee, Unit Trust of India.

S.A. DAVE is Advisor, Industrial Development Bank of India (IDBI) and Former Chairman of Unit Trust of India.

SURJIT S. BHALLA is President, Oxus Research and Investments, New Delhi.

GERARD CAPRIO, JR. is Director, Financial Economics and Manager, Financial Sector Research, World Bank.

STIJN CLAESSENS is Principal Economist, Finance Sector Research, World Bank.

TOM GLAESSNER is Senior Advisor, Soros Management Fund, New York.

Part I

Introduction

India's Financial System: Getting Ready for the Twenty-first Century: An Introduction

JAMES A. HANSON
SANJAY KATHURIA*

India stands at the cusp of the millennium, having largely completed a first phase of financial sector reforms and in need of a second phase to meet some remaining and new challenges. The first phase—liberalization of interest rate and directed credit—began in the early 1990s, hand in hand with real sector deregulation. With prices in the real economy reflecting economic costs more closely and with greater reliance on the private sector, a much larger role for the financial sector in allocating resources to projects with the highest (risk-adjusted) returns naturally became more important. This approach represents a substantial shift from the previous treatment of the financial system as largely an arm of public finance. Cross-country evidence suggests that the new approach should contribute to faster overall development (see Levine, 1997 for a review of the importance of the financial sector in development).

Making this new approach work entails many changes—not just freeing rates and credit allocations but paying more attention to regulation, supervision, and incentives, areas that have been neglected. The changes involve not only individual institutions and sectors of the financial system, but also intersectoral issues.

A fairly rapid change will be needed to allow India to reap, in the near term, the benefits of a financial system appropriate to its development and to the changes that are taking place globally. At the same time,

*The views and interpretations expressed in this paper are those of the authors, and do not necessarily represent the views and policies of the World Bank, or its Executive Directors, or the countries they represent. The authors are grateful to Gerard Caprio, Stijn Claessens, Lloyd Kenward, Ajay Shah, S.S. Tarapore, Marilou Uy, John Williamson, and Roberto Zagha for comments.

there is also concern that the pace and direction of change should minimize the risk of financial distress and macroeconomic instability that has hit many countries (Caprio, this volume). This concern is particularly relevant in light of the East Asian crisis.

Specifically, India faces six interrelated challenges and concerns in its second phase of financial reforms:

1. reducing the fiscal deficit, to lessen the risk of macroeconomic instability and to increase the availability of finance to the private sector;
2. improving banks' credit and risk management, including priority credits;
3. improving systems for identifying and dealing with weak banks;
4. developing capital markets further, in particular developing pensions and insurance to increase finance for long-term investments, including infrastructure;
5. improving financial services to improve the welfare of customers and meet the challenge of globalization of financial services; and
6. managing links to external capital markets.

One key to meeting these challenges and concerns is an incentive framework that encourages individuals and institutions to gather, provide, and prudently use information to make sound decisions, with appropriate rewards for success and penalties for failure and malfeasance. Poor availability and application of information by users of funds is a major factor in bad credit and risk management, and responsible for many weak banks. Such information problems have played an important role in many systemic financial crises, along with macroeconomic instability, excesses of directed credit to favoured borrowers and unproductive projects, and poor regulation and supervision (Caprio, this volume). Of course, improved availability and use of information will not eliminate losses on loans, bonds, and stocks. Some losses will always occur—investment decisions depend on outcomes in an uncertain, unknowable future and are inherently risky. The aim is to reduce these losses and avoid their reaching an aggregate size that generates macroeconomic instability.

Information in financial markets is now recognized as inherently asymmetric—those raising funds inherently know more about the situation than those providing the funds (Stiglitz and Weiss, 1981). It is also important to recognize that information is always changing and needs to be updated; and moreover that although information may not be perfect, it can be gathered and applied with greater or lesser effect. Hence the modern theory of banking emphasizes the role of banks and other financial intermediaries as 'agents' that gather information in order to allocate credit to the highest (risk-adjusted) return (Bernanke, 1983); mutual funds can play the same role in capital markets.[1] Bearing these points in mind, the evaluation of a financial system's performance may need to go beyond the standard static, Pareto-optimality criteria, and apply a more Austrian approach that puts more emphasis on whether incentives appropriately reward good decision making, including the gathering, updating, and application of the necessary information, and penalize bad decision making.

The issue of incentives is especially important in India's financial reforms, particularly given the importance of public financial institutions. India has all the standard problems of the financial sector that result from information asymmetry and 'agency' issues. Moral hazard exists because depositors and lenders count on explicit and implicit government guarantees. Best practice suggests that any guarantees should be very limited, to reduce the disincentives to prudent behaviour from moral hazard, as well as to reduce the risk of macroeconomic instability arising from bailouts. Similarly, best practice suggests that any 'bailouts' should involve substantial costs to bank owners, depositors, and lenders, to avoid giving the wrong incentives.[2] More generally, there is the issue of whether 'fixed' or managed exchange rates also represent an implicit government guarantee, which can generate destabilizing variability in international capital inflows (Bhalla, this volume; Hanson, 1994).

Lack of appropriate incentives in public financial firms adds to these problems. The owner, the government, typically lacks both incentive and means to ensure adequate return on its investment. Political decisions, as opposed to rate of return calculations, are often important in determining resource allocation. Pressures to collect debt service may be low, relative to private financial firms that are longer lasting than most governments. Indeed, political pressures may generate decisions that lead to macroe-

---

[1]Banks and mutual funds also benefit individual savers and the economy by diversifying risks and reducing transactions costs.

[2]See Caprio (this volume); Dziobek and Pazarbasioglu (1997); Rojas-Suarez and Weisbrod (1996); and Sheng (1996). In this regard, India's decision not to provide deposit insurance, *ex post,* to non-bank financial intermediaries was commendable.

conomic instability. Managers and staff in public firms have little incentive to gather and use information to make investment decisions that maximize the risk-adjusted rate of return. Competition to improve services and cut costs is limited within and between sectors. Lenders, investors, and depositors in public banks and mutual funds have little incentive to worry about the use of their funds; de facto there is a public guarantee that taxpayers will make good the promised returns. Illustrating that behaviour is the worldwide tendency, in times of financial crisis, of depositors and lenders to 'flee' from private to public banks, despite the likelihood that public banks have worse balance sheets. All these problems suggest that resolving the issue of incentives will be critical to the success of the second phase of India's financial reforms.

Improved regulation and supervision is another key to meeting the challenges and concerns of the second phase of reform. Prudential regulation and supervision are a major factor in the incentive system, ensuring, for example, that market players have substantial capital at risk.[3] But the role of regulation and supervision goes beyond incentives, to encompass the reduction of systemic risk and possible macroeconomic instability. Private parties may wish to take large amounts of risk and the failure of their activities can generate payments crises that cause system-wide problems/externalities. For this reason, as well as because of the governments' guarantor role in even private sector-dominated financial systems, the government needs to supervise financial intermediaries' risk management and risk taking, limit leveraging relative to

---

[3]Regulation and supervision could also substitute, imperfectly, for incentives in decisions on credit allocation, for example, by defining to whom to lend, how much to lend, and at what prices. But such an approach is a carryover from the old approach to the financial system and the substitution is very imperfect. The asymmetry of information gathering and use between government allocators/regulators and users of funds/the regulated is even greater than between private users and allocators of funds. Government employees have less incentive to find out and use the information than private agents. Regulators must also realize that regulations generate a response by the regulated, to avoid or take advantage of the regulations (Kane, 1993), and take such behaviour into account in framing regulations. In sum, regulation and supervision cannot do what good credit managers do if proper incentives and market frameworks are in place. However, tighter regulation may be needed while a good incentive framework is being put in place. And weaknesses in regulation and supervision can contribute to macroeconomic instability.

capital, and ensure private parties have substantial capital at risk. It also needs to limit lending to related parties and limit lending concentration, which could otherwise be an element of excessive risk taking that could require government bailout.

Regulation and supervision also need to provide market infrastructure of a 'public good' nature. A sound legal framework for collateral and loan recovery is perhaps the most important. Such a framework is a critical part of the government's regulatory apparatus to minimize risks of financial and macroeconomic instability. Regulation and supervision can also encourage competition in the sector. A natural role for the government is encouraging production and dissemination of information, and ensuring that information is correct and timely. For example, the government has an important role to play in auditing and accounting standards. Government can also regulate payments and provide the physical infrastructure for carrying out payments.

The analyses in this volume discuss these challenges and issues, and the reforms that would help deal with them. Preliminary versions of the chapters were presented at a conference that was held in December 1997 and sponsored by the Indira Gandhi Institute of Development Research, the World Bank, and USAID's Financial Institutions Reform and Expansion (FIRE) project. The volume is in some sense a companion to the 1998 Report on the Banking System (the Narasimham II Report) and the prior Report of the Committee on Capital Account Convertibility (Tarapore Report). At the same time, this volume goes beyond those reports in some ways, considering in some detail issues related to the capital market and the pension system, and the challenges posed by financial instability and global financial integration, for example.

THE PRE-REFORM ERA[4]

From the mid-1960s to the early 1990s, India's governments in effect treated the financial system as an instrument of public finance. A complex web of regulations fixed deposit and lending rates and channelled credit to the government and priority sectors at below-market rates. Public institutions dominated the financial system; competition was limited, both within the banking sector and between the banking sector and

[4]For further discussion see Sen and Vaidya (1997), Ch. 1 and Hanson (forthcoming), for example.

capital market and international financial markets. When problems and irregularities developed, regulations were changed to prevent similar outbreaks, without much attention to their impact on the financial system as a whole.

Despite restrictions on deposit rates, India had a relatively 'deep' financial system for a country of its per capita GDP. For example, in 1980 the ratio of broad money to GDP was 36 per cent (World Bank, 1989, p. 188). The stock market was also large in terms of number of listings and market capitalization. For example, in 1985 capitalization (as a per cent of GDP) was similar to Brazil and Korea, countries with much higher GDP per capita (World Bank, 1989, p. 39).

This financial depth partly reflected the avoidance of Latin American style inflation and bank deposit rates that, despite restrictions, roughly matched inflation. For example, the one-year rate on term deposits was kept around the rate of inflation, particularly from 1982 to 1989. Financial depth also reflected the geographic spread of bank offices,[5] stock markets and the reach of salesmen from the Unit Trust of India (UTI, the public sector run 'mutual fund'). In 1983 over 20 per cent of shares were held outside the twelve major cities (Sen and Vaidya, 1997, p. 85). Capital markets grew by providing a (limited) escape valve from financial repression for the larger companies, in terms of ease of listing, higher allowable rates of return, and tax advantages.[6]

On the lending side, financial repression was greater than on the deposit side. Substantial and increasing volumes of credit were chan- nelled to the government at below-market rates through high and increas- ing cash reserve requirements (CRR) and statutory liquidity requirements (SLR), in order to fund a large and increasing government deficit at rela- tively low cost (See Sen and Vaidya, 1997; Hanson, forthcoming). By 1989, these requirements represented 53.5 per cent of deposits. In addi- tion, 40 per cent of advances were to be lent to priority sectors, mainly agriculture and small-scale industry. An additional 10 per cent went to export credit. And credit to fund food procurement averaged about 10 per

[5] See Fry (1988), pp. 142 and 143, for some empirical results linking the spread of bank offices to the ratio of bank deposits to GDP.
[6] See Joseph, Nitsure and Sabnavis (this volume). Trading of stocks and bonds was, however, relatively low. Also, the size of the debt market is difficult to measure. Although large volumes of government debt were bought, buyers were largely the banks, which bought debt and held it to maturity to satisfy the statutory liquidity requirement. Regulations kept interest rates on public sector debt low.

cent of advances during the 1980s. Thus over 80 per cent of portfolio allocations were fixed in broad terms. And interest rates on credits were regulated in minute detail, with the public sector, through the CRR and credits made under the SLR, receiving the largest average cross subsidy (Hanson, forthcoming).

INDIA'S REFORMS OF THE EARLY 1990s

These specifically included financial reform (Ahluwalia, this volume). The idea was to improve resource mobilization and allocate credit more efficiently in broad terms. The first Narasimham Committee Report (November 1991) provided a blueprint for financial reform, particularly in the banking sector. The main recommendations included: (1) reduction in the SLR; (2) reduction in the CRR, payment of interest on the CRR and use of the CRR as a monetary policy instrument; (3) phase-out of directed credit; (4) deregulation of interest rates in a phased manner and bringing interest rates on government borrowing in line with market-determined rates; (5) attainment of BIS/Basle norms for capital adequacy within three years; (6) tightening of prudential norms; (7) entry of private banks and easing of restriction on foreign banks; (8) sale of bank equity to the public; (9) phase-out of Development Finance Institutions' (DFIs') privileged access to funds; (10) increased competition in lending between DFIs and banks, and a switch from consortium lending to syndicated lending; and (11) easing of regulations on capital markets, combined with entry of Foreign Institutional Investors (FIIs) and better supervision.

Broadly speaking these recommendations were gradually implemented, beginning in 1992. The main exception is the continuation of directed credit. Even in this case, the freeing of lending rates (except on loans up to Rs 200,000, where rates have been raised substantially to equal the prime rate) has eased the interest subsidy issue. However, repayment rates on priority lending remain lower than on non-priority lending.

BANKING

Total deposit mobilization increased after reform. However, the additional growth occurred in the non-bank financial companies (NBFCs), where deposits grew over 40 per cent per annum between end 1991–2 and end 1996–7. Banks' deposits did not grow much differently than the previous trend (Sarkar, this volume). At least partly these growth patterns reflected the tightening of monetary policy after liberalization.[7]

Reform strengthened banking institutions (including establishment of debt recovery tribunals), supervision, and regulation. After the initial recognition of the large volume of existing non-performing assets (NPAs), the ratio of NPAs to total assets fell to about 7 per cent, equivalent to about 4 per cent net of provisions.[7] On average, Basle capital adequacy standards were more than met, with 25 of 27 public banks in 1997–8, exceeding the government's new guideline of 9 per cent. Of course, this capital strengthening reflected substantial injections of government funds, which averaged over 0.2 per cent of GDP annually between 1993–4 and 1997–8.

Signs of increased competition included the new banks' rising share of the banking market (partly at the expense of existing private banks), competition between banks and NBFCs, DFIs, and the capital market as sources of funds for industry, and the growth of non-traditional types of lending such as construction and consumer finance. The spread between prime rate and deposit rate also seems to have fallen, even as the interest margin of banks has gone up (Sarkar, this volume). This is suggestive of the combined impact of greater competition in lending to the private sector and more market-based rates on government paper, as well as lower CRR.

FISCAL DEFICIT

The first key challenge for the future is to reduce fiscal deficit and thus, over time, the still high share of government liabilities in the financial sector. The still large deficit raises the risk of macroeconomic instability. The corresponding slower growth of public sector liabilities in total credit would increase the availability of credit to the private sector. Despite reform, the share of government paper in banks' portfolio remains 36–40 per cent of deposits, compared to 37.2 per cent in March 1990 when the SLR was much higher (World Bank, 1998, p. 13). Although the total share of public sector liabilities has declined somewhat, taking into account the fall in the CRR, the decline has been small.[8]

---

[7] Growth played an important role in the decline in the ratio of NPAs to assets. The absolute volume of NPAs rose after the initial tightening of regulations, then fell, but has risen again after 1994–5.

[8] The assessment of banks' credit allocation is complicated by the growth of banks' 'investments' (which do not carry priority sector requirements), as opposed to credit.

The basic reason for the continued large share of public sector liabilities is the history and continuation of large public sector deficits. By 1990–1 central government deficit reached 8.6 per cent of GDP and consolidated public sector deficit 12.3 per cent of GDP. Although by 1992–3 these deficits were reduced, to about 6 and 9 per cent, respectively, they have remained at roughly these high figures ever since (World Bank, 1998, p.8). Thus there is a large stock and flow of public sector debt that continues to have to be held by the financial system; and which crowds out private sector finance.[9] Until public sector deficit is brought down, it will be hard to reduce the large share of public sector debt in the system, and correspondingly, increase the availability of funds for private projects.[10]

With the reduction in directed credit to the public sector, the rate of return on the large public sector debt has risen. However, this rise was dampened by the attractiveness of public sector debt, which has a zero-risk weight under capital adequacy requirements and no priority sector lending requirements. In addition, as Venkitaramanan notes, public banks' credit norms and threat of criminal action by the Central Bureau of Investigation create incentives favouring credit to the public sector.

Other major challenges in the banking sector, identified by Ahluwalia, Sarkar, Tarapore, and Venkitaramanan, are:

- improving credit and risk management of loans to the private sector;
- dealing with weak banks; and
- globalization of banking services and greater capital account convertibility (discussed after the section on capital markets).

[9]Easterly et al., 1994, provide some evidence on this phenomenon across developing countries. When government borrowing is market based, then the crowding-out occurs by raising interest rates above what they would otherwise be. When credit is allocated by fiat, for example as occurred with the high CRR and SLR that existed in India prior to financial sector reforms, the crowding out occurs by forcing banks to hold low interest, public sector debt, and correspondingly generating a high spread between rates on 'free' lending and deposits, in order to make up for low interest rates on public sector debt.

[10]It should also be noted that open market sales to tighten money tend to increase banks' holdings of public sector debt.

CREDIT AND RISK MANAGEMENT

Credit and risk management need substantial improvement in public banks. The 4 per cent ratio of net NPAs to total assets reflects the large volume of government debt in banks' portfolios (and provisions against non-performing assets[11]). However, as a fraction of lending (advances), NPAs are nearly 18 per cent. Although the majority of NPAs reflect pre-reform lending, the ratio of NPAs to advances has remained roughly constant for the last two years, indicating that NPAs are rising about as fast as credit. Moreover, the current industrial slowdown is likely to raise NPAs, as it does in every country. Fears also exist that the quality of loans is even worse than reported, but is hidden by rolling-over bad loans ('evergreening') and loan restructuring agreements. Priority lending accounts for roughly half of the NPAs, but this means that performance of non-priority loans is also not good. India's NPAs are consistent with worldwide experience with public banks, which suggests that public banks find it difficult to lend without generating large non-performing assets.

A substantially improved system of credit and risk management will need to be in place in order to avoid a large increase in NPAs. Best practice suggests that a multipillared approach of better regulation and supervision and better incentives can limit the growth of NPAs while encouraging efficient allocation of resources and faster development (Caprio, this volume).

Improved regulation is needed to limit the riskiness of activities and non-arms length lending, for example. Better supervision is needed to ensure that the regulations are followed and capital is maintained.[12] Moreover, modern approaches to supervision suggest a need to evaluate the whole risk management approach of banks, not just whether their assets are performing or not (Tarapore; Venkitaramanan, this volume), an approach that will entail major upgrading of India's supervisory capacity. Finally, the legal system for recovery of bad debts still needs substantial improvement. In this regard, debt recovery tribunals may be beginning to show some progress, after being tied up in courts.

---

[11]Indian laws make write-offs of loans by public banks, even fully provisioned loans, difficult. Hence NPAs tend to remain on the books for some time and provisions are used to offset them.

[12] For example, in the US, banks are now sold or closed by regulators well before capital is exhausted, if owners are unwilling to inject new funds, in order to reduce losses to the deposit insurance agency.

Better credit management, and incentives to encourage it, are also of major importance in limiting NPAs. As Tarapore points out, banks operating in the same milieu have widely different performances, and that boils down to differences in their credit and risk management. Venkitaramanan also warns that supervision and regulation cannot substitute for good credit management, they can only try to uncover and limit bad credit and risk management, about which the banks being supervised inherently know much more. Owners need the incentive of something at risk, so capital needs to be high and linked to the riskiness of activities (Tarapore, this volume). As noted above, owners, managers, staff, lenders, and depositors should all suffer some loss if NPAs increase too much, in order to provide incentives for prudent behaviour.

Unfortunately, many of the incentive pillars of the multipillar approach are inherently weak in India's largely public sector banking system, as noted above. The owner is the government, which finds it difficult to ensure a sound rate of return on its capital. Indeed, a real issue is whether higher capital ratios in public banks will simply lead the government to provide them more funds that can be used to expand low cost loans. Political pressures abound to lend to favoured clients and in day-to-day decisions. Managers and staff are civil service employees whose salaries are not linked to profit or performance, although selection for higher level positions may be affected by responsiveness to political pressures. Rapid turnover of management, strong unions and limits in control imposed by the large branch network, a complicated administrative network, and poor communications (all mentioned by the first Narasimham Committee) exacerbate the problems of public financial institutions. And, as noted above, depositors in and lenders to India's public banks are even less likely to suffer losses than those in private banks with deposit insurance, as is the case worldwide. Hence the market discipline of public banks is likely to be limited.

A natural approach to resolving these problems is privatization—a reduction in minimum public sector participation below 51 per cent. This would resolve the issue of civil service banker staff. However, unless private management also takes over, i.e. a managing group of private investors holds more of the bank's equity than the government, the government would still control the bank's management. Moreover, privatization is not a panacea. It would require a major improvement in supervision in India, as discussed above, and clear, low limits on deposit insurance. Privatization also faces political and union opposition. Thus far, some Indian public sector banks have sold equity shares. However, legal arrangements are not yet fully in place for directors from the private sector, so ownership functions remain firmly with the government.

PUBLIC SECTOR BANKS

Dealing with weak public sector banks is another major issue. A few banks have much higher levels of NPAs than the average, and low capital, despite large government injections of funds. In India's increasingly competitive financial environment, it is unlikely that weak banks will be able to grow out of their problems. Indeed, attempts to do so, by investing in high return, risky projects, could worsen their situation. To support weak banks, the government has already injected a substantial amount of capital over the last five years. Unless the issue of weak banks can be resolved, the need to provide capital will continue to add to the deficit.[13]

Tarapore asks the fundamental question of whether weak public banks have a 'divine right' to expand credit, that is why should a weak public bank be kept open. Modern banking theory raises one possible answer: that banks are the repository of information on clients and closing them obliterates this information (see, for example, Bernanke, 1983). But the issue is whether Indian public sector banks really have substantial information on clients, given their large holdings of public sector debt, long history of priority lending, and rapid turnover of top management. Another possible answer is that a government-owned bank should not go bankrupt. However, this does not mean that management and staff should not be pushed to improve collections. If they fail, then there is no logical reason to not follow global best practice to the extent possible: replace management, and if necessary merge the weak bank with a sound bank or privatize it after the government downsizes the operation, pays off any public sector loans that are not performing well, and replaces the lost capital as the bank's owner. It is likely that supervision and regulation and laws related to debt recovery too would need improvement. To do otherwise could easily weaken the incentives that do exist for prudent lending and loan payment and, ultimately, raise costs to the government. Moreover, it is possible that India is over-banked. In that context, resuscitating weak banks runs the risk of

---

[13]Government injections of capital took the form of new government debt in exchange for equity, which under Indian budgetary conventions does not add to government spending, nor the deficit. However, the interest on this debt is, of course, part of government spending, and does add to the deficit.

bringing the problems of India's sick industry policy into the banking system—saving the weakest firms in an industry at the cost of jeopardizing the next weakest tier of firms.

Tarapore explores another option—converting weak banks into so-called 'narrow banks', which hold only government paper, and gradually allowing these banks to wither away. Indian banks are already fairly 'narrow', with almost 50 per cent of deposits held in the form of public sector liabilities. And recent replacements of capital have taken the form of more government liabilities. Hence turning weak banks into narrow banks is not as radical a change as it might appear. Although such an approach might imply some annual losses because of the wage bill, it would eliminate any losses from further NPAs. And wage costs could be cut over time by attrition and reduction of branches. Finally, such an approach could provide an incentive to better performance by other banks' management and staff.

An alternative approach to weak banks is an 'Asset Reconstruction Fund' that would take bad loans off the bank's books and try to collect. However, such an approach would still require the government to put funds into banking, either immediately and directly if the Fund buys the assets at or below their provisioned value, or over time and indirectly if the Fund buys the NPAs at par, to cover the Fund's losses. A Fund may also not lead to a change in the management and staff which made the bad loans. Other issues are (a) whether a Fund might actually reduce the collections of existing bad loans in the Indian context, given the possibility of legal challenges to the transfer of loans and associated collateral, and the possibility of losses due to errors in the transfer process; (b) whether the Fund might not actually weaken collections by removing the most experienced collection of personnel from the banks, and (c) whether the Fund might reduce incentives for borrowers to pay and banks to collect, especially since, in the Indian context, such a fund is likely to be long lived. Another question is whether access to the Fund would be limited to the weakest banks, which would put their closest competitors at a disadvantage, or would be system-wide. If system-wide, there may be risks, given the worldwide experience with system-wide Recapitalization Funds (Caprio, this volume), of undermining investor confidence in India's banking sector and macroeconomic stability in general.

CAPITAL MARKETS

Capital markets were relatively large in India at the end of the 1980s, as noted above. This reflected the markets' rapid growth during the 1980s as a source of finance for the larger corporations, especially the debenture market (Joseph et al., this volume). During this period capital markets served as something of an escape valve for the larger corporations from the repressed banking system. Despite the capital markets' size, they suffered from numerous problems (Nayak; and Shah and Thomas, this volume). Information and transparency were limited, reflecting the individual, dealer-based trading system (without market makers), and the associated difficulty in determining the actual price traded, or even highs and lows during the day. Moreover the Controller of Capital Market Issues' regulations on pricing initial public offerings (IPOs) and the time between application and issue kept the IPOs from reflecting the market—limited price discovery. Capital markets were thus ineffective in fulfilling their normal function of providing even basic (price) information, not to speak of the limitations on accounting standards that made it difficult to determine a firm's profitability.

Trading in the capital markets was also costly, reflecting the lack of competition due to the Bombay Stock Exchange's (BSE) dominance,[14] limited number of dealers, and high costs for accessing the market through a system of sub-brokers.[15] Shah and Thomas estimate that direct costs of a small, one-way, retail transaction were about 5 per cent. In addition, execution/settlement of trades was unreliable, with orders difficult to execute on a given day; delivery unsure and slow, particularly outside Bombay; and counterfeit shares a problem. Occasionally, dealers went bankrupt, preventing completion of transactions and, in some cases, leading to a paralysis of payments for the whole market. Not surprisingly, retail trading was low.

Mutual funds can help retail investors improve their access to information and reduce transactions costs, but in India mutual funds were limited until the late 1980s. The government-run UTI had a legal monopoly in the mutual fund market until 1987–8, and then faced competition only from public sector banks until 1993–4. Even from 1988–9 to 1993–4 its resource mobilization still averaged over 80 per cent of the funds put into mutual funds annually (Nayak, this volume). Moreover, the UTI's re-

[14]Arbitrage between the exchanges was weak, reflecting both limited information associated with the dealer system and poor telecommunications

[15]It was illegal for one stock exchange to set up a sub-local in another city.

source mobilization was similar to the size of new issues during much of this period, making it a dominant player in the market.

Capital market reforms began in 1992, reflecting two factors, the general climate of reform and government response to the 'scam of 1992' (Nayak, this volume; Basu and Dalal, 1993). The reforms almost wholly affected the equity market. The bond market, though surprisingly large for a country of India's per capita GDP (see World Bank, 1995), still reflects many of the pre-1993 problems (Nayak, this volume) and would benefit from reforms similar to those that occurred in the equity market.

Equity market reforms took three approaches: (a) the Securities and Exchange Board of India (SEBI) was given regulatory powers in 1992,[16] including regulation of new issues; (b) a new exchange, the National Stock Exchange (NSE), was created in 1992 and began operation in 1994, competing with the Bombay Stock Exchange; and (c) development of a share depository. In addition, FIIs, beginning in 1992, new mutual fund operators since 1993–4, and Indian firms were allowed to issue global depository rights (GDRs) offshore. These additional resources provided finance for India's private-sector-led growth in the mid-1990s, and contributed to a stock market boom.

SEBI took over and liberalized the regulation of new issues, including, recently, allowing book building. It has also increased information requirements for listed shares. It has gradually built up a corpus of regulations. The NSE rapidly attained a much greater volume than the Bombay market, an unprecedented success for a new exchange. Competition from the NSE contributed to substantial reduction in transactions costs, to the point where they are now among the lowest in the world (Shah and Thomas, this volume), and to substantial increase in transparency and liquidity. This reflected the NSE's computer-based, order-matching, which is accessed through a system of satellite-linked terminals throughout the country, a system that the Bombay exchange is also using now.[17] Finally, the depository has eased concerns about counterfeit shares and will eventually improve settlement. Ten stocks, accounting for a substan-

---

[16]It had been constituted in 1988.

[17]To some extent, the Bombay Exchange's failure to embrace modern technology can be attributed to regulations that did not permit a 'city' exchange to expand into another area, and to the poor quality of telecommunications services. At the same time, one can also argue that lack of competition was a major factor in the failure of the Bombay Exchange to expand nationally.

tial part of the exchange volume, are now fully traded through the depository.[18] Reflecting these developments, plus inflows from and trading by FIIs, and unprecedented economic growth, the stock market boomed in the mid-1990s, with a large number of new issues.

Although progress has been great, substantial problems remain in what Nayak calls market 'microstructure'. There is, of course, a need to upgrade information through better auditing and accounting. In the primary market, despite improvements, the new issue process is still limited in its potential use of market information (price discovery) by the length of the process and regulations on underwriting, listings on multiple exchanges, and sales to retail investors.[19] Other methods of pricing new issues, discussed in the chapter by Shah and Thomas and that by Nayak, may lead to better results.

The recent decline in the stock market seems to have hit many of the new issues relatively hard.[20] Trading in many of these issues is negligible and many of the firms have failed to fulfil the information requirements to maintain their listings. Some observers attribute a part of the market's slide and the lack of new issues to investors' disgruntlement with the previous outpouring of new issues. These problems suggest that, in the future, the equity market may not provide much finance for smaller companies. Correspondingly, the number of IPOs is likely to be much smaller than in the past. Venture capital firms may be a more suitable source for financing small companies. In this context, a re-examination of the regulatory framework for venture capital may be helpful.

In the secondary market, the issue is further improvement in the

---

[18]This does not mean that shares cannot be physically held, only that shares would be taken from the depository on purchase, or put back into the depository on sale.

[19]Some research, cited in Shah and Thomas (this volume) and Nayak (this volume), suggests that new issues were underpriced (as measured by their later performance compared to the market) in the first half of the 1990s. However, that result may relate to the period studied and seems to have been more prevalent in smaller issues, where concerns of market manipulation exist (Nayak, this volume). More generally, a market test—the large number of new issues in this period—suggests that the issuers generally did not consider the shares undervalued. Studies of US initial offerings also suggest underpricing, but that it is quickly eliminated (Ibbotson, Sindelar, and Ritter et al., 1989).

[20]In the US, a large number of new issues were also made in the recent bull market; they too have typically done much worse than the market recently, in some cases dropping below their initial issue prices.

settlement process—greater use of the depository, moving to a fixed, shorter, rolling settlement (daily netting, with final settlement at T+5, then T+3, which the 'Group of Thirty' suggested should be the norm), and elimination of counterparty risk. As noted, the benefits of the depository are great. SEBI's intent is to move more stocks to the depository over time. However, until a sufficient volume of shares in a given stock moves to depository trading, the depository actually reduces liquidity, to some degree, by splitting the market into depository and non-depository trades. As the depository comes into greater use, it will make shorter, rolling settlements easier.

The current, lengthy settlement arrangements leave the market subject to what is effectively futures trades. This is exacerbated by '*badla*', a deal between traders that allows a carryover of positions into another settlement period for a negotiated fee.[21] Allowing such activity may provide some additional liquidity and trading. However, the corresponding possibility of highly leveraged trading leaves the market vulnerable to bankruptcies and may be a factor in the Indian markets' periodic payments crises, such as occurred in April 1995 and in June 1998. Moving to rolling settlement will reduce such problems of bankruptcy and foster a more sustained growth of liquidity.

Moving toward rolling settlements, with strict margin requirements, and greater use of the depository will also help resolve another problem of settlement—counterparty risk. Moreover, failure of one party to a trade to meet its payments obligations can cascade into generalized problems for the whole market. Besides requiring substantial capital and limiting margin strictly (which also entails fairly continuous marking to market), counterparty risk can be reduced by setting up a clearing corporation that is counterparty to trades (see the chapters by Shah and Thomas; Nayak).[22] The fund's capital would presumably be provided by exchange members. However, until the settlement process is shortened

---

[21]'*Badla*' is effectively like a futures contract with an uncertain expiration date (in the BSE, moreover, there was no margin requirement until June 1998, when a 5 per cent initial margin was imposed. NSE requires a 15 per cent initial margin). This makes it hard to determine/quote a 'cash' market price. It also is a well-known result that undated futures contracts contribute to 'speculative bubbles' (Shah and Thomas, this volume). SEBI banned '*badla*' in December 1993 but allowed it to resume in late 1997.

[22]So far, only the NSE has a full settlement guarantee fund. The BSE has a guarantee fund if the dealer goes bankrupt.

and margins and marking-to-market are regulated, such an approach would face excessive risks. Such a fund's risks would also be excessive until it is either not held responsible for counterfeit shares, or until trading becomes centralized in the depository.

A final issue is the impact of public 'mutual funds', including one of a large size, on incentives and the market. Generally speaking, well-organized capital markets reduce many of the 'agency' and incentive problems of banking, including those associated with explicit or implicit guarantees of bank liabilities. However, the latter potential benefit is negated to the extent that public institutions, such as the UTI and the public banks' mutual funds, offer market-based instruments bearing guaranteed returns. In this case, the investor in the instrument need pay no attention to the mutual funds' investment strategy, because a public institution has guaranteed it. No private firm can offer such a guarantee, so the regulatory 'playing field' is not level.[23] Finally, such a guarantee represents an implicit government liability which, if called, could add to macroeconomic instability.

The UTI's large size, relative to the markets, means that its activities influence the market. This makes it difficult for the UTI to change its position, without influencing prices.[24] Moreover, its public ownership leaves open the risk that it will operate for political as well as economic goals. These problems suggest that it might be worth exploring ways to maintain the UTI's excellent resource mobilization facilities, but split up and privatize the investment side of the business into smaller units.

PENSION AND INSURANCE REFORM

Pension and insurance reform are keys to mobilizing more long-term funds. India's pension system is still in its infancy (Dave, this volume). A shift towards a more fully funded, transferable pension system would provide more long-term, investible resources for capital markets and good incomes for retirees. Perhaps the largest gains would come from a shift of the public sector's pension system from its current, pay-as-you-

---

[23]The availability or unavailability of derivatives does not change this point. A derivative guaranteeing a high return would cost a lot, making it impossible to guarantee a high return once the cost of the derivative is taken into account.

[24]Again, the issue is not one of the unavailability of derivatives, the size of the UTI means it would have difficulty finding a credible counterparty at reasonable price, if it wished to carry out a trade.

go approach to a more fully funded system. However, the public sector's payment of both its existing pension obligations and its contributions to a fully funded system for the future retirees, not to speak of any extension of coverage, would add significantly to the already large public sector deficit. Hence concerns of macroeconomic stability suggest the need to reduce the current high fiscal deficit as pension reform is undertaken.

Liberalization of the insurance industry would also provide more resources for the long-term capital market. Cuts in liquidity requirements on insurance would mean additional resources for private investment, provided, of course, that a reduced fiscal deficit decreases the government's funding needs. Liberalization of entry into insurance, including foreign firms, would increase competition and thereby improve services, products, and prices facing buyers of insurance. As a result demand for insurance would grow, increasing the resources mobilized by the insurance industry.

FINANCIAL SERVICES

Improving financial services in banking and capital markets, as well as insurance, would yield substantial benefits for Indian firms and households and meet the challenges of the on-going globalization of financial services. As noted above, India has done well in making financial services available. Its 65,000 bank offices and widespread links to capital markets have provided much broader access to the financial system than would be expected in a country of India's size, per capita income, and poor telecommunications. And costs of intermediation in India's banking and stock markets are reasonable by international standards.

Now, however, quality improvements are needed. As in the real sector, it is no longer sufficient just to supply low quality services at low cost. National efficiency and competitiveness demand better, more varied services. For example, improvements are needed in inter-branch and inter-bank linkages, and in payments, which are lagging behind the need for better customer service and transfers and the desired speed-up in settlements of stock transactions. Although public banks' costs are not particularly high by international standards, this reflects India's low labour costs. Overstaffing is the rule, even compared to private banks in India, and service quality is low by international standards. Strong unions have imposed stringent work rules and limited computerization, ATMs, etc. (Sarkar, this volume), to the detriment of users and development. A major upgrade in financial services will depend upon substantial changes such as removal of public financial employees from civil service status and privatization. Without a major upgrade in service and pay-ments systems, as well as reductions in political interference, directed credits, and unprofitable branches, it is difficult to see how Indian public banks can compete internationally without subsidies or protection. As noted above, substantial improvements in settlement arrangements are still needed in capital markets.

Claessens and Glaessner suggest that increased competition in the financial system, in particular allowing greater international competition, would provide an impetus to improve quality and lower costs of financial services, while helping to make the system more robust by encouraging the spread of best practices and standards, the growth of financial information, and ownership by investors with more diversified portfolios who are less subject to single country risk. India lags the East Asian and Latin American countries in opening up financial services to foreign competition, particularly in insurance (Claessens and Glaessner, this volume; Williamson and Mahar, 1998).

LINKS WITH EXTERNAL CAPITAL MARKETS

Managing links with external capital markets and opening up capital account have become highly discussed issues since the East Asian crisis. India maintains controls on international capital movements, notably on the holding or use of foreign exchange by Indian citizens and residents. However, the financial sector reforms have liberalized Indian firms' abil-ity to raise and hold money offshore and foreign investors' and non-resi-dent Indians' ability to invest in India and to repatriate their investments. The 1997 Committee on Capital Account Convertibility (Tarapore Com-mittee) recognized the gains to capital account convertibility, in terms of increased funding for investment and risk diversification.[25] It recom-

[25]See for example Hanson, 1994, for a discussion of these issues and summary of some empirical evidence on them. Obviously, measuring risk diversification is not easy, but one can observe that two-way trade in assets has grown enormously and one explanation is risk diversification. As to the contribution of foreign finance, in industrial countries, well-known studies (e.g. Feldstein and Hororika, 1980) suggest that foreign finance plays a small role, although there is debate on the results. In developing countries, foreign funds seem to represent a larger fraction of investment (although that fraction is still limited by the unsustainability of large current account deficits) and financial intermediation (as measured, for example, by the high ratio of external debt to GDP). Bhalla finds more evidence for the

mended that India move towards capital convertibility over a three-year horizon, at the same time as the fiscal deficit was reduced significantly, the financial system was further liberalized and strengthened, and exchange rate management was shifted to maintenance of a real exchange rate band backed by large reserves.

The Committee's Report was issued about one month before Thailand's floating of the baht made the East Asian crisis obvious. The crisis' spread to countries with capital account convertibility has dampened what had been growing international enthusiasm for opening the capital account, especially since contagion seems to have been limited in countries with more closed capital accounts, like China and India. Of course, it should also be noted, the immediate impact of this was also limited in Latin America, despite Latin American countries' open capital accounts.

Although there is no doubt that openness of the capital account was one factor in the spread of the crisis, openness to flows of capital and goods also probably contributed to Indonesia's, Malaysia's, and Thailand's strong development performance over the previous thirty years.[26] Two other major factors in the crisis were:

- a weakening of the macroeconomic stability and rapidity of adjustment which had been important in East Asia's earlier success

---

impact of foreign capital flows on investment than previous studies, using data on first differences between saving and investment in the major industrial and developing countries.

[26]Over the period 1965–94, GDP growth averaged 6.6 per cent p.a. in Indonesia, 6.9 per cent in Malaysia, and 7.8 per cent in Thailand. Among the other countries with over 20 million population, only Korea averaged over 5 per cent p.a. growth during this period; the next highest growth rate for this period was Turkey's 4.9 per cent and India averaged 4.5 per cent. Obviously many factors contributed to the East Asian economies' performance (see World Bank, 1993, for an extended discussion). Indonesia, Malaysia, and Thailand achieved their high growth rates with much lower rates of investment than Korea (or China which has shown rapid growth in the last twenty years). Two notable differences between Indonesia, Malaysia, and Thailand, *vis-à-vis* China, Korea, and the other countries with over 20 million population, were lower levels of protection and relatively open capital accounts. These three countries had high average current account deficits since the mid-1970s, high ratios of (the present value) external debt to GDP, and large inflows of private equity capital (as well as foreign investment), compared to other large developing countries.

(World Bank, 1993), as measured by substantial increases in already large current account deficits and large actual and potential quasi-fiscal deficits associated with the financial system;[27]

- the channelling of large volumes of external funds through weak financial systems—a recognized hazard (World Bank, 1997)—or directly to firms that chose to borrow offshore rather than in the undersized and costly domestic financial market. Financial institutions were severely under-capitalized/over-leveraged, with large volumes of NPAs. Financial institutions, and non-financial firms, also relied excessively on short-term, external funds. These weaknesses made it difficult to withstand even a small shock or reversal of creditor confidence.

According to Bhalla, the exchange regime also played an important role in the crisis and its spread—East Asia's fixed or managed exchange rates meant that sooner or later a low-cost, speculative opportunity against the currencies would develop. A further question is whether these exchange rate policies also encouraged excessive inflows, by providing implicit exchange rate guarantee to foreign investors and local borrowers (for as long as reserves held out). Thus inflexible exchange rates may have increased the pro-cyclical variability of capital flows (see Hanson, 1994). Bhalla argues that floating exchange rates would be desirable to reduce such problems, as well as to allow markets to play a greater role in the economy and thereby increase economic freedom, which contributes to development.

---

[27]Current account deficits in Indonesia, Korea, Thailand, and Malaysia in 1995 and 1996 were substantially higher than in any other two consecutive years in the previous ten years. Thailand's Central Bank provided roughly $12 billion in credit to the non-bank financial system between June 1996 and June 1997, equivalent to roughly three-fourths of base money in June 1996. This, plus the provision of low interest loans to stock market investors, was a monetary stance at odds with the fixed exchange rate regime. In addition, the Thai Central Bank incurred substantial losses on the forward exchange contracts it had used to defend the baht, after it devalued. In Indonesia and Malaysia, the potential cost of large volumes of non-performing assets, recognized and unrecognized, became a worry to investors once Thailand failed to resolve its problems. Korea channelled an estimated $100 billion of short-term external capital to its industrial firms, in an effort to ease the impact of a recession, while maintaining a relatively fixed exchange rate, and eventually guaranteed a substantial part of the banks' debts; the government, at least tacitly, allowed this inflow by not monitoring it effectively.

In discussing the openness of the capital account and the management of capital flows, it is useful to distinguish between regulations that level the playing field between foreign and domestic funding, and those that are aimed at restricting foreign capital inflows and outflows. One lesson of the East Asian crisis is that excessive dependence on foreign funds can develop if domestic taxes, reserve requirements, and regulations raise the costs of domestic financial intermediation.[28] In East Asia, these policies, and the domestic banks' need to cover their large NPAs, helped make domestic funds more costly than foreign funds, especially given the exchange rate's limited movement.[29] Note also that this level-playing-field argument applies not only to financial intermediaries but also suggests that *firms'* direct borrowings offshore should be subject to charges that approximate the costs of these explicit and implicit taxes on domestic loans or bond issues. In Chile, for instance, offshore borrowings were subject to a 'reserve requirement'.[30] In the Indian context, this approach would mean, for example, that both financial and non-financial firms taking offshore bank loans would be subject to taxes that are equivalent to the costs of the CRR, SLR, and priority lending requirements. Such an approach would not only reduce the attractiveness of foreign funds that arises solely from domestic financial repression, it would also provide greater equality in funding costs/payment of the effective taxes on domestic financial intermediation across non-financial firms.

Capital account controls go beyond levelling the playing field and discriminate against foreign capital inflows. They include limits on holding foreign exchange, limits on foreign exchange exposure, and/or taxes on or minimum holding periods for foreign exchange inflows. Another type of control involves requiring financial institutions to hold

[28]Another factor in the high lending rates in East Asia was the high level of non-performing assets.

[29]It is worth noting that in East Asia even hedged foreign borrowings would have been less costly than domestic bank loans, but few borrowers hedged their exposure. Of course, hedging a substantial portion of the large foreign exchange exposure would have raised the issue of systemic risk because of possible bankruptcy of those taking the risk.

[30]The requirement was setup so that the cost was greater for short-term holdings than for long-term holdings—a fraction of the inflow had to be held in 'reserves' for at least one year, which means a somewhat tougher restriction on (short-term) flows.

additional capital against foreign exchange liabilities, to reflect the systemic risk that external capital adds to the macroeconomy. The arguments for such policies range from avoiding a loss of saving, to increasing the monetary policy's effectiveness under a fixed exchange rate regime (which could also be done by allowing greater exchange rate flexibility), to reducing systemic macroeconomic risk, to curbing speculative flows. Of course, there are costs to capital controls, in terms of reduced access to funding for investment and risk diversification. In terms of public finance theory, many of these policies can be considered taxes that have differential incidence and distortionary implications, particularly in the context of domestic inflation. Finally, there are issues of the implementation and effectiveness of such policies[31] and their impact, if maintained for a lengthy period, including their possible stimulus to corruption. The general conclusion seems to be that capital account controls may be of some help as a short-run, crisis management tool. They also have differences between domestic and international interest rates which, in concert with other types of financial repression, have reduced domestic public sector debt service payments. However, capital controls' ability to affect the composition of the capital account is less clear and attempts to maintain them over longer periods may slow down the needed reforms, stimulate development of mechanisms to avoid the controls, and create a constituency, in the bureaucracy and the private sector, to maintain the controls beyond the time when they are justified by national interests (on these conclusions, see, for example, Claessens, Dooley and Warner, 1995; Dooley, 1995; IMF, 1998; Montiel and Reinhart, 1998).

These considerations and worldwide experience suggest that the policies for managing the links to external markets go much beyond capital account controls. For example, in addition to levelling the playing field, in the case of public firms where the government offers an implicit guarantee to external lenders, the government, as owner, needs to limit offshore borrowing to prudent levels. More generally, the East Asian crisis, and the earlier Latin American debt crisis of the 1980s, highlight the need to maintain macroeconomic stability and sustainable current

---

[31]The issue is not only over- and under-invoicing to obtain foreign exchange. For example, with various forward contracts and derivatives, often off-balance sheet, it is possible to appear to satisfy holding period requirements while actually leaving the system exposed to short-term outflows.

account and fiscal deficits[32] and to strengthen the financial system, particularly incentives for prudent behaviour, the regulatory and supervisory framework, and the long-term capital market. A prerequisite for greater capital account convertibility, as well as, more importantly, rapid, sustainable development, is thus to meet the challenges listed in the introduction, i.e. achieve a low fiscal deficit and sound financial system.

REFERENCES

Basu, D. and S. Dalal. (1993). *The Scam: Who Won, Who Lost, Who Got Away*. New Delhi: UBS Publishers.

Bernanke, B. (1983). 'Non-monetary Effects of the Financial Crisis in the Propagation of the Great Depression'. *American Economic Review*, vol. 73, no. 3 (June), pp. 257–76.

Claessens, C., M. Dooley, and A. Warner. (1995). 'Portfolio Capital Flows: Hot or Cool'. *World Bank Economic Review*, vol. 9, no. 1 (January), pp. 153–74.

Dooley, M. (1995). 'Capital Controls: A Survey of the Literature'. National Bureau of Economic Research Working Paper no. 5352.

Dziobek, C. and C. Pazarbasioglu. (1997). 'Lessons and Elements of Best Practice'. In W. Alexander et al. *Systemic Bank Restructuring and Macroeconomic Policy*. Washington, D.C.: IMF.

Easterly, W., Carlos A. Rodrignez, and Klaus Schmidt-Hebbel. (1994). *Public Sector Deficits and Macroeconomic Performance*. Washington, D.C.: World Bank.

Feldstein, M. and C. Horioka. (1980). 'Domestic Saving and International Capital Flows'. *Economic Journal*, vol. 90, no. 358 (June), pp. 314–29.

Fry, M. (1988). *Money Interest and Banking in Economic Development*. Baltimore, MD.: Johns Hopkins.

Hanson, James A. (forthcoming). 'Interest Liberalization in India and Indonesia'. In G. Caprio, J. Hanson, and P. Honohan (eds), *Interest Liberalization, How Far; How Fast*.

——. (1994). 'An Open Capital Account: A Brief Survey of the Issues and the Results'. In G. Caprio, I. Atiyas, and J.A. Hanson (eds), *Financial Reform: Theory and Experience*. New York : Cambridge University Press, pp. 323–56.

[32]The 1980s Latin American crisis showed the dangers of large fiscal deficits and large offshore borrowing. However, the recent crisis, as well as the experience of Chile in the 1980s, suggests that a small fiscal deficit is a necessary, but not a sufficient, condition for avoiding an external payments crisis—the private sector can still borrow offshore excessively, particularly when there are excessive incentives to borrow offshore rather than domestically.

Ibbotson, R., J. Sindelar, and J. Ritter. (1989). 'Initial Public Offerings'. *Journal of Applied Corporate Finance*, vol. 79 (March), pp. 125–37.

International Monetary Fund. (1998). *International Capital Markets: Developments, Prospects, and Key Policy Issues.* Washington, D.C.: IMF.

Kane, E. (1993). 'Reflexive Adaptation of Business to Regulation and Regulation to Business'. *Law and Policy*, vol. 15, no. 3 (July), pp. 179–89.

Levine, R. (1997). 'Financial Development and Economic Growth'. *Journal of Economic Literature* (June).

Montiel, P. and C. Reinhart. (1998). 'Dynamics of Capital Movements to Emerging Economies During the 1990s'. Mimeo, Williams College, USA.

Rojas-Suarez, L. and S. Weisbrod. (1996). 'The Do's and Don'ts of Banking Crisis Management'. In R. Hausman and L. Rojas-Suarez (eds), *Banking Crises in Latin America.* Washington, D.C.: Inter-American Development Bank. Distributed by Johns Hopkins University Press.

Sen, K. and R. Vaidya. (1997). *The Process of Financial Liberalization in India.* Delhi: Oxford University Press.

Sheng, A. (1996). *Bank Restructuring: Lessons from the 1980s.* Washington, D.C.: World Bank.

Stiglitz, J. and A. Weiss. (1981). 'Credit Rationing in Markets with Imperfect Information'. *American Economic Review*, vol. 71, no. 3 (June), pp. 393–410.

Williamson, J. and M. Mahar. (1998). 'A Review of Financial Liberalization'. South Asia Regional Discussion Paper, no. IDP-171.

World Bank. (1989). *World Development Report.* Oxford: Oxford University Press.

_____ . (1993). *The East Asian Miracle.* Oxford: Oxford University Press.

_____ . (1993). *The Emerging Asian Bond Market.* Washington, D.C.: World Bank.

_____ . (1997). *Private Capital Flows to Developing Countries: The Road to Global Integration.* New York: Oxford University Press.

_____ . (1998). *India: Macroeconomic Update: Reforming for Growth and Poverty Reduction.*Washington, D.C.: World Bank.

Reforming India's Financial Sector: An Overview

MONTEK S. AHLUWALIA*

016

G20

Financial sector reforms have long been regarded as an important part of the agenda for policy reform in developing countries. Traditionally, this was because they were expected to increase the efficiency of resource mobilization and allocation in the real economy which in turn was expected to generate higher rates of growth. More recently, they are also seen to be critical for macroeconomic stability. This is especially so in the aftermath of the East Asian crisis, since weaknesses in the financial sector are widely regarded as one of the principal causes of collapse in that region. Following East Asia, soundness of the financial system has been elevated to a position similar to that of fiscal deficit as one of the 'fundamentals' for judging the health of an economy.[1] Developing countries can expect increasing scrutiny on this front by international financial institutions, and rating agencies and countries which fail to come up to the new standards are likely to suffer through lower credit ratings and poorer investor perceptions. In this background it is both relevant and timely to examine how far India's financial sector measures up to what is now expected.

Reform of the financial sector was identified, from the very beginning, as an integral part of the economic reforms initiated in 1991. As

*The views expressed in this chapter are those of the author and do not necessarily reflect the views of the Commission. Acknowledgements are due to Surjit Bhalla, M. Damodaran, James Hanson, Rajiv Kumar, S.S. Tarapore and C.M. Vasudev for helpful comments.

[1]A weak banking system is viewed with some justification as a fiscal time bomb waiting to go off because banking crises typically force government to recapitalize the banks in order to avoid a larger systemic crisis, involving a fiscal burden which can be quite large as a percentage of GDP (see for example Caprio and Klingebiel, 1996).

early as August 1991, the government appointed a high level Committee on the Financial System (the Narasimham Committee) to look into all aspects of the financial system and make comprehensive recommendations for reforms. The Committee submitted its report in November 1991, making a number of recommendations for reforms in the banking sector and also in the capital market. Shortly thereafter, the government announced broad acceptance of the approach of the Narasimham Committee and a process of gradualist reform in the banking sector and in the capital market was set in motion, a process that has now been under way for more than six years. In this overview, I propose to highlight only some of the more important achievements of financial sector reforms thus far and to focus on the critical issues which need to be addressed if we are to make further progress.

1. LIBERALIZATION AND REGULATION: PARALLEL NOT CONTRADICTORY THRUSTS

Before examining the specific achievements of financial sector reforms in India, it is useful to reflect on the principles underlying these reforms and their congruence with international practice. Financial sector reforms all over the world have been driven by two apparently contradictory forces. The first is a thrust towards liberalization, which seeks to reduce, if not eliminate a number of direct controls over banks and other financial market participants. The second is a thrust in favour of stronger regulation of the financial sector. This dual approach is also evident in the reforms attempted in India and the background and rationale for it need to be well understood.

The case for liberalization of financial markets is based on efficiency considerations similar to those used to justify liberalization in the real sector. The efficiency losses generated by various types of direct controls over banks have been extensively discussed by economists concerned with the problems of 'financial repression' in developing countries.[2] Direct controls on interest rates, high cash reserve requirements, mandatory investments in government securities, and other forms of directed credit policies all amount to a tax on financial intermediation which has the effect of suppressing the level of intermediation below what would

[2]See especially Shaw (1973) and McKinnon (1973) and a more recent review by Fry (1997).

otherwise prevail and also of reducing the allocative efficiency of such intermediation. Both effects lead to a loss of efficiency and lower real growth in the economy. These arguments against financial repression were a reaction to the widespread practice of intrusive and direct intervention by the government in banking systems in most developing countries and played an important role in promoting financial liberalization in Latin America in the late 1970s and early 1980s.

The case for stronger regulation on the other hand derives from the perception that financial markets are different from goods markets in important respects and liberalization of such markets aimed at allowing market forces free play can lead to inferior outcomes.[3] Financial markets are characterized by significant asymmetries of information, moral hazard problems, and principal-agent problems and because of these features a free market equilibrium may not have the efficiency characteristics normally associated with market equilibria in the goods market. For example, assymmetries of information in credit markets lead to market equilibria where interest rates are typically below market clearing levels resulting in excess demand for credit with banks resorting to credit rationing. However, this does not necessarily entail inefficiency as implied in the financial repression literature, to be eliminated by letting interest rates rise to market clearing levels.[4] Similarly moral hazard problems can lead banks under financial stress to engage in high cost mobilization of deposits with risky lending at high interest rates to shore up profitability. Assymmetry of information generates principal-agent problems in capital markets because corporate managements have incentives to behave in a manner which is not consistent with maximization of shareholder value, thus calling into question the efficiency of equilibria in capital markets. Some of these problems, especially those related to information asymmetry and moral hazard, can be mitig by ensuring that banks and capital markets are subjected to strong prudential norms

---

[3]See Stiglitz and Weiss (1981) and Stiglitz (1994). For a skeptical view of the efficiency of stock markets in allocating capital and their role in developing countries, see Singh (1997).

[4]It should be noted however that the particular explanation for a 'repressed' interest rate does not justify repression through government control. It only implies that prudential behaviour by the banks would lead them to restrain interest rates below market levels on their own. If government does fix interest rates, the extent of the distortion is measured by the extent to which this forces banks to repress interest rates below the level they should themselves choose.

with transparent accounting and disclosure requirements and strong external supervision, all of which would encourage banks towards more prudent conduct of banking. Similar considerations apply to the functioning of capital markets. Without such regulation, liberalization leading to free play of unregulated and unsupervised financial markets can lead to suboptimal outcomes.

Financial markets are also special because of possible systemic effects and this provides another justification for regulation. The failure of an individual participant such as a large bank cannot be viewed in the same way as the failure of an individual supplier in the goods market. Closure of a large bank can lead to panic and irrational behaviour by depositors with other banks in the system, regardless of the actual financial health of these banks, because depositors typically do not have full information on these issues. Such panic could precipitate serious liquidity problems which could force otherwise solvent banks to fail, with highly destabilizing systemic effects in terms of a break down in the payments system and a contraction of credit. To avoid such shocks the central bank has to be ready to act as a lender of last resort, willing to provide liquidity to otherwise solvent banks threatened by irrational panic. However, a lender of last resort facility has to be predicated on continuing supervision of the banking system. Such supervision helps identify possible problems at any early stage, when they can be tackled before they reach unmanageable proportions. It also reduces the moral hazard that would otherwise exist if bank managements felt they were free to act in whatever manner they liked while counting on access to last resort financing in the event of difficulty.

The need for regulation in financial markets began to be emphasized in part as a reaction against the problems experienced in the Southern Cone countries of Latin America as a result of excessively enthusiastic financial liberalization in the late 1970s (see Diaz-Alejandro, 1985). To this extent the liberalizing and regulatory thrusts described above are somewhat contradictory, but the apparent contradiction is easily reconciled. Proponents of greater regulation do not necessarily endorse all the direct controls criticized by adherents of the financial repression school. Their main point is that financial liberalization by itself will not achieve the desired results in the financial sector. It may be necessary to remove direct controls in many areas to achieve greater efficiency in financial intermediation but this must be accompanied by stronger regulation aimed at strengthening prudential norms, transparency, and supervision. This is broadly the approach to financial reforms adopted in India and progress can therefore be evaluated in terms of progress achieved on each of these fronts.

2. PROGRESS IN LIBERALIZATION OF THE BANKING SECTOR

On the liberalization side of banking sector reforms significant progress has been achieved in several areas, especially interest rate liberalization and reduction in reserve requirements, but not in the matter of directed credit.

2.1 INTEREST RATE LIBERALIZATION

Interest rates in the banking system have been liberalized very substantially compared to the situation prevailing before 1991, when the Reserve Bank of India (RBI) controlled the rates payable on deposits of different maturities and also the rates which could be charged for bank loans which varied according to the sector of use and the size of the loan. Interest rates on time deposits were decontrolled in a sequence of steps beginning with longer term deposits and the liberalization was progressively extended to deposits of shorter maturity. With effect from October 1997 interest rates on all time deposits, including fifteen day deposits, have been freed. Only the rate on savings deposits remains controlled by the RBI. Lending rates were similarly freed in a series of steps. The Reserve Bank now directly controls only the interest rate charged for export credit, which accounts for about 10 per cent of commercial advances.[5] Interest rates on loans upto Rs 200,000, which account for 25 per cent of total advances, are subject to hybrid control—the rate is not fixed at a level set by the RBI, but is constrained to be no higher than the prime lending rate (PLR) which is determined by the boards of individual banks. The new arrangement implies a considerable reduction in the range of loans with subsidized rates compared to the position earlier.

The rationale for liberalizing interest rates in the banking system was to allow banks greater flexibility and encourage competition. Banks were able to vary rates charged to borrowers according to their cost of funds and also to reflect the creditworthiness of different borrowers. They could also vary nominal rates offered on deposits in line with changes in inflation to

[5]Export credit benefits from availability of refinancing from the RBI at a concessional rate which mitigates the burden of this particular control on the banking system.

maintain real returns. Flexibility to discriminate among borrowers has helped create a more competitive situation. Flexibility on deposit rates has proved to be assymmetrical. Banks are able to raise rates when inflation increases but they are not able to lower deposit rates when inflation declines. This became evident in 1995 and 1996 when inflation varied between 4 and 5 per cent but bank deposit rates remained high. Some observers have attributed this to the fact that expectations of inflation had not fallen even though inflation declined, but a more plausible explanation is that the rates of interest available on postal savings instruments, which are fixed by the central government, have been maintained at high levels. As postal savings are close substitutes for bank deposits, banks find it difficult to lower rates on deposits as long as postal savings rates are not adjusted downwards. Interest rate deregulation requires that interest rates on postal savings be made more flexible, perhaps by linking them to interest rates in the banking system in some way.[6]

Looking ahead, the remaining hybrid control on lending rates for small loans can also be phased out at an early date. The desire to control interest rates for small loans reflects an understandable desire to help small borrowers, but we must recognize that these controls may actually discourage banks from lending to these sectors or alternatively they may encourage corruption in determining access to such loans. There is overwhelming evidence that what matters for low income borrowers is timely availability of credit rather than low interest rates and a policy which keeps rates low but impedes the flow of credit does not help the target group. Banks forced to charge unprofitably low interest rates may also seek to protect their profitability by improving credit quality by insisting on higher levels of collateral than would otherwise be the case, thus effectively excluding precisely the groups which interest rate controls are meant to favour. Some segments of the banking system have already been freed from restrictions on lending rates. Cooperative banks were freed from all controls on lending rates in 1996 and this freedom was extended to regional rural banks and private local area banks in 1997. As the system gets used to higher rates being charged on smaller sized loans by these institutions, it

---

[6]Because the net accretions to postal savings are shared with the states, state governments are likely to resist reduction in these interest rates for fear that it will impede mobilization of resources. This resistance has to be overcome since otherwise the system will not be able to transit to a sustainable low inflation regime.

should be possible to take the next step and remove existing controls on lending rates in other commercial banks.

2.2 RESERVE REQUIREMENTS

Another important area where some liberalization has taken place relates to the cash reserve requirement (CRR) and the separate requirement for mandatory investment in government securities through the statutory liquidity ratio (SLR). At one stage, the CRR applicable to incremental deposits was as high as 25 per cent and the SLR was 40 per cent, thus pre-empting 65 per cent of incremental deposits. These ratios were reduced in a series of steps after 1992. The SLR is now 25 per cent, which appears high, but its distortionary effect has been greatly reduced by the fact that the interest rate on government securities is increasingly market determined. In fact, most banks currently hold a higher volume of government securities than required under the SLR reflecting the fact that the attractive interest rate on these securities, combined with the zero risk-weight, makes it commercially attractive for banks to lend to the government. The CRR has varied between 10 and 11per cent. This is definitely high by international standards and constitutes a tax on financial intermediation in the terminology of the financial repression literature.

The key constraint on reducing the CRR is the continuing high level of the fiscal deficit, which cannot be financed entirely from the market and therefore requires substantial support from the RBI[7]. Reducing the CRR is not a viable option in this situation because the expansionary impact on money supply via the money multiplier (which is a function of the CRR), would need to be offset by a monetary contraction elsewhere. In effect, the RBI would have to refrain from monetizing the deficit to the extent that it does at present which means interest rates on government securities would have to be allowed to rise. The high CRR is therefore the cost imposed on the banking system to allow the fiscal deficit to be financed at a lower cost to the government than would otherwise prevail. Lowering the CRR would of course reduce the

[7]The earlier practice of automatic monetization of the deficit through issue of ad hoc Treasury Bills has been abandoned but as long as fiscal deficit is not controlled, this only forces the RBI to resort to market borrowing to finance the deficit. The RBI is therefore presented with a Hobson's choice—it must either accept the high interest rates generated by government borrowing or moderate interest rates by monetizing the deficit.

implicit tax on the banking system, enabling banks to reduce rates on commercial advances but it would be at the cost of either accepting higher rates for government borrowing or tolerating greater monetary expansion and possible inflation.

2.3 DIRECTED CREDIT

An area where there has been no liberalization thus far relates to directed credit. Directed credit policies have been an important part of India's financial strategy under which commercial banks are required to direct 40 per cent of their commercial advances to the priority sector which consists of agriculture, small-scale industry, small-scale transport operators, artisans, etc. Within this aggregate ceiling there are sub-ceilings for agriculture and also for loans to poverty-related target groups. The Narasimham Committee had recommended reducing the 40 per cent directed credit target to 10 per cent, while simultaneously narrowing the definition of the priority sector to focus on small farmers and other low-income target groups. This recommendation was not accepted by the government and the directed credit requirement continues unchanged.

Should directed credit requirements be phased out? This is an important and potentially controversial question. Directed credit in support of export industries was a part of East Asia's financial policy during the miracle growth period and these policies were generally regarded as successful. However, this is not so for all cases of directed credit. Prevailing international perceptions of best practice in banking are generally against directed credit.[8] The shortcomings of directed credit policies in India are well known and are reflected in the fact that the proportion of non-performing assets (NPAs) in the priority sector portfolio of the banks is significantly higher than in the non-priority sector. However, abandoning of directed credit is unlikely to be a practical option in India in the near future, especially because directed credit in India relates mainly to lending to agriculture, small-scale industry, and poverty groups. If the present level of directed credit has to continue for some more time, we should at

---

[8]Stiglitz (1994) has argued that directed credit may actually promote economic efficiency if it is used to push credit into areas where there are technological spin-off and other externalities. However, this argument is based on the usual argument that government intervention is helpful whenever there is market failure. The problem, as pointed out by Fry (1997) is that market failure does not mean government success.

least consider ways of ameliorating the adverse consequences of this policy as much as possible.

A step in the right direction would be to eliminate the present concessional interest rates applicable to loans below Rs 200,000, most of which fall in the priority sector. If priority sector credit does involve higher cost to the banks we should reflect this in the interest rate allowed to be charged. This would increase the willingness of banks to lend to the priority sector and make the directed credit target less onerous. Another desirable step would be to expand the list of activities eligible under the priority sector as this would increase the range of economically viable activities for the deployment of priority sector credit and thus help improve the quality of the portfolio.[9] We should also consider redefining the priority sector target as a percentage of the total assets of the banking system and not as a percentage of commercial advances as at present. This is because the share of commercial advances in total assets is likely to increase over time as reserve requirements are reduced and fixing the priority sector target as a percentage of commercial advances means a rising percentage of total assets going to the priority sector which may be too onerous.

The quality of directed credit could also be improved if the identification of beneficiaries was left solely to the banks. This is perhaps the most important reform which should be implemented. At present, recipients of priority sector credit under various anti-poverty schemes (which also involve a government subsidy) are identified primarily by the district administration which administers these schemes, and the credit applications of these beneficiaries are then processed by banks. Even where bank officials are involved in the pre-selection, their involvement is perfunctory and the attitude is one of having to meet targets of lending rather than undertaking serious credit appraisal. Many (though not all) of the priority sector schemes oriented towards micro-enterprises have dubious economic viability but banks find it difficult to reject loan applications. Many borrowers tend to view credit extended as part of official anti-poverty programmes as a form of government largesse where repayment is not really intended, making it all the more difficult to fit these schemes within normal banking activity.

A somewhat theoretical sounding possibility, but one which should

---

[9]The Committee on Banking Reforms referred to in the third section of the chapter has suggested including activities related to food processing, dairying, and poultry.

be examined, is that of introducing 'trading' of priority sector perform-ance among banks so that banks which exceed their targets of priority sector lending may be able to 'trade' the excess to the credit of other banks which are falling short. To the extent that some banks are relatively more efficient in priority sector lending than others (e.g. because of broader spread of certain banks in agriculturally prosperous areas), it would enable the banking system as a whole to achieve the priority sector target at lesser cost. This would especially be so if interest rate ceilings are relaxed.

3. REGULATORY REFORM OF THE BANKING SYSTEM

Significant progress has also been made in reform of the regulatory side of the banking sector. Prior to 1991 Indian banks did not follow uniform accounting practices for income recognition, classification of assets into performing and non-performing, provisioning for non-performing assets, and valuation of securities held in the bank's portfolio. Nor were they subject to uniform capital adequacy requirements.

3.1 ESTABLISHMENT OF UNIFORM PRUDENTIAL NORMS

The Narasimham Committee recommended the establishment of uniform prudential norms and standards broadly along the lines recommended by the Basle Committee on Banking Supervision. These recommendations were implemented in a phased manner over a period of three years with the new norms becoming fully operational from 31 March 1996.

Indian banks have adjusted well to the new standards and are in a stronger position today than they were in 1991. Very few banks had a capital adequacy ratio up to the 8 per cent level prior to 1991. By March 1998 only one of the twenty-eight public sector banks fell short of this standard and many banks were significantly above that level. Admittedly, the increase in capital in many cases was achieved only through additional contribution of capital by the government, and to that extent does not reflect an improvement in operational performance, but there were also substantial contributions from internal reserves resulting from improved profitability.[10] Some banks were also able to raise capital from the market reflecting their ability to attract private investors. The new prudential

---

[10]Part of the profitability of banks reflects only the income earned from capitali-zation bonds but there were improvements in profitability even if their contribution is excluded.

norms and the greater transparency they impart to bank balance sheets have also increased consciousness of the need to improve asset quality. Efforts to reduce NPAs show encouraging results with the ratio of net NPAs (i.e. net of provisions) to total advances declining from 16.3 per cent at the end of 1991–2 to 8.2 per cent at the end of 1997–8.[11]

These are impressive improvements but it is also true that following the collapse in East Asia, and subsequent problems in Russia and elsewhere, the standards being demanded for regulating banking systems in developing countries have risen significantly. In anticipation of this development the government, in December 1997, appointed a Committee on Banking Sector Reforms (CBSR) to review the progress made in reform of the banking sector and to chart a course for the future. The Committee has since submitted its report outlining a comprehensive agenda for the second stage of banking sector reforms.

3.2 ALIGNING PRUDENTIAL NORMS WITH INTERNATIONAL PRACTICE

The obvious next step is to align prudential norms as closely as possible with international practice. The CBSR has documented various deficiencies in this regard. For example, loans are classified as substandard when payments become overdue for a period exceeding two quarters, whereas the international norm is one quarter. Similarly substandard assets are downgraded to doubtful if they remain substandard for two years instead of one year internationally. Loans with government guarantees are treated as zero-risk assets and are also not classified as non-performing even if there is a payment default. Government securities are treated as zero-risk assets whereas they are subject to interest rate risk and a modest risk weight is therefore appropriate. No provisions are required to be made for assets classified as standard whereas it would be more prudent to make a small provision even in these cases. Finally the capital to risk-weighted assets ratio is only 8 per cent whereas internationally banks are now aiming at higher levels, especially in view of the greater risks to which banks in developing countries are subject.

The CBSR has made specific recommendations to upgrade standards

---

[11]Figures for gross NPAs are higher but the net figure is more relevant because Indian banks tend to delay writing off NPAs against provisions made. It must also be recognized that NPAs as a proportion of total assets are significantly lower than as a proportion of advances because a substantial proportion of the assets of Indian banks is in the form of government securities.

in these areas. The first step has been taken with the RBI's recent announcement that the capital adequacy ratio must be raised to 9 per cent by 31st March 2000. The CBSR had recommended a 10 per cent level, which will presumably be enforced over a longer time period. A risk weight of 2.5 per cent has also been attached to investments in government securities—half the level recommended by the CBSR. Other recommendations of the CBSR to tighten prudential norms, especially regarding criteria for classifying NPAs, also need to be implemented in a phased manner. It is sometimes argued that NPA recognition norms in India cannot be equated with international norms because the slow pace of the legal system in enforcing bank claims on collateral security makes it inevitable that assets will remain non-performing for a longer time. While this may be true, it represents a real cost in the system and must be explicitly recognized as such. There may be a case for phasing the transition over time but it does not justify accepting lower standards.

Implementation of tighter norms will have an impact on the banking system. It will raise the level of NPAs and force a higher level of provisioning. This would erode the surplus over the minimum capital requirement currently enjoyed by some banks and increase capital deficiency in other cases. Banks are likely to complain that the shrinkage in the capital base will limit their ability to expand commercial credit forcing some of them to become 'narrow banks'. The credit restraining effect is indeed a genuine problem for affected banks, but credit for the system as a whole may not be affected if enough banks have surplus capital, as these banks would expand at the expense of those constrained by capital deficiency. If the net result is a gain in market share for better performing banks at the expense of the others, it is clearly desirable from the efficiency point of view. More generally, we need to recognize that regulatory forbearance in the form of lax prudential norms is not in the interest of the banking system. The experience with banking crises in other countries shows that understatement of NPA levels because of inadequately stringent norms and weak supervision only lulls banks into complacency, making them more vulnerable to crises when they arise. The balance of advantage lies in early announcement of the internationally acceptable norms to which banks must finally adhere, while allowing a reasonable period of time to reach these norms in a phased manner.

3.3 STRENGTHENING SUPERVISION

Along with the introduction of prudential norms it is also necessary to strengthen the system of bank supervision. An important step forward was the establishment of a separate Board for Financial Supervision within the RBI to undertake supervision. The system of supervision is also being modernized to focus on both on-site and off-site surveillance. The role of external auditors has been strengthened as also the role of internal controls and audit. The cycle of inspection and follow-up with bank managements, which earlier often extended over a period of two years, is now completed within twelve months after the close of the fiscal year of inspection. The focus of inspection needs to shift away from a mechanical pre-occupation with the extent of compliance with procedures towards forming an overall assessment of the bank's financial condition and performance under the CAMEL system.

These are welcome steps, but the process of improving supervision is a continuing process especially since banking is likely to become more complex with banks exposed to more complex risks. A great deal will depend upon the ability of the RBI to upgrade the quality of supervisory skills. Bank supervision is an extremely difficult and highly skilled operation and skilled bank supervisors are a rare commodity even in industrialized countries. The Board has greater flexibility for lateral recruitment but a great deal of upgrading of existing personnel skills will be necessary.

4. OTHER ISSUES IN BANKING REFORM

Bringing prudential norms up to international standards is only one part of the reform agenda. The more difficult part is to change the way banks function in practice so that their performance comes up to the more demanding requirements of the new regulatory environment. This means banks must function in a manner which brings NPAs down to acceptable levels while simultaneously showing sufficient profit to ensure growth of reserves to support additional lending. The challenge is all the greater because economic reforms and liberalization in the economy mean that bank borrowers now face greater competition (domestic and international) which increases the risk of commercial failure compared to the situation when banks were lending to clients operating in a protected economy. Banks have to upgrade their credit appraisal methods to ensure that the activities for which they lend are economically viable in the new more competitive environment. A more open economy also implies greater volatility in exchange rates and interest rates and banks must allow for the direct impact of these uncertainties on their balance sheets because of their own exposure and also the indirect effect via the impact on their clients. Banks will have to make changes on several fronts to deal with these challenges including the upgradation of human skills, induction of information technology, an understanding with labour unions to phase out outdated work practices, etc.

4.1 THE ROLE OF COMPETITION

The role of competition in accelerating change is especially important. Banks are more likely to change if they are faced with competition which forces them to become more efficient in order to survive. The creation of a more competitive environment in banking was one of the explicit objectives of the reform and the degree of competition has increased to some extent. Some of the competition has come from outside the system. Because of the development of capital markets and access to international sources of funds, the most creditworthy corporate clients are able to obtain funds from other sources and this puts pressure on banks to improve the cost and quality of their service or risk losing creditworthy clients. Competition within the banking system has also increased. Several new private banks have started operations and foreign banks have also been allowed to expand their branches more liberally than in the past. As a result the share of business of private banks and foreign banks together increased from 10.6 per cent in 1991–2 to 17.6 per cent in 1996–7. Public sector banks still remain in a dominant position, but foreign banks and some of the new private sector banks are ahead of public sector banks in the use of information technology and this will enable them to compete effectively for a larger business share, especially in the high income segment of the market, without having a very wide branch network. Competition among public sector banks is also increasing and this also generates pressures for greater efficiency.

If competition leads to general improvement in efficiency of all public sector banks, strengthening them all equally, we would have an ideal outcome with all participants gaining in the process. In practice, it is more likely that individual banks will respond differently, reflecting long-standing differences in managerial culture and work practices, and some banks will pull ahead at the expense of others. The weaker banks are in any case likely to be held back by enforcement of capital adequacy requirements which will automatically limit the extent to which they can expand credit. This is likely to produce a restructuring of the banking system, with better banks gaining market share at the expense of others. This should be accepted as a natural outcome of competition, even though it may intensify the problem of weak banks.

4.2 THE PROBLEM OF WEAK BANKS

How to deal with weak public sector banks is a major problem for the next stage of banking sector reforms. It is particularly difficult because the poor financial position of many of these banks is often blamed on the fact that the regulatory regime in earlier years did not place sufficient emphasis on sound banking, and the weak banks are, therefore, not responsible for their current predicament. This perception often leads to an expectation that all weak banks must be helped to restructure after which they would be able to survive in the new environment.

The usual recipe for revival of weak banks is to take care of the inherited burden of NPAs through some mechanism, such as, for example, an Asset Reconstruction Company as recommended by the CBSR, and then let the 'restructured' banks, with their cleaned up balance sheet compete with other banks. This approach may be worth trying in some cases but it must be recognized that it does not guarantee revival. Even if the backlog of NPAs is taken care of, many of the weak banks will also need to cut costs by closing loss-making branches and reducing excess staff if they are to have to any hope of surviving in competition with other banks in the more competitive environment of the future when margins will be under pressure. In short, revival may only be possible if it is preceded by a willingness to slim down and cut overheads drastically. It may also need a major overhaul of top and middle management which is not easy to achieve in a public sector bank.

Even after downsizing some weak banks may not be able to survive in competition against stronger banks which have better management cultures, stronger human skills, and better labour relations. In such a situation we must beware of repeated efforts at restructuring aimed at keeping such banks banks alive. The CBSR has recommended that such cases should be handed over to a Restructuring Commission, which can then decide on suitable solutions, including merger with other banks or even closure. Merger in this context should not mean mere arithmetical aggregation of the weak bank with all its staff and branches into another financially sound bank. Mergers have the advantage that they protect depositor interests, which is an important consideration, but they make economic sense only if they are preceded by sufficient effort to reduce cost by further downsizing before the merger. In the competitive environment expected in the future, strong banks are unlikely to be willing to accept merger with a weak bank unless these issues are resolved and they should not be forced to do so.

4.3 GOVERNMENT MAJORITY OWNERSHIP OF BANKS

Perhaps the most difficult issue for the future is whether government should retain majority control over public sector banks. The prevailing international consensus is against government ownership and many developing countries are actively engaged in privatizing government banks as part of financial sector reform. Privatization is obviously not a guarantee against bad banking, as is evident from the many banking crises involving private banks in both developed and developing countries. However this argument is usually countered by conceding that while privatization alone is definitely not sufficient, and must be accompanied by improved regulation and supervision, it is nevertheless necessary because government ownership involves 'politicization' and 'bureaucratization' of banking.[12]

The CBSR considered this issue and has recommended that the government/RBI holding in the public sector banks/State Bank of India be reduced to 33 per cent. Two reasons have been given by the Committee. One is that the capital requirement of banks will expand substantially because of the combined effect of growth of lending and enhanced capital adequacy requirements, and the additional capital needed is much larger than the likely growth of reserves through plough back of profit. Additional capital will, therefore, have to be contributed and maintaining a 51 per cent share in equity for the government will require large contributions from the budget which, the Committee felt, cannot be justified given the many other demands for budgetary funds. The Committee therefore recommended that the additional capital needs of the banks should be met by bringing in new private equity, which would dilute the government's share below 51 per cent. The second reason given by the CBSR is more fundamental and is based on the view that the degree of functional auton-

---

[12]The two phenomena are quite distinct. Politicization in the context refers to politically motivated credit decisions which may range from 'cronyism' in the sense of favouring individual, usually large, borrowers or politically directed populist loan programmes which are not based on sound credit appraisal, or even populist programmes of loan waivers. Bureaucratization refers to the conversion of public sector banks into organizations characterized by a layer of decision making with inadequate delegation which slows down decision making and produces an inability to respond quickly to commercial needs and an insensitivity to customer needs.

omy required for the exercise of sound banking may not be possible as long as government retains a majority share.

Majority government ownership of public sector banks has been an article of faith in many circles in India and it is important to consider carefully whether it is in fact inconsistent with sound banking. Vaghul (1998) has sought to finesse the problem by suggesting that government could retain majority ownership but the management of the bank must be entrusted entirely to a board of eminent professionals, which would appoint (and presumably also remove) the chief executive, and exercise all the functions of supervision over the management. In this arrangement the management would be responsible to the board and the government would deal with only the board which would not include any government officials. The arrangement will appeal to those who retain a preference for public ownership on principle but are willing to delegate power in practice. However, the degree of independence envisaged may not be feasible in practice.

Government accountability to parliament makes it unlikely that government would be willing to distance itself sufficiently from management by delegating all powers of supervision to an entirely independent non-government Board of Directors. In any case, since the board must reflect the interests and perception of shareholders, it is difficult to envisage a board acting completely independently of the government as long as the government is a majority shareholder. In fact, there is real danger that such an arrangement might degenerate into one which gives an appearance of independence but allows informal and unstructured interference in practice. This would only continue the relationship of dependence without the transparency and formal procedures involved when government is formally responsible.[13]

Majority ownership also imposes certain statutory constraints. For example, it implies that majority owned banks will be treated as the state under Article 12 of the Constitution which implies that action can be taken against the bank on grounds of 'natural justice', a feature which limits the freedom available to managements in dealing with personnel matters including promotion. It also implies that the government's anti-corruption machinery has jurisdiction over bank officials in the

---

[13]Reference is appropriate in this context to the view expressed by Jeffrey Sachs to the author that 'the only thing worse than public sector banks is autonomous public sector banks'.

same way as for government officials. The Central Bureau of Investigation (CBI) can therefore initiate investigation of bank officials for suspected malafide actions without complaints from the management and indeed even if the management or board of the bank is satisfied that the impugned actions do not merit investigation. The agencies can also prosecute in such cases even though management may have a different view of the culpability of the action. Since investigations typically take a long time bank officials involved suffer significant costs in the process, including possible suspension and denial of promotion. Vulnerability on this score encourages multiple layers of scrutiny and decision making in public sector banks because bank officials find comfort in concurrence from others. This creates cumbersome systems in which negative views expressed at any stage are unlikely to be countered, all of which introduces rigidity and an unwillingness to take reasonable commercial risks.

It is difficult to imagine Indian public sector banks engaging in innovative banking under these constraints. Reducing the government's equity below 51 per cent should therefore be the next step in banking sector reform.

4.4 LEGAL REFORMS

A major obstacle to the development of an efficient banking system in India is the state of the legal framework governing recovery of bank dues. Realization of dues from sale of collateral is extremely difficult, especially in the case of immovable property. Further, under the Sick Industrial Companies Act (SICA) companies declared sick immediately come under the perview of the Board for Industrial and Financial Reconstruction (BIFR) whereupon legal action for recovery of dues is stayed until the BIFR process is completed. This process is extremely dilatory. An amendment of SICA to make it approximate more closely to internationally accepted standards for bankruptcy legislation is essential. Effective bankruptcy law would provide an incentive to the borrowers to meet their obligations to the banks. The Finance Ministry has appointed an Expert Group to go into these issues. Legal reforms in this area must have high priority.

5. CAPITAL MARKET REFORM

Reform of the capital market was an important part of the agenda of financial sector reforms and action has been taken in this area parallel with reforms in banking. India has a long tradition of functioning capital markets—the Bombay Stock Exchange (BSE) is over a hundred years old—but until the 1980s the volume of activity in the capital market was relatively limited. Capital market activity expanded rapidly in the 1980s and the market capitalization of companies registered in the BSE rose from 5 per cent of GDP in 1980 to 13 per cent in 1990. However the market remained primitive and poorly regulated. Companies wishing to access the capital market needed prior permission of the government which also had to approve the price at which new equity could be raised.[14] While new issues were strictly controlled, there was inadequate regulation of stock market activity and also of various market participants including stock exchanges, brokers, mutual funds, etc. The domestic capital market was also closed to portfolio investment from abroad except through a few closed ended mutual funds floated abroad by the Unit Trust of India (UTI) which were dedicated to Indian investment.

The process of reform of the capital market was initiated in 1992 along the lines recommended by the Narasimham Committee. It aimed at removing direct government control and replacing it by a regulatory framework based on transparency and disclosure supervised by an independent regulator. The first step was taken in 1992 when the Securities and Exchange Board of India (SEBI), which was originally established as a non-statutory body in 1988, was elevated to a full fledged capital market regulator with statutory powers in 1992. The requirement of prior government permission for accessing capital markets and for prior approval of issue pricing was abolished and companies were allowed to access markets and price issues freely, subject only to disclosure norms laid down by SEBI.

5.1 THE REGULATORY FRAMEWORK

Over the years SEBI has put in place a modern regulatory framework with rules and regulations governing the behaviour of major market participants such as stock exchanges, brokers, merchant bankers, and mutual funds. It has also sought to regulate activities such as takeovers and insider trading which have implications for investor protection. The governing structure of stock exchanges has been modified to make the boards of the exchanges more broad based and less dominated by bro-

---

[14]The system forced companies to price new equity issues at levels substantially lower than market prices, ostensibly as a measure of protection for the small investor. However this implicitly penalized firms raising capital from the public and the volume of equity raised in the capital market was relatively small.

kers. The new regulatory framework seeks to strengthen investor protection by ensuring disclosure and transparency rather than through direct control. SEBI acts as a supervisor of the system undertaking supervision of the activities of various participants including stock exchanges and mutual funds and violations of the rules are punishable by SEBI.

The regulatory framework is as yet new and will need to be refined in the light of experience gained and also as gaps and inadequacies are identified. SEBI needs to be further strengthened in some areas and its punitive powers enhanced. However there is no doubt that a good start has been made.

5.2 OPENING THE CAPITAL MARKET TO FOREIGN INVESTORS

An important policy initiative in 1993 was the opening of the capital market to foreign institutional investors (FIIs) and allowing Indian companies to raise capital abroad by issue of equity in the form of global depository receipts (GDRs). Over 500 FIIs are now registered with SEBI, of whom about 150 are active investors, and there has been a cumulative inflow of around $ 9 billion into the capital market through this route up to the end of 1997–8. The GDR route has also seen an inflow of about $ 6 billion.

The cumulative investment of around $ 15 billion in Indian stocks through FIIs and GDRs has effectively linked India's domestic capital market with world markets and has important implications for macroeconomic management. Domestic liquidity conditions and asset prices are now affected by international market perceptions and this must be taken into account in formulating monetary policy. A large inflow of portfolio investment can lead to a sharp increase in domestic liquidity and asset prices as happened in 1994 to 1996, and a reversal can lower asset prices as in 1998. Exchange rate behaviour is now as much determined by developments in the capital account as on current account. Since capital flows are affected by international perceptions, and these perceptions can be triggered not just by developments in India but also by contagion effects from developments abroad, management of the exchange rate has to take these linkages into account. The economy is not as vulnerable to volatile flows as it would be with full capital account convertibility, and this is one reason why India's currency markets were not seriously disrupted in the Asian crisis, but it is certainly more so because of FII and GDR flows. The potential volatility of these flows must be accepted and strategies for exchange market management should take this into account.

5.3 MODERNIZATION OF TRADING AND SETTLEMENT SYSTEMS

Major improvements have taken place in trading methods which were highly antiquated earlier. The National Stock Exchange (NSE) was set up in 1994 as an automated electronic exchange. It enabled brokers in 220 cities all over the country to link up with the NSE computers via VSATs and trade in a unified exchange with automatic matching of buy and sell orders with price time priority, thus ensuring maximum transparency for investors. The introduction of electronic trading by the NSE generated competitive pressure which forced the BSE to also introduce electronic trading in 1995.

The settlement system was antiquated, involving physical delivery of share certificates to the buyer who then had to deliver them to a company registrar to record change of ownership after which the certificates had to be returned to the buyer. This process was very time consuming and also created significant risks for investors.[15] The first step towards paperless trading was put in place by enacting legislation which allowed dematerialization of share certificates with settlement by electronic transfer of ownership from one account to another within a depository. The National Securities Depository Ltd (NSDL) opened for business in 1996. In June 1997 only forty-eight companies, with a market capitalization of Rs 94,000 crore, had signed up enabling dematerialization of their securities. By June 1998 this had increased to 198 companies with a market capital of Rs 288,000 crore. The value of securities actually held in the depository has increased from Rs 2518 crore in June 1997 to Rs 35,000 crore in June 1998. It is expected that the volume of settlements taking place through the depository will expand rapidly.

5.4 FUTURES TRADING

An important lacuna in India's capital market at present is futures markets. A well-functioning market in index futures would help in risk management and provide greater liquidity to the market. A decision to introduce futures trading has been taken and the legislative changes needed to implement this decision have been submitted to parliament.

---

[15] The risks included loss of certificates in transition, fear of fake or forged certificates being involved in stock exchange transactions which would be discovered only much later, and also disputes at the time of registration of new owners on the grounds that signatures of the seller on the certificates did not match signatures in the records of the registry.

Futures trading is expected to commence in 1999 and with this a major deficiency in the capital market will have been corrected.

5.5 SOME PROBLEMS IN THE CAPITAL MARKET

Despite these important improvements in the regulatory framework and trading and settlement systems, the functioning of the capital market in the post-reform period has been the subject of much criticism. Investors, especially small investors who entered the market in the early stages of liberalization, have not found their investments to be good value. There is a widespread perception that many unscrupulous companies took advantage of the removal of government control over issue prices to raise capital at inflated prices, at the expense of inexperienced investors. Merchant bankers and underwriters involved in these issues, some of which were among the better known names in the business, are seen to have misled investors. Nor is disappointment confined to ill-informed small investors greedily venturing into risky investments which they should never have undertaken in any case. Investors who invested in a wide range of blue chip stocks or in mutual funds, including funds managed by some of the best known international names, have also fared poorly because the Sensex has fluctuated widely since 1993 with a dominantly bearish trend in 1997 and 1998. Part of the problem is the change in sentiment among FIIs in this period reflecting a contagion effect from East Asia. Part of it may also reflect the slowing of industrial growth after 1996.

Investor disappointment has led to a withdrawal of ordinary investors from equity markets. The volume of capital (both debt and equity) mobilized from the primary market increased substantially in the initial years of the reforms and reached a peak in 1995–6. The next two years saw a sharp decline in the volume of equity raised in the primary market with offsetting increase in resources raised through debt. This switch away from equity, following the poor experience of investors with equity investment, can be explained as a corrective process but it has created problems for financing of new projects which were begun in the expectation of easier availability of equity.

These problems have drawn attention to the need to restore confidence among small investors and this is indeed an important issue. However the solution does not lie, as is sometimes supposed, in extending a variety of tax incentives to lure small investors back into the market. To some extent it will happen automatically when the industrial cycle shows an upturn. However it also requires deeper rooted institutional changes. Studies conducted by the Society for Capital Market Research and Development show that part of the reason for the reluctance of small investors to enter the market is the low level of confidence about corporate governance in many listed companies. A pre-condition for healthy capital markets which is well recognized in industrialized countries is the existence of institutions which ensure high levels of corporate governance. These include high standards of accountancy to ensure transparency in financial performance, active involvement of institutional investors in monitoring performance based on good quality equity research inputs and also codes of corporate governance which are designed to ensure that managements are subjected to effective oversight by boards and that shareholder interests are protected. India's capital market is as yet far from this ideal. Some corrective processes are however at work. Companies wishing to access capital markets in future will have to price IPOs more reasonably. They will also have to show improvements in corporate governance in line with growing consciousness of our deficiencies on this score.

Issuers of capital must also realize that the capital market should not be viewed as a passive source of equity capital which can be tapped by companies at will to raise equity on favourable terms. Cross-country studies have shown that stock markets in developing countries have been a more important source for financing of new investments through IPOs than in developed countries where financing of new investment has relied mainly on internal generation of surpluses. New companies raising funds have typically relied on venture capital or private placement rather than public issues. To some extent this is made possible by the existence of institutional investors such as insurance and pension funds willing to invest in the capital of new companies based on their own due diligence.

Does the emergence of these problems indicate that the broad thrust of reforms in the capital market has been inadequate? The view is sometimes expressed that perhaps the removal of direct control on issue prices in the primary market was premature and should have been implemented only after greater experience had been gained with regulation of the secondary market. It is difficult to be certain on this issue, but it can be argued that a more drawn out process would not have made much difference. It would certainly not make sense to retain price controls on domestic issuers of capital while also opening up the markets to foreign investors. The solution for protecting the interest of small investors lies less in price control and more in investor education.

Inevitably, some of education comes through actual experience which is not always pleasant.

6. REFORM OF THE INSURANCE SECTOR

No review of financial sector reforms in India can be complete without reference to the need for reforms in the insurance sector. India is one of only four countries—the other three being Cuba, North Korea, and Myanmar—where insurance is a public sector monopoly! The rationale of liberalizing the banking system and encouraging competition among the three major participants viz. public sector banks, Indian private sector banks, and foreign banks, applies equally to insurance. There is a strong case for ending the public sector monopoly in insurance and opening it up to private sector participants subject to suitable prudential regulation.

Cross-country evidence suggests that contractual savings institutions are an extremely important determinant of the aggregate rate of savings and insurance and pension schemes are the most important form of contractual savings in this context. Their importance will increase in the years ahead as household savings capacity increases with rising per capita incomes, life expectancy increases, and as traditional family support systems, which are a substitute for insurance and pensions, are eroded. A competitive insurance industry, providing a diversified set of insurance products to meet differing customer needs, can help increase savings in this situation and allocate them efficiently. The insurance and pensions industry typically has long-term liabilities which it seeks to match by investing in long-term secure assets. A healthy insurance is therefore an important source of long-term capital in domestic currency which is especially for infrastructure financing. Reforms in insurance will therefore strengthen the capital market at the long-term end by adding new players in this segment of the market, giving it greater depth or liquidity.

It is relevant to ask why these developments are less likely if insurance remains a public sector monopoly. One reason is that the industry suffers from a relatively high requirement for mandatory investment in government securities. However this implies that it is the mandatory requirement and not the public sector monopoly which is the real constraint. The fact is that the insurance industry does not fully utilize even the flexibility available at present for investment in corporate securities. This is principally because lack of competition in the insurance sector means there is no pressure to improve the return offered to the investor. Competition will increase the pressure to improve returns and push insurance companies to move out of government securities to seek higher returns in high quality corporate debt. Needless to say, the process would be greatly expedited if fiscal deficit is also reduced resulting in a fall in the interest rate on government securities. Reforms in insurance are therefore more likely to create a flow of finance for the corporate sector if we can simultaneously make progress in reducing fiscal deficit.

The Malhotra Committee had recommended opening up the insurance sector to new private companies as early as 1994. It took five years to build a consensus on this issue and legislation to open up insurance, allowing foreign equity up to 26 per cent was finally submitted to Parliament in 1999. It could not be passed before the dissolution of Parliament and the earliest it can now be passed is by 2000. If approved it will require legislation to remove the existing government monopoly and the earliest that this can be done is some time in 1999. This means new licences to competing insurers can only be issued by the end of 2000 and since the new entrants will have to build up their business from scratch, it will take another 5 to 10 years before private insurance companies, even with foreign partners, can reach significant levels. The sooner we start the sooner we will derive the benefit of providing better service for the consumer, and the sooner it will be possible to finance infrastructure from the capital market.

7. CONCLUSION

The reforms currently under way in the banking sector and in the capital market, combined with the agenda for reform identified for the insurance sector, represent a major structural overhaul of the financial system. It will certainly bring India's financial system much closer to what is expected of developing countries as they integrate with the world economy. As in so many other areas, reforms in the financial sector have been of the gradualist variety, with changes being made only after much discussion and over a somewhat longer period than attempted in most other countries. However the direction of change has been steady and in retrospect a great deal has been accomplished in the past seven years. It is essential to continue these reforms along the directions already indicated and to accelerate the pace of change as much as possible.

Finally, it is important to recognize that financial sector reforms by themselves cannot guarantee good economic performance. That depends upon a number of other factors, including especially the maintenance of a favourable macroeconomic environment and the pursuit of much needed economic reforms in other parts of the real economy. The impact of financial sector reforms in accelerating growth will be maximized if combined with progress in economic reforms in other areas.

REFERENCES

Caprio, Gerard and Daniela Klingebiel. (1996). 'Bank Insolvencies: Cross-Country Experience'. World Bank Policy Research Working Paper 1620, Washington, D.C.

Diaz-Alejandro, C. (1985). 'Good-bye Financial Repression, Hello Financial Crash'. *Journal of Development Economics*, vol. 19 (September–October), pp. 1–24.

Fry, Maxwell J. (1997). 'In Favour of Financial Liberalization'. *Economic Journal*, vol. 107 (May), pp. 754.

McKinnon, R.I. (1973). *Money and Capital in Economic Development*. Washington, D.C.: Brookings Institution.

Shaw, E.S. (1973). *Financial Deepening in Economic Development*. New York: Oxford University Press.

Singh, A. (1997), 'FinanciaL Liberalization and Economic Development'. *Economic Journal*, vol. 107 (May), pp. 771–82.

Stiglitz, J. E. (1994). 'The Role of the State in Financial Markets.' In M. Bruno and B. Pleskovic (eds), *Proceedings of the World Bank Annual Bank Conference on Development Economics 1993*. Washington, D.C.: World Bank, pp. 19–52.

Stiglitz, J.E. and A. Weiss. (1981). 'Credit Rationing in Markets with Imperfect Information'. *American Economic Review*, vol. 71 (June), pp. 393–410.

Vaghul, N. (1998). *Financing Growth: Structural Issues in India—A Look Ahead*. Bombay: Associated Chamber of Commerce and Industry.

Part II
Banking and Financing of Firms

Indian Banking: Preparing for the Next Round of Reform

S.S. TARAPORE

016
G21
G28

INTRODUCTION

It is now six years since the Indian financial sector reforms were launched and it is only appropriate to take stock of the achievements, the weaknesses in the system, the tasks ahead and the desired path of future reform. In the first stage of reform it was recognized that the Indian financial system was following archaic norms which were not compatible with a sound financial system and there was need for much greater transparency of bank operations as well as balance sheets. Reserve requirements on banks (the cash reserve ratio [CRR] and statutory liquidity ratio [SLR]) had reached absurdly high levels but a prerequisite for reform in this area was the containing of fiscal deficit and minimizing of monetization of the deficit. To this effect a major reform on financing of the fiscal deficit was undertaken under which automatic monetization of the fiscal deficit through the instrument of ad hoc treasury bills was discontinued. The reduction of fiscal deficit and its monetization enabled significant reduction in reserve requirements. The move to market-related rates of interest on government paper facilitated the deregulation of interest rates.

In what can be called the second stage of reform, some of the harder issues need to be addressed in the context of globalization. Capital account convertibility (CAC) will impinge on the financial sector. There will be significant intensification of competition not only between banks and non-banks within the country but also severe competition from abroad.

This chapter addresses some of these issues and, inter alia, discusses issues relating to the feasibility of further reduction in reserve requirements, the problem of non-performing assets (NPAs), bank/non-bank competition, a regulatory level playing field, issues relating to supervision, offshore financing, and the question of autonomy. Apart from raising these issues, some specific policy options are set out for consideration.

REDUCTION IN RESERVE REQUIREMENTS

It was earlier felt that a reduction in the CRR to 3 per cent would result in a loss of monetary control. This is not a legitimate fear as reduction in the CRR merely implies a shift from direct to indirect instruments and as such the shift per se does not necessarily mean a loss of monetary control. The reduction in the CRR would be a major boost to a bank's income. Illustratively, a reduction in average effective CRR from the 15.5 per cent level which prevailed in October 1995 to 3 per cent would release about Rs 74,000 crore. Now, if instead of earning 4 per cent on these balances banks invest these resources in 11 per cent gilts, the income of banks would go up by a staggering Rs 5200 crore per annum. In other words, the operating profits of Rs 10,200 crore would, *ceteris paribus*, show an increase of over 50 per cent. A reduction in the CRR would help achieve a more acceptable net return on assets (ROA).

A high CRR is a heavy tax on the banking system and distorts the cost of funds as well as the deployment, and there is a strong case for refraining from a high CRR. It should be the endeavour of policy to ensure that the CRR is raised above 3 per cent only for very short periods, and when monetary conditions stabilize the CRR should be very quickly brought down to 3 per cent. It is pertinent to mention that up to the 1970s this was the approach, but once fiscal deficits were unbridled the Reserve Bank of India (RBI) had no option but to undertake a continuing increase in the CRR. It is best to raise the CRR sharply when required and not remunerate these balances, and bring down the CRR expeditiously when monetary conditions stabilize. Thus the CRR can become a powerful monetary instrument without it becoming a drag on the banking system's profitability.

Progressively, the medium-term objective should be to give up the CRR as an instrument of monetary control. Open market operations as an instrument of monetary control are substantially more efficient than a CRR-refinance regime as the former pick up the liquidity where it is in surfeit and provide liquidity where it is required whereas the CRR-refinance system is a blunt instrument. It should be possible to accelerate the movement to a 3 per cent CRR by abolishing the generalized refinance facility and sector-specific refinance for exports. This could be replaced by a liquidity adjustment facility through primary dealers (PDs) with a system of repos and reverse repos in government securities; this would be a far more efficient system of liquidity management as the RBI would then have better control over the yield curve.

As regards the SLR, there is merit in moving away from a system of preemptions, but this depends on reducing the borrowing requirement of the public sector to a level consistent with lower levels of preemptions. The SLR for the banking system has been rationalized and the present prescription is the statutory minimum of 25 per cent. The element of compulsion is no longer relevant as the actual effective holdings of securities by the banking system are around 35 per cent. The preemptions for the insurance sector and the provident funds are still very high. *Per contra* there is also the question of a level playing field on reserve requirements as applicable to banks and non-banks which is discussed later.

The question of capital flows and how they are handled in terms of the liquidity impact is an important one. At present there is a bias in favour of lower requirements being prescribed for non-resident deposits. A better course of action would be to fix uniform reserve requirements on all liabilities and moreover no liabilities, particularly those emanating from foreign sources, should be exempt from reserve requirements. This approach would create a more level playing field between domestic resource mobilization and offshore funding which is now favoured except for limits on bank offshore borrowing.

THE PROBLEM OF NON-PERFORMING ASSETS

The NPAs of the banking system are perhaps the most worrisome aspect in the second stage of the reform. NPAs lead to wide spreads, inhibit central bank tightening, worsen the fragility of the banking system, and thereby trigger a crisis and represent a potential drain on the government if a bailout becomes necessary. The gross NPAs of the Indian public sector banks at the end of March 1997 were extremely high at an average of 17.8 per cent of advances but the average conceals a wide range from a low of 7 per cent to high of 36 per cent. The net NPAs, i.e. gross NPAs net of provisions, amounted to 9.1 per cent of advances. As a proportion of net demand and time liabilities the gross NPAs were 8.7 per cent and net NPAs 4.4 per cent.

While these numbers do provide some comfort that the problem of the system is not totally intractable, a few caveats are necessary. First, as reserve requirements come down and risk assets rise, the NPAs as a proportion of NDTL could have a tendency to rise and it is, therefore, necessary to ensure that fresh lending does not degenerate into NPAs.

This is easier said than done as it involves a radical change in credit management systems in weak banks. Second, as prudential norms are tightened further NPAs would rise. Third, as mentioned earlier there are wide divergences as between banks and it would therefore be necessary to not only have a system perspective but a concrete plan of action for weak banks to ensure that these weaknesses do not ricochet through the entire system. We cannot take comfort in the fact that the system's average net NPAs are only 4.4 per cent of NDTL, as banks which have the highest gross NPAs are precisely the banks which are not in a position to make adequate provisions. As such, a closer look is necessary to assess the problem of weak banks. Fourth, while the system's gross NPAs have come down from 24.8 per cent in 1993–4 to 17.8 per cent in 1996–7, the reduction is equally attributable to write-offs and recoveries. It hardly need be stressed that a real qualitative improvement would warrant a much larger proportion of recoveries rather than write-offs. In this context the need for an effective legal system of recoveries cannot be overemphasized.

BANK RECAPITALIZATION

When a bank accumulates bad debts, it is incumbent on the owners to recapitalize it. In a system of public sector ownership, and with a history of behest lending, it was recognized that the government had to bear the responsibility. It is in this context that the government of India provided total recapitalization of nationalized banks to the tune of a little less than Rs 17,500 crore, equivalent to 6.3 per cent of the deposits of these banks. To put banks on a sound footing such recapitalization has to be time bound and there must be a clearly delineated time period beyond which there should be no further recapitalization. Open-ended recapitalization would imply that a bank which erodes its capital would in no way be disciplined. There would need to be a system under which banks which do not maintain the stipulated capital adequacy would invite penalties so that there is strong incentive to shrink risk assets.

PROBLEM OF WEAK BANKS

The problem of weak public sector banks is one which has to be faced up front by the government and the RBI. Various options should be discussed in a transparent manner and a resolution sought of this major problem. It is sometimes argued that mergers would be a way out but it must be recognized that what is viable is the merger of two strong public sector banks. Merger of a strong public sector bank with a weak public sector bank or of two weak public sector banks is clearly not viable. Again, liquidating public sector banks, or large-scale closure of branches, or large-scale retrenchment of labour which may be technically desirable are not serious policy options in the Indian context. Nonetheless, within the present constraints, some innovative rationalization of branches should be possible and a gradual reduction of staff undertaken through the process of attrition via superannuation. Although this may appear to be too slow a process of adjustment, it is far better than no adjustment at all.

In a context where the banking system is largely privately owned, it makes sense to use the threat of throwing out management or closing down banks but where the government is owner, such measures just cannot be put in place. This does not mean, however, that there are no solutions to the specific problem of weak banks in India. The Committee on Capital Account Convertibility has recommended that the *narrow bank* concept be used for them. What this means is that depending on the degree of weakness there would be a control on the growth of risk assets of a bank. In other words, the greater the weakness the lower the incremental credit–deposit ratio. Thus, it is not as if credit were suddenly switched off. Again, it is only in extreme cases, where the bank's funds management is reckless, that there would be a control on the growth of bank deposits. The narrow bank concept is not new. It has worked elsewhere and, more pertinently, in the past it has worked in certain individual cases in India.

It is sometimes argued that the concept of narrow banking for weak banks is not sufficient by itself and that more fundamental changes are necessary. It is incumbent on those who do not wish to accept the concept of narrow banking to come out with a better and more viable solution. Denigrating the concept of narrow banking as a mere exercise in damage containment would be an irresponsible response to the most serious problem facing the financial sector.

It is sometimes argued that it is the duty of the government to bail out weak banks because it is behest lending which landed such banks in problems in the first place. The question that has to be considered, however, is why banks operating in the same overall milieu and the same overall geographical area show divergent performances. Ultimately, it boils down to credit management. Credit management does not refer merely to the top management of a bank but the entire credit management team down to the branch level. Rectifying endemic weaknesses in the entire credit management team is not something that can be achieved overnight.

Solutions like an Asset Reconstruction Fund are dangerous in that such an artificial cleaning up of the balance sheet is no assurance that credit management would improve and that fresh NPAs would not emerge. It is for this reason that it is necessary to deal with the root of the malady. Mere cleaning up of the balance sheet is, in a sense, akin to window dressing.

The time has come to stop propping up weak public sector banks. It is not the divine right of these banks to expand credit. Allowing weak banks to undertake unbridled credit expansion, faster than the system, as some of these banks have done, is suicidal and an abrogation of duty by the RBI and the government. The authorities should give the problem of weak banks immediate and overriding priority.

ISSUES OF SUPERVISION

The correct reporting of NPAs is an issue that has been faced by many authorities. The renowned supervisor Aristobulo de Juan, former Deputy Governor of the Bank of Spain, has stressed that banks the world over never reveal the true level of NPAs. Hence in this area it is necessary to strengthen the system of internal and external auditors as well as the supervisory authorities to ensure reasonably accurate reporting of NPAs. While it is necessary to ensure that a sudden tightening of prudential norms does not result in a crisis of confidence, it is equally necessary for the auditors and supervisors to become progressively stricter so that, over time, there is total transparency of operations in the financial sector and balance sheets reflect the true picture.

It is in this context that bank supervisors need to focus attention on the 'good' loan portfolio and not the 'bad' one as it is in the 'good' portfolio that there are errors of reporting. Indian bankers need to take note of the sagacious advice of William J. McDonough, President of the New York Fed, that 'no financial institution should be engaging in activities its senior management does not understand and its board of directors cannot oversee'. Adhering to this principle would save bankers from much trouble. Unsound financing often takes place during the expansionary phase of the business cycle when the authorities sometimes subtly and sometimes overtly urge credit expansion. While banks should no doubt respond to these signals, they should never lose sight of the viability of the borrower. At the same time the authorities do need to allow banks and institutions to take prudent risks even though such risks can result in unanticipated losses. Some mistakes will be made and some financial failures will take place. Failures occur as part of a normal process and should be viewed as a flaw only when the failure rate goes beyond a prudent threshold level. It bears reiterating that the optimal number of failures is not zero and in the real world no one can guarantee a *fail safe* financial system.

It is also necessary that the auditor and supervisor avoid a fixation with figures and pay greater attention to the quality of the loan portfolio, risk management, and the manner of rectification of bad debts. For example, a bank which undertakes rapid expansion when the NPAs are high would automatically bring down the percentage of NPAs as fresh lending would qualify as standard assets. The supervision, however, needs to consider the well-known proposition that rapid expansion and excessive risk taking by banks during booms to undercapitalized and highly indebted corporates carry the seeds of banking crises when there is a tightening of liquidity as a result of a conscious policy of restraint by the central bank. Good auditors and supervisors must judge how well the credit expansion has been managed and whether the credits can withstand such tightening.

Auditors must also ensure that banks report NPAs on a uniform basis and do not use innovative techniques to artificially depress the NPA figure. It is necessary that there should be a stocktaking not only of the gross NPAs but also the loan loss provisioning coverage. It is essential that the NPAs reported by banks reflect the true position. The recent experience of tentative estimates being way off the mark does not add credibility to the system. The supervisory system must evolve procedures which ensure strong disincentives for wrong reporting and auditors should endeavour to develop procedures which would make it virtually impossible to avoid full and correct disclosure.

The Basle Committee on Banking Supervision has set out the Core Principles for Effective Banking Supervision in September 1997. As the Indian economy progressively integrates into the international economy, Indian supervisors and auditors will have to give far greater attention than hitherto to a number of critical issues. The rationale behind the core principles is the increased awareness that banking crises can aggravate recessions particularly in emerging countries where banks play a predominant role in financial intermediation. With the progressive globalization of economic activity, particular attention is necessary for supervision of cross-border banking.

The core principles stress that banks should have in place risk management systems which accurately identify, measure, monitor, and control market risks. Increasingly, there will be a need to take a 'risk-focused' approach to bank supervision with a more targeted approach to identifying the sources of risk in a bank's portfolio. The supervisors' task is to set minimum standards but banks must bear the principal responsibility of adequate risk management.

The Basle capital requirements should be considered as a minimum and in emerging economies higher minimum capital requirements seem appropriate because banks operate in a riskier environment. It is pertinent to note that the minimum capital requirement is 11.5 per cent in Argentina and 9 per cent in Colombia. It is clear that sooner or later it will be necessary for the Indian authorities to consider higher minimum capital requirements.

Again, the core principles emphasize that the supervisors should be satisfied that each bank follows consistent accounting policies and practices. They prescribe that if a bank provides false or misleading information, supervisory action or criminal prosecution should be taken against the individuals involved as well as the institution. They stress that internal and external audit can be an integral part of supervision. The supervisors and the external auditors must have a clear understanding of their respective roles and a framework should be developed for communication between the supervisor and the external auditors. Mr de Swaan, the Chairman of the Basle Committee on Banking Supervision has urged that countries should accord top priority to time-bound implementation of the core principles. In the Indian context it would be best if there is a public debate which would enable corporates, banks, auditors, and supervisors to undertake suitable preparatory steps to implement these core principles.

In an increasingly complex financial system the supervisory authorities need an interdisciplinary team of chartered accountants, financial analysts, lawyers, corporate specialists, economists, and computer specialists to be part of a Supervisory Strategic Strike Force which can respond effectively to the complex supervisory problems thrown up in the financial sector. For the supervisory authority to be effective it would need injection of strategic skills at various levels and the consanguinity of a craft union can clearly undermine the effectiveness of the supervisory authority. A supervisory system would gain respect only if it is able to pick out incipient infringements and take contemporaneous adverse action. But it bears stressing that the regulatory framework should be simple, unambiguous, and codified. The absence of a codified banking regulatory framework—unlike in the area of exchange control where such codification does exist—is a major lacuna which must be rectified on a priority basis. The purpose of such a codification should not merely be to undertake a compilation, but to undertake a meaningful rationalization to keep the regulatory framework simple and unambiguous. Such a regulatory framework would enable expeditious supervisory action as both the central bank and the commercial banks would have a clear reference manual of instructions.

AUTONOMY OF BANKS

In an increasingly competitive environment, public sector banks cannot continue to operate as a monolith. In fact a break up of the monolith is not only inevitable but highly desirable. Public sector banks can no longer use uniform norms for personnel policies, including recruitment and wage policies, upgradation of technology, risk management, and branch network. In effect, within the public sector banking system, the Darwinian principle of survival of the fittest should be allowed to function in that the more efficient would grow and the less efficient would remain stunted. The bank autonomy package recently announced is a step in the right direction. It is reported that banks with net profits for the last three years, having capital adequacy of at least 8 per cent, NPAs below 9 per cent, and minimum net owned funds of Rs 100 crore could be given autonomy in recruitment and freedom to determine their own administrative structure. The recent element of freedom given to banks should be used constructively by the stronger public sector banks. While issues of autonomy are often posed as the regulator/owner giving freedom to the entities, there is also the issue of entities taking their rightful autonomy. Ultimately, it needs to be recognized that autonomy is never given, it is always earned.

Public sector banks which meet certain even more exacting norms on capital adequacy, NPAs, liquidity, risk management skills, etc. should be granted *navaratna* status and provided total flexibility in their operations; the managers in these banks would need to be provided incentives which encourage them to take reasonable risks in lending. In the case of navaratna banks the boards should be so constituted that there is an arms-length relationship with the RBI and the government. For banks granted the navaratna status, the practice of RBI nominee Directors should be discontinued and the government, while withdrawing its officials from the boards, should appoint non-officials with proven track record and eminence as its nominee Directors. RBI nominees should also be removed from other banks. It is not feasible to have the referee (RBI) also double up as a player. As a matter of principle the central bank should not have its employees as nominees on the boards of banks or institutions.

It is sometimes argued that unless the private sector accounts for a sizeable proportion of the total banking system, it will be difficult to introduce a strong element of competition and efficiency of operations. Attempts to alter the Bank Nationalization Act to reduce the government's ownership from the present minimum 51 per cent would inevitably get bogged down in prolonged debate. The more practical approach would be to begin by altering the RBI's minimum holding in the State Bank of India from 55 per cent to say 26 per cent. There is a strong rationale for the central bank not being owner of a bank and besides it would be a case of first in first out. Moreover, it would be a case of privatizing a strong bank which would be meaningful. Again, a part of the ownership of the government in nationalized banks could, in the first instance, be transferred to public sector or other institutional investors

APPROACH TO RURAL CREDIT

The critical issue in the area of rural credit is not a problem of identification or policy prescription; what causes difficulty is policy implementation. A major problem has been the clear delineation between activities which are commercially viable and activities which need to be provided subsidies because the agents are below the poverty line. It is erroneous to give to the rural banking system the role of overall agent of development rather than the specific role of a purveyor of credit. It is paradoxical that there is aversion for higher interest rates in the organized rural credit structure while the alternative of borrowing from the informal market at phenomenally high rates does not invoke similar concerns. The experience in a number of countries has shown that a repeal of interest rate ceilings on lending has not adversely affected the viability of the activities financed. On the contrary, such policies have resulted in greater flow of credit for rural financing. The deregulation of lending rates for advances up to Rs 2 lakh has not had any adverse effect in the case of cooperatives and regional rural banks, and there is a strong case for similar deregulation of lending rates up to Rs 2 lakh for scheduled commercial banks. It has been reiterated that what is important is the timeliness and adequacy of credit and not its cost.

Rapid changes are taking place in the rural economy. There will be an inevitable movement away from traditional food and non-food crops to newer activities, some of which would be credit-intensive. As such large projects in the rural area are bound to emerge and rural financing agencies should not hesitate to finance these operations on commercial terms. This does not imply that the weaker sections would be crowded out. It is, however, necessary that there should be clear delineation between viable and non-viable lending operations. The non-viable operations should not be financed by the banking system as poor recovery and defaults would be inevitable and this can have detrimental contagion effects of viable borrowers becoming chronic defaulters. The viable borrowers should be provided bank credit and the really indigent poor should be provided outright grants through poverty alleviation programmes. Spreading the grant element thinly over a wider area of beneficiaries is not desirable. In terms of the structure of credit a closure of unviable Primary Agricultural Credit Societies (PACS) is unavoidable. The restructuring of the Regional Rural Banks (RRBs) has been debated over a prolonged period. The revamping of RRBs on a stand alone basis would imply a revival of some RRBs and a closure of others and some hard decisions would need to be taken. There are unorthodox ways of improving the productivity of credit such as profit sharing by the employees of rural financing agencies and use of peer group pressure to generate total aversion to loan defaults.

CHANGING ROLE OF FINANCIAL INSTITUTIONS

The non-bank financial sector does have certain serious problems which need attention but these are best separated into issues relating to financial institutions (FIs) and those relating to the non-bank finance companies. The FIs are in a sense a lost tribe looking for an identity. The raison d'etre of these institutions was their special status as long-term development finance agencies. Their objective was to provide longer-term capital at concessional rates. To this end the FIs were provided funds allocated under the market borrowing programme at concessional rates and banks and insurance companies were compelled to invest in these SLR bonds. The RBI also provided concessional loans out of the Long-Term Operations Funds, which in turn were fed from the RBI's profits. As part of the reform, concessional sourcing of funds was discontinued for FIs and, as a logical consequence, the provision of concessional rates of interest to their borrowers was discontinued. The FIs are increasingly providing short-term accommodation to borrowers and also raising short-term resources in the market. Thus the system is moving towards universal banking.

The pertinent question then is one of a level playing field between banks and FIs. The FIs need to be able to fully participate in the payments system and enjoy all the facilities, including that of providing cheque writing facilities for their clients. But equally, they should be subject to the same regulatory framework as banks. In particular, the FIs should be subject to the same reserve requirements as banks. The FIs should be required to maintain reserve requirements on their total liabilities and not merely their deposit liabilities. The appropriateness of the height of the reserve requirement is essential. Assuming, for instance, that the recommendation for banks of a 3 per cent CRR is implemented by the year 2000—and it appears that there is a strong possibility of this being implemented—the FIs can be subject to a 3 per cent CRR by the year 2000 on their total and not merely incremental liabilities. Again in the case of the SLR, the FIs can, over a somewhat extended period, say up to the year 2002, be subjected in a phased manner to the same stipulation as for banks (presently 25 per cent). With these adjustments FIs should be converted into banks and be subject to the same regulatory framework as banks.

Moreover, the substantially diluted prudential norms for FIs have no justification whatsoever. Illustratively, there is a moratorium of two years before an asset is downgraded and substandard assets are provided for only if the provisions required are in excess of the special reserve. Time overruns are also extremely generous for projects financed by FIs and the earlier salutary norms have been significantly diluted. Furthermore, provisions for investment depreciation are much diluted for FIs. It is essential to have a uniform system of prudential norms for FIs and banks.

NON-BANK FINANCIAL COMPANIES

The experience of non-bank financial intermediaries has been unsatisfactory in a number of countries, e.g. Thailand, Indonesia, and the United States. What is uniquely Indian is that non-bank finance companies are allowed to raise deposits on a large scale. The non-bank financial companies' segment is the Achilles heel of the Indian financial system. It would be no exaggeration to say that this is the segment where there could be a major upheaval of large defaults with systemic dangers particularly during a process of financial liberalization. The legislative framework has only recently been strengthened and there is need for early action to ensure that deposit-taking activities of these companies are put on a sound footing. First, the capital adequacy requirements for these companies need to be substantially raised, say from 8 per cent to 16 per cent over a two-year period. Second, the SLR should be raised to 25 per cent over the next two years. Third, such companies that do not meet these requirements during each phase should face a total cessation of incremental deposit mobilization. It is not meaningful to give a company a waiver from prudential norms and in the interregnum allow the company to raise deposits. A temporary breather to attain various norms by a later date is meaningful only if the company is debarred from raising deposits in the interregnum. Fourth, a regime should be developed which actively promotes amalgamation. Visceral memories should tell the regulators that in the 1960s the RBI had a proactive policy of moratorium and amalgamation of weak banks and what needs to be put in place is a special legislation to explicitly facilitate such a rationalization of the finance companies. In the absence of early action the authorities could find themselves sitting on a volcano which could erupt any moment. Lastly, the authorities need to ensure that a system of deposit insurance for finance companies is not sponsored by them. If the authorities were to introduce such deposit insurance, it would not only foster reckless deposit taking but encourage defaults and the RBI and the government would end up picking up the tab.

IMPACT OF LIBERALIZING CAPITAL ACCOUNT ON BANKS

As the Indian economy undertakes an inexorable march to CAC, it is clear that the biggest hurdle would be the inadequacies of the financial sector. With the launching of financial sector reforms since 1991-2, we have, so to say, crossed the Rubicon and there can be no turning back on reform. The adjustments required to strengthen the financial system would be necessary as part of the on-going reform. This is not contingent on the move to CAC, though CAC would throw into bold relief the weaknesses of the financial system.

In an increasingly globalized economy the only choice is between an orderly and a disorderly move to CAC. But given the potential dangers in the financial system there is need for early institution of certain safeguards. First, the present ceiling on external commercial borrowing is an extremely salutary regulation and should be retained to ensure that Indian corporates do not resort to undue and imprudent reliance on such borrowing as these risks, though once removed from banks, would eventually lodge in the banks as corporate accounts become substandard. Second, there should be close examination of the risk management capabilities of banks' borrowers and there must be a system of ensuring that such corporates maintain hedged positions at all times. Banks must be required to set up full-fledged risk management departments and mere asset-liability committees (ALCOs) should not be considered as substitute for comprehensive risk management in banks. Third, while liberalizing capital account, such liberalization should be available only to the stronger elements of the financial sector. It would be dangerous to allow banks with below normal capital adequacy, high NPAs, and total lack of risk management skills to dabble in international money markets. There is great merit in restricting such access only to strong, well-managed banks and FIs.

As part of the reform process, early attention should be accorded to the integration of money, securities, and forex markets as such institutional development takes time. The RBI should give a lead in this matter by integrating its own operations in these areas and the RBI's three Advisory Committees should be merged. This would also signal to banks the need for integrated operations. Such corporates as totally eschew from the cash credit system, should be provided access to the money market. Banks which meet certain stiff criteria on capital adequacy NPAs and risk management skills should be given greater freedom to operate in international money markets. This will broaden supply in the forward exchange market and enable foreign institutional investors to be covered in the forward market for their equity exposures.

While allowing banks and FIs greater freedom to invest and borrow overseas, it would be necessary to set stringent conditions. Likewise while giving corporates the right to raise funds abroad, there should be stringent conditions of viability as a single failure can have adverse repercussions on India's standing in the international market and, more specifically, such failures ultimately get lodged in banks. Thus there is a strong case for continuing a cautious approach on foreign borrowings by corporates.

There are certain important broader financial policy issues which would impinge on the banking system. An artificial and prolonged defence of an unsustainable exchange rate through very high interest rates can damage the banking system as even otherwise viable commercial loans become unserviceable. Furthermore, an unsustainably high interest rate regime because of a very large government borrowing programme could adversely affect the viability of banks. As such the overall health of the banking system is also vitally dependent on a sound overall financial policy.

As the capital account is liberalized, the weaknesses in the financial system will come out into the open. A proactive policy will ensure that these issues are addressed well before the problems reach crisis proportions. It is to this end that this chapter has addressed some issues relating to the financial sector.

India's Banking Sector: Current Status, Emerging Challenges, and Policy Imperatives in a Globalized Environment

JAYATI SARKAR*

1. INTRODUCTION

In India, as in many developing countries, the commercial banking sector has been the dominant element in the country's financial system. The sector has performed the key functions of providing liquidity and payment services to the real sector, and has accounted for the bulk of the financial intermediation process. Besides institutionalizing savings, the banking sector has contributed to the process of economic development by serving as a major source of credit to households, government, business, and to weaker sectors of the economy like village and small-scale industries and agriculture. Over the years, around 30 to 40 per cent of gross household savings have been in the form of bank deposits, and around 60 per cent of the assets of all financial institutions have been accounted for by commercial banks.

An important landmark in the development of the banking sector in recent years has been the initiation of reforms following the recommendations of the first Narasimham Committee on Financial System (NCFS). This Committee was set up in August 1991 by the government of India as part of its economy-wide structural adjustment programme, and in response to the unsatisfactory economic and qualitative performance of public sector banks. In reviewing the strengths and weaknesses

*Acknowledgements: The author would like to thank James Hanson of the World Bank for his insightful comments on earlier drafts of the chapter. This chapter has also benefited from the comments of Subrata Sarkar of the Indira Gandhi Institute of Development Research and that of the participants at the Conference on 'India: A Financial Sector for the Twenty-first Century'. The usual disclaimer applies.

of these banks, the Committee suggested several measures to transform the Indian banking sector from a highly regulated to a more market-oriented system, and to enable it to compete effectively in an increasingly globalized environment. Many of the recommendations of the Committee, especially those pertaining to interest rate and entry deregulation, and institution of prudential regulation and transparent accounting norms, were in line with banking policy reforms implemented by a host of developing countries since the 1970s.

This chapter analyses the response of the banking sector to the reform measures and identifies the emerging challenges facing Indian banking going into the twenty-first century. In particular, the analysis is centred around the following questions:

- What is the current status of the banking sector and how have the reforms impacted its performance and soundness? What are the major findings with respect to portfolio choice, competition, profitability, efficiency, non-performing assets (NPAs), and capital adequacy norms?
- What are the emerging challenges facing the banking sector going into the twenty-first century?
- What are the institutional obstacles to meeting the emerging challenges?
- What do we do about the obstacles? How have other countries coped with some of the problems facing the Indian banking sector today?

To put the analysis in perspective, the chapter begins with a short description of the evolution and structure of Indian banking and an overview of the reforms.

2. EVOLUTION OF INDIAN BANKING

Prior to 1969, all banks, except the State Bank of India and its seven associate banks, were privately owned. However, there was a perception among policy makers that under private ownership too many rural and semi-urban areas remained unserved by banks, whereas the banking industry had to be developed to 'touch the lives of millions'. Further, as India increasingly became a planned economy, policy makers felt that 'it would be difficult to undertake credit planning unless the linked control of industry and banks in the same [private] hands is snapped by the nationalization of banks'.[1] These considerations sparked off the drive

[1] Dr R.K. Hazari, in a report to the Planning Commission on 14 September 1967, on Industrial Planning and Licensing Policy, quoted in Tandon (1989), p. 256.

for 'social control' of banks by the government, and under the Nationalization Act of 1969, the fourteen largest privately owned domestic banks were nationalized. In 1980, under the same Act, the Government of India acquired ownership of six more private banks, bringing the total number of nationalized banks to twenty. The smaller privately owned banks were allowed to function side by side with nationalized banks. Foreign banks were also allowed to continue in the new milieu, but their expansion was stringently regulated.

The spread of commercial banking since nationalization is shown in Table 4.1. All important development indicators such as total deposits mobilized, credit disbursed, per capita deposits, and per capita credit

TABLE 4.1
THE SPREAD OF SCHEDULED COMMERCIAL BANKING 1969–96

	June 1969	June 1985	March 1991	March 1996
I. Number of reporting banks	71	267	272	287
1. State Bank of India and associates	8	8	8	8
(SBI & A)				
2. Nationalized banks (NBs)	14	20	20	19
3. Domestic private sector banks (PVs) of which	36	31	25	34
—New private banks (NPV)	0	0	0	9
4. Foreign banks (FBs)	13	20	23	30
5. Regional Rural Banks (RRBs)	0	188	196	196
II. Total branches in India	8832	53,165	60,646	63,168
1. SBI & A	2602	10,742	12,461	12,968
2. NBs	4617	25,145	29,812	31,177
3. PVs	1,483	4,540	3,703	4,266
—NPVs	0	0	0	76
4. FBs	130	136	139	156
5. RRBs	0	12,602	14,531	14,517
III. Quantitative expansion				
(i) Share of rural branches in total branches	22.2	58.74	58.46	52.4
(ii) Population per office ('000)	64	15	14	15
(iii) Total deposits (Rs bn)	137.8	614.6	1101.2	1448.9
(iv) Total credit (Rs bn)	106.8	406.0	667.0	848.4
(v) Deposits per office (Rs bn)	16.6	12.0	18.3	23
(vi) Credit per office (Rs bn)	13.0	7.9	11..0	13.5
(vii) Per capita deposits (Rs)	261.1	818.2	1296.1	1551.1
(viii) Per capita credit (Rs)	201.7	540.7	784.9	908.1
(ix) Deposits as a percentage of national income	15.5	39.4	49.4	50.6

Notes: (iii)–(viii) are in real terms. Real estimates are obtained by deflating nominal estimates by Wholesale Price Index (1981–82 = 100).

Sources: RBI, *Banking Statistics*, RBI, *Basic Statistical Returns*; and RBI, *Annual Report*, all several issues.

availability point to very significant expansion of the banking sector in real terms between 1969 and 1996. The spread of banking to the masses is evident from an increase in the share of rural branches, a drastic reduction in the population served per bank, increases in per capita deposits and credit availability, and an increase in deposits and credit per office.

Notwithstanding the positive role played by the banking sector since nationalization in institutionalizing savings and becoming a source of credit to the small borrower, the cumulative effect of excessive focus on quantitative achievement and social obligations, often at the expense of achieving profitability and efficiency, took its toll. Rates of return became low by international standards, the capital base was eroded, NPAs were on the rise, and customer service was below expectation. These conditions led to the realization that progressive deregulation in the policy environment was necessary to bring about improvement in the performance of the banking sector. The government in 1991 under which controls on trade and industry were being liberalized also deemed deregulation of the sector necessary in view of the adoption of the structural-adjustment-cum-stabilization programme. For the market-oriented reforms in the real sector to succeed, it was important to ensure that the financial sector was liberalized so that scarce investible funds were drawn to the most productive uses and the cost of investible funds to the real sector declined. All these considerations led to the gradual liberalization of banking sector operations since the mid-1980s and culminated in the initiation of fundamental banking sector reforms in 1992 with the acceptance of key recommendations of the Narasimham Committee.

Consequently, a major change in the institutional set-up of the banking sector followed when the Reserve Bank of India (RBI), the country's central bank, allowed the entry of new private sector banks with the objective of generating increased competition in the banking system. To this effect, the RBI issued guidelines in January 1993 for the establishment of these banks, and several new private sector and foreign banks commenced operations. Finally, as proposed in the Union Budget for 1996–7, guidelines were issued in August 1996 for setting up of new private local area banks (LAB) with jurisdiction over two or three contiguous districts to provide competition in rural banking. In January 1997, the RBI granted 'in principle' approval to two LABs.

The present institutional set-up of the Indian commercial banking sector is shown in Chart 4.1. The banking sector is dominated by scheduled commercial banks, which account for nearly 95 per cent of all banking operations. Among the scheduled banks are public sector banks, namely the State Bank of India and its seven associates (SBI & A), the 19 nationalized banks (NBs), and 196 Regional Rural Banks (RRBs), as well as 24 old domestic privately owned banks (DPVs), 9 new private sector banks (NDPVs), and 30 foreign banks (FBs). The SBI&A and NB together account for nearly 85 per cent of banking operations. RRBs, although much larger in number, account for only 5 per cent of total operations.

CHART 4.1
INSTITUTIONAL SET-UP OF THE INDIAN COMMERCIAL BANKING SECTOR

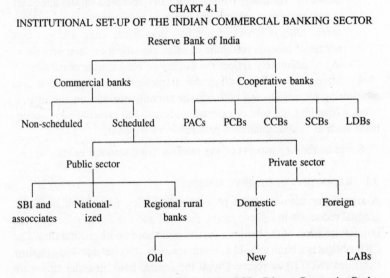

Notes: PACs: Primary Agricultural Credit Societies; PCBs: Primary Cooperative Banks; CCBs: Central Cooperative Banks; SCBs: State Cooperative Banks; LDBs: Land Development Banks; LABs: Local Area Banks.

3. KEY ASPECTS OF BANKING SECTOR REFORMS

The banking sector reforms, initiated in 1992, have aimed at increasing the profitability and efficiency of public sector banks as well as improving their safety and soundness. The RBI, till date, has adopted a four-pronged approach for this purpose (see Annexure at the end of the chapter).

1. It has deregulated the existing policy framework aimed towards removing the external constraints bearing on the profitability and functioning of commercial banks. This was done through

gadually reducing the cash reserve ratio (CRR) and statutory liquidity ratio (SLR) to bring down the appropriation of bank resources by the RBI, freeing interest rates on deposits and loans, liberalizing branching policy, and eliminating quantitative restrictions on credit allocation by banks.

2. Created a competitive environment by allowing entry of new private and foreign banks, and directing nationalized banks to rely on the capital market for supplementing their equity base.

3. Sought to improve the financial soundness and credibility of banks by instituting (i) internationally accepted capital adequacy norms requiring commercial banks to maintain a capital to risky assets ratio (CRAR) of not less than 8 per cent, and (ii) new norms of income recognition, asset classification, and provisioning to accurately reflect the quality of banks' loan portfolios.

4. Strengthened the institutional framework for supervision and monitoring by introducing both off-site surveillance and on-site inspections, expanding the role of external auditors, and creating new institutions such as ombudsman and debt recovery tribunals.

Some of the key aspects of the reforms are discussed below.

3.1 REDUCTION IN RESERVE RATIOS

A significant feature of the post-reforms policy framework has been gradual reduction in reserve ratios, the CRR and the SLR to decrease the implicit taxation of the banking system and shore up its profitability. The CRR obligates a bank to hold a certain fraction of its net demand and time liabilities (NDTL) as reserves with the central bank in order to ensure liquidity of the banking system. The SLR requires banks to invest a pre-determined proportion of its NDTL in government and other approved securities. While these requirements serve as instruments of monetary control, they also pre-empt lendable resources of banks and distort portfolio choice. As these reserves earn no, or relatively low, rates of interest, the maintenance of high reserve ratios impinges on the income earning potential of banks. Often this leads to high interest spreads as banks, being able to lend only part of the deposits mobilized, have to charge substantially higher lending rates compared to deposit rates to cover the cost of funds.

The CRR, which was 15 per cent in 1991–2, has been gradually reduced over the years and is, as of April 1998, at 10 per cent (see Table 4.2). The base SLR that stood at 38.5 per cent in 1991–2 has also been reduced to a uniform level of 25 per cent (see Table 4.2), and the system of multiple prescriptions for the SLR has been withdrawn. Finally, since October 1997, all cash balances maintained by banks with the RBI on account of the CRR have been earning a uniform interest of 4 per cent, as against earning an effective interest rate of 3.5 per cent earlier under a two-tier formula.

TABLE 4.2
TRENDS IN CASH-RESERVE RATIO (CRR) AND STATU-
TORY LIQUIDITY RATIO (SLR) 1991–2 TO 1997–8

	CRR (as % of NDTL*)	Base SLR (as % of NDTL*)
1991–2	15	38.5
1992–3	15	37.75
1993–4	14	34.75
1994–5	15	33.75
1995–6	14	31.5
April '96	13	31.5
July '96	12	31.5
October '96	11.5	31.5
January '97	10	31.5
October '97	9.75	25.0
January '98	10.5	25.0
April '98	10.0	25.0

Note: *Net demand and time liabilities

Source: RBI, *Annual Report*, various issues, and RBI, *Credit Policy*, October 1997 and April 1998.

3.2 INTEREST RATE DEREGULATION AND
FLEXIBILITY IN OPERATIONS

Prior to the reforms, interest rates on both deposits and loans were fully administered by the RBI and were 'highly complex and rigid'. The RBI stipulated maximum deposit rates on both savings and time deposits of all maturities, as well as minimum lending rates on loans of all maturities and sizes. This guaranteed banks a minimum interest rate spread and a measure of protection against increasing cost of operation. Along with interest rate regulation, the RBI also regulated credit allocation by banks through various mechanisms such as the Capital Authorization Scheme (CAS), Credit Monitoring Arrangement (CMA), consortium financing, and the lead bank system. Under the CAS, banks were expected to obtain prior authorization from the RBI before fresh or additional credit limits to large clients were sanctioned. Under the CMA, which replaced the CAS in 1988, banks were required to report to the RBI credit facilities sanctioned to large borrowers, i.e. those enjoying term loans of Rs 50 million or above, for post-sanction scrutiny. Under the scheme of consortium financing, the RBI ruled that if the credit limit of a single borrower from any bank exceeded 1.5 per cent of that bank's deposits, then formation of a consortium was obligatory to reduce the bank's credit risk. The largest lender in the consortium was designated to act as the lead bank which was responsible for credit appraisal, monitoring, and supervision, sharing other banking business of the borrower with participant banks in agreed proportions and taking the lead in arranging for reconstruction or rehabilitation of problem accounts. Besides establishing credit allocation mechanisms for the large borrower, the RBI also prescribed norms for working capital loans by industrial subsector and firm location under the Maximum Permissible Bank Finance (MPFB) scheme. Under the MPBF, the RBI in effect decided how much of working capital a bank could lend to each and every borrower, and laid down inventory norms stipulating exactly how much stock of raw materials, finished goods and receivables would be financed by banks in a vast majority of industries.

Interest rate controls as well as stringent credit allocation mechanisms eliminated the scope of price competition among banks and destroyed their incentive to allocate resources according to highest value use. To this extent, the phased deregulation of interest rates has been one of the cornerstones of the reform process. Deregulation of interest rate was also expected to enable banks to compete more effectively for funds with the capital market and other financial intermediaries that had no restrictions on their pricing of loans.

The first step in deregulating lending rates was taken in October 1994, when rates were deregulated for advances greater than Rs 200,000. Banks have, however, been advised to announce and maintain a specified band over the prime lending rate (PLR) to keep the range of lending rates across different types of risks within reasonable limits. Lending rates for loans less that Rs 200,000 have also been partially deregulated since April 1998 in order to remove the disincentive to the flow of credit towards small borrowers. As against the earlier regulations under which interest on credit limits up to Rs 25,000 was prescribed at 12 per cent and for credit limits between Rs 25,000 and Rs 200,000, the rate was not to exceed 13.5 per cent per annum, under current regulations, interest on all loans below Rs 200,000 should not exceed the PLR which is available to the best borrowers of the concerned bank.

Deregulation in lending rates has been accompanied by liberalization of various quantitative restrictions on credit allocation, giving banks more operational freedom to evolve their own methods of assessing working capital requirements of borrowers, but within the prudential guidelines and exposure norms prescribed by the RBI. Accordingly, all instructions relating to MPBF and CMA have been withdrawn since April 1997. Similar deregulation have also been made with respect to term finance, where the RBI has withdrawn its stipulations both on the time and quantum of loans that can be granted by banks either individually or in consortia for a single project.

The process of deregulating deposit rates in phases began in April 1992 and has gathered momentum in recent years. Deregulation of term deposit rates first took the form of the RBI switching from prescribing a single rate for each category of term deposit (determined by maturity period) to announcing a ceiling rate below which banks were free to fix their deposit rates. Since July 1996, the RBI has been abolishing the ceiling for deposits of different maturities, starting from those with the highest maturity, and by April 1998, interest rates on deposits beyond fifteen days have been freed. Banks can now charge differential rates on deposits of similar maturity but different sizes. However, interest rates on savings deposits continue to be administered by the RBI. Interest rates on NRI term deposits under the Non-Resident (External) Rupee Accounts (NR(E)RA) scheme have also been deregulated, and banks have been given the freedom to determine their own interest rates on deposits under the Foreign Currency Non-Resident Accounts (Banks) (FCNR(B)) scheme subject to a ceiling that is prescribed by the RBI from time to time. Besides, banks are no longer required to obtain prior concurrence of the Indian Banks' Association (IBA) or prior approval of the RBI for introducing new deposit mobilization schemes, except for NRI deposits. However, the banks are required to obtain prior approval of their respective boards and follow the directives on interest rates, premature withdrawal, sanction of loans and advances against deposits, etc. issued by the RBI from time to time. The phased reduction in interest rates since the reforms and as of 21 October 1997, is shown in Table 4.3.

3.3 ENTRY DEREGULATION

Entry of private banks was deregulated in January 1993. Between January 1993 and March 1997, 19 new private sector banks—9 domestic, and 10 foreign—were started, increasing the total number of scheduled commercial banks, excluding specialized banks such as the RRBs, from

TABLE 4.3
STRUCTURE OF INTEREST RATES 1994-6

Rates	1994		1995			1996			1997		
	18 Oct	1 Nov	10 Feb	18 Apr	1 Oct	2 July	20 Aug	20 Oct	16 April	26 June	21 Oct
Lending rates:											
Size of credit limit											
(i) Up to and Rs 25,000	12.0	12.0	12.0	12.0	12.0	12.0	12.0	12.0	12.0	12.0	12.0
(ii) Above Rs 25,000 - 200,000	13.5	13.5	13.5	13.5	13.5	13.5	13.5	13.5	13.5	13.5	13.5
(iii) Over Rs 200,000	Free	Free	Free	Free	Free	Free	Free	Free	Free	Free	Free
	(14)	(14)	(15)	(15.5)	(15.5)	(16.5)	(16-16.5)	(14.5-15)[e]	(14-14.5)	(13.5-14)	(13-13.5)[b]
Deposit rates:											
(i) Current	0	0	0	0	0	0	0	0	0	0	0
(ii) Savings	5.0	4.5	4.5	4.5	4.5	4.5	4.5	4.5	4.5	4.5	4.5
(iii) Term											
(a) 46 days to 3 yrs & over	Max 10	Max 10	Max 10	Max 10	–	–	–	–	–	–	–
(b) 46 days to 2 yrs	–	–	–	–	Max. 12	–	–	–	–	–	–
(c) Above 2 yrs	–	–	–	–	Free	–	–	–	–	–	–
(d) 30 days to 1yr	–	–	–	–	–	Max 11	Max 11	Max 10	Not > bank rate minus 2%	Not > bank rate minus 2%	Free
(e) Above 1 yr	–	–	–	–	–	Free	Free	Free	Free	Free	Free
Inflation Rate[a]	8.9	9.7	11.7	10.0	8.4	5.7	6.6	6.5	6.3	4.7	3.5
Bank Rate	12	12	12	12	12	12	12	12	11	10	9

Notes: 'Free' means banks are free to charge interest rates decided by them; –: Not applicable; Figures in brackets denote the Prime Lending Rate (PLR) of five major scheduled commercial banks. a: Annualized monthly rate. b: PLR of three major scheduled commercial banks as of end October 1997.

Sources: RBI, *Annual Report*, several issues, RBI, *Busy Season Credit Policy*, October 1997, Centre for Monitoring Indian Economy, *Monthly Review*, several issues.

73 in 1991–2 to 92 in 1996–7. The RBI has sought to ensure that the new entrants are professionally managed, financially viable, and technologically strong, and that there are no adverse consequences such as concentration of credit. Capital norms of foreign banks have also been substantially liberalized. Joint ventures between foreign and Indian banks have been permitted for the first time since Independence, with foreign banks being allowed to own up to 20 per cent of equity.

3.4 PRUDENTIAL REGULATIONS

The RBI has taken major steps towards liberalizing the operating environment of banks in order to improve their financial health and credibility. To this effect, it has introduced internationally accepted prudential norms relating to income recognition, asset classification, provisioning, and capital adequacy. These norms are recognized world over and are considered fundamental in ensuring the soundness and solvency of commercial banks.

Capital adequacy norms require commercial banks to maintain a capital to risky assets ratio (CRAR), of not less than 8 per cent, as recommended by the Bank of International Settlements (BIS). Further, at least 4 per cent of risk-weighted assets were to be in the form of pure capital (Tier I), that is equity capital and free reserves. Such norms were expected to minimize the problem of inadequacy of capital compared to risk exposure that has persistently plagued public sector banks. It was hoped that institution of the BIS standard would provide Indian banks with a comfortable cushion against insolvency, thereby ensuring market stability. New norms of income recognition, asset classification, and provisioning were introduced to reflect more accurately the quality of the loan portfolios, and to obtain a true picture of the financial situation of each bank. By one estimate (MOF, 1993), the profits of twenty-eight public sector banks were reduced by 45 per cent due to a switch to the new accounting norms.

Prudential regulations have been increasingly strengthened over the years. This has been especially with respect to the classification of assets into four categories: standard, substandard, doubtful, and loss assets. In India, standard assets are defined as credit facilities with respect to some of which interest or principal or both are paid by due date, and for others, where the amount due is paid within thirty days of the due date. NPAs are non-standard assets. Under current regulations an asset is treated as an NPA if it remains 'past due', for a period of two quarters. While initially, banks were not required to classify accounts with outstandings below Rs 25,000 into four categories, but were required to make provisions at a flat rate, presently these advances have also come under the purview of detailed classification. Prudential guidelines for agricultural advances have also been made more stringent.

3.5 INSTITUTIONAL STRENGTHENING

Strengthening of the institutional framework has come in the form of (1) strengthening the supervisory process, and (2) creation of new institutions like the Board of Financial Supervision, ombudsman, and debt recovery tribunals. The present supervisory system attempts to make a substantial improvement over the earlier system in terms of frequency, coverage, focus, and tools of supervision.

Currently, the RBI supervisory strategy comprises both off-site surveillance and on-site inspections. A detailed off-site surveillance system based on a prudential supervisory reporting framework on a quarterly basis covering capital adequacy, asset quality, loan concentration, operational results, and connected lending has been made operational. On-site inspection, to be conducted annually since July 1997, involves the evaluation of the total operations and performance of banks under the CAMELS (viz. Capital Adequacy, Asset Quality, Management, Earning, Liquidity, and System) system followed in many countries including the US. This involves the evaluation of capital adequacy, asset quality, management, earnings, liquidity, and internal control systems of banks. The role of external auditors has also been enhanced and enlarged whereby auditors are now required to verify compliance with SLR computation and prudential norms and also report serious irregularities to the RBI.

Over the years, the RBI has also taken a number of measures to improve transparency and disclosure norms in the published accounts of banks. From 1996–7 disclosure under 'provisions and contingencies' in the profit and loss account has become more detailed with banks now being required to separately list the provision for bad and doubtful debts, provision for diminution in the value of investments, and provision for taxes, instead of showing them as a conglomerate item. Banks are also required to disclose the capital adequacy ratio, as well as percentage of net NPA to net advances that were not required earlier.

In order to supervise financial institutions more effectively, the Board of Financial Supervision became operational in November 1994, and its supervisory scope was gradually extended to include first commercial banks, then development financial institutions and, finally, non-bank financial institutions. To facilitate the recovery of loans, debt recovery tribunals have been set up in major cities. However, their operations as well as constitutional validity have been challenged in some courts. Finally, in a bid to be more responsive to customer needs and complaints, the Banking Ombudsman Scheme was instituted in 1995 for expeditious and inexpensive resolution of customer complaints about deficiencies in banking services. Presently fourteen ombudsmen are functioning in the country.

4. REFORMS AND PERFORMANCE

What has been the response of the banking sector to the reforms? Let us look at the different aspects of bank performance which have been targeted by the reforms. These are:

  (i) deposit mobilization;
  (ii) portfolio choice;
  (iii) competition;
  (iv) profitability;
  (v) efficiency;
  (vi) capital adequacy;
  (vii) NPAs.

4.1 DEPOSIT MOBILIZATION

Since bank nationalization, deposit mobilization by public sector banks has been impressive with the ratio of currency and time deposits with banks to gross domestic product (i.e. M3/GDP) increasing steadily at a rate of between 14 and 17 per cent per annum in the last decade or so (Figure 4.1). The M3/GDP ratio reflects the extent of the public's willingness to hold the claims of the banking system as an investment, and determines the quantum of savings in the economy that can be channelled into investment by banks. As is evident from Figure 4.1, growth in the ratio in the post-reform years have been part of the earlier trend, and has closely followed the monetary policy regimes pursued by the RBI. The fluctuations in the reform years have been due to the tight monetary policy in the initial years, and later, on account of an easy monetary policy pursued by the RBI when the CRR was gradually being brought down. Further, since the reforms, as deposit rates were being deregulated progressively, market forces that are conditioned by the monetary and credit policy of the RBI have also increasingly determined the rate of deposit mobilization.

Estimates of trends in real deposit growth in the last three years reveal that the rate of growth has fluctuated, slackening between 1994–5 and

TABLE 4.4
GROWTH RATES OF KEY BANKING VARIABLES (1981–2 = 100)

Item	Per cent				
	1980-1–1989-90	1990-1–1995-6	1993-4–1994-5	1994-5–1995-6	1995-6–1996-7
1	2	3	4	5	6
Aggregate deposits	9.8	6.8	10.7	4.1	6.3
Time deposits	10.2	6.5	8.1	5.8	7.2
Bank credit	8.7	4.2	–1.6	9.3	–1.9
Investments in government securities	10.5	10.3	22.9	4.3	9.6

Notes: Compound annual growth rates. All estimates are in real terms.

Sources: Computed from RBI, *Annual Report, 1996–7*, and *RBI Bulletin*, several issues.

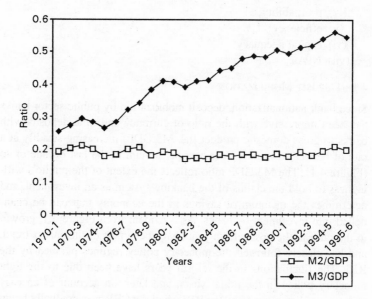

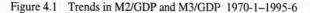

Figure 4.1   Trends in M2/GDP and M3/GDP 1970-1–1995-6

Notes: M2 = Currency (M1) + post office savings bank deposits.
M3 = M1 + time deposits with banks.
The dashed line marks the beginning of reforms.

Source: RBI, *Report of Currency and Finance*, several issues.

1995–6, but picking up during 1996–7 (Table 4.4). Between 1995–6 and 1996–7, total deposits increased in real terms by 6.3 per cent with time deposits registering an increase of 7.2 per cent. While nominal deposit rates have been decreasing during the latter period, real rates increased due to continuous decline in the rate of inflation.

One of the factors behind the recent growth in deposits has been increased mobilization of different types of NRI deposits. Recent trends in NRI deposits show that net inflows have shown a significant spurt in the last year, recording a three-fold increase over the preceding financial year. Along with increase in net inflows, there has been a change in the composition of the deposits, in favour of rupee denominated deposits. Some of the factors behind the spurt in NRI deposits in recent years have been (i) the existence of large differentials between domestic interest rates on these deposits and international interest rates of comparable maturity; (ii) the expectation of a stable exchange rate; (iii) the cost-effectiveness of these deposits relative to domestic liabilities as many of these deposits until April 1997 have been subjected to much lower CRR and SLR preemptions; and (iv) the deregulation of interest rates on NR(E)RA term deposits, and the increasing freedom given to banks to determine their own interest rates on deposits under the FCNR(B) scheme.

4.2 Portfolio Choice

On the assets side of the balance sheet, the two major sources of income for banks are credit and investment. Bank credit consists of food and non-food credit and bank investments comprise investment in government securities, bonds/ debentures/shares issued by public sector undertakings (PSUs), and private corporate sector and commercial paper.

The choice between the two alternative assets, credit and investment, depends on their relative risk and return. With the deregulation of interest rates on loans, and gradual reduction in CRR and SLR requirements, one would expect banks to alter their asset portfolios in favour of loans. However, post-reforms trends in credit and investment suggest otherwise.

As is evident from Table 4.4, the rate of growth of real credit has significantly declined in the years following the reforms, compared to the average growth rate in the ten years prior to reforms. The rate of growth of credit in the last three years has fluctuated, being negative in two out of the last three financial years. The rate of growth of non-food credit between 1995–6 and 1996–7 was a negative 0.7 per cent,

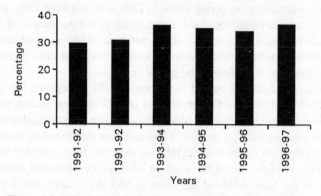

Figure 4.2   Investments in Government Securities as Proportion of
Major Earning Assets 1992–7

Source: Indian Banks' Association, *Performance Highlights of Banks*, several issues.

compared to a healthy growth rate of 11.6 per cent between 1994–5 and 1995–6. The decline in the rate of growth of credit has occurred concurrently with an increase in the rate of growth of investments in government securities (Table 4.4) and an increase in the proportion of government investments in major earning assets (Figure 4.2). While a comparison of growth rates of investment in government securities in real terms over the pre-reform (1980–90) and reform years (1991–6) does not reveal substantial differences between the two subperiods, it is important to note that increases in investments in the latter period took place in the context of declining SLR requirements. This has conse-quently resulted in commercial banks holding government securities above SLR requirements, while industry and trade complained of a lack of availability of credit.

Post-reform trends in credit and investment allocations of Indian banks bear some consistency with the credit crunch hypothesis. Accord-ing to this hypothesis, reforms characterized by relatively large increases in riskless interest rates are more likely to see a substitution away from riskier loans—a flight to government paper that can be described as 'credit crunch' (Caprio et al., •1997, p. 54). Such flight can be reinforced under prudential norms that require provisioning for risky assets such as loans in contrast to zero provisioning for riskless assets such as government securities. Some recent theoretical and applied work (Thakor, 1996) has shown that capital adequacy requirements linked solely to credit risk can increase equilibrium credit rationing and lower aggregate lending. This might be expected as the system moves from an environment of moral hazard and directed credit (by rule and suasion), to reflect a truer price of risk.

In India, recent trends in (riskless) interest rates and provisioning requirements closely conform to the underlying assumptions of the credit crunch hypothesis. Returns on government securities have risen sharply to move closer to the PLRs of banks. During 1996–7, while the yields in primary auctions of dates securities ranged between 13.40 and 13.85 per cent for stocks of two- to ten-year maturity, the PLR ranged between 14.5 and 16.5 per cent. Provisioning norms have also been been tightened in the recent years. Besides maintaining a capital adequacy ratio of 8 per cent for risk-weighted assets, banks have been required to classify all loans and advances into four categories and make appropriate provisions for NPAs. As mentioned earlier, such provisioning requirements have been increasing every year. In contrast, government securities have been always classified as risk-free and hence exempted from any provisioning requirements. Investments in government securities have also been exempted in calculating the capital adequacy requirement whereas regular bank advances have been attached a weightage of 100 per cent.

Notwithstanding the fact that there are legitimate grounds in subscribing to the credit crunch hypothesis, several competing hypotheses have been put forward to explain the decline in credit growth. One of these is the apparent stickiness of government securities investment and the inability of banks to adjust their investment portfolio to changes in regulatory and market conditions due to the absence of an active secondary market for such securities. The other is a demand side explanation that relates the slowdown of credit growth to the slowdown in economic conditions. For example, a recent analysis (Bhaumik and Mukhopadhyay, 1997) concludes that a significant part of the first half of 1996–7 witnessed a lack of adequate demand for credit, as opposed to credit rationing by banks. The RBI has also maintained that the introduction of capital adequacy requirements has not been the prime reason for higher investments in government securities as non-food credit expanded by more than 20 per cent in the years 1994–5 and 1995–6 when pressure was great to maintain capital adequacy requirement. The share of gross non-food credit going to industry between 1992 and 1996 has also improved marginally (Figure 4.3). Moreover, while there has been conspicuous shift in the asset portfolio mix of banks towards investments, the flow of funds to the commercial sector has

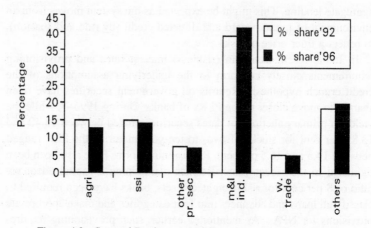

Figure 4.3 Sectoral Deployment of Gross Non-food Bank Credit

Notes: agri–agriculture, ssi–small scale industry, other pr. sec.–other priority sector, m and l ind.–medium and large industry, w. trade–wholesale trade.

Source: RBI, *Annual Report*, several issues.

increased in recent years through investments in commercial paper, bonds, and debentures issued by the corporate sector.

The debate on the proximate causes of the slowdown of credit off-take and credit crunch is likely to continue for some time. The RBI, under the presumption that credit crunch is a demand side problem, has sought to tackle it through infusing greater liquidity in the banking system under the Busy Season Credit Policy of 1997. Such infusion, following a period when the RBI had slowed money growth from a rapid pace, is expected to lower lending rates and stimulate demand. However, one cannot downplay the possible negative impact that changing relative rates of return and prudential regulations can have on a bank's decision to lend. This is especially so in the case of public sector banks on which the burden of provisioning is especially large, and for whom the problem of bad loans and loan recovery are more acute.

4.3 COMPETITION

Competition in the banking sector was expected to come from two channels. The first was from within the banking sector as incumbent banks competed with each other as well as with new entrants in an increasingly deregulated environment. The second was from outside the banking sector as both the incumbents and entrants competed with non-bank financial intermediaries.

Competition among Banks

There have been some limited signs of competition within the banking sector. With the entry of new private banks, the market shares of public sector banks in the deposit and advances market have declined by close to 4 percentage points from around 90 per cent in 1991–2 to around 85 per cent in 1995–6 (Table 4.5). The 5-bank concentration ratio has also declined from 47.2 per cent in 1992 to 44.1 per cent in 1996–7. There are also apparent signs of price competition, with public sector banks vying with each other and with private banks to cut lending rates from time to time. However, such cuts have mostly coincided with RBI credit policy announcements. Bank spreads have also declined in the last one and a half years in nominal terms (Figure 4.4). However, it is not *a priori* clear as to what extent the decrease has been triggered by an increase in liquidity (due to lower CRR) and to what extent it reflects genuine price competition.

There have also been apparent signs of service competition as public sector banks have been increasing their use of computer and telecommunication technology to provide improved and faster banking services. As Bhatt (1994) has noted, centralized decision making through directives and direct controls on credit allocation that existed prior to the reforms did not leave adequate scope for experimentation, innovation, and full use of widely dispersed information. Bank managements were concerned more with their dealings with the RBI and government than with good customer service and sound decision making relating to credit transactions. Innovations had also been resisted for long by bank unions, especially in the public sector banks.

In recent years, a number of public sector and old domestic private sector banks have been setting up ATMs, introducing tele-banking, increasing the number of branches providing specialized services, and introducing credit card operations. The computerization of branches of commercial banks has gathered momentum since 1993, and of the 2866 public sector bank branches identified for full computerization by 1997, about 2197 had been computerized by March 1997. However, computerized branches still remain a very small fraction, 5 per cent, of the total number of branches of these banks. All commercial banks (excluding RRBs) have also been advised to provide certain functional facilities at their non-branch/stand alone ATMs, such as PIN changes, requisition for

TABLE 4.5

SHARE OF BANK GROUPS IN DEPOSIT MARKET:
PRE- AND POST-REFORMS

Bank Group	1991–2	1996–7
State Bank and associates	28.9	27.4
Nationalized banks	60.6	55.5
Old private sector banks	4.7	7.3
New private sector banks	0	2.5
Foreign banks	5.8	7.3

Source: Computed from Indian Banks' Association,
Performance Highlights of Banks, several issues.

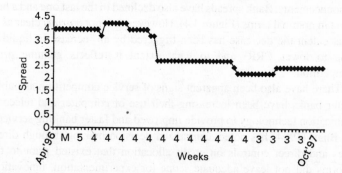

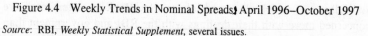

Figure 4.4   Weekly Trends in Nominal Spreads, April 1996–October 1997

Source: RBI, *Weekly Statistical Supplement*, several issues.

cheque books, statements of accounts, balance inquiries, and inter-account transfers for customers with accounts at centres where ATMs operate. The foreign and new domestic private banks, for whom accessibility has been a major drawback because of limited branch network, have attempted to overcome this by introducing services such as 'anywhere banking', 'home banking', and 'convenience banking'. Finally, under the Banking Ombudsman Scheme, ombudsmen have settled 2253 consumer complaints.

Competition from Other Financial Intermediaries

Other types of financial intermediation include capital market, development financial institutions, non-bank financial companies (NBFCs), and mutual funds. Before the reforms, the ability of these financial institutions, especially that of the NBFCs, was significantly limited by a host of RBI and Government of India regulations that favoured banks in the mobilization of deposits. Along with interest rates of Development Finance Institutions (DFIs) being regulated, entry of the private sector into financial services was strictly regulated. The capital market also remained weak and underdeveloped largely because of high transaction costs and lack of transparency in markets dealings.

The NBFCs and the capital market have experienced impressive growth in the first half of the 1990s. In 1992, the Securities and Exchange Board of India (SEBI) came into being as an agency to protect the interests of investors in securities and to promote a transparent and strong regulatory structure for the efficient functioning of the capital market. Merchant bankers, brokers, portfolio managers, and mutual funds were all brought under SEBI and RBI regulations. Such developments have somewhat increased the confidence of the small investor in non-bank deposits and investments.

The relative importance of commercial banks *vis-à-vis* NBFCs with respect to deposit mobilization has steadily declined over the years (Figure 4.5) even as deposit mobilization by banks has increased steadily. The regulated deposits of NBFCs as a proportion of total deposits mobilized by scheduled commercial banks has increased continuously from 1.2 per cent in 1991–2 to 7.6 per cent in 1995–6. The

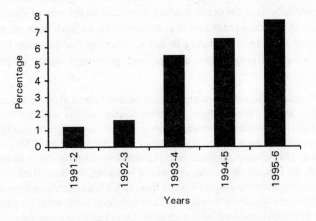

Figure 4.5   Regulated Deposits of NBFCs as a Percentage of
Total Bank Deposits 1992–6

Source: RBI, *Trends and Progress in Banking*, several issues.

attractiveness of NBFCs relative to banks lies in the fact that the former are in a position to offer higher rates of interest on deposits than commercial banks as these are mainly engaged in hire-purchase and leasing finance which allows them to charge higher interest rates on their loans. Moreover, the NBFCs, unlike banks, benefit from a lesser preemption of loanable funds due to their lower reserve requirements on their liabilities, and hence are in a position to provide finance at more attractive terms compared to banks engaged in similar lines of activities. The downside of the NBFCs has however been that these are perceived by depositors as having greater risk of failure due to less stringent regulatory oversight by the central bank and not being covered under any deposit insurance scheme unlike banks. The former perception is vindicated by several scams involving the NBFCs, the latest being the CRB Capital Market Limited group of finance companies, in which the total exposure of liabilities has been close to Rs 9.3 billion.[2] While the impact of the CRB scam on the financial system and on the confidence of the small depositor in the NBFCs has been quite adverse, the government has correctly avoided the short-run solution of giving *ex post* deposit insurance and has instead focused on the more fundamental issue of strengthening regulation and supervision of the NBFCs through enacting a new set of NBFC regulations.

Apart from competition from the NBFCs and corporates on the deposit side, commercial banks have also been facing competition from these institutions in the credit market, especially in the area of short-term finance. While cash credits from commercial banks have been the major source of short-term financing in India, other options for such finance have been emerging where a large and growing number of private

---

[2]CRB Capital and its sister concerns covered the entire gamut of financial activities including leasing, hire-purchase, corporate finance, project advisory services, fixed deposit mobilization, foreign exchange services, and securities trading. The CRB scam broke out when the State Bank of India discovered that CRB paid out almost Rs 470 million as dividends to its shareholders with no money in its account to cover the cheques. When cheques started bouncing, the State Bank of India notified government investigators. Since then, all CRB accounts have been frozen and a liquidator appointed for recovery. The break-up of liabilities of the company is Rs 1.33 billion to the banking system alone. Other parties to whom the company owes money include the Gujarat government (Rs 0.2 billion), Rs 1 billion, in inter-corporate deposits, mutual fund investors (Rs 1.86 bn), depositors in the company's fixed deposits (Rs 1.86 billion), and Rs 2.6 billion from public issues.

financial institutions are becoming engaged. These are bill discounting, factoring, issue of commercial papers for 90 days, and raising unsecured deposits from the public for periods ranging from 6 months to 3 years. An active short-term money market for inter-corporate borrowings has also been emerging which threatens to dry out some of the lending opportunities of commercial banks. Finally, while commercial banks are making forays into long-term project financing, DFIs like the IDBI and ICICI, are trying to make some headway in short-term financing. However, in this case, the relative position of commercial banks *vis-à-vis* the DFIs has remained unchanged, with the assets of commercial banks being nearly twice those of the DFIs.

The other areas of competition for banks from private financial institutions have been with respect to non-fund-based services such as capital market advisory services, foreign exchange services, investment consultancy, portfolio management, factoring, and leasing and venture capital (see Box 1). However, recent policy changes have strengthened

BOX 1
BANKS *VIS-À-VIS* OTHER FINANCIAL INSTITUTIONS

	Commercial Banks	DFIs	Investment Institutions	NBFCs
Major players	SBI & associates, nationalized banks, old private banks, new private banks, foreign banks.	All India term lending institutions such as the IDBI, ICICI, IFCI, NABARD, and IRBI.	LIC, GIC, UTI, public and private sector mutual funds.	HDFC, LIC, housing finance, equipment leasing and hire-purchase agencies, nidhis and chit funds.
Primary nature of activity	Working capital financing, and recently in long-term project financing following enhancement of limits for term lending. Recent forays in non-fund-based services such as factoring, hire-purchase, equipment leasing, forex dealings, housing finance, funds management, mostly through subsidiaries.	Long-term project funds for industrial projects and agricultural development. Recent forays into short-term financing.	Insurance and funds management.	Hire-purchase, equipment leasing, housing finance, capital market intermediation, etc.

the scope of commercial banks in these activities as the RBI has waived the limit on the period of lease financing by commercial banks. It has allowed banks to take long-term exposures in parabanking activities like equipment leasing, hire-purchase financing, and factoring services. Till recently banks were allowed to take only five-year exposures in lease financing in normal circumstances and seven years in exceptional cases. Banks have now been given freedom in regard to the period of lease finance provided. The diversification of commercial banks into non-fund-based activities has shown up in an increase in the share of non-interest earnings as a proportion of total income. Between 1991–2 and 1995–6, this share has increased from around 12.31 per cent to 16.79 per cent for the State Bank of India group, from 9.72 per cent to 10.85 for nationalized banks, and from 9.62 per cent to 16.02 per cent for domestic private sector banks.

As with regard to NBFCs, the relative position of banks has also somewhat declined *vis-à-vis* capital markets since reforms in the capital market gained momentum. While assets intermediated by banks have grown by nearly 3 per cent, those by the capital market, as measured by market capitalization of the Bombay Stock Exchange (BSE), have grown by about 9 per cent. Consequently, the share of banks in total assets intermediated by banks and capital market has gone down from 75 per cent in 1990 to around 47 per cent in 1996.

4.4 PROFITABILITY

There is some debate about whether profitability measures are appropriate indicators of performance of public sector enterprises that are required to produce socio-economic outputs that cannot be reflected in balance sheets. This is especially relevant in the case of public sector banks in India whose overriding objectives have been social rather than economic. However, with the onset of reforms, policy makers have laid increasing emphasis on profitability as an important benchmark against which the performance of public sector banks is to be judged in the post-reforms era (MOF, 1993). Further, as some public sector banks are already listed in the stock market and more banks are likely to approach the capital market to mobilize additional funds, improvements in profitability are being sought by public sector bank management in order to signal good performance to existing and prospective shareholders.

Cross-country trends in profitability following banking sector deregulation and reforms do not reveal any clear-cut effect on bank profitability.

This is perhaps because of the fact that the multitude of reform measures that are introduced tend to pull a bank's bottom line in different directions. On the one hand, changes in regulatory norms that facilitate entry and expansion are expected to pull down profits and spreads as increased competition would push up deposit rates and pull down loan rates. On the other hand, changes in regulatory norms that reduce preemption of bank resources by the government and give greater freedom to build up more market-determined loan portfolios are likely to have a positive impact on profits. Accordingly, it is difficult to make a clear-cut inference by looking at the variation in profitability immediately before and after deregulation. In addition, variation in bank profitability is likely to be a bank-specific phenomenon, especially during the initial years, as the ability and skills to adjust to changes in operating environment are likely to vary across banks.

Figure 4.6 shows the return to working funds in percentage terms for both public and private sector banks since 1985. The pre-reform years are, however, not strictly comparable with post-reform estimates due to the lax income recognition and asset classification norms prevailing in the former period. Post-reforms trends in profitability show significant variability for all groups of banks except that of private sector banks that has experienced a continuous increase in bottom line. The variability has been especially noticeable for public sector banks. While there was marked improvement in the profitability of public sector banks between 1993–4 and 1994–5, such improvement remained short-lived as the profitability of public sector banks as a group suffered a setback in 1995–6. Latest estimates for 1996–7, however, show a turnaround, with public sector banks as a whole wiping out the loss of Rs 3.71 billion in 1995–6 and turning a net profit of Rs 30.95 billion. The number of loss-making banks has also decreased from eight in 1995–6 to three in 1996–7.

Comparing among bank groups, new private sector banks are the most profitable followed by foreign banks and domestic private sector banks. Public sector banks are still significantly less profitable than private sector banks (Figure 4.6). It is important to note that there is considerable heterogeneity in performance among public sector banks, and that the persistent underperformance of a bunch of banks has neutralized the achievements of the performers and has thus caused public sector bank profitability as a whole to remain at relatively low levels. For instance, in 1995–6, the losses of eight banks exceeded the profits of nineteen banks, resulting in a loss for public sector banks as a whole.

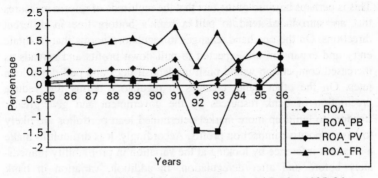

Figure 4.6   Trends in Profitability of Commercial Banks 1985–96

Source: Computed from Indian Banks' Association, *Financial Analysis of Banks,* and *Performance Highlights of Banks*, several issues.

4.5   EFFICIENCY

There are various measures of cost efficiency that one might consider in the context of the banking sector. Four important efficiency measures are presented in Table 4.6. These are: (i) the net interest margin (NIM), defined as the difference between interest income earned and interest payments expended divided by average total assets, which measures the core earning capacity of the bank;[3] (ii) operating profit to staff expense (OPSE), defined as operating profit divided by total staff expense, which is an indicator of labour productivity; (iii) operating cost ratio (OCR), defined as total operating cost divided by average total assets, which measures a bank's ability to economize on total costs; and (iv) staff expense ratio (SER), defined as total staff expense divided by average total assets, which is a measure of manpower expenses.

[3]Although the terms NIM and spread are sometimes used interchangeably as measures of operating efficiency (Barltrop and McNaughton, 1992), the technical definitions of the two are different. While NIM is defined as the difference between interest income and interest expense as a percentage of total assets, spread is defined as the difference between interest rate on loans and interest rate on deposits. While spread, by excluding the impact of non-interest bearing demand deposits, capital and non-remunerated reserve requirements on net interest earned, isolates the effect of interest rates on bank profits, NIM, by measuring interest differential income as a percentage of total assets, identifies the core earning capacity of the bank. Thus a change in spread following a change in preemptions through the CRR may not necessarily imply a change in NIM.

TABLE 4.6
TRENDS IN EFFICIENCY OF BANK GROUPS 1993–4 AND 1996–7

	1993–4				1996–7				
	SBI&A	NB	PV	FR	SBI&A	NB	PV	NPV	FR
Net interest margin as per cent of average assets	3.2	2.3	3.4	5.6	3.5	3.0	3.0	2.9	4.1
Operating cost as per cent of average assets	3.1	2.9	3.1	2.1	2.9	2.9	2.5	1.9	3.0
Staff expenditure as per cent of average assetS	2.1	2.0	2.2	0.7	2.1	2.1	1.5	0.3	1.0
Operating profit/staff expenses	0.9	0.4	0.9	11.8	1.0	0.6	1.2	1.0	3.4

Notes: SBI&A: State Bank of India and associates; NB: nationalized banks; PV: old domestic private banks; NPV: new domestic private sector banks; FR: foreign banks.

Source: Computed from Indian Banks' Association, *Performance Highlights of Banks, several issues.*

An increase in competitive pressures in an industry is expected to improve efficiency levels as would be manifested in a decrease in the NIM, an increase in the OPSE, a reduction in the OCR, and a reduction in the SER. Comparing efficiency levels across bank groups between 1993–4 and 1996–7, one finds that there is no noticeable improvement in the efficiency of any bank group. However, the State Bank group and the old domestic private banks have fared relatively better than nationalized and foreign banks. A possible reason for the operating cost of public sector banks in the reform years could be the computerization and technological upgradation of bank branches that have been undertaken by these banks to increase efficiency in the long run. The proportion of staff expenditure to working funds has increased for most bank groups in part due to the upward revision of wages of bank employees during this period. There has, however, been marginal improvement in the income earned per employee in nationalized banks and old private banks, but, as in the case of other efficiency measures, is still way below that of foreign banks and the new private sector banks.

4.6 CAPITAL ADEQUACY

As of 1996–7, out of the twenty-seven public sector banks, twenty-five have attained the BIS norm of an 8 per cent risk-weighted capital to assets ratio. Thus the target set by RBI, of all banks attaining the BIS norm by 1996–7 has nearly been met. However, as is evident from Table 4.7, banks have been helped in this regard through substantial infusion of capital, i.e. recapitalization by the government. The government has also contributed towards writing down the capital base of several banks against their accumulated losses.

TABLE 4.7
QUALITATIVE PERFORMANCE OF PUBLIC SECTOR BANKS

	1993–4	1994–5	1995–6	1996–7
1. Percentage of NPAs to total advances	23.6	19.5	17.3	17.75
—State Bank of India and associates	22.3	18.5	15.3	n.a.
—Nationalized banks	24.3	20.0	18.5	n.a.
2. No. of banks with NPAs more than 20 per cent	16.0	10.0	10.0	n.a.
3. Volume of gross NPAs (Rs bn)	410.4	384.2	416.6	435.8
4. No. of banks attaining capital adequacy ratio	–	13.0	19.0	25.0
5. Recapitalization of banks (Rs bn)	57.0	52.9*	8.5	15.1
6. Number of banks capitalized	19.0	13.0	6.0	6.0

Note: *Includes Rs 924.58 crore under World Bank assistance for the financial sector development loan.

Sources: RBI, *Trends and Progress in Banking*, several issues, and RBI, *Annual Report, 1996–7*.

The attainment of the BIS norm apparently indicates an improvement in the soundness of the Indian banking sector. However, it is important to keep in mind the fact that the quality of capital is only as good as the quality of asset or loss provisioning. In case asset provisioning is inadequate, high nominal capital-asset ratios are deceptive. This proposition finds good support in debacle of the Indian Bank in 1995–6. The Indian Bank was a bank which had attained the minimum capital adequacy ratio, but whose net worth, including reserves, was wiped out by a high incidence of NPAs.

Another point that needs to be kept in mind while evaluating the implications of attaining the BIS norm is that banks may find ways to attain the CRAR that compromise on their lending activities. Capital adequacy ratios can easily be shored up by banks through investing in government securities and loans guaranteed by the central and state governments which carry zero percentage weight for computing risk, while other investments and advances are assessed at 100 percentage weight. The downside to the substitution of credit by investment is that spreads may get squeezed as government securities offer lower returns than the traditional lending business. But they obviously have not.

4.7 NON-PERFORMING ASSETS

In India, NPAs are defined as a proportion of total advances, while standard international practice is to define NPAs as a proportion of total assets. Given that there is a significant pre-emption of loanable funds in India in the form of the CRR, SLR, and 'free investments' in government securities, and that the level of provisioning for taxes, contingencies, and loan losses is fairly high, all of which are counted as part of assets, the quoted NPA figures for India are somewhat inflated relative to international estimates. However, it is also important to recognize that the definition of NPAs in India is very liberal compared to international standards as India recognizes NPAs only after 180 days of default, while the international norm is 90 days to 45 days. ·

Table 4.7 presents the trends in NPAs in the post-reform years. In 1993–4, the average percentage of NPAs to total advances for twenty-seven public sector banks was 21.89. This has declined to 19.5 per cent in 1994–5, and 17.75 per cent in 1996–7. Net NPAs (i.e. gross NPAs net of provisioning) in 1996–7 stood at 9.8 per cent of total advances. Moreover, the number of public sector banks with gross NPAs over 20 per cent has declined from 18 in 1994–5, to 10 in 1995–6, and remained unchanged at 10 in 1996–7. However, what is worrisome is that the volume of gross NPAs has remained more or less the same over the last three years at a significant level of Rs 400 billion.

According to RBI estimates, 47 per cent of NPAs in 1996–7 originated in the priority sectors. Further, the percentage of NPAs for small advances of less than Rs 25,000 was around 3 per cent of total NPAs in March 1996, implying that most of the NPAs are on account of large loans. Apart from these estimates, there is very little published disaggregated information on the nature of NPAs, the sectors in which NPAs are concentrated, and the list of defaulters. Neither is the recovery performance of NPAs obtainable at a disaggregated level. Consequently, the RBI estimates have been challenged many a time by some observers and agencies as also bank unions. For instance, the international credit rating agency, Standard & Poor (S&P), has estimated the real NPAs of the Indian banking sector anywhere between 35 and 70 per cent of its total outstanding credit.[4] According to the agency, much of these

[4]According to Ken McLay, Director, Financial Institutions Ratings, S&P, if a meltdown like the one that occurred in East Asia happens in India, most of the assets now shown as good assets would turn bad. S&P has placed India's banking system at the bottom of the pile in a ranking on the risk profile of various Asian nations. The Indian banking system is rated high risk and features alongside Indonesia and is placed lower than crisis-riddled Korean and Thai banking systems (*Indian Express*, 19 August, 1998).

NPAs—up to 35 per cent of total banking assets—would be accounted as NPAs if rescheduling and restructuring of loans to make them good assets in the book are not taken into account.

Notwithstanding the fact that the proportion of NPAs has been coming down in the past few years, the ratio in India still seems to be high relative to the target of a minimum of 5 per cent by the year 2000 set by the Tarapore Committee as a precondition for capital market convertibility. Moreover, there are several reasons why the existing level of NPAs, at 17.75 per cent gross and 9.8 per cent net could be underestimated currently and increase in future. These are:

- Banks with relatively high NPAs may have undertaken rapid expansion of credit to bring the percentage of NPAs down as fresh lending would qualify as standard assets. Such rapid expansion, while artificially lowering current NPAs, may carry the seeds of future NPAs. Figure 4.7 bears an indication of this, showing that while the operating income of banks has steadily increased over time, the return on assets which is arrived at by deducting provisions and contingencies from operating income, has declined. This suggests that while banks have generated more income, the provisioning burden has more than proportionately increased.

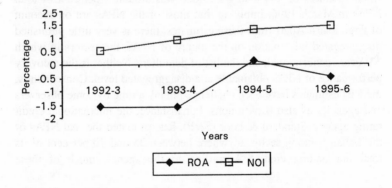

Figure 4.7   Trends in Return to Assets and Gross Operating Profit of Public Sector Banks, 1991-2–1995-6

Notes: ROA: Return to assets for all bank groups; NOI: Net operating income (gross profit).

Sources: Computed from Indian Banks' Association, *Financial Analysis of Banks,* and *Performance Highlights of Banks,* several issues.

- Banks may have rolled over bad debts by continuing to make loans to borrowers who are 'too big to fail' through the process of 'ever-greening' in order to cover up the extent of damages from NPAs. This is why the worst loans are often considered those that are reported as 'current' as banks roll over NPAs. In the Indian case, around 53 per cent of NPAs originate in the corporate sector and around 70 per cent of total advances of public sector banks are accounted for by cash credits and overdrafts.

- While provisioning norms for NPAs have been standardized, some reports suggest that public sector banks have been following a less stringent approach in declaring the existence of doubtful and loss assets as compared to their foreign counterparts.

- While the average NPAs for public sector banks are at 17.75 per cent, it is important to keep in mind that 10 of the 27 banks (around 37 per cent) have NPAs higher than 20 per cent and this number has remained constant in the last two years. This is not a trivial number, and a repeat of the Indian Bank crisis may create a domino effect to undermine depositor confidence in the Indian banking system.

- With a decline in reserve requirements over time, the amount of loanable funds with banks can be expected to increase. Given that NPAs as a proportion of lending are now 17.5 per cent, an increase in 'free lending', with other operational parameters remaining constant, could cause this proportion to become the figure for the entire portfolio, i.e. total assets of banks.

Taking these factors into account, it is not clear whether the reforms have ushered in a higher level of asset quality in the banking sector. As a rule of thumb, financial distress is likely to be systemic when non-performing loans, net of provisions, reach roughly 15 per cent of total loans (Sheng, 1996). While the Indian banking system is currently not too close to such a yardstick, the current estimates of its NPAs, and the absence of any significant decline in their volumes in recent years certainly do not suggest that the system is out of the 'danger zone'. That the problem of NPAs in India continues to be a cause for concern is evident from the recent government directive to public sector bank managers to bring NPAs down to 10 per cent in the immediate future.

Among the factors that have been considered responsible for the persistence of the NPA problem are inadequate credit appraisal skills, on-site and off-site monitoring and supervision of bank-assisted projects, both small and large. With regard to small loans, which are mainly disbursed to priority sectors, banks have principally concentrated on meeting quantitative targets and credit allocation directives rather than on promoting sound schemes of farm and small enterprise development (Bhatt, 1994). The consortium system of lending for large borrowers may also have created perverse incentives for monitoring, especially for the smaller banks in the consortium, which would have a tendency to free-ride on the lead bank in the consortium, given that it is the largest bank in the consortium which is assigned to take the lead in reconstructing or rehabilitating problem-ridden borrowers. Recognition of such problems[5] may have guided the RBI to recently change regulations with respect to consortium lending under which 'complete freedom' has been given to banks in the matter of credit dispensation without obligation on the part of banks to form a consortium subject to observance of exposure limits. Syndication is also allowed if the arrangement suits borrowers and financing banks.

Finally, a major factor that has impeded the desired reduction in NPAs has been inadequate loan recovery by public sector banks. While the recovery of advances has improved somewhat over the years, such improvement has at best been marginal. The recovery rate for direct agricultural advances, for example, has improved from 56 per cent in 1993 to 59.6 per cent in 1995. One of the factors preventing successful recovery in rural areas is the expectation of the borrowers that some of the loans may ultimately be waived through loan waiver schemes of the government. Currently, the recovery of advances in the industrial sector is slightly better than that in the agriculture and services sectors, but here too nearly 40 per cent of loans are unrecoverable. A substantial portion of industry's unrecoverable loans is reportedly accounted for by sick public sector undertakings. With respect to the recovery of small loans, out of the 5642 cases involving an amount of Rs 39.9 million filed with the district authorities, as many as 4937 cases (88 per cent) amounting to Rs 27.4 million were pending with them.

The recovery of NPAs has been an ongoing problem despite putting in

---

[5]Bhatt (1994, p. 513) quotes a letter by Chief Officer, Department of Bank Operations and Development to all scheduled commercial banks which states that 'deviations (from guidelines) have been in various areas such as entering the formal consortium arrangements, joint appraisal, exchange of information, holding of meetings and the level of representation there at, sharing of business (including ancilliary business) and stipulation of uniform terms and conditions'.

place several institutional arrangements such as debt recovery tribunals and specialized task forces. This is evident from the constant attempts by public sector banks and government agencies to launch joint efforts in recovering loans made by banks and other government agencies. Several public sector banks have recently set up special recovery cells to address the NPA problem on an urgent basis.

5. EMERGING CHALLENGES AND OBSTACLES

The analysis in the foregoing section regarding the impact of reforms on the performance and the soundness of Indian banking leads to the following conclusions:

- There are signs of a portfolio shift of banks from credit to riskless government securities.
- There have been limited signs of increased competition within the banking sector. Public sector banks have attempted to improve the quality of services through technology upgradation, but such attempts still remain small by relative standards. In spite of new entry and expansion of private sector banks, the oligopolistic dominance of public sector banks continues.
- While the rate of deposit mobilization by commercial banks has increased, there are signs of disintermediation in the deposit market with banks facing increasing competition from the DFIs, the capital market, and the NBFCs.
- Trends in profitability and efficiency indicators of public sector banks do not conclusively suggest an improvement in their performance. Significant differences in profitability and efficiency between public sector banks and the new private sector and foreign banks persist.
- Performance in terms of asset quality also leaves much to be desired. The volume and proportion of NPAs continue to remain significantly higher than the desired levels in spite of some visible attempts to improve valuation and recovery of loans.
- While most public sector and old private sector banks have attained the BIS capital adequacy norm of 8 per cent, this achievement is somewhat neutralized by the existence of high volumes of NPAs, periodic injections of capital by the government, and the absence of sound banking practices. Credit may have been rationed in the process of attaining the capital adequacy norm and there has been a shift in banks' asset portfolio in favour of investments in risk-free government securities.

The above points suggest that while the winds of change are blowing in the Indian banking industry, such changes have not translated into large improvements in performance. Changes appear to be more on the surface than coming from within. One might argue that four to five years of reforms—dubbed as the 'first phase' of the reforms process—is too short a time for fundamental changes to take root and attain the reform objectives of better performance and increased soundness, and that such objectives will be attained once the 'second phase' is completed. While such a scenario is indeed plausible, going by cross-country experiences on banking sector reforms, it is important to highlight that certain *structural impediments* have continued to stand in the way of meeting the reform objectives. This is especially so with respect to the functioning of public sector banks. These impediments will loom larger than before in view of the emerging challenges facing the Indian banking sector in the coming years.

5.1 EMERGING CHALLENGES

Foremost among the emerging challenges facing Indian banks is the increasing globalization of the banking sector. These challenges will rise exponentially as the government, on the recommendations of the *Committee on Capital Account Convertibility* (the Tarapore Committee), proposes to move towards full capital account convertibility in a few years. Presently, banks are allowed to participate in a limited way in the global financial market through loans and borrowings from overseas banks and correspondents, short-term investment in overseas money markets (ceiling of $10 million), providing fund- and non-fund-based facilities to Indian joint ventures and wholly owned subsidiaries abroad, and a few other miscellaneous activities. However, banks are not allowed to accept deposits and extend loans denominated in foreign currencies from or to individuals except for those under existing foreign deposit schemes.

The progressive dismantling of exchange controls under capital account convertibility would imply an increase in the inflow of both portfolio and foreign direct investment. This in turn would generate increased competitive pressures for the banking system. Banks have to compete not only with their counterparts in foreign markets but also with other financial institutions as borrowers (mainly the corporates) and depositors access international markets for loans and investments. Country-wide experiences suggest (see Sheng, 1996) that the most marked change following capital account convertibility has been the increasing strength of non-banks relative to banks, powered mostly by capital markets. In five Asian countries, market capitalization in the equity market became much larger than the domestic currency assets of the banking system after reform, and non-bank financial intermediaries in the Republic of Korea have more deposits and assets than the highly regulated banks.

While banks remain a significant part of the financial sector in India even with the rather rapid growth of the capital market and NBFCs, their modes of operations and bottom lines are likely to be significantly affected by increased competition from domestic financial institutions, signs of which are already apparent, and from increased financial flows. For one, the increased flow of funds consequent on capital account convertibility would put a downward pressure on lending rates, and a bank's ability to respond to supply pressures would depend on its cost of funds and operations. The failure to remain competitive in the loans market would lead to a loss of clientele, with corporates and individuals accessing financial markets abroad. An exit of blue chip borrowers, who are the main source of income for banks, may lead to an increase in the riskiness of the loan portfolio and exacerbate the problem of NPAs. As the foregoing analysis suggests, the process of bank disintermediation has started in India, and it will only gather momentum through increased integration with global financial markets. Because of securitization and financial innovation (e.g. derivatives), the cost of intermediation through capital markets is significantly lower than through bank credit, and US experience suggests that whereas spreads on bank loans are nearly 200 basis points, spreads on funds obtained through the debt market could be only 50 basis points.

On the deposit side, banks would feel increased pressures to offer attractive and remunerative products to individual depositors as the latter are given access to invest in international markets. Upward pressures on the deposit rate due to increased competition may in turn force banks to increase their lending rates to remain solvent, hence triggering off adverse selection and raising the cost of loans, with consequent adverse effect on the cost of borrowing by corporates. In general, banks would be increasingly vulnerable to the volatility of the financial market, with small differences in rates of return in the domestic and international markets leading to sudden inflows and outflows of capital. In addition to being exposed to credit and interest rate risk, the business of banks would be susceptible to country risk, where expectations of poor performance of the economy may cause banks to lose business overnight as investors, aided by improved telecommunications and technology, can quickly shift funds into a variety of products to protect their total return.

Given such market pressures, it is easy to understand why the Tarapore Committee has suggested the need for banks to meet certain preconditions and 'signposts'. Critical among these are the need for reducing the NPAs of the banking system from the 13.7 per cent level (as provisionally estimated by the Committee) to 5 per cent in three years, reducing effective CRR from 10 to 3 per cent by the year 2000, better risk management by banks (and non-banks), the development of an effective supervisory system, and granting administrative autonomy and operational flexibility to public sector banks to enable them to effectively respond to market signals. My analysis of the impact of reforms on the banking sector suggests, however, that these banks, which still control around 85 per cent of commercial banking operations, are still a long way from reaching these signposts.

Along with the challenge posed by the integration of the Indian financial sector with global markets, are challenges thrown up on the domestic front as the RBI is slowly moving away from micro-management to taking on a more supervisory role. In the process, banks are being given increasing freedom in their deposit mobilization and credit disbursement activities. Interest rates have been deregulated and several credit allocation programmes have been liberalized, and thus decision making has become more market oriented. This in turn has required banks to fix the rates on deposits and loans depending on overall liquidity conditions and demand factors.

The management of the investment portfolio of commercial banks will henceforth require greater attention, since the prices of the securities will be affected by changes in interest rates. Therefore the maturity patterns of a bank's liabilities, its investment and loan portfolios, and the distribution of assets according to risk and return, are matters in which banks will have to gain expertise. Thus, compared to the pre-reform years, a more comprehensive approach of asset liability management (ALM) will have to be adopted.

5.2 THE OBSTACLES

There are several *structural* factors inherent in public sector banks that continue to impinge on their performance and soundness. Many of these had been identified in the Narasimham Committee Report, but very little progress has been made in removing them. Key among these, are:

- overmanning
- trade union
- absence of a level playing field *vis-à-vis* competitors
- lack of administrative autonomy
- relatively complex administrative structure

Overmanning

In 1995–6, public sector banks accounted for around 93 per cent of total bank officers, total bank clerks, and total bank subordinates. Judged by any criteria, public sector banks are significantly overmanned. To get an idea of the extent of overmanning, let us look at two ratios and their trends between 1985–96 for the three major bank groups. These are: (i) the employee to asset ratio, disaggregated by officers to assets, clerks to assets, and subordinates to assets; and (ii) the proportion of staff expenses to total operating costs. While the first ratio is based on physical count of labour, the second ratio is based on total resources spent on labour and is more suitable when comparing labour with heterogeneous quality.

Trends in the employee to asset ratio show that this ratio, for all classes of employees, has been declining steadily over the years for *all* groups of banks (Figure 4.8). This implies that banks in general have been hiring at a lower rate compared to their growth in assets. This is understandable given the increased use of technology in banking operations. However, the extent of overmanning of public sector banks, as well as of the old domestic private sector banks, is clear when we look at the trends in the ratio of officers to assets and employee to assets of these banks *normalized* by the corresponding ratios of foreign banks (Figure 4.9).

The following facts emerge from Figure 4.9:

- The extent of overmanning is similar for public and domestic private sector banks.
- In 1995–6, the ratio of officers to assets for both public and private banks was *5 times* that of foreign banks. The ratio of employees to assets was still higher, *7 times* that of foreign banks. The difference in the two ratios implies that the extent of overmanning is significantly higher at the lower levels (clerks and subordinates).
- While in 1985, the ratios for domestic private banks were higher than those of public banks, these have come down since the early

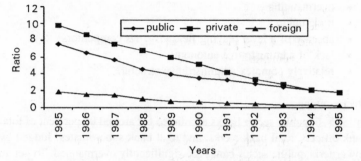

Figure 4.8   Employment to Asset Ratio of Major Bank Groups 1985–95-6

Sources: Computed from Indian Banks' Association, *Financial Analysis of Banks,* and *Performance Highlights of Banks*, several issues.

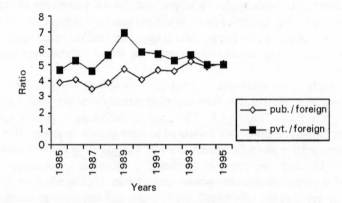

Figure 4.9   Trends in Officer to Assets of Public Sector and Private Sector Banks Relative to Officer to Assets of Foreign Banks 1985–95-6

Notes: Pub./foreign: officer to assets of public banks/officer to assets of foreign banks. Pvt./foreign: officer to assets of private banks/officer to assets of foreign banks.

Sources: Computed from Indian Banks' Association, *Financial Analysis of Banks,* and *Performance Highlights of Banks*, several issues.

1990s. On the other hand, the ratios for public banks have *increased* systematically during the same period.

A related indicator for understanding the extent of overmanning in public sector banks is the ratio of wages and salaries to total operation costs. While this ratio has been increasing for all groups of banks in recent years mainly on account of periodical wage revisions, what is instructive is that the ratio for public sector banks is almost *double* that of foreign banks. In 1995–6, while this ratio was around 35 per cent for foreign banks, it was as high as 73 per cent for public sector banks, and 68 per cent for old domestic private sector banks. Finally, an international comparison of the asset to employee ratio for top banks across countries drives home the extent of overmanning in Indian banks relative to international standards, even with respect to countries with abundant labour and relatively low wages like China (Table 4.8). These comparisons highlight the potential cost savings that banks can achieve by trimming their manpower, thereby improving their profitability as well as competitive position.

TABLE 4.8
ASSETS PER EMPLOYEE IN TOP BANKS IN
SELECTED COUNTRIES

Country	Assets (US$ '000)
Brazil	638
China	1,122
France	5,321
Germany	7,562
Korea	4,348
Taiwan	7,909
US	3,478
UK	2,755
India	167

Source: Indian Banks' Association, *Indian Banking Review, 1995–6*, Mumbai.

Trade Unions

There are a total of nine trade unions of officers and workmen in the banking industry. The Indian Banks' Association (IBA), an advisory service organization of nearly all banks, negotiates wages and service conditions on behalf of bank management with the unions and associations of bank employees. Bipartite negotiations between the IBA and bank unions are conducted on issues related to the settlement of wages and service conditions, pensions, computerization, etc. Important among the unions are the All India Bank Employees Association which account for 50 per cent of organized workmen in the industry, and the All India Bank Officers' Confederation which accounts for 70 per cent of organized bank officers.

110 / *India: A Financial Sector for the Twenty-first Century*

It has been contended that trade unions have from time to time opposed profitability and efficiency inducing changes in the industry. Union opposition has been regarded as an important bottleneck to the speedy computerization of public sector banks. While the Computerization Settlement of October 1993 signed between the IBA and bank employees' unions helped overcome the initial hurdles to computerization, the scope of the settlement (under which banks will be able to computerize 2500 to 3000 branches in urban and metropolitan centres), is woefully inadequate relative to the total branch network. However, it is to be noted in this context that the Narasimham Committee, while blaming organized labour for resisting speedy mechanization and computerization of work technology, has also put part of the blame on to the management of banks which did not appear to have exerted itself sufficiently in furthering the process of technological upgradation. One reason for management laxity could be that in the absence of any flexibility in restructuring employment in the face of automation, little cost savings can be achieved.

Recently, industrial relations in the banking industry have taken a turn for the worse. Through a spate of strikes, unions have put forward several demands, most of which run counter to the RBI's attempt at infusing competitiveness in the banking industry. The more recent demands by the unions relate to the:

- setting up of Local Area Banks
- closure of Non-Banking Finance Companies (NBFCs)
- removal of ceiling in the Bonus and Gratuity Act
- extension of pension to private sector banks
- permitting wage revision in RRBs at par with the banking industry

Reports also suggest that unions are apprehensive of the government buckling under pressure from international funding agencies to retrench bank staff as has been done in neighboring Pakistan. Bank unions have also strongly opposed the idea of bank-specific wage settlements instead of an industry-wise wage settlement as proposed by the IBA.

Absence of a Level Playing Field

One of the reasons behind the superior performance of foreign banks is that these banks have been subject to less stringent regulations compared to domestic banks, particularly public sector banks. The inefficiency of public sector banks also stems from the structural characteristics that they have inherited from the regulations of the pre-reforms era. It is only recently that foreign banks have been mandated to meet priority sector obligations, but the requirement of 32 per cent is still less than the minimum 40 per cent required for domestic banks. Moreover, domestic banks have been much more involved in agricultural lending where NPAs and non-recovery of loans are significant. Also public sector banks have not been able to close a large proportion of non-viable rural branches that were forced on them as part of the quantitative expansion of banking since nationalization. Finally, the business of public sector banks has been predominantly retail in nature as compared to the whole-sale nature of business of foreign and new private sector banks, and the service charges of the former are significantly lower than those of the latter. This implies higher transaction costs of servicing accounts for public sector banks and it is only since April 1998 that banks have been allowed to set deposit rates that vary not only with maturity but also with the size of accounts.

Apart from the absence of a level playing field among commercial bank groups, there is the lack of a level playing field between commercial banks as a group and other competing financial intermediaries, specifically the NBFCs. The growth of non-bank institutions has been implicitly encouraged over the years to bring about financial deepening, diversification of financial assets, and an easing of the informal credit markets. Going by the transitional experiences of other countries (Box 2), while some amount of bank disintermediation resulting from increased growth and competition from other financial institutions and increasing overlap in the activities and products offered by different financial institutions is inevitable, banks appear to be the most regulated among the institutions in terms of reserve requirements and prudential regulations. This has been a typical feature across many countries. While several measures have been introduced by the RBI under the RBI (Amendment) Act, 1997 to ensure a more healthy growth of the NBFCs, instil depositor confidence, and create a more level playing field between banks and NBFCs, the regulatory requirements in general are still relatively less stringent in case of the latter group.

According to the new regulatory framework, the NBFCs accepting public deposits are now subject to entry requirements (public deposits can be accepted only with a minimum net owned fund of Rs 2.5 million), credit rating requirements (at least an 'A' rating), an interest rate ceiling of 16 per cent per annum, compliance with prudential norms nearly at par with banks, and maintenance of liquid assets. However, the regula-

---

BOX 2
THE NBFCs VERSUS BANKS: THE KOREAN EXPERIENCE

The NBFCs in Korea are subject to less stringent prudential regulations and other operational restrictions. The growth of the NBFCs was encouraged by the government in order to control the growth of a large informal curb market. The government's conscious promotion of the NBFCs led to an erosion of commercial banks' intermediation role. Disintermediation out of banks was particularly pronounced after substantial interest rate reductions in June 1982. The lagging growth in the banking sector constrained the government's practice of using bank credit as a major incentive in its industrial policy.

In an effort to correct this situation, the government responded to narrow the interest rate differentials between banks and non-banks. The government also sought to help banks by introducing new non-fund business. Negotiable certificates of deposits were introduced by banks with interest rates higher than those of ordinary time deposits in the hope of strengthening the banks' position in mobilizing short-term funds.

In spite of such efforts, the NBFCs have grown much faster than banks, although the new financial products have slowed the erosion of their position. Between 1972 and 1990, the share of banks in total depos- its mobilized by banks and non-banks declined from 91.4 per cent to 45.8 per cent.

Source: Nam Sang-Woo. (1997). 'Korea's Financial Reform since the Early 1980s'. In Caprio, Atiyas and Hanson (eds), *Financial Reforms:Theory and Experience*. New York: Cambridge University Press.

---

tory requirements for the NBFCs are still considerably softer relative to banks as is, for instance, evident from the fact that the NBFCs are required to maintain liquid assets at 12.5 per cent of public deposits from April 1998 and 15.0 per cent of deposits from April 1999. Investment in any unencumbered approved security can be used for this purpose. This is much less than the total reserve requirements (CRR + SLR) for all commercial banks. The NBFCs are also not required to meet any priority sector obligations. Entry point norms are also less stringent for NBFCs compared to banks. The presence of less stringent regulations enables non-bank financial intermediaries to offer high rates of returns on deposits, notwithstanding the ceiling on NBFC rates. This puts pressure on banks to hike up their deposit rates with consequent upward pressure on lending rates. Although such a trend is not evident at present, with operations of commercial banks being almost nine times those of the NBFCs, there is a distinct possibility of strong competition in interest rates as the operations of the latter expand over time.

Lack of Administrative Autonomy

There is more or less a consensus among policy makers and bank management that public sector banks are seriously constrained in their operations due to a lack of autonomy in decision making. This has also created an uneven playing field between public and private sector banks. The Narasimham Committee has noted in this context that autonomy in internal decision making is *critical* to the functioning of a competitive and efficient banking system. The RBI Governor too, in a recent speech on the future course of banking reforms, has highlighted that

in depth corporate planning combined with organizational restructuring are necessary prerequisites towards achieving desired results in terms of productivity and profitability... To achieve all these goals public sector banks need to be given greater autonomy with respect to recruitment and promotion of personnel and in general management of staff and in determining the organizational structure.

The lack of autonomy of public sector banks has mainly stemmed from excessive government intervention in day-to-day decision making, especially with regard to loan disbursements (politically influenced credit disbursements, for example), political appointment of the chief executive and management boards, and absence of flexibility in recruitment and promotions. Of particular importance has been the absence of any autonomy regarding recruitment of suitable staff and the 'rigidities' in the system with respect to rewards and punishment. The common ownership of public sector banks has generated the need for identical service conditions and recruitment procedures and has necessitated the adoption of common eligibility criteria and standards for recruitment of bank personnel. This led to the establishment of the Banking Service Recruitment Boards in 1978 that were assigned the functions of recruitment. Currently, there are fifteen of these Boards functioning in different parts of the country. The fall-out of such a procedure has been that individual banks, despite being heterogeneous in terms of structure and performance, have not been able to use market mechanisms to recruit personnel according to their special requirements. Moreover, seniority rather than ability has been considered the main criterion for promotions. Such a system has obviously generated perverse incentives and has culminated in a significant outflow of top and middle ranking bank personnel to foreign and new private sector banks that offer much more attractive terms of remuneration and perquisites.

Complex Administrative Structure

The Narasimham Committee had highlighted the need to rationalize the complex administrative structure of public sector banks that has evolved over the years as a result of their quantitative expansion. Notwithstanding the benefits that have been achieved as a result of such expansion, efficient coordination, supervision, and monitoring of bank activities have been adversely affected. The geographical spread of public sector banks is manifold wider than that of private sector and foreign banks. The old private sector banks are located mainly in southern India, and the new private banks and foreign banks, in metropolitan areas. Thus private banks tend to bear less in terms of coordination costs, costs of delayed decision taking, and monitoring and supervision costs. The Narasimham Committee had noted that 'lines of command and control have lengthened to the point of weakening the central office supervision without effectively decentralizing decision making and operations'. Currently, all nationalized banks, big or small, are following a uniform four-tier organizational structure, consisting of branches, regional office, zonal office, and a central office. The complex administrative structure will prove to be more of a barrier now when the RBI is in the process of increasing the scope of central bank supervision through both off-site and on-site monitoring, internal, and external audits.

6. POLICY IMPERATIVES

The analysis of the existing challenges and obstacles points to certain obvious policy imperatives. These are:

 (i) Adopt a multi-pronged approach to reduce the incidence of NPAs.
 (ii) Weaken the hold of organized labour by encouraging bank-level rather than industry-level negotiations. Reduce overmanning by freezing fresh hiring and possibly through creating voluntary retirement schemes.
 (iii) Create a level playing field among different financial intermediaries through institution of similar reserve requirements and prudential regulations.
 (iv) Tackle the problem of endemically weak banks through consolidation or privatization.
 (v) Improve the performance of the stronger public sector banks by granting them more autonomy in operations.

6.1 TACKLING NPAs

Reform experiences of several countries suggest different approaches to reducing the incidence of NPAs (Box 3). In the Indian context, a combination of several workable approaches can be tried as the dimension of the NPA problem is not uniform across banks so that 'one policy fits all' may not be the best way. Some NPAs have been the product of the pre-reform years (old NPAs) and some have been acquired since the reforms (fresh NPAs), and the incidence of old and new NPAs is likely to vary across banks. With respect to old NPAs what is presently happening is gradual provisioning and write-offs depending on the level of profits. At this rate, it will take years before the balance sheets of many public sector banks are restored to an even keel. Several possible approaches can be used for old NPAs, either separately or in conjunction.

- Chronically sick accounts can be *carved out* to a centralized agency. A centralized asset recovery approach permits consolidation of skills and resources in debt restructuring and debt workout within one agency. In India, this model can be followed through the institution of the Asset Reconstruction Fund (ARF) as suggested by the Narasimham Committee. Bad debts can be transferred to the fund at book value. In return, the ARF would issue government-guaranteed bonds to public sector banks. The ARF route can put banks with a heavy backlog of old NPAs back in business. The success of carve outs would, however, depend on whether banks with the erstwhile sick accounts now have the requisite credit appraisal skills and loan recovery mechanisms that would prevent re-accumulation of NPAs. If banks are structurally deficient in this respect, these banks, in the absence of a viable exit policy, may, as a second best solution, be turned into 'narrow' banks and allowed to lend or invest only in assets of the highest credit quality.

- A decentralized debt workout by banks can be tried out under which banks can undertake case-by-case resolutions of problem accounts. This will work effectively in cases where NPAs are concentrated in few big accounts. This method assumes that banks have sufficient skills and administrative infrastructure to deal with these problems. Recently, some public sector banks have announced the setting up of special recovery cells to tackle NPAs on a case-by-case basis. Separate subsidiaries for dealing

BOX 3
RESOLVING THE NPA PROBLEM: CROSS-COUNTRY
EXPERIENCES

- *Korea*: Writing off some NPAs by the government, by funds raised through recapitalization via a booming stock market, favourable impact of cyclical industrial upturn and increase in the value of property held as collateral. Accumulated write-offs during 1986–9 were equivalent to 1 per cent of total credit outstanding. Net worth of banks grew dramatically from 3.5 per cent of total assets to 11 per cent. The recent banking and currency crisis has seen the setting up of the Korea Asset Management Corp that will use the bailout fund to purchase non-performing bank assets and repackage them for sale, while helping companies under restructuring sell their corporate assets. Banking officials say the government could give the green light for the repackaged loans to be sold as asset-backed securities.

- *Poland*: Decentralized debt work-outs by banks through case by case resolution.

- *Germany, the US, Ghana, and Japan*: Carve-outs through centralized agency. In Germany, funding is concentrated in one agency with state guarantee, and in the US it is the US Resolution Trust Corporation. Japan followed a private sector variant through the Japanese Cooperative Credit Purchasing Company established by Japanese banks which bought NPAs from individual banks at a market price.

- *Malaysia*: Enterprise rehabilitation fund set up by the central bank to reduce overhang of NPAs. Seed capital was provided to many of the recession hit indigenous enterprises. Specialist turnaround groups evaluate the viability of eligible enterprise and recommend assistance under the fund.

- *Yugoslavia*: The Bank Rehabilitation Agency was created to provide across the board help in both asset and income rehabilitation operations. Asset rehabilitation included writing off $962 million in foreign debt, refinancing $400 million of selective credits and rescheduling some of the $300 million in credits from Soviet Union.

- *Chile*: Two major rescheduling of loans for a term of ten years with five years grace period, of 'productive' sectors covering about 25 per cent of the financial system's loans. Emergency lines of credit and other credit programmes provided to banks by the central bank, and carve out efforts undertaken by the central bank through direct purchase of substandard loans. Commitment was obtained from shareholders to buy back the carved out loans rather than passing on such loan liabilities to the taxpayers.

Source: Compiled from A. Sheng (ed.). (1996). *Bank Restructuring: Lessons from the Eighties*, World Bank, and Caprio et al., (1997), 'Policy Issues in Reforming Finance: Lessons and Strategies', in Caprio, Atiyas and Hanson (eds), *Financial Reform: Theory and Experience*, Cambridge University Press.

with bad loans can also be created. Rolling over bad debts could be a potential problem under the decentralized approach as was the case in Chile and US Savings and Loans industry.

- There could be the securitization of debt by the government. Under this approach, debts of public sector units that are showing up as NPAs of the banks are to be converted into low-interest government bonds. Since a significant proportion of bad debt has originated in public sector units, it can be logically argued that the responsibility of reducing NPAs should be thrust back on the shoulders of the government. However, the flip side to this argument is that if debts are written down in the government's books, banks will simply stop trying to recover their dues and public sector units will make no attempt to make themselves financially more viable. The finance ministry has reportedly categorically ruled out any possibility of such securitization due to the moral hazard problem inherent in such an approach.

- The government can recapitalize banks in exchange for performance obligations. This has been the route adopted *de facto*. However, given the significant loss of political and financial rating of the government associated with bank failures, such performance obligations may not be credibly implemented. One possible way out could be to turn endemically problem banks into 'narrow banks' and suspend fresh credit disbursement activities until existing problems are sorted out. This had been the first response of the government to the Indian Bank debacle, but ultimately the government has decided to bail out the bank through recapitalization.

- Fixing of accountability and responsibility on bank officers for bad advances should also be undertaken in a comprehensive manner.

- Appropriate incentives for assessment and monitoring in the case of consortium advances could be created . Under current guidelines, banks are free to classify consortium loans according to the health code of an individual bank's account unlike the erstwhile guidelines of classifying an account as non-performing even if the account was an NPA for any one of the consortium members. The latter would create incentives for sharing information and assessment skills within the consortium.

- The judicial process for the borrowal accounts has to be revamped and speeded up and special courts such as debt recovery tribunal should be urged to dispose NPA cases faster. Presently, the constitutional validity of debt recovery tribunals has been questioned in some courts.

Approaches to deal with fresh NPAs should take into account the fact that the potential of such NPAs to increase is quite high at present time because of the presence of additional liquidity in the banking system, and the recessionary conditions prevailing in major commodity industries. The incidence of fresh NPAs can be reduced by taking the following steps.

- Judicious lending should be encouraged and proper accountability should be maintained. In-house credit appraisal techniques should be upgraded in line with the pressures of a deregulated environment.
- Banks may utilize the expertise of credit rating agencies for evaluating proposals as well as hone up in-house expertise in credit evaluation.
- Transparency should be present in demarcating between fresh and existing NPAs. Lending that covers financial distress will tend to be concentrated in the same sectors as previous lending and will not respond to changing economic conditions. Comparison of bank lending patterns between the pre-reforms and post-reforms-period is essential. The practices of ever-greening can then come to light.
- Overexposure to specific sectors should be avoided.

6.2 Tackling Labour Opposition and Overmanning

Several steps have been taken by management in different countries to reduce resistance from organized labour. Some of these have been direct steps such as fragmenting union power through the encouragement of rival unions, whereas others have been more indirect like the casualization of labour through contract employment, and cutting back on hiring. More extreme steps like the dismantling of unions have sometimes been adopted as in some of the Latin American countries. These have not necessarily yielded results because of continuing imperfections in other markets, and because of the fact that labour institutions were only symptomatic of the underlying political economy problems rather than being responsible for slowing structural adjustment and growth (see Box 4).

The steps that can be taken for mitigating labour problems in the Indian banking industry are:

- Encourage bank-level settlements in place of the present system of industry-level settlement. This suggestion has been recently mooted by the Indian Banks' Association, but vehemently opposed by the unions. This could be a way to weaken the bargaining position of industry-level unions that presently act as a monopsonist (single seller of labour services) especially with respect to public sector banks. Bank-specific wage settlements can also address the problem of labour inefficiency in the sense that less productive labour would not be in a position to demand higher wages. However, bank-specific wage settlements can be time-consuming and may also lead to industrial disputes and litigation.
- Freeze fresh hiring, a trend that is already evident in terms of a decline in employee to asset ratio for all bank groups.
- Offer incentives to workers to take voluntary retirement and not substitute them by fresh recruitment.

BOX 4
STRUCTURAL ADJUSTMENTS AND ORGANIZED LABOUR

Organized labour in most countries is seen as a potential obstacle to labour market adjustments that are part and parcel of a process of industry-level and economy-wide structural adjustment. Yet in some countries, labour confederations have cooperated with the government and employers to facilitate adjustment. What makes organized labour confront or cooperate, and what empowers it to slow or stall attempts at adjustment? What political circumstances and approaches have persuaded organized labour to acquiesce in the past? Both theory and evidence on these questions are fragmentary, especially with respect to developing countries.

Comparisons between the structural adjustment processes in Latin American countries show that dismantling labour institutions is neither necessary (Costa Rica) nor sufficient (Bolivia) for success. In Costa Rica, for example, a higher degree of social consciousness allowed a union-backed president to undertake some of the painful initial steps towards successful adjustment.

The Asian countries followed highly interventionist strategies to curb the power of unions. For example, in South Korea, the right to strike was banned in 1971 and only recently reinstated, and unions need government permission to undertake collective bargaining. In Malaysia, union power is similarly limited and unions are banned in some sectors. Unions in Thailand are also weak except in the public sector.

Source: Compiled from S. Horton, R. Kanbur and D. Mazumdar (eds). (1994). *Labor Markets in an Era of Adjustment*. EDI Development Studies, World Bank.

- Evolve a more *participatory work environment* once settlements are made at bank level. This can include joint consultations between labour and management on major corporate decisions. Building a cooperative relationship, though costly in the short run, can reap benefits in the long run. The crucial element in gaining workers' cooperation is to make them believe that short-term sacrifices in wages and employment will contribute to long-term gains, and that union resistance to technical change can lead to substantial long-term losses. A participatory approach has special appeal in the face of increased private sector and international competition where both unions and management are forced to realize that their joint adversary is a competing firm against which they have to put up a collective fight.

6.3 ENSURING A LEVEL PLAYING FIELD

Notwithstanding the fact that commercial banks are still a force to reckon with in spite of the growing competition from other financial institutions, some cross-country experiences suggest that banking sector disintermediation can gather strong momentum in view of the increasing overlap in their activities. In some countries, increasing financial integration has destroyed many of the unique characteristics of banking institutions, while government protection and relatively stringent regulation have made it 'impossible for them to evolve into enterprises compatible with the new environment' (Pierce, 1991).

As many analysts have noted, the key to making banks operate effectively in the new milieu does not lie with tightening the intensity and scope of bank regulation because that may only lead to more banking activities being conducted outside of conventional banking. If the objectives of an efficient financial system is to achieve stable and reliable sources of credit, avoid undue risk taking, honour its liabilities, and avoid exposure to future government bailouts, then it is necessary to extend our thinking beyond the specific institutions that provide financial services and instead focus on the particular services that are provided by these institutions. That is, regulation should target the type of financial service in question and not who provides the service. Thus reserve requirements should be uniform across all types of financial institutions with respect to a particular type of financial activity. Similarly, the application of deposit insurance should be extended to cover all financial institutions rather than being restricted to only banks.

'Regulation by function rather than by institution' can be an effective way to generate a level playing field between banks and other financial intermediaries in the Indian context. The specific policy measures that can be followed in this context are:

- Bring down existing CRR and SLR differentials between banks and non-banks, especially 'bank-like non-banks'. Parity in reserve requirements can also be brought about with respect to the capital market and offshore borrowing.
- Subject retail funds and wholesale funds to different reserve requirements irrespective of which type of institution mobilizes these funds. The difference in reserve requirement should reflect the differential costs of obtaining such funds.
- Extend the scope of priority sector financing to NBFCs and reduce priority sector lending for banks. A portion of NBFC funds can be earmarked for exports and small-scale industries, as has been required from foreign banks. Infrastructure can also be declared as a priority sector across all financial institutions including DFIs. As in the case of reserve requirements, bringing all institutions into the priority sector net would reduce the average incidence of policy lending on commercial banks.

6.4 HANDLING PROBLEM BANKS

The track records of a number of public sector banks in the last four years suggest that these banks need to be dealt with decisively as they are pulling down the performance of the banking sector as a whole. Even in 1996–7, the government has had to recapitalize six banks, with the recapitalization amount going up in the last year over the preceding year. Endemically weak banks not only put pressure on the government budget, but also can destabilize the banking system as the recent experience of several East Asian countries suggests. This, in turn, leads to adopting drastic measures such as liquidation and closure, as has happened in the case of Indonesia and Japan.

As Box 5 highlights, one would face several policy dilemmas in tackling the weak-bank problem in the Indian context. However, one could consider two ways in which problem banks can be tackled. These are:

- bank consolidation through mergers and acquisition or through setting up of 'narrow banks'
- privatization of weak banks

BOX 5
POLICY OPTIONS AND DILEMMAS WITH RESPECT TO
ENDEMICALLY WEAK BANKS

- Consolidate through merger? But strong banks may be adversely affected in the absence of freedom to restructure.

- Continue to recapitalize them and write off bad assets? Unlikely to solve structural problems in the long run and destroy incentive for improvement.

- Turn them into 'narrow banks'? Profits could be further eroded, given little freedom to trim down expenditure (on staff, etc.) in consonance with lower income generating capacity.

- Privatize them? Would be difficult to find takers, given high volume of NPAs and little freedom to restructure branch network and workforce.

- Liquidate them? But banks are relatively large in terms of deposit base and branch network, and this may destabilize the banking system through erosion of depositor confidence.

- Give more autonomy? May exacerbate problems given that management of such banks is weak in the first place.

- Privatize management in the sense of firing 'non-performing management'? Likely to be resisted by officers/managers who too are organized into unions.

Consolidation

The Narasimham Committee has recommended bank consolidation through mergers and acquisitions as one of the ways to bring about greater efficiency in operations. The Committee was apparently 'struck' by the broad spectrum of support from representatives of labour and industry to the idea that the number of public sector banks should be substantially reduced. The optimal banking structure in the view of the Committee should comprise (i) 3 to 4 large banks (including the State Bank of India) which could become international in character, (ii) 8 to 10 national banks with a network of branches engaged in general and universal banking, (iii) local banks whose operations would generally be confined to a specific region, and (iv) rural banks whose operations would be confined to rural areas.

The relationship between structure and efficiency is complex, but one can observe that in many countries the expansion in the range of services offered by financial institutions has grown with increased concentration in financial markets, suggesting the possible presence of economies of scale. Select evidence from developed countries does suggest that banking systems with high levels of concentration tend to have lower margins and operating costs as well as higher profits (Vittas, 1991). However, the overall evidence on the presence of economies of scale and scope, or efficiency gains from mergers, has been far from conclusive in empirical studies in developed countries, particularly the US where the banking industry has experienced an 'unprecedented' level of consolidation.[6]

Studies on the relationship between structure and performance are rare in the context of Indian banking as banking decisions were not market determined prior to the reforms. However, given that public sector banks, weak or strong, have large branch networks, and given the difficulty in closing down a significant number of branches upon merger (due to resistance from unions, etc.), the scale economies are likely to be marginal. On the other hand, merger between a strong and a weak public sector bank can drag the former down as evidenced in the case of the merger between the Punjab National Bank and the New India Bank. The potential synergies from mergers in terms of greater accessibility, bigger customer base, etc. also seem to be minimal given that all public sector banks are already well spread out. An alternative can be to break up a weak bank into several subgroups and merge each subgroup with one of the stronger banks. This way, the bottomline of the taker will not be severely affected. Sub-groups (like rural branches, or SSI branches) can also be merged with specialized banks or development financial institutions. In this context, it may be instructive to highlight one of the less ambiguous conclusions of the research on bank mergers and consolidation in the US that can have implications in the Indian context. It is that the gains from bank consolidation depend on the *ex-ante* efficiency of participating banks. Berger (1998), for instance, finds in his empirical analysis of US bank mergers that when the merging banks, particularly the small ones, are below median efficiency, the average improvement in efficiency rank is substantial and is statistically significant.

An attractive alternative to the merger and acquisition route that has been increasingly considered by Indian policy makers is the proposal of turning many of the weak public sector banks into 'narrow banks'. According to the proposal which has been discussed in some detail in

[6]See the collection of papers on bank mergers and acquisitions in Amihud and Miller (1998) for an extensive review of the recent literature.

the *Report of the Tarapore Committee on Capital Account Convertibility*, the narrow banks would be allowed to engage only in the safest of activities, offering say only transactions accounts and investing only in government securities. However, one potential problem with turning weak public sector banks into narrow banks is that while their income earning capacity will be severely curtailed through the narrowing of activities, the banks will be saddled by excessive staff if the staff cannot be retrenched. This would erode the bottomline of the already weak banks. In the absence of an exit policy, narrow banks may have to increasingly depend on the government.

Privatization

All public sector banks have been demanding greater autonomy in decision making from the government. However, it is not very clear if greater autonomy in decision making will lead to better performance on the part of weak banks. Given that all public sector banks face the same regulatory environment, the fact that some banks have been endemically weak point to the existence of more structural reasons like poor management or low labour efficiency behind their weakness. Hence, giving more independence in decision making to such banks may only exacerbate their problems. This line of reasoning is perhaps at work behind the recent proposal of the Finance Ministry regarding the issue of greater autonomy to public sector banks. The Ministry has proposed to link the extent of autonomy or operational freedom to performance. Stronger banks would qualify for autonomy while the weaker ones will not. However, this proposal does not consider the possibility that banks that are currently strong may become weak in the near future. The Indian Bank debacle points to the possibility that the fortunes of even 'strong' banks can change drastically for the worse.

Given that autonomy may not be enough to shore up the performance of weak banks, one possible option is privatization. Cross-country experiences have suggested that 'banking is no exception to the general rule that autonomy, competition and hard-budget constraints cannot be achieved without privatization' (Joshi and Little, 1996), and privatization of banks has been an option exercised in countries such as Korea, Chile, Hungary, and Poland. Evidence from a recent study (Sarkar, Sarkar, and Bhaumik, 1998) from the Indian banking sector on the issue of whether a change in ownership would positively impact performance of public sector banks reveals that private domestic banks are significantly superior to public banks with regard to return on assets. However, the study finds that there are no significant differences in cost efficiency between public and private banks. Most interestingly, the study finds that the performance of different bank groups is correlated to the extent to which they are linked to the market for corporate control, suggesting that bank privatization in developing countries like India should be accompanied by a concerted effort to strengthen the institutional framework, like developing a market for corporate control, or a managerial market, the efficient functioning of which is fundamental to the superior performance of private enterprises in any economy.

One of the most important issues related to privatization is who is going to buy the public sector banks, especially the endemically weak ones? One possible solution is that the government can recapitalize these banks or write off all bad loans once for all and then offer them for private ownership.

6.5 ADMINISTRATIVE AUTONOMY

The Finance Ministry has recently proposed that the better public sector banks will be granted autonomy in decision making. According to the proposal, banks would be provided greater autonomy to improve performance and accelerate the credit off-take provided they fulfil the criteria to be laid down by the government. The Ministry has decided to fix four criteria and those banks which meet all the criteria will be given eleven categories of autonomy, that will be worked out soon. The larger the number of criteria they meet, the greater will be their autonomy and the smaller the number of criteria they meet the lesser will be the autonomy.

The moot question in this case is what are the dimensions of autonomy? What the Narasimham Committee emphasized in its report was that autonomy should mean the end of political interference and day-to-day involvement of the government in public sector bank operations. Would the banks get freedom in recruitment and in restructuring? Can banks refuse to lend to public sector enterprises, especially the sick ones? Would banks have freedom to deal with their NPA problems in a more bank-specific, decentralized way? An answer in the affirmative to such questions would be a way to ensure that banks would benefit from increased autonomy.

While granting up to eleven categories of autonomy may take care of the problem of the involvement of the government in the day-to-day operations of public sector banks, it is unlikely that political interference which is largely 'informal' in nature can be credibly eliminated so long as government representatives sit on the board of public sector banks and the government is the *de facto* owner. Such a concern was voiced in a dissent note in the Narasimham Committee Report that remarked that in the 'prevailing political culture' of the country, the autonomy of banks cannot be credibly granted unless the government desists from having representatives on the boards of public sector banks. It is only under these circumstances that the government can send a 'strong message' of autonomy to the banking system and create a climate conducive for efficient bank operations.

7. CONCLUSIONS

This chapter analysed the response of the Indian banking sector to the reform measures that were initiated in 1991 as part of the economy-wide structural adjustment programme, and as recommended by the first Narasimham Committee on Financial System. It also identified some of the emerging challenges facing the sector going into the twenty-first century and recommended ways to overcome them.

An analysis of post-reform trends with respect to key indicators such as profitability, efficiency, and asset quality suggests that although there have been some important changes, such changes have not yet translated in a perceptible way into strong, sustained performance. Also, the existing improvements have been limited to only a few large public sector banks, with endemically weak banks continuing to under-perform. Structural impediments like overmanning, trade unionism, and lack of administrative autonomy, continue to hinder the efficient functioning of public sector banks. These impediments are likely to loom larger than before in view of the emerging challenges facing the banking sector in the coming years.

Foremost among the emerging challenges is the increasing globalization of the banking sector. Such exposure is expected to increase manifold as the government gradually moves towards full capital account convertibility in a few years and inefficient banks become increasingly vulnerable to international competitive pressures. As the recent East Asian crisis shows, the consequences of continued structural weaknesses and inefficiencies in the banking sector can be devastating both for the financial sector as well as for the real sector. The lessons learnt from the East Asian crisis should certainly form the background of the 'second generation' of banking reforms in India.

ANNEXURE

BANKING SECTOR REFORM: PROGRESS TO DATE

Status Before July 1991	Status in April 1998
Interest Rate Controls	
Bank lending rates fixed according to loan size and sector-specific categories (loans over Rs 200,000 had an interest rate floor).	Interest rate structure simplified. Lending rates above Rs 200,000 deregulated. Interest on all loans below Rs 200,000 should not exceed the prime lending rate (PLR). Banks advised to announce maximum spread over PLR for all advances other than consumer credit.
Bank deposit rates fixed according to account types and maturities.	Deposit rates for term deposits above fifteen days deregulated. Banks can now charge differential rates on deposits of similar maturity but of different sizes.
NRE deposit rates regulated.	The maximum deposit rate (up to thirty days) of scheduled commercial banks linked to the Bank Rate. Deposit rates on NRE term deposits of over one year, and FCNR(B) deposits deregulated.
Government Preemptions	
Preemption of large proportion of bank reserves through CRR and SLR: CRR of 25 per cent and SLR of 38.5 per cent of deposits.	Preemptions lower due to lower CRR (9.75 per cent) and lower SLR (28.2 per cent). Rationalization of CRR and SLR requirements.
High monetization of government debt.	Monetization reduced. Issue of *ad hoc* Treasury Bills for monetization of fiscal deficit discontinued. Scheme of *Ways and Means Advances (WMA)* put in place to take care of temporary mismatches between government receipts and payments, provided such advances outstanding at any time do not exceed the mutually agreed upon limit.
Priority Sector Lending	
Forty per cent of bank credit channelled to priority sector at concessional rates.	Number of directed credit categories and interest rate subsidy element reduced. Weaker sections in priority sector redefined. Foreign banks advised to increase priority sector advances to 32 per cent of net credit.
Prudential Regulation and Bank Supervision	
Inadequate and non-uniform norms concerning income recognition, provisioning, and capital adequacy. Bank profits not reflecting 'true' health of banks.	Regulations on asset classification, income recognition, and capital adequacy strengthened, made uniform and transparent. Banks required to attain 8 per cent of capital to risk-weighted ratio as per international norms. Recapitalization of banks undertaken. Board for Financial Supervision (BFS) operational to strengthen bank supervision.

Status Before July 1991	Status in April 1998
	Reports submitted by three expert Groups constituted by the Department of Supervision, viz. the Group to review the system of on-site inspection of banks (Padmanabhan Committee), the Group to review the internal control and audit system in banks (Jilani Committee) and the Group for designing supervisory framework for NBFCs (Khanna Committee) were deliberated upon and adopted by the BFS.
	In response to the need for having in place an effective legislative framework in respect of NBFCs that was strongly advocated by various Committees in the past, the RBI (Amendment) Act, 1997, was passed in March 1997, putting in place an effective legislative framework in respect of NBFCs.
Private Sector Banks Restriction on entry and expansion of domestic private and foreign banks.	Entry and expansion of private sector banks deregulated to increase competition: 19 new private banks: 9 domestic and 10 foreign opened since 1994–5. Entry of more banks approved by the RBI.
	Guidelines issued for setting up new private Local Area Banks (LABs) with jurisdiction over two or three contiguous districts and a minimum capital base of Rs 5 crore. 'In-principle' approvals given to two LABs.
Branch Licensing Branch expansion rigidly controlled by the RBI branch licensing policy. No bank allowed to open branch without prior permission.	Branch licensing policy liberalized. Specifically, domestic banks satisfying certain performance criteria such as achieving capital adequacy ratio of 8 per cent, etc. need no prior permission for branch expansion. Other proposals to be considered on case by case basis.
	In line with the Bhandari Committee's recommendation, the branch licensing policy for RRBs was modified to free 70 RRBs from Service Area obligations and given freedom to relocate loss making branches. Mergers of loss making branches subject to certain conditions also allowed.
	Customer services Implementation of a number of measures to strengthen customer service as recommended by the Goiporia Committee on Customer Service in Banks.
	For expeditious and inexpensive resolution of customer complaints against deficiency in banking services, the Banking Ombudsman Scheme 1995 introduced.

Status Before July 1991	Status in April 1998
	The Electronic Clearing System (ECS) being used at four metropolitan centres by about 20 corporate customers for servicing dividend, interest, refund order, salary and pension payment transactions, extended to other metropolitan centres.
	Technological issues
	Recommendations of the Saraf Committee set up to study technology issues relating to payment and settlement system in the banking industry, are at various stages of implementation.
	The Shere Committee Report, set up to study all aspects of Electronic Funds Transfer, submitted.
	Under the World Bank's Financial Sector Development Project, participating banks can obtain a modernization and institutional development loan of US \$150 million for extending *inter alia*, automation and computerization of banking operations.
	Others
	Amendment of Banking Companies (Acquisition and Transfer of Undertakings) Acts, 1970/1980, permitting public sector banks to raise capital up to 49 per cent from the public.
	Banks permitted to trade in shares in the secondary market.
	A 'Loan System' for Delivery of Bank Credit for working capital purpose introduced to bring greater discipline in credit utilization and better control in credit flows.

REFERENCES

Amihud, Y. and G. Miller (eds) (1998). *Bank Mergers and Acquisitions.* Boston/London/Dordrecht: Kluwer Academic Publishers.

Barltrop, C. and D. McNaughton. (1992). *Banking Institution in Developing Markets.* Washington D.C.: World Bank.

Berger, A. (1998). 'The Efficiency Effects of Bank Mergers and Acquisitions: A Look at the 1990s Data'. In Amihud and Miller (eds), pp 79–111.

Bhatt, V. V. (1994). 'The Lead Bank Systems in India', In M. Aoki and H. Patrick (eds), *The Japanese Main Bank System: Its Relevance for Developing and Transforming Economies.* Oxford and New York: Oxford University Press.

Bhaumik, S.K. and Mukhopadhyay, H. (1997). 'Has Credit Crunch Led to Industrial Stagnation?: A Disequilibrium Approach'. *Economic and Political Weekly*, vol. 32, no. 18, pp. 964–7.

Caprio, G. (1997). 'Banking on Financial Reform? A Case of Sensitive Dependence on Initial Conditions'. In G. Caprio, I. Atiyas and J. Hanson (eds), *Financial Reform: Theory and Experience*. New York: Cambridge University Press, pp. 49–63.

Caprio, G., I. Atiyas, and J. Hanson. (1997). 'Policy Issues in Reforming Finance: Lessons and Strategies'. In Caprio, Atiyas, and Hanson (eds), *Financial Reform: Theory and Experience*. New York: Cambridge University Press, pp. 413–40.

Indian Banks' Association. (1995). Indian Banking *Yearbook, 1994–95*. Mumbai.

―――. (1996). *Indian Banking Review 1995–96*. Mumbai.

―――. (several years). *Performance Highlights of Public Sector Banks*. Mumbai.

―――. (several years). *Performance Highlights of Private Sector Banks*. Mumbai.

―――. (several years). *Performance Highlights of Foreign Sector Banks*. Mumbai.

Joshi, Vijay and I.M.D. Little (1996). *India's Economic Reforms 1991–2001*. Delhi: Oxford University Press.

Horton, S., R. Kanbur, and D. Mazumdar (eds). (1994): *Labour Markets in an Era of Adjustment*. EDI Development Studies, World Bank.

Ministry of Finance (MOF). (1993). 'Public Sector Commercial Banks and Financial Sector Reform: Rebuilding for a Better Future'. Discussion paper, Government of India, New Delhi.

Pierce, J.L. (1991). *The Future of Banking*. London: Yale University Press.

Report of the Narasimham Committee on Financial System (NCFS). (1991). Government of India, Mumbai.

Report of the Tarapore Committee on Capital Account Convertibility. (1997). Government of India.

Reserve Bank of India (RBI). (several years). *Trends and Progress in Banking*. Mumbai.

―――. (several years). *Annual Report*. Mumbai.

―――. (several years). *Report of Currency and Finance*. Mumbai.

Sarkar, J. and P. Agrawal. (1997). 'Banking: The Challenges of Deregulation'. In K. Parikh (ed.), *India Development Report, 1997*. New Delhi: Oxford University Press.

Sarkar, J., S. Sarkar, and S. Bhaumik. (1998). 'Does ownership always matter?—Evidence from the Indian Banking Industry'. *Journal of Comparative Economics*, vol. 26, pp. 262–81.

Sen, K. and R. Vaidya. (1997). *The Process of Financial Liberalization in India*. Delhi: Oxford University Press.

Sheng, A. (1996). 'Post-liberalization Bank Restructuring'. In A. Sheng (ed.), *Bank Restructuring: Lessons from the 1980s*. Washington, D.C.: World Bank.

Tandon, Prakash. (1989). *Banking Century: A Short History of Banking in India and the Pioneer—Punjab National Bank*. New Delhi: Penguin (India) Books.

Thakor, A. (1996). 'Capital Requirements, Monetary Policy and Aggregate Bank Lending: Theory and Empirical Evidence'. *The Journal of Finance*, vol. 51, pp. 279–324.

Vittas, D. (ed.). (1991). *Financial Regulation: Changing the Rules of the Game*. Washington D.C.: World Bank.

World Bank. (1989), *World Development Report*. Washington. D.C.: World Bank.

_____. (1996). *World Development Report*. Washington, D.C.: World Bank.

Regulation and Supervision Issues: Banks and Non-Banks

S. VENKITARAMANAN

1. OVERVIEW

The question of regulation and supervision of banks and non-banks has been a vexed one. Whenever there is a large failure of banks or non-banks, the public gets exercised over the efficiency and effectiveness of supervision. Regulators, who are also often the supervisors, get blamed for errors of omission and commission which may be mainly those of the managements of the banks/non-banks.

The public has a highly exaggerated expectation of the regulator's role. It expects the regulator to be able to identify, as well as prevent, frauds. The gap between these high expectations and the reality explains much of the criticism levied, often unjustly, against regulators and supervisors.

Management of financial institutions inherently knows more about the institutions than regulators and supervisors. Every system of regulations has its inadequacies, making the system vulnerable to exploitation by those who are seeking to take advantage of the loopholes and indulge in fraud. Thus there is an ongoing tussle between the regulators and those who would take advantage of the loopholes in regulations. India's 1992 'securities scam' showed how systemic scams can surprise and shock the supervisors. Supervisors may get blamed for not knowing what even the bank management may not know.

The new emphasis has, therefore, been not only on improving regulation and supervision, but on relating it to a structure of incentives that will make banks themselves perform with greater prudence, and on improving banks' own systems of risk management. Banks are a locus of borrowers and depositors and lenders. As institutions, incentives are needed to make sure banks are careful in lending to borrowers. And those who lend to and deposit in banks should see the advantages of exercising caution in depositing with risky banks. Only then will regulators' job become easier. Of course, this is more easily said than done.

Various prudential norms, stipulations on connected lending, capital related to risky assets, exposure to specific sectors, etc. can be devised to provide incentives to banks to take adequate care in expanding their assets. Deposit insurance, where it exists, can be extended at more favourable rates to those banks with a better record. Capital adequacy norms should be strictly enforced so that shareholders of banks have something to lose if banks lose. Managements will then be encouraged to behave more prudently.

All this presumes a structure of banks in which incentives and disincentives can work efficiently. In India, 90 per cent of banks are in the public sector, with no 'risk' of loss of capital faced by the managers. The sovereign government invariably fills up the losses. India's public sector banks, therefore, present a major problem, precisely because of the built-in difficulties of using incentives and disincentives.

The hard reality is that public sector banks cannot be allowed to fail. As a result, lenders and depositors have less incentives to be careful. 'Autonomy', the oft-cited remedy, is essential, but not sufficient. There is a need to develop a framework, which involves more autonomy with greater accountability.

Currently, managers and staff of public sector banks are treated as if they are employees of the 'state'. They are under the same regime of protections and sanctions as government employees. The incentive and disincentive structure of the banks suffers from this handicap. In addition, representatives of the government continue to sit on banks' boards, although the Narasimham Committee had objected to this approach. Although, in principle, there can be no objection to government *qua* shareholder having representation on the boards of public sector banks, it is something that has led to considerable abridgement of autonomy. Such is the nature of government representation that in spite of or because of it many public sector banks are weighed down with heavy losses! The government, so long as it has majority, or even minority, shareholding in banks, has to find a way whereby its representatives on the boards of banks do not constrain the boards' operational freedom. This mindset, which regards public sector banks as more or less captive institutions of government, must change.

At the same time, autonomy will have to coexist with much greater accountability. Accountability, the obverse of autonomy, should carry with it the threat of severe penalty in cases where crimes are proved, albeit after due process. At the same time, the undue publicity now given to the process of investigation should be avoided. The glare of exposure without sufficient proof destroys executive morale. However, the fact remains that poor judgement and bad performance with regard to business risk should carry disincentives. Obviously, where moral turpitude is involved, severe penalties should be imposed. Equally, good performance should be rewarded. Rigidities of the public sector system, however, accentuate the negative and do not emphasize the positive.

This chapter does not for a moment argue that India's public sector managers should be exempted from investigations. On the contrary, it suggests that there should be a specialized cadre of investigators for white collar crime in financial matters. These should consist of special teams of experts, as have been set up in the UK under the Special Bureau of Frauds. Their focus should be on sifting essentially business risks from collusive actions leading to fraud and/or loss to banks and society. They should fix responsibility for and penalize criminality in banks and other financial sector institutions.

2. REGULATION AND SUPERVISION

Banks in India are governed essentially by the Banking Regulations Act (1949) and the Reserve Bank of India Act. They also come under various acts and regulations covering foreign exchange transactions as well as securities. India's lead regulator and supervisor in the case of banks has always been the Reserve Bank of India (RBI). Non-banking finance companies have also been regulated and governed by the RBI, except to the extent that they come under the jurisdiction of the Securities and Exchange Board of India (SEBI) or the Companies Act.

The Indian financial scene is generally 'over-regulated and under-managed'. Early in India's economic development, partial preemption of bank resources for meeting the government's resource gap became part of the national financial agenda. 'Statutory liquidity requirements' which started as a legitimate safeguard against bank failures, were converted to mandatory contributions to meet gaps in government finance. Over time, the statutory liquidity ratio (SLR) was raised to as high as 38.5 per cent of all deposits and time liabilities. Only recently, after the inception of the 1992 financial sector reforms, has it come down, but even now it remains at 25 per cent. This credit repression resulted not only in the banks having lower resources to lend to the businesses at large, but also in depressing their earnings.

The recent welcome spate of deregulation saw the freeing of interest rate structure both on deposits and lending, interest rates till then being subject to a series of regulations. Rates of interest depended not only on the purpose but also on the magnitude of loans given.

Reserve Ratios

Until the credit policy of April 1997, the RBI had more or less ignored the 'bank rate' as a monetary policy instrument. Its usefulness is, even now, none too clear. It has been the cash reserve ratio (CRR) and the SLR to which the RBI has resorted as the main policy instruments over the years. The CRR started at 3 per cent of demand and time liabilities. In June 1989, it reached 15 per cent, rising to 25 per cent in the crisis period of 1990–2. The CRR has since been brought down further, and is currently at 11 per cent. Since it was recognized that the high CRR rates formed an indirect tax on banks, there was pressure to increase rates of interest paid on the reserves, which was objected to as attenuating monetary control. The RBI has recently paid an interest of 4 per cent on eligible reserve balances. The levy of CRR on inter-bank borrowings was also removed in the credit policy of April 1997.

One aspect of the RBI's regulations regarding the CRR and SLR is that the application of different rates on various types of liabilities distorts the operation of these monetary tools. This has been rectified, to a considerable extent, in recent modifications of policy. However, the changes in the CRR and SLR, as applied to foreign currency non-resident deposits, have shown a flip-flop phenomenon. The rates have moved from 0 to 7.5 per cent to 15 per cent and back again to 7.5 per cent, all within a period of three years. Once in between, it touched zero for a while. These changes, which were a reflection of the RBI's attempts to manipulate foreign exchange flows, show an unclear stance in relation to banks raising funds abroad.

Micro-management by Regulators

Over time, banking regulations in India became so detailed that they often intruded even on managerial discretion of banks. A typical instance was branch licensing. Even today, banks have to apply to the RBI for new branch licences or permission to open branches. At one time, even ATMs were defined as branches and could be opened only with the

RBI's clearance. Even the size and scale of expansion of staff is laid down by the RBI.

Until 1996–7, regulations went so far as to prescribe even 'maximum permissible bank finance', as a result of which bankers' judgements were subordinated to a mechanistic regulation by a guideline, which laid down how much could be lent by each bank. This was a certain recipe for delays and bottlenecks.

Another aspect of regulatory intervention which in the view of some observers constrains the further development of Indian banking is the concept of 'priority sector'. As much as 40 per cent of lending has to be towards specified types of economic activities, such as agriculture and small industry. While it is true that such directed lending exists in many other economies and may be socially justified, lending at lower than cost of funds and high default rates has led to cross-subsidization of the priority borrowers and higher interest costs for other sectors. Moreover, banks, subject to 'priority' sector requirement, are more constrained than other intermediaries. These are just a few examples of micro-management through regulation. Most internationally competitive banking systems, particularly in the developed world, do not have such requirements.

Costs of Regulations

The response of most countries to banking crises has been to ask for stricter regulation. Regulation *per se* is not 'costless'. Every regulation involves both direct and indirect costs—the direct costs to the regulator and indirect costs to the regulated entity and the economy, which can be much higher. There are many inefficiencies associated with the pheno-menon of over-regulation. The number of steps which are to be taken in order to enforce any regulation inevitably involves delays as well as inefficiencies.

Over-regulation is often the result of a desire to avoid *all* errors. In the process of trying to prevent every single error, many correct business decisions of bankers may be ruled 'out of court'. The protection of depositors and consumers by regulation and supervision therefore comes at high cost. Regulation should not become an end in itself.

Control systems, such as regulation, also have their moral hazards. They tend to give a wrong impression to the public that once there is a regulator, all will be well and that depositors and lenders to banks need not be cautious. Further, regulators do not pay for their own failures, which are not infrequent. Accountability for regulatory mistakes should be well defined.

It has been commented that forbearance should be a necessary quality of a good regulator. A regulatory system has to beware of attempting too much. More rules do not necessarily mean a better system. Since supervisors are not held responsible for their regulatory actions, they have little incentive to worry about its possible negative impact (which can sometimes be serious) on the system.

The cost of regulation may tend to be much higher than appears on the surface mainly because of the excessive safeguards which over-regulation induces. Supervisors, therefore, have to use their powers with caution. 'Supervisors can sometimes induce even recessions by their over-drive', said Albert Wojenflower, a distinguished US central banker. Often, supervisors impose a dull uniformity of behaviour on banks, because their guidelines have led to failure to distinguish between potential good credits and bad risks. There is no court of appeal against supervisory errors.

2.1 HISTORY OF SUPERVISION IN INDIA

When the RBI first started to inspect banks, its role was unpopular with commercial banks. They even protested against the vesting of such authority in the central bank. The Banking Companies Act (1949), which was introduced after detailed debate, faced strong criticism. Even some Governors of the RBI in those early days felt that the invisible hand of the market might do it all. One of them even said that he did not want to be accused of 'nationalizing banks by the back door through excessive inspections'. This scenario seems far different from today's enthusiastic assumption of the regulatory and supervisory burden of the RBI.

The RBI's Department of Banking Operations (DBOD) was set up in 1945. The first head of department went to the US Federal Reserve for training in bank examinations. Once set up, the Department dealt with all problems relating to scheduled and non-scheduled banks and carried out, on behalf of the government, inspections of banks applying for inclusion in the second schedule. The Department remained the nerve centre of supervision until the reforms of 1992–3 when a separate Department of Supervision and a Supervisory Board were set up.

One of the first cases of bank failure to test the RBI in its early years—even before the DBOD was set up—was the Travancore National and Quilon Bank in 1938. Although the Travancore National and Quilon Bank had been a defaulter in respect of its statutory reserves, the legislation at the time did not empower the RBI to take any penal action. It had to refer the issue to the government. In 1960, when Palai Central Bank, a premier private bank of Kerala, faced a run on deposits, the RBI had to swing into action once again. The Banking Companies Act was amended to enable the RBI to ask for and obtain relevant information to monitor banks' activities. The Banking Companies Act (1949) was renamed the Banking Regulations Act (1949) with certain amendments in 1965. The pressure for supervision as a central bank's responsibility thus gained support, mainly because of the realization that some private banks were mismanaging their resources.

2.2 THE 'SECURITIES SCAM' AND THE REGULATORY RESPONSE

The securities scam of 1992, the culmination of a series of irregularities that seem to have been going on for years, came as a shock both to the Government of India and the RBI. It was interpreted as a rebuke to those associated with supervision over the years. While the securities scam has been generally ascribed to 'systemic failure', its origin actually seems to have been a skilful manipulation of regulatory loopholes. In particular, there was a misuse of payment and settlement systems, which had, over the years, suffered benign neglect. Among banks which lost heavily in the scam were one or two otherwise well-run foreign banks with a reputation for good internal control systems. While the scope of this chapter does not extend to the history and causes of the securities scam, it is worth noting that the extent of 'exposure' of banks to losses as a result of speculative operations involving collusions of some of their own officials was not known even to their top managements until the scam broke.

The use of 'bank receipts' as substitutes for securities being sold (bought) by one bank to (from) another, was the principal *modus operandi* of the scam. On the 'security' of these bank receipts, which were assumed to represent underlying gilt-edged securities, certain bankers undertook repo-like transactions—ready forward sale and purchase of securities. These transactions involved bankers borrowing from each other under cover of sale and repurchase of securities. Inter-bank borrowing, on the basis of sale and purchase of bank receipts, was attractive mainly because at the time such sales did not attract reserve requirements. They were treated as investment transactions, although in substance they involved borrowing between banks. Once the scam broke, those banks that had lent money against non-existent bank receipts found they had no way to recover the money. Some brokers had used money obtained through such repo transactions—both legitimately and illegitimately—to boost stock prices, leveraging them to the hilt. They found they had no funds to pay when the margin calls came. The exchanges reacted sharply. Stock prices fell. The speculators who had led the exchanges on an upward spree were caught with losses. In turn, banks which had placed funds with the speculators in pursuit of quick gains were severely trounced. In some of the banks, there was a failure of payment and settlement systems, which was fortunately stopped from spreading further.

Questions were raised as to what the supervisors of the RBI at various levels had been doing and why the RBI had not been able to prevent these abuses in time. Accusing fingers were pointed at the alleged failure of supervision by the RBI. Enthusiastic investigators unnecessarily spent time on why and where a particular file was delayed at a specified supervisor's desk and for how long. Unjustified attribution of motives and publicity became part of the game, ignoring the cardinal truth that supervision cannot substitute for micro-management. Also ignored was the issue of incentives—the fact that profits could be and were made by taking advantage of the regulatory loopholes. The costs of the potential failures are not yet fully known. To an extent, they were borne by the public sector banks. However, all the glare and the publicity did lead to an overall emphasis on the need for better supervision.

2.3 RECENT REVIEWS OF SUPERVISION AND REGULATION

As early as 1991, a Working Group chaired by Shri S. Padmanabhan, former Chairman of the Indian Overseas Bank, had reviewed the system of inspection of banks by the RBI. By and large, the recommendations of the Group were accepted by the RBI. Following the number of changes that took place in the Indian financial system in the period since 1991, a second review of the system of supervision was initiated in 1995 by a second Working Group, again under Shri S. Padmanabhan.

The report of this second Padmanabhan Group clearly defines the role of both preventive and protective prudential regulations. While preventive regulation is designed to prevent the wrong type of business enterprises getting into the banking sector and undertaking non-prudential behaviour, the report also emphasizes protective regulation needed to protect depositors. The Padmanabhan Group has given importance to off-site supervision, within a strategy of continuous supervision and periodic inspection. 'Off-site supervisory returns and supplementary examination in between statutory examinations' form the core of the recommendations.

While the Padmanabhan Committee returns to centre stage, the traditional CAMELS approach, viz. capital adequacy, asset, quality management, earnings analysis, liquidity and systems, also emphasizes a new style of inspection. Inspection is expected to focus more on policy, systems, and procedures than on details of advances given. While, in principle, such a shift of emphasis does look attractive, the supervisor cannot draw general conclusions without looking at some details.

Guidelines have recently been issued by the RBI following these recommendations. They lay particular stress on the role of statutory auditors, who are to certify compliance by banks with certain regulatory aspects. Banks have also been asked to set up a system of concurrent audit, 'covering 50 per cent of their advances and deposits and 100 per cent in respect of their investment operations'. Compliance Officers to ensure strict observation of all regulations have also been mandated.

An Audit Committee of the board of banks is to be set up and made responsible for the effectiveness and efficiency of the internal control systems in banks. While the Audit Committee is to be chaired by a non-official Chartered Accountant Director, the Chairman and Managing Director is to be excluded from the Committee. This recommendation seems impractical, since in most of our banks there are no separate finance officers, unlike the case of other corporates. The Audit Committee will have only the external auditor to assist, if the Chairman and Managing Director are not sitting on it.

The new supervisory paradigm devised by the Padmanaban Committee demands a very high level of competence and skills on the part of the examiners/inspectors. Examiners are expected to assess not only the quality of non-performing assets, but also to comment on papers, such as the investment policy document approved by the bank's board. They are also to produce an evaluation of the functioning of the board itself—the Management Committee and the Audit Committee of the board—in terms of both content and process. In addition, they are to evaluate systems and procedures. However, all this is expecting too much of the RBI supervisors, who are relatively junior functionaries. The range and complexity of the subjects that are to be continually appraised by the staff is, indeed, quite challenging. The evaluation of complicated businesses, such as foreign exchange transactions, for instance, may well be beyond the ken of the average inspector. The need for substantial training of regulators and supervisors is obvious.

The Bank of International Settlement's 1997 document on the twenty-five core principles for effective banking supervision, issued by the Basle Committee on the eve of the 1997 IBRD–IMF meeting, largely reiterates the original objectives of the 1988 Basle Committee's recommendations on bank regulation and supervision. Many of the core principles enunciated therein implicitly assume that supervision and regulation should be in the same agency and that supervision of the banks has necessarily to be closely related to the location of the lender of last resort. A monetary authority which does not have access to what happens inside the banks would be very much handicapped, if it is insulated from information on the real world, because of the decision to divest it of supervisory functions. Importantly, the core principles affirm (a) the need to involve a pre-commitment on entry conditions into banking as also on criteria for major new acquisitions, (b) the need for banking supervisors to set prudential norms as well as norms for minimum capital adequacy, and (c) strict regulation of connected lending. Recent instructions issued by the RBI following the Padmanabhan Committee report seem broadly consistent with the twenty-five core principles.

3. ISSUES IN REGULATION

One key issue that can be posed is: can the rigour of regulation be reduced without sacrificing its objectives? For example, can incentives do the job?

Different avenues for using incentives are possible. Thus it might be possible to reduce the intensity of regulatory oversight if, for instance, banks have higher than the prescribed capital. Clear guidelines need to be set for dealing with banks which become under-capitalized or fail to maintain sound risk management procedures.

Can bankers be their own policemen? Voluntary self-regulation is not easy if only because self-regulatory organizations have no enforcement power. It is also possible that self-regulatory agencies can be captured by the regulated.

Capital Adequacy

High capital provides an incentive to owners to ensure sound performances, at least in private banks. The higher the capital, the greater the potential loss to the owners and, hopefully, the greater the prudence they will demand from the managers and themselves. Supervision is needed, however, to ensure that capital is really there and systems are in place to maintain it.

Capital adequacy norms, generally based on the Basle Committee recommendations, were introduced in India following the Narasimham Committee I recommendations. One criticism levied against them is that the risk weights attached to the different categories of lending other than to the government do not 'discriminate' according to the quality of credit. This may be one factor in the tendency of banks to constrain lending to non-government borrowers. The RBI and the government should examine the possibly perverse consequences of the capital adequacy formula.

Another aspect of capital adequacy to be considered is its relevance in countries with underdeveloped capital markets. In developed countries, which have mature capital markets, banks find it easier to meet the capital adequacy norms as they can raise more equity. This is not so in developing countries. As against this point of view, some observers feel that banks in emerging economies need a tighter set of capital adequacy norms than in developed countries, because risks in small markets are greater.

How exactly the banks' extra capital is contributed is also important. In the case of public sector banks, capital adequacy has become something of a ritual. Granted, public sector banks need capital adequacy to meet internationally accepted standards. But, quite often, the Government of India puts in equity and asks the banks to reinvest in special securities of the government, although the Basle norms did not intend injections of capital to be so used.

Deposit Insurance

It has been argued that deposit insurance *per se* reduces incentives for depositors to monitor banks. In certain circumstances, it may allow even weak banks to attract deposits by offering to pay higher interest. Deposit insurance may thus pose a 'moral hazard' by giving perverse incentives to depositors. Given the comfort of deposit insurance, bank managements may undertake more risky lending than otherwise, in the expectation that, ultimately, deposit insurance will pay off depositors. This argument is, however, weakened where deposits are insured only up to a ceiling, namely only for small depositors, leaving larger depositors, especially the corporates, uncovered. It is important, in order to avoid the risk of moral hazard, that the government stick to a 'limited' deposit insurance under which large depositors do not see an opportunity to collect, especially by splitting deposits.

Public sector banks present a special type of problem where deposit insurance is concerned. It is hard to provide incentives or disincentives for deposits with them from the point of view of security. The general public assumes that governments do not normally default and, therefore, nationalized banks are safer, even when they are incurring losses. Deposit insurance may therefore offer only symbolic protection for public sector banks. This position will, however, change as public sector banks continue to divest more and more of their shares to private shareholders.

A special issue to be considered with regard to deposits with public sector banks is that of off-shore lenders/depositors. Foreign currency deposits of India-based banks represent external currency liabilities. The extension of explicit insurance to such deposits is subsumed within a larger question to the extent that all public sector banks are seen to have government guarantee. Prudential exposure norms should be introduced for such offshore borrowing represented by non-resident deposits (FCNR [B]).

If deposit insurance is to be effective, the Deposit Insurance Corporation (DIC) has to go beyond its current role of offering insurance and asking for annual reports of compliance. Like its counterpart in the USA, the Indian DIC may also need to undertake inspections or examinations of banks to satisfy itself that what it has insured is worth insuring.

It may be argued that this will lead to multiple inspections. One way to avoid multiple inspections is for the DIC to entrust such inspections of banks to specialized rating agencies. 'Bank rating' agencies, which are common in other economies where bank equity is widely held, need to be encouraged by the RBI and DIC.

An important question is whether deposit insurance should be extended to select non-bank finance companies (NBFCs) also. Should it be offered at least in respect of NBFCs above a certain size and meeting certain specified criteria? The pleas for such insurance have become more insistent, after the recent collapse of a few large NBFCs. Increasingly, NBFCs are taking on the character of banks. Prudential norms, capital adequacy, liquidity ratios, etc.—most of the defining characteristics of banks are also being extended to non-banks. The larger NBFCs are today as much under the watchful eye of the supervisors, as are banks. The real issue may well be why with all this monitoring and regulation, strong NBFCs cannot become banks themselves. This is a question which I turn to later.

An alternative that has been suggested in place of public insurance is that deposit insurance should be offered by private agencies instead of either government or government-related agencies. There is, however, a strong case for public insurance as against private insurance. A well-designed deposit insurance scheme sponsored and run by the government seems well worth the while, provided it is limited to small depositors

Bank Failures: Closure versus Merger

How should bank failures be handled? Should failed banks be closed or merged with stronger banks? Should the central bank 'forbear' before closing a weak bank?

There has been a spate of bank failures around the world recently. The answers to banking crises in India will have to be a blend of different approaches which have been successful in other countries.

It has been the experience the world over that whenever a big bank fails, even if it is in the private sector, governments have often had to bear the burden of rescuing them. The financial is intertwined with public interest in this sector to the extent that governments cannot always disown their ultimate responsibilities, except where there is a proven case of fraud. 'Too big to fail' is often broached as the guiding principle of governments dealing with banks in crises. Governments cannot ignore the social costs of bank failures, when they are too big. There have been exceptions to this rule as in the case of the BCCI in the UK, when the bank was, indeed, allowed to fail. However, the usual rule is intervention by the government, as in the case of the Continental Illinois Bank of the USA, a major bank that the government of USA did not allow to fail, although it swept out the old management and shareholders. In effect, it had to virtually 'nationalize' the bank, contrary to its own public philosophy and posture of laissez-faire, protecting all depositors and lenders and only later selling it back to the private sector. In Japan also, many recent bank and non-bank failures have resulted in the government having to take over their liabilities and ultimately bearing part of the bill.

While a few of India's public sector banks have had losses that wiped out almost their entire equity in recent years, there has been less panic because they have been publicly owned. However, the very size of non-performing assets of Indian public sector banks, which stands at nearly Rs 40,000 crores, will put many of them under pressure. The Government of India may have to transfer more funds to make up for impaired equity. Otherwise, some of them will not meet the RBI's prudential norms and capital adequacy ratios.

Conversion of impaired banks to 'narrow banks' has been advocated as a solution to the problem of India's weak banks. This concept involves a bank or even separated parts of the same bank being required to hold a limited set of highly liquid assets, such as gilts. Only such a highly liquid and safe bank or narrow bank can be given 100 per cent deposit insurance. While risk averse depositors can be expected to choose such narrow banks, others can choose the riskier banks which can, in turn, lend to riskier clients and therefore offer higher interest rates on deposits. The narrow bank concept has the defect that it may diminish an already losing bank, both in terms of asset size and scope. Borrowers to whom it had earlier lent will now have to go to other banks. While there is undoubted merit in curtailing asset expansion of banks which have incurred heavy losses, it can be argued that such a step may be self-defeating. It does not seem to be prudent to confine the business of weak banks only to lending to government or equally riskless clients, which means a much narrower spread. After all, successful banking requires a portfolio of diversified assets. A bank which becomes a narrow bank and therefore has both its asset size and deposit base reduced, will also find it difficult to build up momentum and further growth.

In defence of the concept of narrow banks, it has been strongly argued that banks which have proved themselves unable to collect should also forfeit their right to continue as broad banks. If they die, so the argument goes, let them. One cannot, however, find a strong historical basis for the argument that narrow banking can itself fully solve a banking crisis. It will need enough broad banks, which can take up the function of intermediation.

Let us now turn to 'merger', which is one of the methods adopted to solve banking crises in mature market economies. Most mergers between banks have also been characterized by strong and successful efforts at reducing the workforce and enforcing other economies. Such a strategy cannot, however, be easily operated in India today. Rationalization through reduction of staff and elimination of overlapping branches will be a non-starter, given the Indian political mindset against reduction of staff. There will be strong trade union pressure to absorb surplus staff/branches in stronger banks, which will only make them weaker.

A feasible option for handling weak banks in India appears to be the 'asset reconstruction device', although I note that Dr C. Rangarajan has not been in favour of this approach; the Narasimham Committee had specifically recommended such a device on a national scale. Dr Aristobulous de Juan, the Spanish expert who has had a successful experiment with asset reconstruction in Spain has written extensively about this in his various articles and studies. The Resolution Trust Corporation, which was set up by the Federal Government to handle the Savings and Loans crisis, belongs to this category. Ideally, an asset reconstruction approach in India should also start with a 'catch all' national-level asset reconstruction fund. But such a national-level asset reconstruction undertaking may not be feasible in India, given the different cultural traditions in various banks.

A way out could be that the balance sheet of each impaired bank be first cleaned up by transferring the sticky loans to a special purpose vehicle (SPV) to be created by each bank separately. Such SPVs should, however, be operated at arm's length from the by now 'healthy' bank. The asset reconstruction vehicle should be duly empowered to carry on a work-out operation to recover the banks' 'non-performing' loans.

One argument advanced against such asset reconstruction devices is that bank staff which lends would also be in a better position to collect than staff with the new entities and that there is no specific incentive for persons in asset reconstruction agencies to collect on the old loans. These criticisms are not quite valid. First, the relatively sticky assets, which require more intensive attention, would be transferred to the asset reconstruction device, which can concentrate on them. Second, the argument that only staff that lends money in the impaired bank will be able to collect may not always be correct. The precedent of successful separation of lending and collecting exists in devices like factoring and other similar procedures. It is, therefore, worthwhile trying the asset reconstruction device, at least in respect of a few banks.

In order that bank managements and asset reconstruction agencies are enabled to arrive at quick decisions on impaired assets, it could also become necessary to set up an advisory council, for working out 'compromises' or settlements. In the current atmosphere in which every credit decision is subject to *post facto* evaluation, laced with suspicion, such a special device will help. It may be headed by a judge, as has been done in the case of the Indian Bank exercise on settlements. Such a council can hopefully handle the sticky loans with greater expedition than banks themselves can.

Banking crises and failures cannot be wished away. When the BCCI came and went, no one had imagined that Leeson's contribution to

Barclay's failure was around the corner. Credit Lyonnais was yet another story of a bank that went down because it could not say 'No'. Every single banking crisis has its own special characteristic. Regulators have to be ready to find ways of confronting crises, however much their rules and regulations were designed to avoid them.

Above all, a healthy macroeconomic situation is obviously one of the prerequisites for minimizing bank failures and crises. Not that bank failures *per se* do not occur in healthy economies. They are, however, more likely to take place in economies that are weak.

Culture Shock in the Indian Financial System

One of the important features of Indian banking's regulatory structure is actually outside the usual regulatory paradigm. Excessive investigative zeal and the resulting atmosphere of suspicion have led many bank officials of the public sector to rely on caution for safety. They prefer treading a safe track in lending. Unlike decisions not to lend, decisions to lend can be held against them, especially if the latter end up in a loan turned sour, albeit for bona fide and unforeseen reasons. Investigators become super regulators.

While this chapter has pointed to the adverse consequences of excessive investigative zeal on bankers' actions, it does not suggest, even remotely, that bankers who commit serious errors that lead to frauds and losses to banks, should be left untouched. The point rather is that there should be an adequate screening mechanism staffed by experienced bankers and others who can sift criminal from intent bona fide error. The fear of reckless attack by ever present vigilantes, who tend to hound bank staff, officers, and supervisors should be removed. In response to criticism of such overzealous investigation, a Screening Committee has been set up at the Reserve Bank of India under former Deputy Governor Shri S.S. Tarapore's chairmanship to ensure that cases of genuine errors of judgement are not pursued by investigators.

4. ISSUES IN SUPERVISION

Consolidated Supervision

The changing face of banking has been a global phenomenon. Many banks have established merchant banking subsidiaries. Profits from merchant banking activities have in fact contributed a substantial share of the growth of revenues of many global mega banks. As elsewhere, banks in India have been extending their reach beyond the customary sphere of deposit taking and lending, and can be expected to become increasingly 'universal' in character.

Different parts of such banks may therefore come under different supervisory agencies and present problems of overlapping jurisdictions. Such problems have already cropped up in respect of merchant banking and mutual fund subsidiaries of scheduled Indian banks. In so far as security-related and merchant banking activities are concerned, even now commercial banks have to submit themselves to more than one agency of regulation.

Although the concept of 'lead supervisor' has become increasingly relevant, certain recent episodes of failure in respect of NBFCs, which also manage mutual funds, have cast doubts on the viability of divided supervision. There is a possible loss of information in transmission between different supervisors. Entities that do not pass the test of one supervisor, can sometimes succeed in getting permission from another.

Role of Auditors

Statutory auditors have an important role to play in the new structure of supervision. Quite often, auditors of banks in India, as elsewhere, suffer from various built-in systemic inefficiencies. First, since they are appointed by the boards or institutions which they audit, they depend on these very boards for their continuance as well as for enhancement of remuneration. This occasionally results in 'client' capture—extra sensitivity to concerns of clients. Further, auditors necessarily have to go by the documentation and information that are furnished by the audited banks. They are not expected to take into account any extraneous sources of information. The supervisor should have the right to insist on minimal compliance with regard to provision of adequate information to auditors as well as examiners from the supervisory agency. Failure to provide adequate information should be subject to mandatory punishment. Equally important is the need to give exemplary penalty to auditors who deliberately fail in their duties. Auditors who collude with erring institutions should face the threat of discontinuance of further auditing assignments, unless of course they are able to prove that the mistakes are *bona fide*.

In this connection, reference should be made to the important recommendations of the Jilani Committee set up by the RBI in 1993. In particular, it recommended that internal audit and vigilance systems should remain separate. Unfortunately, the Committee did not suggest specialization of audit. In other words, internal inspectors and auditors are to be interchangeable.

Internal audits can play a significant role in helping supervisors and auditors. Although internal audit is different in quality from inspection, the Jilani Group has favoured the two being together. This may not be appropriate. Audit of accounts is necessarily different from inspection. Inspection cannot substitute for audit. The skills required for the two are different.

The report proceeds on traditional lines in so far as its recommendations on vigilance are concerned. According to the report, this is justified because vigilance has a detective and investigative aspect, while inspection and audit involve both preventive and detective work. This appears to be a distinction without a difference. In fact, one of the reasons for the current shyness of lending is said to be the excessive fear of post mortems of decisions, especially by vigilance personnel. One cannot press the brake and accelerator at the same time

Supervision and New Financial Products

Derivatives and other sophisticated financial instruments for risk management, although comparatively new to India, represent an important area of supervisory concern. The latest amendment to the Basle Accord takes special note of derivatives and associated products. India's banks are also indirectly exposed to the new products, such as derivatives, both in the foreign exchange and in respect of global fund flows. A number of people who function in the foreign banks operating in India are themselves well equipped in handling these new techniques. With increasing integration into the global economy, it would be difficult for any emerging market to escape the impact of global players who can and do use the new tools of derivatives and risk management.

Location of Supervision in the RBI and Frequency of Supervision

In 1991, the Narasimham Committee recommended an alternate model of supervision. Until then, given the high credibility of the RBI as an institution, location of supervision in the RBI had seemed the only option. Following the recommendations of the Narasimham Committee, a Board of Supervision has now been set up at arm's length from the RBI, but serviced by its newly created Department of Supervision.

Broadly speaking, there are four possible institutional models for bank supervision with minor variations to consider. One is the current

Indian version of the central bank as lead supervisor with a board of Supervision. Another is the German/continental model wherein the Ministry of Finance takes on the responsibility of bank supervision. A third would be the setting up of a separate agency, as in the latest UK reforms—separate and distinct from the central bank. A fourth possibility is the US system where there are multiple supervisors ranging from the Federal Reserve to the state's own bank examiners and including the Controller of Currency as well as the Federal Deposit Insurance Corporation. The Basle Committee implicitly assumes that regulation and supervision should be undertaken by the same agency and closely tied to the lender of last resort.

What model should India follow? Those in favour of change emphasize the desirability of distancing supervision fully from the monetary authority so that conflicts between the role of central bank *qua* monetary authority and as supervisor can be avoided. While it is argued that the results of monetary tightening may be contrary to the interests of banks, it is also clear that the central bank, as lender of last resort, will have to know the conditions of the banks that may approach it for help. This will be more easily possible if a central bank is supervisor, as it will maintain continuous touch with banks. Thus a supervisory role will be helpful for the central bank's task as a monetary authority and lender of last resort. Above all, a central bank in any country is usually the best reservoir of talented people in the field of banking. A new institution situated outside the RBI would still have draw on people from the RBI, at least initially. For instance, the new mega-regulator in the UK is itself proposing to draw liberally on personnel from the Bank of England. However, the current structure of the Board of Supervision in the RBI is well designed. It has to be given time to grow to its full stature, before new experiments are undertaken.

This is not, however, to deny that the problems of on-site and off-site supervision of both banks and the NBFCs continue to be formidable and growing, both in view of their magnitude and complexity. One issue here is the frequency of inspection. One possibility is to adjust the frequency of inspection according to the rating of the bank/non-bank, the percentage of non-performing assets it has, and its capital adequacy in excess of norms. Obviously, such a structure would depend on the accuracy of information furnished by auditors/rating agencies and other factors.

5. OTHER ISSUES

NBFCs

Over time, the NBFCs have gained an important place in India's financial sector. As at the end of March 1996, the total deposits of the non-banking finance sector came to nearly Rs 100,000 crore, distributed over 9060 companies. In July 1996, the RBI announced a package of measures relaxing controls over the NBFCs, provided they comply with its restrictions and guidelines. Under this liberalized dispensation, the NBFCs were allowed to raise more deposits for the same capital provided they complied with the controls. In April 1997, restriction on lending by banks to the NBFCs in certain multiples of the net owned funds was removed for those NBFCs which comply with registration, prudential norms, and credit rating requirements.

The problems of the NBFCs and their supervision have been studied by many Committees. Important among these were the Bhabatosh Datta Study Group (1971) set up by the Banking Commission, the James Raj Study Group (1975), the Sukhamoy Chakravarty Committee Report of 1987 and the Narasimham Committee Report of 1991. The Dr A.C. Shah Committee recommended the present framework of the RBI's relations to NBFCs in 1992 . An important milestone was the report of the Expert Group by Shri P.R. Khanna for recommending a framework for supervision of the NBFCs through an off-site surveillance system. More importantly, a number of amendments were introduced in the RBI's Act so that control of the central bank over the NBFCs is made comprehensive. Under these amendments, the RBI took authority to register all NBFCs. No unregistered NBFC can hereafter carry on business. An important new requirement is that the NBFCs, like banks, need to maintain liquid assets in specified securities on a daily basis 5 per cent in respect of certain categories of NBFCs and 10 per cent for others. The reserve requirements that were earlier applied only to banks have now been extended to the NBFCs also, reducing thereby the advantage to a NBFC as compared to banks. The RBI has also assumed the power to direct the NBFCs on issues relating to disclosures and prudential norms. The freedom that the NBFCs have in respect of credit decisions can also be subject to regulation.

The RBI may not itself be in a position to handle supervision for all NBFCs given the large numbers. It has already proposed the use of special auditors for the purpose as a second tier of inspection. This is worth pursuing. It may also be appropriate for the RBI to consider sharing its responsibility for supervision of NBFCs below a certain size by the agencies to be set up by state governments.

One suggestion in regard to NBFCs (already referred to) is that the best way to end the current confusion of roles may be to allow NBFCs, which satisfy certain criteria, to become banks. From the point of view of those NBFCs that are healthy, such a transition makes sense. Such a prospect can also induce better and more prudential performance from other NBFCs, that seek to graduate to the status of banks. But in the current situation, and for a very long time to come, bank finance with all its rigidities cannot fully replace non-bank finance. Many studies have shown the important role that informal finance plays in most emerging markets. Non-bank financial companies fill an important gap in the financial structure of countries like India, in as much as their lending decisions are based more on local knowledge and trust. Their non-performing assets are, by and large, lower in proportion to their total asset base, compared to the larger and impersonal banks. Conversion of some NBFCs to banks will not solve the problem that the credit delivery system, in general, faces today because of the rigidity of existing bank financing.

Technology and Supervision

Technology is changing the face of banking. Computerization, satellite link-ups, the internet, and other technological changes have dramatically transformed the finance function. Even branch banking is no longer the same. Supervision of computerized banking needs specialized skills and training. For instance, during the securities irregularities of 1992, supervisors had to grapple with the skills of those who used computers and electronic devices to suborn the system. The knowledge base of the supervisor has, in particular, to constantly keep up with the agile minds of those who are always on the lookout for loopholes in the financial system.

Today, billions of dollars move across the country and between countries in microseconds, thanks to progress in information technology. This has also spurred the rapid growth of both credit cards and now debit cards. Sophisticated variations, such as 'smart cards', which utilize the fuller potential of electronic chips have become quite common in developed economies. These innovations, which change the very structure of banking, will soon be part of the Indian financial scene as well. Supervisory guidelines have to take them into account.

The regulatory and supervisory guidelines of today lag behind this increasing sophistication of the technology of finance. This is particularly so because the financial sector around the world has made heavy investments in information to the central banks. Supervisors have not kept pace with these changes in environment. The normal career path in the RBI does not, for instance, expose an inspector or examiner to the growing and invasive role of computers in banking.

Computer frauds are another important area for regulators and supervisors to focus. Embedded in the very speed of transactions are prospects of greater fraud by scamsters, who can make quick get-aways. Regulators need to specially focus on instilling into bank managements the need to develop adequate backups and training systems to prevent, trace, and bring to book attempts at computer frauds. Here again, regulators and supervisors can only do so much. The main burden has to fall on the internal management of banks.

Changes in Regulation and Supervision with Capital Account Convertibility

The extant exchange controls on both current and capital accounts represent an important element of continuing regulation of the banking sector. Recently, there has been considerable discussion on the impact of the contemplated move towards capital account convertibility on regulation and supervision (see the Tarapore Committee report on capital account convertibility).

There will be need to tune India's regulatory and supervision systems fully to the evolving scenario. A radical change in the approach of exchange control and supervision is called for. Many of the current requirements of exchange control may need to be reviewed and eliminated. This review has to take into account the fact that as a monetary authority, the RBI will continue to need certain minimum data for its information requirements, regarding foreign exchange exposures of banks and financial institutions. Indeed, with the growth of the derivatives and hedge markets, there will be greater need for more rather than less vigilance on the external front. The Leeson episode showed how a mere dealer or assistant in the derivatives desk could deal a death blow to a well-known financial institution.

The RBI is rightly engaged today in the task of refining its norms for the growing exposures of individual banks on the foreign front. Supervision should move in this direction. Bank managements at all levels need to become more aware of the risks on this front and to update their own skills, both in respect of risk management and control. No amount of external regulation can substitute for lax internal controls on exchange risk management.

6. LOOKING TO THE FUTURE

India's banking and non-bank finance are today at the point of transition to greater complexity as a result of globalization. With the increasing importance of foreign capital, these changes will become even more compelling. Traditional methods of supervision, using various ratios of performance, may not work in a situation in which functional lines are blurred and portfolio adjustment is much faster both within and outside the national economy. Although there must always remain a role for external regulation and supervision, there is no alternative to placing greater reliance on internal risk management by each financial entity. The first and foremost requirement of the supervisory regime has therefore to be to shift focus from external supervision to better internal governance.

Banks are in the business of raising funds and intermediating between different sectors of the economy. Risks are inherent in the process. So are the burdens of how to allocate resources to those areas where returns, and therefore spreads, are highest. These involve judgements on the future profits of projects and entrepreneurs. They are necessarily clouded by uncertainty. There can be no sure remedy for the problems which such prognoses of the future, in conditions of imperfect information, impose on the banker. It is similarly not possible to impose regulations to ensure that there will be no risk at all. The structure of governance of banks and non-banks has to take into account risk taking, which is part of the business.

Indeed, as the financial sector gets more mature, one can visualize greater recourse to credit enhancement through devices that can hedge risks. These do not come without costs. Derivatives of various kinds will play a role in this.

Can better regulation of the derivatives market reduce risks? Opinion differs. Some eminent experts believe that an attempt to hedge against hedges would be unprofitable and unproductive. The Bank of International Settlements has brought in a number of guidelines which can be of use to banks in handling the risks in the uncharted area of derivatives.

A second major area of emphasis for the improvement of supervision and regulation of the bank and non-bank sectors is the role of auditors. Reference has already been made to the need for setting up audit committees in the boards of banks. Auditors are essentially experts in post mortems. While they can identify the causes of crises, they can also serve a limited purpose in anticipating problems. This said, there can be no denying the role of better audit. Auditors have not covered themselves with glory in banking crises either in India or abroad. They have often left out clues of significance, and pursued superfluous objectives. In view of this, the Government of India should set up a separate cadre of professional auditors specializing in financial sector audit. This cadre, which should be under the Comptroller and Auditor General (CAG) and paid for by the banks audited, should be at the disposal of the RBI or the supervisory agency. It can be used for special or supplementary audit of banks and non-banks. Since this cadre of auditors will be specially trained in various facets of the financial sector, it will be possible for it to help anticipate various potential misuses and misapplications of discretion. This cadre can also be authorized not only to audit particular banks or non-banks but follow through claims of linked transactions in other banks.

With a greater thrust and move towards universal banking, the question of connected lending will assume greater importance. Not only lending but also investments can suffer if banks deploy their not inconsiderable resources to propping up share prices of related firms. Bank regulators must make it compulsory that such connected lending is immediately reported and action taken.

Prudential norms of exposure to particular groups and sectors will play an important role in regulation and supervision in the future. As particular sectors, like automobiles or petrochemicals or property, become a larger part of bank exposure, the volatility in those sectors will affect the balance sheets of banks. In fact, recent experience in Thailand and Japan has reaffirmed the importance of caution in lending to the real estate sector, particularly when an economy is booming. Regulators and supervisors have to refine the tools of control of exposures of the banks and non-banks to particular sectors. It is always tempting to lend or invest more in a sector which is in fashion. When the trend reverses, banks are left with non-performing assets.

Group exposure norms are vital for the continued health of banks and non-banks. The experience in India has been that many group companies are able to continue to avail of fresh credits when some of their own firms languish. Many groups have indulged in large investments in new start-ups even while some of their existing companies are sick. The banks should insist on the promoter group bringing in additional funds to revive the sick firms before embarking on new units with bank help.

Transparency of accounting practices also needs to be stressed by regulators and supervisors. Considerable changes in accounting norms have been introduced following the economic reforms of 1991–2 and thereafter. With increased private shareholding in the State Bank of India and nationalized banks as well as the emergence of private banks, the importance of setting the right accounting policies increases. The culture of quick enrichment, which is the bane of the financial sector, is paid for by depositors, customers of banks, and ultimately the government.

Looking into the future of banking, it is apparent that it will be increasingly dominated by technology. Even branch banking will become less and less important. On-line banking and the combination of 'smart cards' with other developments in communications may change the face of bank–customer relationships.

Regulators have to come to terms with a new world of banking, where banks will merge with communications systems and card purveyors. Internet itself offers prospects of a sea change in banking. As a recent review in *The Banker* points out, 'On-line banks only need one presence on the Internet to serve the whole world, costing a fraction of the traditional overheads in staffing, heating bills and security expenses'. How will the regulator undertake off-site inspection of such banks? The distinction between providers of communication networks, like DoT and VSNL and the organizers of payments and settlement or credit delivery, like banks, will grow thin. Sufficient effort has yet to be devoted to analyse the role of regulation in such a system. Although it is possible that, as happened in the case of nationalized banks, Luddite resistance from labour can try to turn back the age of new technology, global competition will force the change. Otherwise, Indian banks have no future. The Indian non-banks will move fast into the modem information age. Foreign banks have already automated most of their branches. Private banks will also follow quickly. Public sector banks may have no alternative except to catch up.

One interesting but unfortunate offshoot of the information wave will be the disconnect between customers and banks. Personal contacts, which were the core of branch banking in earlier times, will now be less and less important. The build-up of trust, which had characterized banking through the middle of the twentieth century, will increasingly give way to numerate verification and computerized checks. How will a regulator hold a branch manager responsible when a computer becomes manager!

7. CONCLUSION

The regulator of tomorrow cannot confine himself to the problems of his or her country. The increasingly interconnected world has led to changes in one part of the world having a sharp impact on the financial sector in another. Recent events in East Asia emphasize the challenge before regulators in economies with open capital accounts. It is not only the hedge funds that try to make profits out of speculation. Many global banks and even some Indian banks derive substantial profits from proprietary trading in foreign exchange. Indian regulators have naturally to take care of the dangers that this presents not only to banks, but also to the country's financial system as a whole. In the years to come, financial specialists have to take special care to evolve systems and procedures to limit volatility of markets.

In conclusion, it is too much to expect a regulator to always come to the rescue of every bank in distress or identify the problems beforehand. The new paradigm for regulation will have to be one in which banks and other financial entities will be motivated to better performance by incentives and disincentives. It is no longer possible, or sufficient, for regulators to lay down the why and wherefores of every detail of banking. In short, regulators and supervisors should not, and cannot, become managers of the entities they are to regulate and supervise.

ANNEXURE I

EVOLUTION OF FINANCIAL SECTOR REFORMS: IMPORTANT LANDMARKS

1. *Capital Adequacy Norms*

In 1992–3, all Indian banks with international presence were asked to achieve a capital to risk asset ratio of 8 per cent by 31 March 1994, later extended to 31 March 1995. For other banks, the rates were set at 4 per cent to be reached by 31 March 1993 and 8 per cent by 31 March 1996.

2. *Recapitalization of Nationalized Banks through Provision of Additional Funds in the Union Budget Starting from 1993–4*

The recipient banks were, however, asked to invest the government's capital subscription in government bonds, known as 10 per cent Recapitalization Bonds 2006. Total sum thus provided nearly Rs 11,000 crore.

3. Income Recognition and Provisioning

In April 1993, a prudential system of income recognition, classification of assets, and provisioning for bad debts was put in place beginning financial year 1992–3. 'Non-performing assets' were defined as credit facilities with respect to which interest has remained 'past due' for a period of four quarters ending 31 March 1993, three quarters ending 31 March 1994 and two quarters ending 31 March 1995 and onwards. Banks were instructed not to charge and take to income account interest on all non-performing assets (NPAs).

In March 1993, banks were advised to make 100 per cent provision in respect of lost assets and not less than 30 per cent in respect of substandard and doubtful advances with outstanding balance of Rs 25,000 for the year ended 31 March 1993. Provision requirement for NPAs was progressively tightened in the years 1994–5, 1995–6, and 1996–7.

4. Regulatory and Supervisory Issues

In May 1993, a decision was taken to set up a Board for Financial Supervision (BFS) within the RBI.

In December 1993, the Department of Supervision was set up. From 16 November 1994, the BFS became functional with the Deputy Governor as Vice-Chairman and two members of the BFS were inducted in January 1995.

In April 1995, the BFS started supervising all-India financial institutions. In February 1995, a committee under Shri Rashid Jilani was set up on internal controls in banks. It submitted its report in September 1995. The Padmanabhan Committee was also set up in February 1995 to review the system on on-site supervision.

5. Private Sector Banks

In January 1993, guidelines were issued by the RBI for establishment of new banks in the private sector. In February 1994, the Banking Regulatory Act was amended, raising the ceiling of voting rights of individual shareholders in private banks from 1 per cent to 10 per cent. Ten new private banks were authorized. In August 1996, guidelines were issued for new private local area banks.

6. Frauds and Malpractices

In February 1997, an advisory board on bank frauds was set up under Shri S.S. Tarapore, to advise the RBI on cases referred by the CBI for investigation/regis-tration of cases against bank officers of the rank of GM and above.

7. Reforms in NBFCs

Began in 1993–4. Detailed prudential guidelines to NBFCs were issued in June 1994. A code for financial supervision was issued to extend supervision to NBFCs from July 1995. Maintenance of liquid assets increased from 10 to 15 per cent of deposit liabilities for equipment leasing on hire purchasing finance companies and other NBFCs registered with the RBI.

In April 1995, an expert group headed by Shri P.R. Khanna was set up to recommend a comprehensive supervisory system over the operation of NBFCs.

In July 1996 ceilings on deposits of NBFCs, hitherto restricted to 10 times of net owned funds, were removed. There was also a reduction of the ratio of liquid assets to deposit from 5 to 12.5 per cent. Freedom to determine interest rates on deposits of one year and up to five years. Overall ceiling on deposits for registered loan/investment companies, complying with credit rating requirement and prudential norms, hitherto equal to Net Owned Funds (NOF) was increased to twice the NOF.

In January 1997 an ordinance for amending the RBI Act for regulating the activities of NBFCs and unincorporated bodies was passed.

8. *Term Lending Institutions*

Term lending institutions, viz. IDBI, IFCI, ICICI, IRBI, and Exim Bank were required to achieve capital adequacy norm of 4 per cent by end March 1994. Financial Institutions having dealings with agencies abroad were required to achieve a norm of 8 per cent by 31 March 1995.

ANNEXURE II

IMPORTANT CHANGES IN RESERVE AND LIQUIDITY REQUIREMENTS

1992–3

17 April 1992   Scheduled commercial banks exempted from the maintenance of 10 per cent incremental CRR over the level of net demand and time liabilities as on 17 April 1992.

1993–4

15 May 1993   Average CRR on NDTL was reduced from 15 to 14 per cent in two phases—from 15 to 14.5 per cent beginning 17 April and 14 per cent from 15 May 1993.

11 June 1993   To sterilize expansionary effect of the surge in foreign currency assets, CRR increased from 14 to 15 per cent in three phases.

1995–6

CRR reduced from 15 to 14.5 per cent from 11 November 1995 and further to 14 per cent from 9 December 1995.

1996–7

CRR reduced from 14.5 to 13.5 per cent from 27 April 1996 and 13 per cent from 11 May 1996. Further reduced to 12 per cent from 6 July 1996. CRR further reduced to 10 per cent in four phases in 1996–7.

1997–8

October 97   CRR to be reduced in eight phases from 10 to 8 per cent.

STATUTORY LIQUIDITY RATIO (SLR)

1992–3   SLR frozen at 38.5 per cent of outstanding NDTL as on 3 April 1992. For any increase in domestic NDTL over the 3 April 1992 level, SLR reduced to 30 per cent.

SLR on the level of outstanding domestic NDTL as on 3 April 1992 reduced to 37.75 per cent in three phases.

1993–4   (1) Further reduced to 37.25 per cent in two stages.

(2) SLR on any increase in domestic NDTL over the level as on 17 September 1993 was reduced from 30 to 25 per cent.

1994–5   SLR reduced to 33.75 per cent in two stages.

1997–8   All scheduled commercial banks required to maintain a uniform SLR of 25 per cent on their entire net demand and time liabilities.

ANNEXURE III

A BRIEF SUMMARY OF REPORTS OF VARIOUS COMMITTEES ON NBFCs

Bhabatosh Datta Group Report (1971)

The Group set up by the Banking Commission recommended that

(i) keeping in view the difficulties in regulating a very large number of institutions, regulations should aim at reducing the number of entities to be regulated, if possible, by inducing them to form themselves into corporate bodies; and

(ii) that the RBI or any other regulatory authority which might be set up, should build up and strengthen its inspection machinery so that NBFIs could be inspected at least on a sample basis.

James Raj Study Group (1975)

The Group recommended that the situation as prevailing at the time called for regulation and not prohibition of deposits acceptance by NBFCs. The regulatory framework suggested by this Study Group aimed at keeping the magnitude of deposits accepted by NBFCs within reasonable limits and ensuring that they subserved the objectives of monetary and credit policy and safeguarded, to the extent possible, the interests of depositors.

Chakravarty Committee (1987)

The Committee recommended that

(i) regulations aiming at NBFCs should curb that part of their activities which was not in conformity with credit policy, but not that which genuinely helped trade and industry; and

(ii) a system of licensing appeared to be essential to protect the interests of depositors of the NBFCs and in view of their large number and administrative considerations, a suitable cut off point could be laid down in regard to the level of their business so that those which exceeded that level would be under legal obligation to obtain a licence.

Narsimham Committee Report (1991)

The Committee recommended that minimum capital requirements be stipulated for NBFCs. It also desired that prudential norms and guidelines in respect of the conduct of NBFC business should be laid down. A system of supervision based on periodic returns was suggested; this is to be undertaken by the board of Supervision recommended by the Committee.

Shah Committee (1992)

It emphasized

(1) the need for a well-integrated regulatory framework;

(2) category-wise classification to be abolished;

(3) regulatory attention to be confined to larger size companies; particularly those over net owned funds of more than Rs 50 lakhs should compulsorily register with the regulatory authority;

(4) entry norms of net owned funds of Rs 50 lakhs to be enforced;

(5) regulations of asset side, such as limits on credit concentration and prohibition of undesirable investments;

(6) capital adequacy standards to be laid down;

(7) interest rates on deposits accepted by NBFC to be 2 to 3 per cent points more than those offered by commercial banks—so long as interest rates on bank deposits are regulated;

(8) credit rating for NBFCs every year.

Khanna Committee (1995)

(1) Existing statutory powers of RBI to be enhanced to ensure orderly functioning of NBFCs with special reference to

    (a) entry point conditionalities

    (b) compulsory registration

    (c) investment in approved securities

    (d) creation of reserve fund

(2) A comprehensive supervisory framework to cover all NBFCs will focus on those with net owned funds above Rs 100 lakhs.

(3) Need for off-site surveillance system, whether or not entity is registered with the RBI.

(4) Scope of auditors' responsibilities clarified.

(5) An annual statement on operational data.

(6) Supervisory rating system for registered NBFCs.

(7) NBFCs on the watch list (High Risk) should be subjected to immediate on-site inspection.

(8) Responsibility on the part of auditors to inform the RBI of any aspect which might warrant qualification or withholding of certificates of audit or failure to comply with regulatory or other guidelines.

REFERENCES

I have benefited a great deal from discussions with officials of banks and the RBI as well as with businessmen.

Bank for International Settlements. (1997). *The Core Principles of Banking Supervision*. Basle Committee on Banking Supervision.

Goodhart, Sir Charles, Philip Hartman, David T. Llewelyn, Lilian Rojas Suarez, and Steven R. Weisbrod. (1997). 'Financial Regulation, Why, How and Where?'. A monograph for the Commonwealth Central Bank Governors' Conference, 6 June.

Guitian, M. (1997). 'Keeping Banking Systems Sound Calls for Modern Approaches to Supervision'. *IMF Survey*, vol. 26, pp. 60–4.

Juan, de, A. (1991). 'Does Bank Insolvency Matter and What to Do about It?'. Economic Development Institute Working Paper, World Bank, Washington, D.C.

Reserve Bank of India. (1971). *Bhabatosh Datta Group Report*.

———. (1975). *James S. Raj Study Group*.

———. (1985). *Report of the Committee to Review the Working of the Monetary System*. (Chairman: S. Chakravarty).

———. (1991). *Report of the Committee on Financial System*. (Chairman: Narasimham).

———. (1992). *Report of the Committee on Financial Companies*. (Chairman: A.C. Shah).

————. (1995). *Report of the Expert Group for Designing a Supervisory Framework for Non-Banking Financial Companies.* (Chairman: P.R. Khanna).

Vittas, D. (1992). 'Financial Regulation—Changing the Rules of the Game'. EDI Development Studies Working Paper, World Bank, Washington D.C.

Financing of Indian Firms: Meeting the Needs and Challenges of the Twenty-first Century

MATHEW JOSEPH, RUPA R. NITSURE,
and MADAN SABNAVIS*

The decisive role of the financial system in mobilizing and allocating the resources needed for capital formation has been well established by many empirical studies. However, the issue of the relative roles of capital markets (equity and bond markets) and credit markets (banks and financial institutions) in influencing economic growth is not conclusively resolved in the policy-related research. In this chapter, an attempt has been made to examine the evolution of corporate financing pattern in India with a view to identifying the type of financial structure (comprising financial markets and intermediaries) that is supportive of long-term growth.

The chapter is divided into five sections. Section 1 describes in detail the institutional structure of the Indian financial system. Section 2 deals with the regulatory and legal framework within which the Indian financial system has functioned. Section 3 presents the theory and collects the evidence from international experience with respect to patterns of corporate financing. Section 4 analyses the changing pattern of corporate finance in India over the last twenty-five years. In this section the macroeconomic analysis is followed by detailed analysis of the financing pattern of project cost of companies. Further, the changing pattern of sources and uses of funds (based on the balance sheet analysis)

---

*The views expressed in the chapter are those of the authors and not of the organization to which they belong. The authors would like to thank Nachiket Mor, K. Ramaswamy, N. Jadhav, S. Kathuria, and J. Hanson for their valuable comments on an earlier version of the chapter and Mrs Oliver for able typing assistance.

is discussed for the period from 1972–3 to 1995–6. A quick survey is also carried out on the current scenario, based on patterns observed in 1996–7 and 1997–8 through a questionnaire. Section 5 lists the main findings of this study against the backdrop of international experience on corporate financing patterns and discusses the policy implications.

1. INSTITUTIONAL FRAMEWORK

Indian firms have been raising funds from a variety of sources—debt, equity, and mixed securities. However, their dependence on different sources has varied substantially across time, with the evolution of the Indian financial system.

Though a developing economy, India is characterized by a large network of commercial banks, financial institutions, stock exchanges, and a wide range of financial instruments. The provision of working capital finance is dependent primarily on commercial and cooperative banks. Following financial sector reforms since 1992, many new private sector and foreign banks have been granted banking licences with the resultant increase in the number of market players. In recent years, commercial banks have diversified into several new areas of business like merchant banking, mutual funds, leasing, venture capital, factoring, and other financial services. In addition, there is a wide network of cooperative banks and cooperative land development banks at state, district, and sub-district levels. Commercial and cooperative banks hold around two-thirds of total financial assets of the Indian banks and financial institutions taken together.

Medium- and long-term finance is largely provided by a few large all-India development banks or development financial institutions (DFIs) along with a spectrum of state-level financial institutions. The development banks in India were originally sponsored by the government (often supported by the World Bank's participation or line of credit) to give a primary impulse to economic expansion in important sectors where private enterprise was not forthcoming. They were set up to finance the requirements of the corporate sector in the fields of large and small industries, shipping, tourism, exports, housing, and development of backward regions and new entrepreneurs. They came mostly in the 1950s and 1960s, as commercial banks were not willing to divert into term finance (World Bank, 1989, pp 54–5) given their short-term liability profile, while capital markets were too underdeveloped to provide large sums required for promoting rapid industrialization. Besides the DFIs, there are the investment institutions which include the Unit Trust of India (UTI), a mutual fund, and the Life Insurance Corporation (LIC) and the General Insurance Corporation (GIC) which are insurance companies. These institutions also deploy part of their funds in long-term financing of projects. The UTI, set up in 1964, has been the first mutual fund in India. During 1987–92, seven new mutual funds were established in the public sector. A change in government policy in 1993 led to the entry of private corporates and foreign institutional investors into the mutual funds segment, taking the tally of mutual funds to thirty-two by March 1997. In addition, there are over 12,530 private sector non-bank financial companies (NBFCs) in India which undertake para-banking activity in the area of hire-purchase and leasing (RBI, 1997, p. 212).

Over the years, significant growth has taken place in the domestic capital market in terms of volume of transactions and also of new types of participants and products. Compared with Rs 2 billion raised from the capital market in 1980–1, as much as Rs 155 billion were raised in 1996–7. In this, the share of the private corporate sector was Rs 105 billion (Rangarajan, 1997 and RBI, 1997, p. 93). The balance amount was raised by public sector units. Household sector savings, which are a major source of finance for the capital market, increased from 11.3 per cent of GDP in 1970–1 to 20.3 per cent of GDP in 1996–7. The average share of household sector's financial savings in the form of 'shares and debentures' increased from 2.8 per cent of GDP in 1971–6 to 12.2 per cent in 1986–91 (Table 6.1). This share declined to 8.3 per cent in

TABLE 6.1

CHANGING COMPOSITION OF HOUSEHOLD SECTOR'S
FINANCIAL SAVINGS*

Period	Bank Deposits	Shares and Debentures	Government**
1971–6	35.0	2.8	46.3
1976–81	37.7	3.9	38.9
1981–6	31.2	7.5	46.7
1986–91	22.1	12.2	50.0
1991–7	37.9	8.3	53.8

Notes: *Total financial savings are inclusive of currency.
**Government includes net claims on government, life insurance funds, and provident and pension funds. (See Nagaraj, 1996).

Source: CSOS, *National Accounts Statistics*, various issues and RBI, *Report on Currency and Finance, 1996–7.*

1991–7 mainly due to the dormancy of capital markets during 1995–7. However, it hovered around 12.5 per cent during 1992–4.

A new dimension has been added to the Indian capital market with the liberalization of international capital flows since 1992. Funds raised by Indian companies through global depository receipts (GDRs), offshore funds and others, during the period 1991–2 to 1996–7, amounted to US$ 6.2 billion, and the net cumulative investment made by foreign institutional investors (FIIs) in the Indian stock markets during January 1993 to March 1997, amounted to US$ 7.1 billion (*RBI Annual Reports*). At the end of 1996, the International Finance Corporation (IFC) ranked India twentieth in terms of market capitalization, and eighteenth in terms of total value traded among forty countries with developed as well as developing markets. In terms of the number of listed domestic companies at the end of 1996, India (with 8800 firms listed on the domestic stock exchanges) is ranked first ahead of the US. These trends show substantial resource mobilization through the capital market by the private corporate sector in India.

In recent years, in addition to the traditional methods of raising resources through public and rights issues, 'private placement' has also gained ground wherein resources are raised through arrangers (merchant banking intermediaries) who place securities with a small number of financial institutions, corporates and high net-worth individuals. This method is considered as being both cost and time effective, as it does not require detailed compliance with formalities needed in public or rights issues. Private placement accounted for as much as 49.1 per cent of total resources mobilized by the government and non-government companies during 1996–7. The private placement market has been witnessing the introduction of several innovative debt instruments like step-down/step-up debentures, liquid income debentures, and subordinated bonds (RBI, 1997, p. 94).

Three credit rating agencies (set up at the initiative of financial institutions) are also operational in guiding investors regarding the credit risk associated with debt instruments. Their indication of the relative capacity of a corporate entity to service its debt obligations within a specified time period and with reference to a particular debt instrument being rated, has great impact on the resource mobilization efforts of the corporate sector.

During the 1980s, the Indian financial system witnessed the introduction of several new products. Convertible bonds were already popular in the capital market. Commercial papers (CPs) and certificates of deposits

(CDs) started circulating in the money market towards the end of the 1980s. These products were introduced in order to help highly rated corporate borrowers to diversify their sources of short-term borrowings as also to provide additional financial instruments to investors.

2. REGULATORY AND LEGAL FRAMEWORK

Since the early 1990s, the focus of financial regulation has started shifting from 'the control over financial products/prices' to 'prudential regulation, supervision and promotion of competition'.

During the 1950s and 1960s, the necessary legislative framework had been developed in India to facilitate reorganization and consolidation of the financial system. In this period, the cooperative credit structure was strengthened and new institutions set up to provide long-term finance to agriculture and industry.

The year 1969 became a major turning point in the Indian financial system when fourteen large commercial banks were nationalized. The main objectives of bank nationalization (Jadhav, 1994, p. 218) were:

(i) reorientation of credit flows so as to benefit priority sectors like agriculture, small-scale industries, and small borrowers;
(ii) widening of branch networks of banks, particularly in the rural and semi-urban areas; and
(iii) greater mobilization of savings through bank deposits.

The Indian financial system and more particularly the banking system has evolved in an environment of administered interest rates and mandatory stipulations on credit distribution. These were primarily intended to provide specific sectors and economic activities with cheap credit. They also helped the government to finance the budget deficits at relatively low cost. An element of cross-subsidization implicit in an administered system of lending rates also meant that certain borrowers have had to pay higher rates than others. Furthermore, the actual realization of interest income in banks has been much lower because of the high level of non-performing assets (Rangarajan, 1997, p. 74).

Moreover, the government imposed reserve requirements consisting of the cash reserve ratio (CRR) and statutory liquidity ratio (SLR). While the former defines the proportion of total deposits banks have to deposit with the central bank, the latter defines the proportion of deposits banks are obliged to hold in government and other approved securities. By 1991, statutory preemptions under the CRR and SLR, on an incremental basis, reached a level of 63.5 per cent, and even of the balance 36.5 per cent, there were preemptions under the priority sector of 40 per cent, export credit, food credit, and other formal and informal preemptions (Tarapore, 1996, p. 54). The credit allocation schemes accompanied by the reserve requirements severely restricted the freedom of intermediation of banks.

The existing legal framework also implied wide geographical coverage of banks, which, in turn, lengthened the lines of supervision and control. Retail lending to more risk-prone areas at concessional interest rates has raised costs, affected the quality of bank assets, and strained their profitability.

The first attempt at reforming the financial sector was undertaken with the release of the Chakravarty Committee Report in 1985, which reviewed the working of the monetary system. Later, against the backdrop of the balance-of-payments crisis in 1991 and the macroeconomic adjustment, the Narasimham Committee was appointed with a view to promoting a diversified and competitive financial system as part of the overall structural reforms. The recommendations of the Chakravarty and Narasimham Committees resulted in many new steps by the Reserve Bank of India (RBI) to move away from direct monetary policy instruments to indirect monetary control (Ajit and Bangar,1997). The level and structure of interest rates have been rationalized in a phased manner, with banks enjoying the freedom to determine their own prime lending rates. In 1995, all controls on deposit rates above one-year maturity have been removed. Steps had been initiated for bringing down the CRR and SLR. Prudential norms and regulations had been introduced to ensure the safety and soundness of the financial system and at the same time to encourage markets to play dominant roles. For improving recovery-related performance in banks, special Debt Recovery Tribunals were established after 1992–3. Bank branch licensing policy was also amended by the RBI with a view to helping banks to rationalize their branch networks and deal effectively with the loss-making branches. The concept of priority sector advances has undergone various changes and, to improve supervision, a new system of offsite surveillance has been put in place. In general, the reform measures have been mainly directed towards removing the liquidity constraints of corporates and making finance available at competitive rates.

A number of steps have been taken to develop transparent and efficient capital and money markets. India's capital market witnessed rapid growth from the 1980s. Policy changes such as permission to raise partly convertible debentures and permission to public sector enterprises to raise resources through bonds led to substantial increase in total resource mobilization from the primary market (CMIE, 1995, p. 7). The growth of the 'equity-cult' began in the mid-1980s, as a consequence of the partial liberalization of the industrial sector. The most important policy decision which channelled household savings into shares and debentures was the abolition of the Controller of Capital Issues (CCI) in May 1992. With a stated objective of investor protection, the CCI, in the past, laid stringent controls over public and rights issues and their pricing. Implicit in the pricing system had been substantial underpricing, relative to market fundamentals. The abolition of the CCI has left companies free to decide the price of issues. As a result, there has been substantial increase in the number and volumes of issues floated. Between 1991–2 and 1995–6, new capital issues by non-government public limited companies increased from 514 to 1684, while the total amount raised increased from Rs 61.9 billion to Rs 163 billion. (RBI, 1996, p. 152). However, the primary segment of the capital market remained highly subdued during 1996–7 and 1997–8.

An important constituent of the reforms strategy adopted in the 1990s was the opening up of the economy to foreign investment—both direct and portfolio (SEBI, 1997, p. 115). As part of this strategy, the government invited foreign portfolio investment in the Indian securities market through FIIs, who have been required to register with the Securities and Exchange Board of India (SEBI). SEBI had been given statutory powers in January 1992, through the enactment of the SEBI Act, which is mainly based on the concept of investor protection and regulation of intermediaries. Indian firms have also been allowed to raise capital abroad through issues of GDRs and foreign currency convertible bonds (FCCBs). Foreign participation has also been allowed by the government in various areas of financial services through joint ventures.

The broad segments of the Indian financial market, i.e. the money market, government securities market, and the foreign exchange market, have responded favourably to the reform measures with growing inter-linkages (RBI, 1997, p. 104). This has facilitated faster liquidity pass through. For example, improvements in liquidity in 1996–7 were translated into significant softening of various money market rates, interest rates on government papers—particularly those at the shorter end (Table 6.2).

TABLE 6.2

RELATIVE RATES OF RETURN IN MAJOR FINANCIAL MARKETS

(per cent per annum)

	Last Week/Fortnight of March					
	1992	1993	1994	1995	1996	1997
Call money rate (Mumbai)	30.6	17.4	6.4	16.1	16.3	3.7
91-day T bills (cut-off yield)	–	11.0	7.5	11.9	13.0	8.0
182-day/364-day T bills (cut-off yield)	9.3	11.1	10.0	11.9	13.1	10.1
CDs (middle rate)	14.5	14.5	9.6	12.5	17.1	11.4
CPs (middle rate)	16.5	15.9	11.5	14.5	20.2	11.9
1–3 year deposit rate*	12.0	11.0	10.0	11.0	12.0	10.0
MLR/PLR (banks)**	19.0	17.0	15.0	15.0	16.5	14.5–15.0
Coupon rate of 10-year GOI securities	11.0	12.8	12.5	12.4	14.0	13.7
Capital market (ordinary shares)						
(a) Gross yield (all industries)	1.4	2.3	1.8	2.1	3.6	4.9
(b) Change in RBI share price index (all Industries)	181.4	–39.9	49.3	4.0	–18.3	–6.2

Notes: CDs: Certificates of deposits

        CPs: Commercial papers

        *Up to October 1995 a ceiling was put on deposit rates for all maturities. Subsequently, the ceiling held only for deposits with a maturity of up to 2 years and interest rates on other deposits were freed. In July 1996 deposit rates for maturities above one year were freed.

        **Since October 1994, the concept of MLR (minimum lending rate) was abolished for credit limits over Rs 0.2 million and the concept of a PLR (prime lending rate) was introduced.

Sources: RBI, *Report on Currency and Finance*, vol. 1, 1996, and RBI, *Annual Report, 1996–7.*

Another impact of financial sector reform has been the breakdown of segmentation of financial markets. The system of specialized institutions providing specialized services to particular categories of borrowers/industry segments has slowly been disappearing. Thus commercial banks have now been allowed to extend term loans, invest in shares and bonds, and provide merchant banking and forex loans. Financial institutions have been permitted to diversify their activities into working capital finance, lease finance, venture capital, and capital market-related products/services along with term finance. They have also been putting in place their own networks to access cheaper 'retail funds' like commercial banks, as such funds provide a more stable pool.

The operation of financial institutions and commercial banks in the same market is slowly evolving into universal banking rather than purely commercial or development banking.

In short, financial sector reforms resulted in opening up several new sources of funds for the corporate sector. Increased reliance on market forces for determining the cost and availability of funds enabled the corporate sector to make an optimum combination of different sources of funds.

3. CORPORATE FINANCE: THEORY AND EVIDENCE

Contrary to the 'pecking order' pattern of finance observed for advanced country corporations, developing country corporations mainly depend on external sources of finance, with a significant share coming from the stock market.

The issue of optimal capital structure of firms has been intensively researched in policy-related works on financial structures. Historically, firms have raised funds from a variety of sources—internal finance, external debt, and new equity. However, their dependence on these sources has varied both across time and countries.

The issue of optimal capital structure is closely related to the question of whether the development of capital markets (equity and bond market) *vis-à-vis* banks (both commercial and development banks) can influence economic growth. As noted by Berthelemy and Varoudakis (1996, pp. 33–5), the debate on capital markets versus financial intermediaries has been constantly fuelled by the differing economic experiences of countries which first concentrated on capital markets (like the UK and the US) and those which gave priority to the system of universal banks (like Germany). However, in spite of the differences in their financial systems, developed (industrialized) countries appear to have more or less converged on a common method of financing the real sector. A cross-country study by Mayer (1990), covering the period 1970–85, demonstrates that internal funds constituted almost two-thirds on average of investment financing in developed countries like the US, the UK, Japan, Germany, France, Italy, Canada, and Finland. The relative share of external funding through equity and bonds was quite small in all these countries, lying systematically below 10 per cent of the total investment expenditures and even becoming negative at times—on the basis of net operations—due to the impact of takeovers and restructuring within the corporate sector.

Such reliance on internal finance can be rationalized from at least two theoretical perspectives: (i) the managerial approach which emphasizes agency costs arising out of the separation of ownership from control and the role of internal finance in facilitating managerial discretion; and (ii) the information-theoretic approach that emphasizes asymmetries in information between insiders (managers) and outsiders (suppliers of capital) giving rise to credit rationing faced by firms (see Samuel, 1996). Stiglitz and Weiss (1981) have shown that in the presence of informational asymmetries, equilibrium may take the form of 'credit rationing'. This is explained as follows. Borrowers have projects with different degrees of risk, but the riskiness is unobservable. Therefore lenders cannot distinguish between good and bad borrowers and cannot price discriminate (i.e. vary interest rates) in a loan contract. If they raise interest rates, this can be self-defeating, since relatively good borrowers will find the loan offer unattractive and drop out of the market and lenders are left with only the weakest borrowers, which will increase the possibility of default and perhaps decrease lenders' expected profits. In equilibrium, therefore, lenders may set an interest rate that leaves excess demand for loans, which leads to rationing of some borrowers.

Also, in a world of incomplete information, a new equity issue may signal bad news to existing investors, suggesting that the firm does not have enough retained earnings to rely on internal financing. In the OECD countries, the price of outstanding shares usually drops when a firm announces a new equity issue. Announcement of an increase in debt has a similar, though less strong, effect on the share price. This perhaps explains why managers will first use internal financing, turn to debt if this is not possible, and use equity issue only as last resort (Cornelli, Portes, and Schaffer, 1998).

Among developed countries, there are noticeable differences in preferences for various sources of external finance. Damodaran (1997) documents evidence that US companies are more heavily dependent on debt than equity for external financing than their counterparts in other countries like Japan, Germany, France, Italy, the UK, and Canada. However, based on the analysis of small firms in the US, Petersen and Rajan (1994) show that firms with strong relationships with intermediaries have better access to bank credit at reasonable cost than other firms. Hoshi, Kashyap, and Scharfstein (1990) find that firms in Japan with close ties to their banks are less likely to be liquidity-constrained in their investments than firms which do not have such ties. On the choice between debt and new equity, theory says that tax considerations should induce firms to increase their debt exposure, so as to benefit from the tax shield. On the other hand, bankruptcy increases the cost of having a large debt exposure, and, therefore, should limit the optimal amount of debt held (see Cornelli, Portes, and Schaffer, 1998).

The trends in certain developing countries are very different from what has been observed in Western industrialized economies. According to the estimates of Singh and Hamid (1992), the contribution of external sources to the financing of net fixed capital formation in the 1980s was well over 50 per cent (reaching as much as 90 per cent in Korea for the biggest enterprises), with a significant share coming from the stock market. Based on data from more countries, more companies, and a longer time series, Singh (1995) shows that in five out of the ten sample countries (the Republic of Korea, Thailand, Mexico, Turkey, and Malaysia), more than 70 per cent of the growth of corporate net assets during the period 1980–91 was financed from external funds. Similarly, the importance of equity financing for the developing countries' corporations is indicated by the fact that in five of the nine sample countries (Republic of Korea, Mexico, Turkey, Malaysia, and Zimbabwe), more than 40 per cent of the growth of net assets in the 1980s had been financed by new share issues. In another two countries (Jordan and Brazil), equity finance accounted for more than 20 per cent of corporate asset growth during the relevant period. Many factors can explain the preference of developing countries' corporations for equity rather than debt financing. Some of this dependence can be attributed to government regulations that directly discourage the use of debt, by constraining the debt ratios of firms to below specified limits, or indirectly by limiting the deductibility of interest. In some countries, the absence of corporate bonds market may lower overall debt dependence.

Concentrating on the stock market, Singh (1997) shows that between 1982 and 1992, total market capitalization of companies quoted on stock exchanges in a number of developing countries increased by a factor of 20. The issue of financing through stock markets is important to the whole debate about financial liberalization. A major point of departure in the financial sector literature is the McKinnon (1973) and Shaw (1973) 'financial repression paradigm'. This paradigm views interest rate ceilings, high reserve ratios, and directed credit programmes as sources of financial repression, which necessarily result in low savings, credit rationing and low investment. In financially repressed economies, even the quality of investment suffers, as the available funds are not rationed on the basis of marginal productivity of investment, but at the lender's discretion. The Mckinnon–Shaw paradigm had a major impact through the work of the IMF and the World Bank, both of which encouraged financial liberalization in developing countries as part of economic liberalization. Their thesis was further extended by Cho (1986), who argued that financial market liberalization may remain incomplete without an efficient market for equity capital as a means of spreading risk (and reward). In principle, stock markets allow efficient risk sharing, as they induce information gathering. This gets reflected in stock prices. These prices also act as powerful signals for managerial incentives and corporate governance.

In a series of papers, Stiglitz (and Weiss 1981; 1994) criticizes the financial liberalization thesis on the grounds that financial markets are prone to market failures. The thesis has also been challenged for the central position given by it to stock markets in resource allocation. Mayer (1992) found, on the basis of company balance sheet data, that internal resources finance bulk of corporate (physical) investment in major OECD countries and the stock market's role (net of redemption) is very limited.

Singh (1997) examines the implications of rapid growth of market capitalization in developing countries between 1982 and 1992 to conclude that financial liberalization, by making the financial system more fragile, is not likely to enhance long-term growth in developing countries. Singh (1998), after examining the implications of stock market development for economic growth, recommends that less developed countries should promote bank-based systems, influence the scale and composition of capital inflows, and prevent a market for corporate control from emerging. Mishkin (1996) notes that adverse selection[1] and moral hazard[2] problems arising from asymmetric information in investor–firm relationship necessarily create disruptions in financial markets, leading to inefficient allocation of investible funds. Mishkin feels that banks (or intermediaries) rather than capital markets might be a solution to these problems. He regards factors such as increased interest rates,

---

[1]Adverse selection means 'hidden information' problems which arise from the asymmetry of information about the riskiness of investment projects before investment occurs.

[2]Moral hazard means 'hidden action' problems which arise because investors cannot distinguish the effects of managerial actions from the effect of events that management cannot control.

stock market declines, increased uncertainty due to exogenous shocks, and the consequential worsening of the balance sheets of firms and banks as the ones that are instrumental in generating financial crises.

Aoki (1996), however, points out that the factors which Mishkin posits as triggers of adverse selection and moral hazard are often the consequences of the moral hazards of banks and firms. So it is the over-optimism of economic agents, especially financial intermediaries, during the booming phase of the economy that leads to adverse selection problems ultimately resulting in interest rate increases and stock market declines.

The recent revival of interest in the analysis of factors which determine growth, has led to a closer study of the implications of stock market development for intermediation and economic growth. Levine (1991) and Bencivenga, Smith, and Starr (1996) show that stock markets may affect economic activity through creation of liquidity. Liquid equity markets make investment less risky and more attractive because they allow quicker and cheaper acquisition or sale of an asset (equity). Also, companies enjoy permanent access to capital raised through equity issues. By facilitating longer-term, more profitable investments, liquid markets improve the allocation of capital and enhance the prospects of long-term growth. Risk diversification through internationally integrated stock markets is another vehicle through which stock markets can positively affect growth (Obstfeld, 1994).

Demirguc–Kunt and Levine (1996) also examine the interaction between stock market development and financial intermediaries. After constructing individual measures of bank, non-bank, and financial system development, they also construct aggregate indices of financial intermediary development based on the individual measures of bank and non-bank development. They find that across countries, the level of stock market development is positively correlated with the development of financial intermediaries. Thus stock markets and financial intermediaries are generally complements, and grow simultaneously.

Demirguc–Kunt and Maksimovic (1994) also empirically investigate the effect of stock market development on financing choices of firms. They observe that firms in countries with underdeveloped stock markets first increase their debt–equity ratios as their stock markets develop. This means that not only do they issue new equity, but they also borrow more. This relationship changes as stock markets develop. These findings are consistent with the theory that during early stages of market development, improvement in stock market functioning tends to improve information quality, monitoring, and corporate control, such that these improvements induce intermediaries to lend more. For these firms, debt and equity finance are complementary.

This chapter will analyse the Indian corporate financing pattern within the two competing frameworks. First, the financial liberalization and deregulation thesis that accords capital markets an important role in resource allocation, and, second, the asymmetric information framework that relates information failures to the failures of intermediaries and stock markets, thus arguing for government intervention.

4. CHANGING PATTERN OF INDIAN CORPORATE FINANCE

4.1 DATA AND METHODOLOGY

This section analyses historical data relating to the non-financial, non-government corporate sector for the years 1971–2 to 1995–6, with a view to ascertaining changes in the pattern of financing. As a first step, data at the macroeconomic level are examined and subsequently, data on financing project costs and corporate balance sheet information.[3]

The analysis aims at presenting intertemporal comparison rather than a static scenario. Earlier studies (described in Section 3) on the subject have based their findings either on cross-sectional information or on average values emerging from the long time-series data.

4.2 MACROECONOMIC ANALYSIS

The saving-investment gap of the private corporate sector has steadily increased over the span of the last twenty-six years.

Table 6.3 presents the magnitude of the five-yearly average of the private corporate sector's deficit, i.e. excess of gross investment over savings as a per cent of GDP. It indicates that the deficit as a per cent of GDP for the private corporate sector increased substantially in the first half of the 1980s and further in the first half of the 1990s. It declined somewhat in the second half of the 1980s. A long-term trend (based on decadal values) clearly indicates that over a twenty-six-year period (from 1971–2 to 1996–7), there has been a secular decline in the share of the corporate

---

[3]The analysis is primarily based on data in various issues of the following: (i) *National Accounts Statistics*, Central Statistical Organisation (CSO); (ii) *Report on Currency and Finance*, RBI; (iii) *Report on Development Banking*, Industrial Development Bank of India (IDBI); and (iv) *Financial Performance of Companies*, Industrial Credit and Investment Corporation of India (ICICI).

sector's own savings in its physical investment. This points to the growing reliance of the private corporate sector on external financing.

TABLE 6.3

DEFICIT OF PRIVATE CORPORATE SECTOR

1971–2 TO 1995–6

(per cent of GDP)

Period	Gross Domestic Savings	Gross Domestic Investment	Deficit
1971–6	1.64	2.76	1.12
1976–81	1.64	2.33	0.69
1981–6	1.72	4.50	2.78
1986–91	2.28	4.38	2.10
1991–7	3.65	7.46	3.81

Source: CSO, *National Accounts Statistics*, various issues.

RBI data on flow of funds in the private corporate business sector give information on the composition of external sources of funds for the corporate sector. It reveals that the private corporate sector, in its attempt to plug the growing resources gap, has heavily depended on banks and other financial institutions, followed by the household sector. However, it should be noted that the data employed in the flow of funds analysis are less reliable than those in company accounts, as flow of funds are constructed from a variety of different sources that are rarely consistent. (Samuel, 1996, p. 2).

4.3   ANALYSIS OF FINANCING PROJECT COSTS

Over the years, the complementary and competitive interaction of various players in the financial system has greatly impacted the sources of finance for the corporate sector.

Besides the 'flow of funds' information, the RBI also provides detailed information on the financing of project costs (or capital expenditures) of both new and existing companies. Every company needs financing to expand or modernize existing projects and to take on new ones. Table 6.4 presents this information on financing patterns for projects. This information is not given in the usual form of internal versus external sources of finance, as for projects the component of retained earnings from operations is not very large. However, this table sharply brings out the combination of sources of funds used by the companies in different periods.

TABLE 6.4
FINANCING OF PROJECT COST OF COMPANIES

(per cent share of various sources)

	1971–2 to 1980–1	1981–2 to 1990–1	1991–92 to 1995–6
No. of companies (average)	83	319	530
Share capital (Indian)	28.5	37.5	41.1
(a) Equity	26.5	37.5	41.0
(b) Preference	2.0	0.1	0.1
Share capital (foreign)	0.2	0.1	5.5
(a) Equity	0.2	0.1	5.5
(b) Preference	0.0	0.0	0.0
Reserves and surplus	11.8	3.4	1.6
Subsidy from central govt.	0.5	0.9	0.2
Debentures/bonds	4.5	18.2	6.1
Deferred payments	1.2	0.4	0.2
Loans	53.3	39.6	45.3
(a) DFIs (IDBI, ICICI, IFCI)	24.1	22.5	12.1
(b) UTI, LIC and GIC	4.0	1.7	0.3
(c) SFCs and SIDCs	5.3	1.6	1.4
(d) Banks	15.5	6.6	10.0
(e) Promoters, directors & friends	0.6	1.0	8.7
(f) Other sources (foreign & Indian)	3.9	6.3	12.8
Total	100.0	100.0	100.0

Source: RBI, *Report on Currency and Finance*, vol. II, various issues

The data as set out in Table 6.4 over a twenty-five-year period (from 1971–2 through 1995–6) reveal that the relative importance of domestic equity capital (consisting of both promoters' contribution and external equity) in project expenditure steadily increased, from 28.5 per cent in the 1970s to 37.5 per cent in the 1980s and to almost 41.0 per cent in the first half of the 1990s.

The proportion of project financing obtained through debentures and bonds increased sharply in the 1980s to 18.2 per cent from 4.5 per cent in the 1970s, while that through bank loans declined from 15.5 per cent in the 1970s to 6.6 per cent in the 1980s. This is consistent with what had earlier been seen during the 1980s when the composition of the household sector's financing savings shifted away from bank deposits to 'shares and debentures'. Loans (which include in addition to bank loans, loans given by DFIs, investment institutions, state-level corporations, and other domestic and foreign sources) remained the most dominant source of funds in the 1970s but their importance declined significantly in the 1980s, when the capital market boomed and a large amount of capital was mobilized in the form of 'debentures and equity'. This decline in the share of the loan component was more pronounced in the second half of the 1980s.

All-financial Institutions and Capital Market

The share of all-financial institutions, i.e. the DFIs, investment institutions, and state-level finance corporations, declined somewhat (under the loans component) in the 1980s and sharply after liberalization. This, however, does not truly reflect the total share of these institutions in project financing. In addition to loans, the all-financial institutions (AFIs) also offer assistance by way of underwriting or direct subscription of shares and debt securities.[4] This assistance has not featured under the 'loans' category in Table 6.4. This assistance extended by AFIs to projects, is included in the 'domestic share capital' and 'debentures/bonds' categories.

As the capital markets expanded to provide support to projects, AFIs also channelled their funds increasingly via the capital markets by raising their share of assistance through underwriting and direct subscription of issues for project construction in the 1980s and the 1990s. The share of this assistance in total disbursements of AFIs rose from below 7 per cent during the 1970s to 11 per cent in the 1980s to 20.2 per cent in the post-reform period (Table 6.5).

TABLE 6.5

AFIs' CAPITAL MARKET CONTRIBUTION AND ROLE IN GROSS FIXED CAPITAL (GFCF) OF THE PRIVATE CORPORATE SECTOR

	% Share of Underwriting, Direct Subscription, etc. in Disbursements	% Share of Disbursements in GFCF
1971–2 to 1980–1	6.7	45.8
1981–2 to 1990–1	11.0	54.5
1991–2 to 1996–7	20.2	48.0

Sources: CSO, *National Accounts Statistics*, various issues; RBI, *Report on Currency and Finance*, vol. II, various issues; and IDBI, *Report on Development Banking*, various issues.

[4]Actually banks can also do this, and with more relaxed norms after liberalization their investment in shares and debentures was about 6.3 per cent of the total flows of funds to the commercial sector as on end-March 1997.

The contribution of AFIs to gross fixed capital formation of the private corporate sector can also be seen from Table 6.5. Their average share increased by almost 9 percentage points, from 45.8 per cent in the 1970s to 54.5 per cent in the 1980s. In spite of the heightened competitive pressures in the financial sector and the resultant improvement in the mechanisms for resource pooling, the AFIs have financed on an average around 48 per cent of gross fixed capital expenditure of the private corporate sector in the first six years of the 1990s.

Impact of Liberalization on the Sources of Finance

The sub-period, 1991–96 represents a period of rapid transition. The government liberalized domestic financial markets as part of a larger economic liberalization programme in the early 1990s. There has been enhanced competition in the financial system as a result of the opening up of the market for new entrants from within and outside the country. The choice of external funds widened with the free pricing of domestic capital issues on the one hand and a freer flow of direct and portfolio inflows from abroad, on the other. In this period, the average share of foreign equity capital sharply increased to 5.5 per cent from its negligible share in the 1970s and 1980s. The relative share of bank loans in project cost somewhat increased, while that of debentures and bonds sharply declined after liberalization.

Furthermore, the share of equity capital (both domestic and foreign) in total financing increased to 46.6 per cent and that of total borrowings (via loans) to 45.3 per cent in the first half of the 1990s, from their respective shares of 37.6 per cent and 39.6 per cent in the 1980s. Together, equity capital and debentures/bonds, total capital mobilized from the capital market financed around 53 per cent of the total project cost during the post-reform period. Within the loan component, the relative importance of loans taken from sources like promoters, directors, and friends as well as other domestic, and foreign sources increased sharply after liberalization.

4.4 ANALYSIS OF CORPORATE BALANCE SHEETS

There has been a secular decline in the share of internal sources of funds during the last twenty-five years despite an increase in the share of reserves and surplus. Within external funds, the 'share premium' rose sharply after 1987–8 while the share of debentures fell after showing substantial growth in the 1980s.

Corporate balance sheet accounts bring out more sharply the issue of internal versus external funding for the corporate sector. Internal funds are essentially funds generated from within the firms and cover reserves and surplus and depreciation. External funds are those mobilized from other sources and include long-term borrowings, debentures, paid-up capital, sundry creditors, unsecured loans and deposits, bank borrowings for working capital, and other current liabilities.

The main issues addressed here are the following: (i) Has there been any discernible change in the pattern of finance for the private corporate sector between internal and external funds? If so, why did it occur? Further, within internal and external sources of funds, are there any changes in preferences? (ii) What have been the factors affecting the corporate sector's pattern of finance? (iii) Does the size of the firm have any bearing on the pattern of finance? Do firms make greater use of internal funds on account of higher retention and do they have better access to borrowings from various sources as well as equity markets?

To explore these issues, a twenty-five-year period has been selected from 1971–2 to 1995–6. This period has been further classified into three sub-periods: 1971–2 to 1979–80 signifying the 1970s when conservative policies were being pursued; 1980–1 to 1987–8, which was the earliest phase of liberalization, albeit, at a gradual pace; and the third phase between 1988–9 and 1995–6 when the economy witnessed the equity boom amidst a continuous series of reforms in all spheres.

The main source of data are the ICICI's studies on corporate performance entitled *Financial Performance of Companies: ICICI Port-*

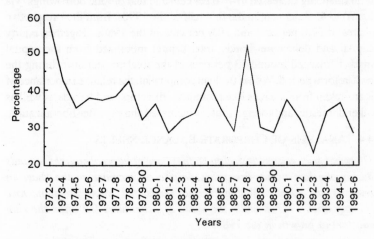

Figure 6.1   Internal Sources of Funds (per cent in total)

Source: ICICI, *Financial Performance of Companies*, various issues.

folio. These studies have been conducted from 1971–2 and cover a representative sample of companies in the private corporate sector. The sample of companies included in the latest study for 1991–2 to 1995–6 accounted for 38.5 per cent of value added in registered manufacturing and 43.8 per cent of gross fixed capital formation in the private corporate sector in 1995–6.

Table 6.6 presents information on the sources and uses of funds for various samples of ICICI-assisted companies over the chosen periods. All the items in the table are calculated as increments in the balance sheet accounts of assets and liabilities of the corporate sector.

It can be seen from Table 6.6 that the share of internal sources declined from 40.5 per cent in the 1970s to 31.4 per cent in the 1990s. The falling trend in the share of internal funds of the corporate sector is

TABLE 6.6

SOURCES AND USES OF FUNDS

(Average Shares in Total)

(per cent)

	1972–80	1980–8	1988–96
No. of companies	417	417	615/675*
Sources of funds	100.0	100.0	100.0
Internal	40.5	36.0	31.4
Depreciation	27.6	21.0	14.8
Reserves and surplus**	12.9	15.1	16.6
External	59.5	64.0	68.6
Paid-up capital	8.9	4.2	4.5
Share premium	0.5	1.4	11.6
Debentures	1.3	10.1	7.3
Long-term borrowings	6.7	12.6	12.7
Bank borrowings for working capital	9.1***	7.1	7.9
Unsecured loans and advances	6.3***	6.4	5.8
Sundry creditors	22.5***	19.0	13.0
Other current liabilities	3.3***	3.4	5.9
Uses of funds	100.0	100.0	100.0
Gross fixed assets	51.1	56.2	52.1
Inventories	22.4	16.8	13.9
Financial investments	1.1	3.0	7.6
Other current assets	25.4	24.0	26.5

Notes: *The number of sample companies are 615 for the period 1988–92 and 675 for 1992–6.

**Excludes 'share premium reserves'.

***These figures refer to 1976–80 as data for 1972–6 are not available.

ICICI data on share premium is clubbed with reserves and surplus. As share premium constitutes an external source of funds and not internal, the same has been estimated with additional information from RBI company studies and CMIE data with similar coverage of sample companies.

also evident from the annual data plotted in Figure 6.1. The rise in external sources of funds to the corporate sector is shared by debentures and long-term borrowings (mainly from financial institutions) in the 1980s and mainly by capital markets in the late 1980s and 1990s.

External Sources

The capital market assumed more importance in the 1980s, which continued in the 1990s. In fact, if all resources from the capital market are considered, then the share of paid-up capital, share premium, and debentures rose from 10.7 per cent in the 1970s to 15.7 per cent in the 1980s, and further to 23.4 per cent after 1987-8. However, the interesting part of this change has been the gradual shift from paid-up capital to debentures to share premium[5] to meet the funding requirements of the corporate sector in the three distinct phases. The share of debentures roses sharply from 1.3 per cent in the 1970s to 10.1 per cent in the 1980s. This reflected the growing popularity of debt securities in the 1980s. From the point of view of subscribers, debentures were attractive as the return was higher than that on alternative modes of savings. Furthermore, they also had the advantage of being convertible into equity. The borrowing companies also preferred debentures on account of their convertibility as it would help to realign their debt–equity position. But they became less important in the period following 1987-8 even though interest rates were on the decline especially after 1992-3 since companies were able to pick up substantial additional funds in the form of share premium from equity issues.

Internal Sources

The share of reserves and surplus rose throughout this period, from 12.9 per cent in the 1970s to 16.6 per cent during 1988-96. The rise can be attributed to increasing profitability of the corporate sector. The concept that is pertinent here is the ratio of retained profits to profits after tax, also called the profit retention ratio. Table 6.7 shows that there was continuous increase in the profit retention ratio from 52.6 per cent in the 1970s to 62.9 per cent in the 1980s to 70.7 per cent during 1988-96.

[5]Share premium is the extra amount collected by a company coming up with an equity issue and it reflects the difference between the issue price and face value of the share. In the immediate post-liberalization phase, companies were able to mobilize share premium which was of the order of a multiple times the face value of equity.

Thus the high profit retention ratios had been responsible for the continuous increase in the proportion of reserves and surplus. This is also indicative of the fact that the corporate sector had been ploughing back ever-greater portions of their profits for reinvestment purposes. It is interesting to note that there had been continuous decline in the effective tax rate (ratio of tax provisions to profits before tax) from 48.6 per cent in 1972–80 to 31.0 per cent in 1980–8, and further to 22.7 per cent in 1988–96. This, along with a higher profit retention ratio, had been instrumental in increasing the share of reserves and surplus. However, the share of total internal funds in total sources declined because of a fall in the share of depreciation.

TABLE 6.7
AVERAGE PROFIT RETENTION RATIO

Period	Retained Profits as % of PAT*
1972–80	52.6
1980–8	62.9
1988–96	70.7

Note: *Profits after tax.

The share of depreciation in total sources of funds declined from 27.6 per cent in 1972–80 to 14.8 per cent in 1988–96. There could be at least two reasons for the declining share of depreciation: (a) with the progressive replacement of old machinery by the new and with the easy availability of modern imported machinery since liberalization, industry finds the need of provision for depreciation above the statutory minimum less and less; and (b) as the capital market emerged, the ability to tap it as a cheaper source of finance emerged, and less provision for depreciation could show higher profitability. However, these are tentative explanations and would require further inquiry.

Long-term borrowings include borrowings from financial institutions, banks, and other long-term sources. Table 6.6 also shows that there was a sharp increase in the share of long-term borrowings in the second period, followed by the maintenance of that share in the last period. This indicates that long-term borrowings have been important despite the growing importance of the capital market. In the 1980s, there was a debenture boom, but the share of long-term borrowings also rose during this period. Further, in the late 1980s and early 1990s when equity markets boomed, long-term borrowings still maintained their share in the financing of the corporate sector. In fact, if the last period is split into two four-year phases from 1988–9 to 1991–2 and 1992–3 to 1995–6, it can be seen that the share of long-term borrowings rose initially to 13.3 per cent in the first sub-phase and then declined somewhat to 12.1 per cent during the phase of economic reforms.

In this context, it is worthwhile to examine the factors that determined long-term borrowings. One factor is the average interest rate paid by the corporate sector on all its borrowings and the other, the comparative returns on equity. The borrowings include long-term borrowings, debentures, unsecured loans, and bank borrowings for working capital. Table 6.8 shows that the average effective interest rate rose from 11.8 per cent in the 1970s to 13.3 per cent in the 1980s. Interest rates peaked at 14.0 per cent during 1988–92 and then declined sharply to 12.2 per cent during 1992–6. The decline in effective interest rate has been on account of two factors: (a) a general decline in interest rates after a peak was attained in 1991–2, and (b) sourcing of funds by companies from cheaper avenues such as Euro-markets, intercorporate deposits, and commercial paper.

TABLE 6.8
COST OF CAPITAL, RETURNS ON EQUITY, AND CORPORATE TAX RATE

Period	Effective Interest Rate*	Total Dividend Rate*	Average Change in Share Price Index**	Effective Corporate Tax Rate*
1972–80	11.8	10.8	5.7	48.6
1980–8	13.3	14.9	12.8	31.0
1988–92	14.0	17.6	39.7	27.2
1992–6	12.2	22.2	15.7	18.1

Notes: *Computed from the ICICI's *Financial Performance of Companies*, various issues.
   **As calculated by the Reserve Bank of India.

It is interesting to note that long-term borrowings have been resilient to interest rate changes. Their share rose sharply in the 1980s when interest rates rose distinctly. And when interest rates rose further in the late 1980s and early 1990s, the share of long-term borrowings increased marginally. In fact, in 1992–6, when the cost of borrowings fell, the share of long-term borrowings somewhat declined. It is possible to say that the dependence on long-term borrowings is not linked to interest rates alone. Recourse to long-term borrowings would also depend on the cost and availability of alternative sources of funding including the state of equity markets. Booming equity markets imply easy availability of share premium, which brings down the need to borrow from institutions even though interest rates are low.

Corporate tax generally encourages debt financing *vis-à-vis* equity because interest is paid from income before tax whereas dividends are paid from income after tax (Rajan and Zingales, 1995). However, it has been found that a definite relationship between debt finance and tax rates cannot be established from the Indian data. The effective tax rate fell continuously over the period of study. During the 1980s, there was an increase in debt finance (long-term borrowings and debentures). Lower tax rates could have induced the corporate sector to borrow less during this phase. During 1988–96, effective tax rate came down further and debt finance declined. This was more due to the equity market boom than fall in tax rate.

If companies have to mobilize funds through equity, it has to be attractive in terms of a primary return in the form of dividend and a secondary return in terms of capital appreciation. The former can be captured by the total dividend rate and the latter by changes in share prices. Both the dividend rate as well as share prices have risen during the period under consideration thus indicating that equity capital has become progressively attractive to investors. The average total dividend rate rose successively from a low of 10.8 per cent in the 1970s to 22.2 per cent during 1992–6. The average capital appreciation on equity was as low as 5.7 per cent in the 1970s which moved up to 39.7 per cent during 1988–92 before moving down to 15.7 per cent during 1992–6.

The relative attractiveness of equity issues to the corporate sector has been enhanced by the fact that it has been able to obtain a premium on such issues. This was mainly on account of the abolition of the Controller of Capital Issues (CCI) in 1992, which facilitated the free pricing of equity issues by companies. The nearly stagnant share of long-term borrowings in total sources in the late 1980s and early 1990s can be attributed to the rise in popularity of equity markets. During this period, companies have, typically, been able to raise a substantial amount of funds in the form of share premium from the market, which is directly linked with returns from equities.

The other sources of funds for the corporate sector are bank borrowings for working capital, unsecured loans and advances, and sundry creditors. Sundry creditors have shown a declining trend in the whole period under study as cheaper sources of finance emerged and inventory levels came down with better management. Bank borrowings for working capital did lose importance in the 1980s, but recovered somewhat after 1987–8. This is significant as it shows that dependence on bank credit remained notwithstanding the fact that there were alternative sources available such as intercorporate deposits and commercial paper, which were, typically, cheaper avenues. Unsecured loans and advances have been declining during the last ten-year period.

4.5 SIZE-WISE ANALYSIS

A size-wise analysis of companies shows that smaller firms relied more on internal sources of funds compared with large and medium size firms. The larger firms had higher proportions of share premium, debentures, and long-term borrowings relative to small and medium size firms.

To examine the relationship between the size of firm and the pattern of finance, companies have been divided into three size groups, based on their gross fixed assets. Companies with gross fixed assets of between Rs 50 million and Rs 200 million have been called 'small', while those with gross fixed assets of between Rs 200 million and Rs 500 million 'medium', and those with gross fixed assets of over Rs 500 million have been termed 'large'. This exercise would throw light on the resource-raising pattern of companies, based on size. Table 6.9 provides information on the main sources of funds for firms in the three size categories for the period 1988–96.

TABLE 6.9

CORPORATE SOURCES OF FINANCE BY SIZE 1988–96

(AVERAGE SHARES IN TOTAL)

			(per cent)
Source	Small	Medium	Large
Internal	33.0	30.1	31.3
Reserves & surplus	13.3	15.5	16.4
Depreciation	19.7	14.6	14.9
External	67.0	69.9	68.7
Paid-up capital	8.2	7.0	4.4
Share premium	6.7	6.7	12.8
Debentures	1.9	4.9	7.9
Long-term borrowings	8.7	10.1	13.1

Note: Individual items under external sources of funds are not exhaustive and exclude mainly short-term sources of finance and, therefore, do not add up to the total.

The Table reveals the following:

(1) Small firms had higher dependence on internal funds relative to medium and large companies.

(2) The share of reserves and surplus in total sources of funds rose along with size, reflecting partly, the higher profits being earned by larger firms.

(3) The share of depreciation was highest for small firms.

(4) The share of equity capital was higher for small firms and this, therefore, declined with size. However, the proportion of 'share premium' was higher for large-sized firms relative to medium and small firms, indicating thereby that large firms had been able to raise more premium on a lower level of equity. Hence the magnitude of share premium was directly related to the size of firm.

(5) The share of debentures in total sources also rose with size and was as high as 7.9 per cent for large size companies which supports the observation made in (4) that the size of company had a bearing on access to the capital market (both equity and debt).

(6) The share of long-term borrowings was also highest for large firms and this kept rising with size.

The analysis indicates that it is large companies that have more access to share premium and the size of company has a direct bearing on the ability to raise equity or debentures in the capital market as well as loans from the financial institutions. As a corollary, it follows that small firms tend to have greater recourse to internal funds.

The analysis of the corporate balance sheets can now be summarized as follows. The corporate sector has witnessed a change in the pattern of financing from internal to external sources. Within external sources, the share of capital market instruments has risen. The 1970s were dominated by paid-up capital, followed by debentures in the 1980s, succeeded by equities after 1987–8. During the last period, i.e. 1988–96, the importance of share premium increased. The share of long-term borrowings also increased; it grew substantially in the 1980s and maintained its share in the last phase. In the last period, companies, mainly large and medium, had greater access to share premium through equity, as well as long-term borrowings. The corporate sector has reduced its dependence on sundry creditors continuously during the entire period of the study. The share of bank borrowings for working capital has been maintained throughout the period even though there has been an upsurge in the issue of commercial paper and intercorporate deposits in the recent period.

Uses of Funds

While the corporate sector channelled a substantial proportion of its funds for capital formation there was a tendency to divert funds towards financial investment in the period of equity market boom.

While sourcing of funds is important, it is also interesting to look at the uses of funds. It can be seen from Table 6.6 that the share of gross fixed assets rose from 51.1 per cent in the 1970s to 56.2 per cent in the 1980s. Thereafter, it declined to 52 per cent. This phase also witnessed a decline in the share of inventories in total uses of funds. The corporate sector deployed a progressively larger part of its resources to financial investments in the capital market during the period under study. The share of financial investments rose from 1.1 per cent in the 1970s to 3.0 per cent in the 1980s and then a much larger 7.6 per cent in the third phase. This trend has been contemporaneous with movements in the proportion of share premium in total sources of funds. Therefore, the equity boom of the late 1980s and 1990s served a double purpose for the corporate sector: it helped raise cheap funds and also aided in increasing its 'other income'.

1996–1997 Results

There has been a shift in the pattern of finance from external to internal resources in 1996–7. However, the share of long-term borrowings and debentures has increased, while that of equity (paid-up capital and share premium) has declined.

The year 1996–7 has been a difficult year for industry with growth being substantially lower than in 1995–6. Capital markets remained subdued but interest rates began to decline with additional infusion of liquidity in the market through reduction in the RBI's CRR and also through reduction in bank deposit rates. Under these circumstances, it can be expected that the financing pattern of companies has undergone a change. To understand the pattern of financing of the corporate sector in 1996–7, the preliminary results of 566 companies have been used. The companies selected are not representative of ICICI-assisted companies, but of the total corporate sector. Table 6.10 brings out the sources and uses of funds of these companies for 1996-7 in comparison with the averages of the previous period, 1992–6.

In 1996–7, there has been some shift in the pattern of finance from

TABLE 6.10
SOURCES AND USES OF FUNDS 1996–97
(PRELIMINARY RESULTS)

(per cent share in total)

	1992–6	1996–7
Sources of Funds	100.0	100.0
Internal	30.6	34.0
Depreciation	12.3	16.3
Reserves & surplus	18.3	17.7
External	69.4	66.0
Paid-up capital	4.8	1.6
Share premium	20.7	6.6
Debentures	5.6	8.6
Long-term borrowings	12.6	24.4
Bank borrowings for working capital	7.5	6.3
Fixed deposits	0.5	1.3
Sundry creditors	9.6	9.3
Other current liabilities	8.0	7.9
Uses of Funds	100.0	100.0
Gross fixed assets	51.9	62.6
Inventories	11.4	8.4
Financial investments	9.7	7.2
Other current assets	27.0	21.8

Source: CMIE data

external to internal sources. The share of internal funds rose from 30.6 per cent in 1992–6 to 34.0 per cent in 1996–7. This has been entirely due to a sharp rise in the share of depreciation provisions from 12.3 per cent to 16.3 per cent during this period. This can be attributed mainly to the sharp rise in the share of gross fixed assets in total uses of funds from 51.9 per cent in 1992–6 to 62.6 per cent in 1996–7. The share of reserves and surplus fell. This can be explained by the lower profits earned by the sample companies in 1996–7. While the corporate sector's recourse to external funds as a proportion of total funds declined in 1996–7, there has been distinct move towards debt from equity. The share of paid-up capital declined accompanied by a large dip in the proportion of share premium. This shows that the dormant capital markets meant less equity being raised and those successful in raising equity picked up less in the form of share premium. As seen earlier, phases of high share premium have been associated with high financial investments up to 1995–6. Hence in 1996–7, a fall in the share of equity funds has been associated with resources being channelled more towards creating real capital assets rather than financial investments. The share of inventories, financial investments, and other current assets declined sharply during 1996–7. The share of long-term borrowings rose sharply from 12.6 per cent during 1992–6 to 24.4 per cent in 1996–7 while that of debentures increased from 5.6 per cent to 8.6 per cent during this period.

The share of bank borrowings for working capital and sundry creditors declined during this period. The share of inventories in total uses of funds declined from 11.4 per cent in 1992–6 to 8.4 per cent in 1996–7. This could be due to a fall in inventories of raw materials, presumably on account of lower production that year. This lower holding of inventories could be partly responsible for the decline in share of bank borrowings for working capital and sundry creditors.

Bank credit to industry (medium-, large- and small-scale) has turned volatile in the 1990s while the disbursements from AFIs have been steadily rising (see Figure 6.2). This is in accordance with the differing

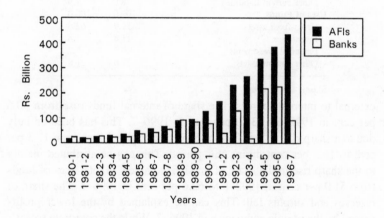

Figure 6.2   AFIs' Disbursements versus Bank Credit to Industry

Source: RBI, *Annual Report*, various issues.

nature of assistance provided by these two types of institutions. While bank credit is directed towards working capital requirements, the assistance extended by AFIs finances physical investment.

4.6   CURRENT SCENARIO: A QUICK SURVEY

A questionnaire-based survey shows that financial institutions (FIs) are the most preferred source of long-term finance followed by external commercial borrowings (ECBs) and banks. However, banks are still the most preferred source of short-term finance.

The shifts in financing pattern in 1996–7 could be an aberration considering the particularly difficult time industry went through in that year. To understand the current situation, a quick survey was carried out during September–November 1997 on industry's views in this regard through a questionnaire.

The sample contained eighty-eight companies covering a wide spectrum of industries with different sizes. In the questionnaire, companies were asked to rank the various sources (long-term and short-term) of funds. In order to find out the consolidated rank of every source, a weightage system was applied, whereby weights of 1, 1/2, 1/3, 1/4, 1/5, 1/6, and 1/7 were applied for ranks 1, 2, . . . , 7. Thus the number of companies assigning a particular rank to a source was multiplied by the reciprocal of the rank (i.e. the weight), to arrive at the weighted score for a source. The source with the highest weighted score is the most preferred source.

The main findings are as follows:

1. The sample showed a preference for external funds over internal funds. However, the smaller firms had a tilt towards internal funds.

2. Table 6.11 below presents a quick look at the preferences of companies among the different sources of external funds. The sample showed the strongest preference for financial institutions (FIs) followed by ECBs, banks, debentures, ordinary capital, preference capital, and GDRs. However, the larger firms had the highest preference for ECBs followed by FIs, debentures, banks, preference shares, ordinary shares, and GDRs. This is clearly due to their better access to cheap foreign funds. The medium- and small-sized firms preferred the more traditional channels of FIs and banks, followed by ordinary capital.

3. The major factor behind such preferences in (2) was the low cost of funds.

4. The sample also preferred private placement to public issues due to cost and time effectiveness and an assured subscription. However, the medium-sized firms were balanced in their preferences between the two.

5. The preferences within short-term funds are presented in Table 6.12. Notwithstanding the diminished share of bank borrowings

for working capital in 1996–7 compared with 1992–6, the companies surveyed preferred banks as the main source of short-term funds followed by CPs, FIs, and inter-corporate deposits (ICDs).

TABLE 6.11
SIZE-WISE RANKING OF SOURCES OF EXTERNAL FUNDS

Source	All Companies (Number: 88)	Large (Number: 60)	Medium (Number: 19)	Small (Number: 9)
FIs*	1	2	1	2
Banks	3	4	2	1
Debentures	4	3	5	6
GDRs**	7	7	7	7
ECBs***	2	1	4	4
Ordinary Capital	5	6	3	3
Preference Capital	6	5	6	5

Notes: *FIs: Financial Institutions.
**GDRs: Global Depository Receipts.
***ECBs: External Commercial Borrowings.

TABLE 6.12
SIZE-WISE RANKING OF SHORT-TERM FUNDS

Source	All	Large	Medium	Small
Banks	1	1	1	1
CPs*	2	2	4	3
ICDs**	4	3	3	2
FIs***	3	3	2	3

Notes: *Commercial Paper.
**Inter-corporate Deposits.
***Financial Institutions.

6. While 25 out of 88 companies did report problems in raising money from banks, it was seen that this difficulty was independent of size. The problems faced by companies were mainly in the form of time delays and rigidity in adhering to rules.

7. Legal and institutional bottlenecks were perceived by companies in the form of rigidity in rules, delays in getting clearances, discretionary procedures, red tapism from the government side and too many clearances from the SEBI, RBI, and Foreign Investment Promotion Board (FIPB).

4.7 COMPARISON WITH INTERNATIONAL EXPERIENCE

The Indian financing pattern emanating from the present study may now be compared with the international experience given in Section 3. As in other developing countries, Indian firms rely more heavily on external rather than internal financing. Over the years, this dependence on external sources has steadily increased. Until the early 1990s, due to the absence of a widespread and buoyant equity market, Indian corporate growth has been essentially loan based and the policies have encouraged high leveraging. Since the beginning of the 1990s, the new equity issues and share premium have assumed importance in financing corporate growth. However, similar to the research findings of Demirguc–Kunt and Maksimovic (1994), both the credit and capital markets have emerged as complementary sources of corporate finance in India in the post-liberalization period. There could be two reasons for this. First, financial institutions and more recently banks as well have fuelled capital market expansion by channelling their funds increasingly via the capital market in the form of 'underwriting and direct subscription' assistance. Second, the fact that banks and financial institutions stipulate a certain amount of promoter's contribution (fresh equity) as a precondition for making fresh loans has facilitated simultaneous growth of credit and stock markets. Borrowings from commercial banks for working capital needs have also been maintained, despite the upsurge in the issue of CPs and ICDs. As funding requirements for investment expenditure greatly exceed internal generation of funds for Indian firms, the heavy dependence on external financing is unavoidable. Within external sources of finance, the continued dependence on the banking sector (both commercial banks and financial institutions) can be explained in terms of more stability and easy availability associated with this source.

5. CONCLUSIONS AND POLICY IMPLICATIONS

In India, much has been achieved from a series of financial sector reform measures, undertaken during the 1990s. Between 1986–91 and 1991–6, the average domestic savings rate of the household sector increased from 17.9 per cent to 18.8 per cent of GDP, whereas that of the private corporate sector increased from 2.3 per cent to 3.6 per cent of GDP. For the corporate sector, represented by the ICICI-assisted companies (i.e. the medium- and large-scale companies), the average savings rate (measured by the 'retained earnings to value-added ratio') increased from 10.9

per cent in 1987–92 to 20.4 per cent in 1992–6. However, the public sector's savings rate declined on an average, from 1.8 to 1.6 per cent of GDP between these sub-periods, pointing to the inadequacy of fiscal reforms.

The average domestic investment rate of the private corporate sector also increased sharply from 4.4 per cent of GDP in 1986–91 to 7.2 per cent of GDP in 1991–6. The average rate of growth of fixed investment for ICICI-assisted companies increased from 19.8 per cent in 1988–92 to 25.6 per cent in 1992–6. Thus the liberalization of financial markets has produced the first round of expected results with respect to increased domestic savings rate in the economy and higher rate of investment by the private corporate sector.

With regard to the productivity of investment, nothing much can be said at this stage, as sufficient time has not elapsed to account for the lagged effect of investment on output. The first half of the 1990s was a period of investment boom and large amounts of domestic and foreign resources had been mobilized for building up capacities. The sharp growth of investment has been accompanied by an increase, albeit marginal, in the fixed capital-output ratio from 2.8 to 3.0 for ICICI-assisted companies between 1988–92 and 1992–6.

With regard to the pattern of financing of the corporate sector, the long-term trend indicates a decline in the share of internal finance in corporate investment over the last twenty-five years. This corroborates the findings by other studies such as Samuel (1996), Nagaraj (1996) and Singh (1995 and 1997) regarding the relative importance of internal sources in overall financing of the corporate sector. However, the findings emerging from our study regarding the relative importance of various sources of external finance and their respective contribution to growth are different. The study brings out the complementary roles played by credit markets (consisting of loans raised from banks, DFIs, investment institutions, and other sources) and the capital market (through bonds/debentures and equity) in financing the corporate sector's physical investment. The shifts between different sources of finance have not really led to the growth of any one source at the expense of another.

During the 1970s and the early 1980s, the credit market played a dominant role. However, since the mid-1980s, the capital market started assuming increasing significance. The first half of the 1990s was also marked by increased inflows from the rest of the world besides the above-mentioned domestic sources. The growth of domestic capital market induced the all-financial institutions to channel an increasing proportion of their investible funds through the capital market in the 1980s and 1990s. Several new financial products came into existence in the 1980s, signifying a wider choice for the corporates. The fixed investment boom of the first half of the 1990s was thus supported by both the capital and credit market expansion. Also, since the early 1990s, the focus of financial regulation has shifted from the control over financial products/prices to prudential supervision and promotion of competition, resulting in the emergence of structured products at competitive prices.

In the initial couple of years of financial sector reforms, the flow of funds from banks to the corporate sector slowed down as a result of increased flows from other newly emerging domestic and foreign sources. However, bank credit to the corporate sector picked up in the subsequent years. The industrial slowdown of 1996–7 again negatively affected bank credit to the corporate sector, which is mostly for working capital requirement. This can also be interpreted as a technical correction by banks to the high credit expansion of the preceding two years, as periodic booms in credit expansion give rise to adverse selection. However, the overall buoyant mood of investment in 1996–7 was supported by the segment of credit market specializing in long-term finance, as capital market activity was dormant.

It has been argued in the earlier studies like Singh and Hamid (1992), Nagaraj (1996), Singh (1995 and 1997), and Samuel (1996) that the capital market boom in developing countries is not associated with improved corporate profitability and, therefore, may not help achieve quicker industrialization and faster long-term economic growth. That observation does not find support from the data of the ICICI sample companies. The ICICI sample covers those companies which have better access to finance from the credit market as well as the domestic and foreign capital markets as they are mostly medium- and large-scale companies. The profitability of at least this section of the corporate sector has shown consistent improvement since the 1970s (Table 6.13). Both 'net profits to total assets' and 'net profits to net worth' ratios show a dip in the second half of the 1980s. However, both have registered substantial improvement in the post-1992 period, a period of equity boom in the Indian economy.

As regards the financial structure, in broad terms economies can be categorized either as stock market oriented (like the UK and the US economies) or as bank oriented (like the Japanese and German econo-

TABLE 6.13
PROFITABILITY OF ICICI-ASSISTED COMPANIES
1971–96

Period	Net Profits to Total Assets	Net Profits to Net Worth
1971–6	4.1	11.2
1976–81	4.1	12.3
1981–6	4.1	14.2
1986–91	3.9	13.4
1991–6	5.9	16.2

mies). From the 1970s to the early 1990s, the financial structure of most large- and medium-scale Indian firms has been similar to that in Japan, South Korea and Germany, as there had been limited growth of a widespread and buoyant equity market, due to the conservative stance taken by the Office of the Controller of Capital Issues with regard to pricing of capital issues. Thus, in form, the Indian situation closely approximated the situations in Japan, Korea, and Germany, where development banks/banks have been the largest debt holders and shareholders of firms. Industrial growth in India has been essentially loan based and high leveraging has been encouraged. This has given plenty of opportunities to intermediaries, especially the term-lending institutions to acquire major strengths in the form of large asset base, large client base, project appraisal skills, and close ties with the firms. These strengths have helped the financial institutions considerably to maintain their market share at 48 per cent of corporate fixed investment even during the heightened competitive environment of the first half of the 1990s.

During the post-liberalization period there has been a gradual convergence of activities of banks and financial institutions. However, a move towards universal banking is expected to take some time, given the strict compartmentalization followed in the past fifty years. In the Indian context, even today financial institutions are in an somewhat advantageous position to cope with adverse selection and moral hazard problems, due to their expertise in project evaluation, credit analysis, and interim monitoring. However, as pointed out by Diamond (1984) *ex-post* monitoring is also important and this is not currently done in India. This kind of monitoring includes such activities as verifying the outcome of investment projects (the financial state of the firm) and taking (controlling) action contingent on the outcome.

In recent years, the prominence of the capital market has increased considerably in the Indian financial market. As shown by our analysis, in both project financing as well as in the ongoing operations of the corporate sector, the importance of equity capital has risen. With the entry of foreign institutional investors, mutual funds, and overseas country funds, the market is bound to expand further. In any economy, a specific corporate governance structure is defined by a particular combination of debt instruments and equity holdings. In the stock market dominated economies, investors are represented by shareholders and their agents (the Board of Directors). In such economies, competition in the market for corporate control provides the ultimate discipline. In bank-dominated economies, banks are the principal monitors. In the Indian financial system, financial institutions are better suited for this purpose with their project appraisal skills and monitoring ability. In the emerging financial scenario, it is expected that both the credit and the capital markets will play an important role in India in developing the corporate governance structure.

REFERENCES

Ajit, D. and R.D. Bangar. (1997). 'Banks in Financial Intermediation: Performance and Issues'. *Reserve Bank of India Occasional Papers*, vol. 18, nos. 2 and 3, pp. 303–49.

Aoki, M. (1996). 'Comment on Understanding Financial Crises: A Developing Country Perspective by F.S. Mishkin'. In M. Bruno and B. Pleskovic (eds), *Proceedings of the World Bank Annual Bank Conference on Development Economics 1996*. Washington, D.C.: World Bank, pp. 63–8.

Bencivenga, Valerie R., Bruce D. Smith, and Ross Starr (1996). 'Equity Markets, Transaction Costs, and Capital Accumulation: An Illustration'. *The World Bank Economic Review*, vol. 10, no. 2, pp. 241–65.

Berthelemy, Jean-Claude and A. Varoudakis. (1996). 'Financial Development Policy and Growth'. Long-term Growth Series of the Development Centre Studies. Paris: OECD.

CMIE (Centre for Monitoring Indian Economy) (1995). *The Primary Capital Market*. Mumbai.

Chelliah, Raja. (1996). 'Financial and Fiscal Reforms in Asian Countries'. In Chelliah, *Towards Sustainable Growth: Essays in Fiscal and Financial Sector Reforms in India*. New Delhi: Oxford University Press, pp. 68–81.

Cho, Y.J. (1986). 'Inefficiencies from Financial Liberalisation in the Absence of

Well-functioning Equity Markets'. *Journal of Money, Credit and Banking*, vol. 18, no. 2 (May), pp. 191–200.

Cornelli, F., R. Portes and M. Schaffer. (1998). 'Financial Structure of Firms in the CEECs'. In *Different Paths to a Market Economy: China and European Economies in Transition*. Paris: Centre for Economic Policy Research, OECD, pp. 171–88.

Damodaran, A. (1997). *Corporate Finance: Theory and Practice*: New York: John Wiley & Sons, pp. 387–542.

Demirguc–Kunt, Ash, and Ross Levine. (1996). 'Stock Market Development and Financial Intermediaries: Stylized Facts'. *The World Bank Economic Review*, vol. 10, no. 2, pp. 291–321.

Demirguc–Kunt, Ash, and Vojislav Maksimovic. (1994). 'Capital Structures in Developing Countries: Evidence from Ten Countries'. WPS 1320, World Bank Policy Research Department, Washington, D.C.

Diamond, D. (1984). 'Financial Intermediation and Delegated Monitoring'. *Review of Economic Studies*, vol. 59, pp. 393–414.

Hoshi, T., A. Kashyap, and D. Scharfstein. (1990). 'Corporate Structure, Liquidity and Investment: Evidence from Japanese Industrial Groups'. *Quarterly Journal of Economics*, vol. 106, pp. 33–60.

Jadhav, Narendra. (1994). *Monetary Economics For India.*, New Delhi: Macmillan India Limited, pp. 211–31.

Levine, Ross. (1991). 'Stock Markets, Growth, and Tax Policy'. *Journal of Finance*, vol. 46 (4 September), pp. 1445–65.

Mayer, Colin. (1990). 'Financial Systems, Corporate Finance and Economic Development'. In R.G. Hubbard (ed.), *Asymmetric Information, Corporate Finance, and Investment*. NBER; Chicago: Chicago University Press.

———. (1992). 'Corporate Finance'. *The New Palgrave Dictionary of Money and Finance*, vol. 2. London: Macmillan.

McKinnon, R.I. (1973). *Money and Capital in Economic Development*. Washington, D.C.: Brookings Institution.

Mishkin, F.S. (1996). 'Understanding Financial Crises: A Developing Country Perspective'. In Bruno and Pleskovic (eds), pp. 22–62.

Nagaraj, R. (1996). 'India's Capital Market Growth: Trends, Explanations and Evidence'. *Economic and Political Weekly*, Special Number (September).

Obstfeld, Maurice. (1994). 'Risk-Taking, Global Diversification, and Growth'. *American Economic Review*, vol. 84 (5 December), pp. 1310–29.

Petersen, M. and R. Rajan. (1994). 'The Effect of Credit Market Competition on Lending Relationship'. *Quarterly Journal of Economics*, vol. 110, no. 2 (May), pp. 407–43.

Rajan, R. and L. Zingales. (1995). 'What Do We Know about the Capital

Structure? Some Evidence from the International Data'. *Journal of Finance* (December).

Rangarajan C. (1997). 'Indian Financial System: The Emerging Horizon'. In Raj Kapila and Uma Kapila (eds), *Banking and Financial Sector Reforms in India*. New Delhi: Academic Foundation, pp. 69–88.

RBI (Reserve Bank of India) (1996). *Report on Currency and Finance, 1995–6*. vol. II. Mumbai.

———. (1997). *Annual Report*. Mumbai.

SEBI (Securities and Exchange Board of India) (1997). 'Indian Securities Market, Agenda for Development and Reform'. In Kapila and Kapila (eds), pp. 105–41.

Samuel, Cherian. (1996). 'The Stockmarket as a Source of Finance: A Comparison of US and Indian Firms'. World Bank Policy Research Working Paper, (1592), Washington, D.C.

Shaw, E.S. (1973). *Financial Deepening in Economic Development*. New York: Oxford University Press.

Singh, Ajit. (1995). 'Corporate Financial Patterns in Industrializing Economies: A Comparative International Study'. *Technical Paper 2*. Washington, D.C.: International Finance Corporation, World Bank.

———. (1997). 'Financial Liberalization, Stock Markets and Economic Development'. *The Economic Journal*, vol. 107 (May), pp. 771–82.

Singh, Ajit and Javed Hamid. (1992): 'Corporate Financial Structures in Developing Countries'. *Technical Paper 1*. Washington, D.C.: International Finance Corporation, World Bank.

Singh, Ajit and B.A. Weisse. (1998). 'Emerging Stock Markets, Portfolio Capital Flows and Long-term Economic Growth: Micro and Macroeconomic Perspective'. *World Development*, vol. 26, no. 4 (April), pp 607–22.

Stiglitz, J.E. (1994). 'The Role of the State in Financial Markets'. In M. Bruno and B. Pleskovic (eds) *Proceedings of the World Bank Annual Bank Conference on Development Economics 1993*. Washington, D.C.: World Bank, pp. 19–52.

Stiglitz, J.E. and A. Weiss. (1981). 'Credit Rationing in markets with Imperfect information'. *American Economic Review*, vol. 71 (June), pp. 393–410.

Tarapore S.S. (1996). 'The Second E.F. Schumacher Memorial Lecture, Nagpur, April 29, 1996', *RBI Monthly Bulletin* (May).

World Bank. (1989). *World Development Report 1989: Financial Systems and Development*. Oxford: Oxford University Press.

Part III

Capital Markets, Pensions

Developing the Indian Capital Market

AJAY SHAH and SUSAN THOMAS*

1. MARKETS AND BANKS IN INDIA'S FINANCIAL SYSTEM

The financial system in a country serves to link up the savings of households with the investment objectives of firms, and improve welfare by redistributing risk across the economy. It has broadly two major institutional mechanisms: banks lending funds to companies, and markets through which shares of companies are bought and sold. In understanding the financial system, a unified approach encompassing both institutional alternatives is required. Neither banks nor markets are important as ends in themselves; they are a means for obtaining efficiency in intermediation, risk allocation, and intertemporal welfare maximization. From this perspective, at a policy level, we focus upon their *functions* in the economy (Merton and Bodie, 1995a) instead of focusing upon the *institutions*.

If banks and markets are alternative vehicles for financial intermediation, in what way do they differ? There are some differences which are fairly superficial. One of the differences pointed out in India is that banks are unique in giving households the convenience of writing cheques and using ATMs. However, elsewhere in the world, there are mutual funds which offer investors these facilities.[1] Banks in India have typically focused on debt financing, as opposed to markets which work with both

*Presented at the World Bank–IGIDR–USAID Conference, 'India: A Financial Sector for the 21st Century', Goa, December 1997.

[1]Money market mutual funds in most countries offer cheque-writing facilities. In 1993, Wells Fargo Bank pioneered a facility in the US whereby account holders would be able to move money between a savings account and an index fund using an ATM. The Reserve Bank can easily allow mutual funds to participate in cheque clearing and in the payments system, thus eliminating this special feature of banks.

equity and debt financing. But in the recent past, there are banks in India, and many abroad, which do take an equity stake in projects that they finance. Increasingly, these differences are not of essence.

The *essential* feature that differentiates markets from banks is the 'technology' of financing projects. The crux of the problem in project financing is asymmetric information and divergent objectives between the investor and the managers of the firm. Banks can be viewed as an effort to overcome this asymmetric information through a close bank–borrower relationship. Markets are an effort to overcome the asymmetric information by giving speculators incentives to conduct research and information search, which brings information in the form of publicly visible prices in a state of 'market efficiency'.

Therefore, while markets rely upon anonymous investment and anonymous evaluation—the investor and the firm do not know each other directly and the valuation is in the prices arising out of secondary market trading of the securities—banks rely upon direct contact with the firm and evaluation of the projects that are being funded.

By this definition, financial intermediaries like venture capital funds lie in the category of banks, even though they are not regulated by the RBI, do not offer cheque-writing facilities, and do not have reserve requirements. Similarly, India's 'development financial institutions' would be viewed as banks because of their direct involvement with projects.

1.1 INTERMEDIATION SERVICES OF BANKS AND MARKETS

Banks and markets compete in the operational costs of intermediation, and in the quality of information processing that they use in resource allocation. The comparison between banks and markets on these is summarized in Table 7.1.

A major problem inhibiting efficient information processing in India's banking system is *agency conflicts*, where employees of banks do not share the interests of the owners. Another direct factor inhibiting the functioning of banks is the existence of reserve requirements.

Markets, in contrast, accomplish information processing by rewarding successful speculators with trading profits. A large mass of individuals (working independently and therefore without agency conflicts) do research and analysis and trade on securities markets, therefore bringing information into market prices to produce informational efficiency. There is considerable empirical evidence, especially for the more liquid securities of the country, that this process appears to be producing a fair degree of 'market efficiency' (Shah and Thomas, 1994, 1996; Thomas, 1995).

When secondary market liquidity is poor, market prices can sometimes lose touch with reality, leading to distorted resource allocation.

TABLE 7.1

INTERMEDIATION SERVICES OF BANKS AND MARKETS

Banks	Markets
Operational Costs	
Elevated by reserve requirements, labour problems, and poor automation, and perpetuated by entry barriers.	The various transactions costs faced when using securities markets. These have dropped sharply in recent years for large capitalization securities, but remain high for smaller capitalization securities.
Information Processing	
Information processing is hampered by credit allocation policies and agency conflicts. In public sector banks, credit analysis is fairly weak.	India's markets appear to be fairly informationally efficient for securities with good market liquidity. Markets can become a morass of poor information and market manipulation when liquidity is poor. Given the small role of institutional investors in India's markets, agency conflicts are much less of a problem in price discovery.

The subject of bank versus market orientation in the financial system of a developing country has often been debated in the literature (Singh, 1997; Levine and Zervos, 1996). The central feature of India's financial system is the race between

- institutional development of the securities industry which improves liquidity (Shah and Thomas, 1997), thus improving the intermediation of markets; and
- reforms of the banking sector (Sarkar and Agrawal, 1997) which reduce reserve requirements and diminish agency conflicts, thus improving the intermediation of banks.

As of today, there appears to be a middle road where India's markets are performing better intermediation for liquid securities. On India's equity market, there are around 800 securities where liquidity might be considered acceptable.[2] This suggests that the equity market is presently

[2]This estimate is based on a fairly weak notion of asset liquidity: that both buy and sell orders are found in the market limit order book with at least 90 per cent probability. There are around 800 securities on the NSE which meet this criterion.

able to perform intermediation reasonably effectively for the largest 800 companies of the economy. These are generally firms with large market capitalization and dispersed ownership; this set of 800 firms accounts for around 80 per cent of the market capitalization of all listed companies of the country. In the future, improved market mechanisms could be used in India's securities industry to better obtain liquidity amongst smaller securities.

For smaller securities, banks might well perform information processing better than illiquid markets, especially through organizational structures which minimize agency conflicts, such as private banks and venture capital funds. The future development of the financial system could see benefits from specialization by banks and markets into these non-overlapping roles.[3]

India's households face a portfolio allocation problem, where they can use either markets or banks as avenues for investing their financial assets. As of 1990, households relied more on banks than on markets: bank deposits in the country amounted to Rs 1.7 trillion as against market capitalization of the equity market of Rs 0.6 trillion. By 1996, households seemed to be allocating their wealth more evenly between the two alternatives, with Rs 4.2 trillion in bank deposits and Rs 4.7 trillion as the market capitalization of the equity market. These estimates understate the importance of markets by ignoring the market capitalization of the corporate debenture market. This change in the structure of portfolio choices of households reflects the increased importance of markets in India's traditionally bank-oriented financial system.

1.2 PROBLEMS IN CAPITAL MARKETS: THE PERSPECTIVE OF THE FIRM

The difficulties of resource mobilization using India's capital markets, from the firm's point of view, may be expressed as follows:

1.   When the firm uses the primary market for conducting an initial

---

[3]The relationship between banks and markets should not be viewed in adversarial terms; synergies also exist. Banks, like other lenders, would prefer to deal with a firm which is listed on markets, so that the price discovery that takes place on markets is available as a free input into credit evaluation and monitoring. This is consistent with the empirical evidence (Demirguc–Kunt and Maksimovic, 1996) that in developing countries, improvements in the functioning of stock markets are associated with *increased* leverage by firms.

public offering (IPO) or a seasoned equity offering (SEO), the primary market generally requires a significant *underpricing* from the secondary market value of the securities (Shah, 1995a). This underpricing is a hidden cost of capital for the firm. In addition, issue costs on the primary market are high. Firms have a strong incentive to use the primary markets outside India to reduce issue costs and obtain better prices.

2. Once securities list on the secondary market, liquidity is poor for many securities. Investors require a 'liquidity premium' in the form of a higher expected rate of return for illiquid securities. This problem is worst for issues of debt instruments, where fragmentation of liquidity often takes place. Only a few corporate bonds are traded by the secondary market.

3. Illiquid securities additionally run the risk of being ensnared in a variety of manipulative efforts on the market.

4. The firm incurs significant costs on an ongoing basis through settlement procedures with physical certificates.

1.3 Problems in Capital Markets: The Household Perspective

Traditionally, participation in financial markets has been restricted to a small fraction of India's population. The limited wealth of most households typically generates poor diversification and, therefore, poor risk–reward outcomes. In addition, limited knowledge has attracted a variety of malpractice. This susceptibility to malpractice was partly owing to mechanisms in trading, clearing, and settlement in the securities industry which were fraught with dangers for the relatively uninformed household. Today, the best practices available in India's securities industry (screen-based trading, novation at the clearing corporation, and the depository) make it a much safer place for uninformed investors. However, less reliable practices continue to survive on many stock exchanges in the country. It may take years before the ingrained mistrust of securities transactions amongst most Indians is diminished.

The world over, *indirect* investment into the securities markets is a much more common mode of access for households. Here, the mutual fund industry is a crucial intermediary, which would be able to attract the savings of households into capital markets. Mutual funds are diversified in their investments and could add value through their fund management abilities. In an environment where households are uncomfortable about directly using securities markets, mutual funds could be useful intermediaries.

The track record of mutual funds in India is poor (Warburg SBC, 1996; Shah and Thomas, 1994; Thomas, 1995; Thomas, 1998a). As is the case with most OECD countries, around 80 per cent of India's mutual fund schemes underperform the index on a risk-adjusted basis, irrespective of whether they are Indian or foreign mutual fund companies. This lack of value-added by professional managers partly reflects the informational efficiency of securities markets in India, which makes 'beating the market' difficult. In addition, mutual funds are vulnerable to agency conflicts that inhibit their functioning: as with banks, employees of the mutual fund might often have objectives which are not in the best interests of investors (Shah, 1998d).

These twin problems of market efficiency and agency conflicts are both squarely addressed by index funds. Index funds generally yield risk-adjusted returns in the top quartile of mutual funds. Additionally, the ease of monitoring the actions of the fund manager—the returns via NAV each day have to exactly equal the percentage change of the index—serves to eliminate principal–agent problems. Hence the development of index funds is a vital direction for establishing the credibility of the mutual fund industry in the eyes of the investor.

Pension reforms are an initiative which will initiate large-scale institutional investment into financial markets. Through the aegis of pension funds, savings of households can obtain higher returns through the capital market, and the growth of a large mass of institutional investors can commence. The world over, equity investment is an ideal alternative for pension investments given the long time horizons involved. India's mutual fund industry has experienced many problem, but pension funds investing into index funds are intrinsically easier to manage and regulate. Hence a policy initiative to greatly enlarge equity investments on the part of pension funds, subject to the caveat of only using index funds, may be a safe and effective way to embark upon the development of the pension fund industry.

Finally, the risk reallocation function of capital markets is critically linked to the development of financial derivatives. Economic agents in India would face a less risky environment if derivatives markets could rapidly come about.

1.4 IMPLICATIONS OF CONVERTIBILITY ON THE CAPITAL ACCOUNT

The discussion so far has been conducted in terms of comparing India's banking system and India's securities industry as alternative vehicles of financial intermediation. Convertibility on the capital account (Tarapore, 1997) enlarges the budget set for India's households and firms by additionally making foreign banks and foreign securities markets directly available to them. In so far as this enlarges the opportunities of firms and households, convertibility can only improve the financial services available to both.

Firms already have limited access to offshore capital, through Euro-issues and through FII investment in India. Convertibility would be a truly new phase for India's households, for whom international diversification will produce a dramatic reduction in portfolio risk.[4] When enough households take advantage of this risk reduction, it would reduce the volatility of consumption in India and thus help stabilize India's macroeconomy. If households lack expertise in investing in foreign financial instruments, mutual funds could play a major role in accelerating this process by offering internationally diversified products.

Convertibility and India's Securities Industry:
Threat or Opportunity?

Financial market participants sometimes exhibit a degree of protectionism when viewing the inroads made by foreign market intermediaries and markets into what was once a monopoly for Indian firms.[5] The success of foreign brokerage firms and investment bankers (see Section 5.6) has been the source of much resentment. The growth of foreign banks operating in India has effectively been blocked by policy. The rise of Indian firms listing on the Global Depository Receipts (GDR) market, with some situations like shares of VSNL where the GDR market is more liquid than the National Stock Exchange (NSE), has been criticized as 'exporting the Indian securities markets'. From the viewpoint of India's economy, such protectionism is unjustified in so far as the most important objective of the financial system is to deliver financial

---

[4]Diversification is the only free lunch known in economics. The calculations on page 183 of Shah and Thomas (1997) illustrate the gains from even the most limited notion of international diversification, between investing in an NSE-50 index fund and an S & P 500 index fund.

[5]The entry of foreign brokerage firms into India is a significant success in the political economy of liberalization. India is significantly more open towards FDI into the brokerage industry as compared with many East Asian countries, where domestic brokers have been able to maintain significant barriers against such entry.

intermediation to India's firms and households at the lowest possible cost and highest possible market efficiency; the nationality of the intermediaries or markets involved is not an objective.

At the same time, there is considerable merit in the argument that India's securities industry is a skill-intensive and labour-intensive industry where Indian firms have comparative advantage as compared with financial service providers elsewhere in the world. India's financial industry has the same advantages as India's software industry, and has the potential to be a high-wage, export-oriented sector. Bombay has the potential to become a centre of international finance, provided markets and institutions of international standard develop rapidly. As soon as convertibility comes about, India's financial markets could commence trading in Sri Lankan government bonds, Bangladeshi index futures, and options on the Thai baht.

This perspective induces an urgency in reforms and modernization of India's financial markets. Equity derivatives on the Indian market index could trade in Singapore in the future, and a non-deliverable forward market trades the rupee forward in Hong Kong today. These markets *do* meet the objectives of India's economy, once convertibility comes about. However, such developments imply lost opportunities for the development of a high-wage industry in India.

1.5 POLICY ISSUES

The problems faced by firms accessing resources on India's capital markets would be addressed by

- improved procedures on the primary market (Section 5);
- improved market liquidity on the secondary market (Section 3);
- improved functioning of the bond market; and
- complete adoption of the depository (Section 3.3).

The problems faced by households supplying resources into India's capital markets would be addressed by

- complete adoption of the depository (Section 3.3);
- development of index funds;
- pension reforms; and
- markets for financial derivatives (Section 4).

The onset of convertibility has the following implications:

- India's securities industry will face strong competition from the worldwide financial industry;
- the transition into settlement through depositories, T+3 rolling settlement, and derivatives is urgently required to obtain international competitiveness;
- a close attention to enabling infrastructure (Section 6) would also be valuable in producing Indian firms in the financial sector which are competitive by international standards;
- if progress towards convertibility takes place at a faster pace than the institutional development of India's securities industry, then India's financial intermediation would mainly take place through the international financial system, and India's securities industry would be relegated to a less important role.

2. THE OBJECTIVES OF THE SECURITIES INDUSTRY

The objective of the securities industry is to produce trading arrangements which involve the lowest possible transactions costs. In Section 1.2, we spell out the importance of low transactions costs for the economy.

Transactions costs are greatly influenced by the design of market mechanisms. Radical changes of market mechanisms are often the best way to produce dramatic reductions in transactions costs. Such reforms have traditionally always faced opposition from individuals who possess skills in *existing* market mechanisms. The political economy of reform is the subject of Section 2.2.

In Section 2.3, we decompose the total transactions costs faced by users of financial markets into several components. Policy analysis can proceed by evolving market mechanisms which minimize each of these components (Shah, 1998a).

Finally, Section 2.4 deals with common misconceptions about market quality.

2.1 THE IMPORTANCE OF LOW TRANSACTIONS COSTS

From an economic perspective, *transactions costs* are the essential source of divergence between the ideal frictionless market of theoretical economics, and markets which are observed in the real world. A highly liquid market is one where transactions involve low costs. To understand the consequences of transactions costs, it helps to classify users of financial markets into two categories: *informationless users* and *speculators*:

- *Informationless users* of markets require liquidity services; they need to convert funds into securities or securities into funds for reasons external to market prices. One simple example of informationless users in a market is that of importers and exporters who trade on the foreign exchange market as a side consequence of their core activities; most orders placed by them are not attempts at obtaining speculative profits.

  For informationless users, the equity and debt markets make it possible to participate in long-term projects while retaining the option of asset liquidation. This role of financial markets in providing liquidity has been known ever since John R. Hicks. A modern extension of this argument is the idea of the *liquidity premium*, whereby investors require a higher rate of return (at equilibrium) when transactions involve large costs (Amihud and Mendelson, 1986).

- *Speculators* invest in research and information gathering, form forecasts about the future risk and return of financial assets, and take positions on markets. By their activities, speculators make markets informationally efficient.

  Transactions costs reduce the profits of speculators: thus high transactions costs inhibit the allocation of resources to research and information gathering, and reduce the speed with which information flows into prices. By this argument, asset liquidity is important in the modern economy in order to enable a high degree of market efficiency.

These ideas suggest that asset liquidity, i.e. low transactions costs, is the end product which the securities industry creates. Alternative modes of functioning in the securities industry should be judged in terms of differences in transactions costs.

2.2 THE POLITICAL ECONOMY OF INSTITUTIONAL CHANGE

Policy issues concerned with institutional arrangements in the securities industry are fraught with controversy. Market participants possess skills which are specific to existing institutional arrangements, and often stand to lose from institutional change. Hence major market participants are often conservatives who resist institutional change. This resistance is most pronounced when a new form of market organization directly hurts revenues of intermediaries—e.g. through improved market transparency or through reduced entry barriers into intermediation.

The conservatism of market participants is not peculiar to India; it is observed in every country. A striking example of the resistance to change is seen in the US, arguably one of the pioneers of modern securities exchanges. The major markets of the US (NYSE, NASDAQ, CME, and CBOT) continue to use market mechanisms which were designed many decades ago. Hence they fail to exploit contemporary technology in computers and communications.

Similarly, the US treasury bill market has many deficiencies which derive from its organization around a small club of primary dealers. The worldwide foreign exchange market operates in a distributed dealer market, something approaching an institutional vacuum. It lacks basic qualities like price–time priority, centralization of order flow, and public visibility of liquidity.

The most important new idea in market organization of the last two decades is computerized order matching, which is also called the open electronic limit order book market (Black, 1971; Glosten, 1994). Electronic order matching first appeared in small markets like Toronto and Mexico, or new markets like the NSE. These successes paved the way for adoption in larger markets like Paris, Tokyo, and London (Domowitz, 1990; Melamed and Tamarkin, 1996). In November 1997, the London Stock Exchange commenced trading through order matching, and Indian readers of *The Financial Times* witnessed a replay of the debates which took place in India's equity market in 1993 and 1994. In each situation, the introduction of computerized order matching has encountered the same fierce political opposition which was seen in India, from existing intermediaries who face the prospect of reduced revenues.

A focus upon transactions costs provides a secular foundation for an analysis of market mechanisms. In Section 2.3, we decompose the total transactions costs faced by users of a market into many components. Each component is a direct outcome of the form of market organization that is chosen by market administrators and policy makers. From a policy perspective, the most important question is that of *identifying the forms of market organization which yield the lowest transactions costs, and evolving India's financial markets towards these market mechanisms* (Shah, 1998a). The best market mechanisms seen in such an analysis will often prove to be *different* from existing market mechanisms in major markets of the OECD countries. The major question we face today is not a comparison of India's existing markets against those of the major OECD countries, but a comparison of India's existing markets against the best practices that are available in the world.

2.3 COMPONENTS OF TRANSACTIONS COSTS

The transactions costs that markets impose upon users are of twelve kinds. The objective of the securities industry, and of economic policy in connection with the securities industry, is to evolve systems covering the full life-cycle of the trade which minimize all these costs and completely eliminate some of them. An approximate depiction of India's equity, fixed income, and foreign exchange markets in terms of these twelve components is presented in Table 7.2.

TABLE 7.2
TRANSACTIONS COSTS ON INDIA'S MARKETS

Component	Equity		Fixed Income	Foreign Exchange
	1993	1997		
Trading				
Denial of access	High	Low	High	High
Market downtime	High	Low	Low	Low
Fees to intermediates	High	Low	High	High
Unreliable order processing	High	Low	High	High
Market inefficiencies	High	Low	High	Low
Market impact cost	High	Moderate	High	Moderate
Clearing				
Counterparty risk	High	Low	Low	Low
Initial margin	0	Moderate	0	0
Settlement				
Back office costs	High	Moderate	High	Moderate
Bad certificates	High	High	Low	0
Delays in payment	High	Moderate	Low	Low
Transaction taxes	Moderate	Low	Low	0

Note: The terms used in this table are approximate. They reflect both a comparison between the transactions costs seen on these markets, and a comparison of how different these transactions costs are as compared to what they could be given improved market mechanisms.

Denial of Access

Inter-bank markets are an example where users are unable to directly access the market and are forced to go through a small club of market participants. India's fixed income and foreign exchange markets are dominated by intermediaries (a broker or a dealer) based in Bombay.

Another example is India's equity market before 1994, where users outside Bombay had significantly inferior access to the market. This led to domination by Bombay in the equity market. Today in India's equity market, the NSE's VSAT-based trading system has made the market directly accessible in 200 cities in the country. We now have a remarkable situation where only 36 per cent of the NSE's trading volume originates in Bombay.

This is perhaps suggestive of the way India's fixed income and foreign exchange markets might be able to gain liquidity by spreading to locations outside Bombay, when superior trading technology is implemented. This also has welfare implications, by improving utility of individuals outside Bombay.

Market Downtime

This cost occurs when a user wants to access liquidity services but is unable to do so because the market is closed (either because of holidays, a strike by exchange staff, a payments crisis, or a technical breakdown). The NSE's recent experience with unreliable satellites has generated massive transactions costs for many market participants.

Market Impact Cost

Market impact cost is the cost faced by a user who places a market order as compared with the ideal price.[6] Buyers pay impact cost over and above the ideal price, sellers obtain the ideal price less impact cost.

Market impact cost is the largest component of the transactions costs which are faced in most transactions, except for retail users working with the fifty most liquid shares in the equity market. In all other cases— either less liquid securities or larger transaction sizes—market impact cost is likely to be the most important component of transactions costs.

Market Inefficiencies

When a user buys or sells shares at prices which stray from the true value, this generates additional risk. Specifically, when market manipulation is present, the typical user normally loses money (on average) when trading in the presence of manipulative efforts. These costs are transactions costs faced by users of the market.

---

[6]This is defined as (bid + ask)/2.

Unreliable Order Processing by Broker

When users place an order with a broker, which is not reliably executed, it is a risk for the user. Traditionally, on India's equity market, intermediaries attached a low priority to small investors, and gave them unreliable services, driving up the transactions costs faced by small investors.

Reliable order processing is generally a question of the degree of automation of trading and associated support systems in brokerage firms. The degree of competition in the brokerage industry is also important in giving incentives to intermediaries to improve systems and be able to cope with a wide variety of users. Eliminating entry barriers into brokerage services would thus help reduce transactions costs.

Fees to Intermediaries

We will distinguish between two components of brokerage fees: the fees directly charged which the user observes, and the less visible costs which users are charged in the form of prices which are different from the best prices available on the market.

The latter is possible when markets are organized in ways which lack transparency: if the best bid and offer in the market are not easily known to users, cross-checking the claims of the intermediary is not possible. This was a common abuse with floor-based trading on India's equity market, where it was called *gala*. A related malpractice is frontrunning, which is also directly related to the non-transparency of prices and liquidity on a market.[7] These problems are also prevalent in India's fixed income and foreign exchange markets, which are presently organized as distributed dealer markets.[8]

---

[7]A principal (the user) asks the agent (the intermediary) to buy 10,000 shares. The agent first places an order for 1000 shares on his own account, then places an order for 10,000 shares for the principal (which generates some price impact), and then sells off his position of 1000 shares. This is called frontrunning. Frontrunning serves to drive up the impact cost that users face in actual trades as opposed to the impact cost that the limit order book might normally convey.

[8]The RBI has made special efforts to ensure that the quotes of dealers in the foreign exchange market are close to the truth. Hence the best bid and best offer that are seen on a Reuters terminal are fairly accurate indicators of the price on the market for small trades. However, such a state of affairs is not a natural outcome in a distributed dealer market, where price–time priority is intrinsically lacking. The special efforts of the RBI were only able to have an impact owing to the small number of dealers that currently exist on the foreign exchange market.

Going beyond the best bid and best offer on the market, which typically pertain to small transaction sizes, *transparency of liquidity* is important to large users. The only form of market organization presently known where liquidity can be made transparent is the open electronic limit order book market, where the entire limit order book can be displayed to the public.[9] Using the limit order book, any user can calculate the true impact cost at any desired transaction size, and the intermediaries cannot introduce markups.

The second component of the costs of brokerage that users pay is the direct brokerage fee. Brokerage fees are strongly a function of entry barriers into the brokerage industry.

In the case of India's equity market, the BSE (Bombay Stock Exchange) traditionally restricted membership of the stock exchange, which helped elevate brokerage fees. The ownership structure of the NSE has enabled a policy of free entry into the brokerage industry, which has generated a sharp fall in brokerage rates, from around 1 per cent to 0.3 per cent. Free entry into the brokerage industry, in turn, would not be possible without the credit enhancement services of the clearing corporation.

India's fixed income and foreign exchange markets are dominated by a few large banks, and thus feature elevated fees.

Counterparty Risk

When a trade is completed, and the counterparty defaults, this exposes the user of a market to risk. India's equity market has a long tradition of payments crises which often halted the functioning of markets.

The modern approach to coping with counterparty risk is the idea of 'novation', where a clearing corporation interposes itself into every transaction, buying from one leg and selling to the other. Through this,

---

[9]This statement is inaccurate in two respects:

- Limit order book markets like the NSE have often chosen to not display the complete limit order book, only the best five buy and sell prices are displayed. While this has some economic justification, the NSE's reasoning seems to be primarily motivated by India's telecom policies.
- In addition to the limit order book market the electronic call auction market inherently involves zero impact cost. Hence, in an electronic call auction market, as long as the 'notional equilibrium price' is revealed to users in realtime, there is no scope for malpractice.

the clearing corporation serves as a credit enhancement agency, eliminating the risk to each side of bankruptcy of the other.

India's fixed income and foreign exchange markets are effectively restricted to a small club of banks, and hence feature low counterparty risk. Entry into these markets would not be possible without a clearing corporation.

Initial Margin

The credit enhancement of a clearing corporation is not achieved at zero cost; it requires that both sides pay collateral to the clearing corporation.

When users have to put up initial margin associated with positions that they take, the cost of capital on this initial margin is a part of the cost of liquidity services that they face.

Margin payments are hence a trade off between the cost of capital of the funds which are blocked as initial margin versus the costs implied in the risk of bankruptcy.

From a policy perspective, the initial margin charged by a clearing corporation should be the *minimum* level at which adequate safety can be obtained. Mistakes in either direction are common—margin levels are either too low, which makes the clearing corporation vulnerable, or too high, which imposes excessive transactions costs upon users.

Back Office Costs

When users are forced to put labour and capital into their back office tracking, this is a cost associated with trading on the market. Back office costs are particularly high in India's fixed income market through the lack of netting and a clearing corporation.

An important innovation at the NSE's clearing corporation (the NSCC) is 'nationwide clearing', whereby funds and securities are partly handled at regional clearing centres (in four major cities). This greatly helps reduce the costs faced by the numerous NSE members who are outside Bombay.

On the equity market, the introduction of the depository is the final solution to the back office problem.

Resolving Bad Certificates

When markets suffer from stolen or fake certificates, this generates costs for the user.

The introduction of the depository is the final solution to the bad paper problem on India's equity market. The probability of getting bad paper drops to zero for trades that take place with the depository.

Delays in Payments

When users are forced to pay in funds early, and receive funds late, they lose the time value of money. These delays derive from India's slow payments system, and from administrative inefficiencies which exacerbate the time elapsed between funds pay-in and securities pay-out, and the time elapsed between securities pay-in and funds pay-out.

Transaction Taxes

Transactions taxes serve to reduce market liquidity (i.e. raise transactions costs). There are three forms of transactions taxes in India today: stamp duty, service tax on brokerage, and the SEBI transaction fee. The stamp duty has been abolished for trades settled through the depository. Stamp duty is particularly onerous on the real estate market.

The flat transactions tax of Rs 1000 per contract note in the fixed income market ensures that a large mass of small users cannot develop.

2.4 WHAT MARKET QUALITY IS NOT

This discussion, which defines market quality as a state of low transactions costs, immediately suggests the difficulties with some alternative measures of market quality which have been commonly used in India:

1. Trading Volume: Trading volume is often correlated with transactions costs (when transacting is cheap, economic agents tend to trade more). However, trading volume does not directly measure asset liquidity.
2. Delivery Ratios or Delivery Volume: Debates about capital markets in India have often focused upon delivery ratios or delivery volume. Delivery ratios have little to do with transactions costs and hence should not be viewed as a measure of market quality.[10]

---

[10]Modern market microstructure theory suggests that market impact cost is reduced when a large supply of informationless orders comes to the market (Glosten and Milgrom, 1985). Hence a profusion of delivery-based transactions, which are generally non-speculative, would help diminish impact cost and thus make markets more liquid. However, this perspective does not support the notion that high delivery ratios are an end in their own right.

Delivery ratios in India have reflected the asymmetry between transactions costs faced within the settlement period—which dropped sharply once the NSE and NSCC came about—and the high transactions costs faced in making delivery. These high costs derived from the paperwork and risk associated with physical certificates, and the absence of modern facilities for borrowed funds or shares.

Trading strategies would hence be expected to evolve towards minimizing deliveries, thus generating low delivery ratios. This is not a direct indication of a malfunctioning market; it should instead be viewed as a *symptom* of the asymmetry between the low costs in trading as compared with the high costs of making delivery.

In markets outside India, low delivery ratios are often found. Writing in 1995, Perold (1995) shows delivery ratios of 30 per cent (in Paris using monthly settlement) and 25 per cent (in the US using T + 5 settlement). These figures do not greatly differ from the 18 per cent delivery ratio seen on the NSE, a figure which is likely to increase once all settlement goes through the depository and borrowed funds/securities become available.

3. SECONDARY MARKET FOR EQUITY

India's secondary market for equity has seen revolutionary changes over the period from November 1994 (the launch of equity trading at the NSE) to November 1996 (the launch of the NSDL). The major events of this period[11] may be summarized as follows:

- The introduction of the open electronic limit order book market by the NSE (November 1994) and other exchanges (from middle 1995 onwards).
- The emergence of a single nationwide market through the spread of NSE VSATs to 150 cities.
- A sharp fall in brokerage fees, and improved brokerage services, through the entry of NSE members, and foreign direct investment into the brokerage industry.
- The elimination of counterparty risk through novation at the clearing corporation, which commenced at the NSCC in April 1996. The NSCC is a major break with tradition on India's equity

[11]See Shah and Thomas 1997 for details about these changes.

market in the strict enforcement of margins and exposure limits.
  Other attempts at reducing counterparty risk include the elimination of long-present blemishes like *badla* and *kapli*, and 'trade
guarantee funds' which several exchanges have now introduced.
- The launch of the depository, in November 1996.

These developments have had a sharp impact upon transactions costs.
One attempt at *quantifying* transactions costs is shown in Table 7.3.
Here, we see a sharp reduction in transactions costs in trading and
clearing as of 1996 as compared with 1993. Costs at settlement have
actually worsened, owing to a spread of skills in counterfeiting share
certificates over this period.

TABLE 7.3
TRANSACTIONS COSTS ON INDIA'S EQUITY MARKET

(in per cent)

Component	India			New York Today
	Mid-1993	Today	Future	
Trading	3.75	0.75	0.40	1.23
Brokerage	3.00	0.50	0.25	1.00
Market impact cost	0.75	0.25	0.15	0.23
Clearing				
Counterparty risk	Present	In part	0.00	0.00
Settlement	1.25	1.75	0.10	0.05
Paperwork cost	0.75	0.75	0.10	0.05
Bad paper risk	0.50	1.00	0.00	0.00
Total	5.00 (+ risk)	2.50	0.50	1.28

Note: This table attempts to quantify transactions costs faced by retail investors (i.e.
    with small delivery-oriented transactions).

Source: Shah and Thomas (1997).

While these changes are a significant accomplishment, India's equity
market continues to experience serious problems. The important questions which India's equity market now faces are:

- Cash Market Organization: How will the cash market evolve
  into a true spot market? How will weekly settlement give way to
  rolling settlement? How will equity derivatives come about? How
  will the SEBI establish minimum safety standards for margins

which eliminate competition between exchanges to dilute margin requirements? How should price discovery and liquidity of the institutional and retail markets be better integrated?

- Settlement: How will the equity market evolve towards a state where all settlement is done through the depository?

We will address these questions in Section 3.2. However, before we can analyse these problems, it is useful to review some ideas and jargon. This is taken up in the next section.

3.1 BACKGROUND

In this section, we deal with some ideas and introduce jargon which serves as a valuable backdrop for Section 3.2 which directly addresses the policy issues of the secondary market.[12] In turn, we will take up:

1. defining a spot market;
2. futures style settlement and the difficulties therein;
3. *badla*;
4. safety in clearing;
5. rolling settlement;
6. margin trading; and
7. the network externality aspect of market liquidity.

Defining a Spot Market

A true spot market is one where the buyer and seller exchange goods for money 'on the spot', the moment the trade is matched. A forward market is one where the buyer and seller agree on a price and quantity, but agree to exchange goods for money at a stated future date.

Futures Style Settlement

India's cash market for equity uses 'futures style settlement' where trading takes place with netting through the settlement period. At the end of the settlement period (i.e. on the expiration date), open positions turn into delivery and payment.

Futures style settlement on the cash market is uncommon by world standards, but it is not unique to India. Trading on the Paris bourse mainly takes place through a thirty-day settlement period. Similar practices once existed in the UK (fortnightly settlement) and Italy (monthly settlement).

---

[12]Other background material may be found at http://www.igdr.ac.in/~ajayshah.

On the NSE, a weekly cycle is used, from Wednesday to Tuesday. On the BSE, the weekly cycle from Monday to Friday.

Trading under futures style settlement resembles the functioning of a futures markets. A person who goes to an NSE terminal on Wednesday to buy shares will make the payment fourteen days hence and get the shares fifteen days hence. If, prior to closing time on Tuesday, he sells off his position, then he will have no purchase obligation. The transactions are hence forward transactions rather than spot market transactions.

Problems of Futures Style Settlement

As in all forward markets, the secondary market price under futures style settlement equals the 'spot price' (which is unobserved in this case) plus the cost of carry (Solnik, 1990). Hence the price should drop every day by the cost of carry. Prices on the NSE are at their lowest on Tuesday, where payment is only seven days away, and jump up on Wednesday morning to reflect the fact that payment is fourteen days away.[13] These price fluctuations do not reflect the valuation of firms and hence detract from market efficiency. However, if interest rates are publicly known, it should not be difficult for economic agents to infer a 'true spot price' by observing the market price and number of days till payment.

In the words of Perold (1995), futures style settlement

creates a blurring of transactions in physical securities and transactions in forward contracts. Lagged settlement is economically nothing other than a simple forward contract. It is priced in the same manner as a forward contract, it has the same type of credit risk, and investors use it the same way they use forward contracts to obtain netting over time—that is to obtain short-run exposure to fluctuations in the market price of a physical instrument without having to deliver or take delivery of the actual instrument.

The credit risk that goes along with forward contracting has long afflicted India's cash market for equity. If no margins are charged within a settlement period, then a person who buys on the first day of the settlement and sells on the last day of the settlement obtains infinite *leverage*.[14] If no upfront margin is charged, then a person who buys shares in the morning and sells them in the evening has effectively

---

[13] The NSE-50 index rises by 0.83 per cent from Tuesday close to Wednesday close, on average.

[14] Basu and Dalal (1993, p. 32) describe an episode in 1991, where DB Finance (an infant finance company floated by Deutsche Bank and Brooke Bond), a firm formed with equity capital of Rs 10 million had a long position of Rs 10 billion.

accessed infinite leverage. In this sense India's 'cash market' is a unique market by world standards in offering leveraged trading on individual securities. This generates credit risk, as is attested by the long history of payments crises on India's stock exchanges, where the functioning of the market was disrupted by bankruptcies.

This leverage can also assist market manipulation. A small amount of capital could adopt large positions on the market, to potentially serve manipulative objectives, using this leverage.

Badla

The concept of *badla* went along with futures style settlement in European markets (e.g. Williams and Barone, 1991) analyse *badla* on the Milan stock exchange, which is called *riporti*). The operation of *badla* is illustrated by the following example:

1. On the expiration date of futures style settlement, there are long positions of 1000 shares which do not want to take delivery, and short positions of 1200 shares which do not want to make delivery.
2. We focus on the imbalance, i.e. there are an excess of 200 shares of a short position.
3. The *badla* financier steps in to lend 200 shares, at a rental fee.
4. The remainder of the long and short positions (1000 shares long and 1000 shares short) are netted against each other. This is in sharp contrast with other mechanisms for securities lending or moneylending where no such netting takes place.
5. The positions of +1000 and −1200 shares are automatically re-opened at the start of the next settlement period.

The problems of futures style settlement are particularly applicable with *badla*. In addition, once *badla* is present, it becomes harder to infer the 'true spot price' by observing market prices, because no clear expiration date is associated with the trading on the cash market.[15]

Badla is also an unusual form of securities lending (or moneylending)

[15]Some observers have suggested that *badla* is like a futures contract without an expiration date, and it should hence be viewed like a futures market. There is a well-known result in economics, which suggests that markets with *undated* futures, i.e. futures markets without an expiration date, are vulnerable to speculative bubbles (Neuberger, 1995).

In any case, price discovery on the spot market is not improved by merging it with a futures market. Hence even if the risk of speculative bubbles was not an issue, the market mechanism of *badla* has weaknesses.

in that borrowers do not always pay a rental fee. At every *badla* session, we have one of two outcomes: either the borrowers of funds are charged a negative rental fee, or the borrowers of securities are charged a negative rental fee.

Safety in Clearing

The credit risk inherent in futures style settlement is best addressed by the institutions of the futures market: novation at the clearing corporation, daily mark to market (MTM) margin, and initial margin. These concepts were functional in India at the National Securities Clearing Corporation (NSCC) from April 1996 onwards.

The strength of a clearing corporation depends upon (a) the initial margin and (b) the daily MTM margin. The initial margin needs to be large as compared with the potential one-day movement in prices. Both kinds of margins need to be rigorously enforced.

If the payments system is slow (see Section 6.3), and it takes n days for the MTM margin to be paid to the clearinghouse, then the initial margin needs to be $\sqrt{n}$ times larger, to pay for the multi-day risk which the clearing entity is exposed to.

One of the unsatisfactory aspects of India's equity market, as of today, is the phenomenon of exchanges competing in lowering margin requirements in an attempt to attract trading volumes of traders who desire high leverage. There is a role for regulation here, by way of establishing minimum standards of safety, to eliminate the incentives for exchanges to gain market share by reducing safety.

Rolling Settlement

Rolling settlement is an alternative which avoids the problems of futures style settlement. The functioning of a market with rolling settlement is illustrated by Table 7.4. The netting of trades which takes place over an entire week in India today would be replaced by netting within the trading day. With $T + 5$ settlement, open positions at the end of each day of trading would turn into delivery and payment within five working days.

A cash market with rolling settlement is closer to the ideal spot market as compared with a cash market which uses futures style settlement. Rolling settlement eliminates the fluctuations of prices which take place around settlement dates. In a world without novation at the clearing corporation, rolling settlement is safer than futures style settlement. If strong clearing corporations exist, rolling settlement would reduce the working capital requirements of brokerage firms.

In 1993, the 'Group of Thirty' put out guidelines which suggested that all markets move to T + 3 rolling settlement. This was an impetus for the NYSE to move from T + 5 to T + 3 rolling settlement. Futures style settlement, and *badla*, have been eliminated in the UK, which now uses rolling settlement. France and India are now the last major stock markets of the world which have not yet switched to rolling settlement.[16]

TABLE 7.4

FUTURES STYLE SETTLEMENT VERSUS ROLLING SETTLEMENT

Date	Weekly Settlement	T + 5 Rolling Settlement
1	Buy 200 shares	Buy 200 shares
2	Sell 100 shares	Sell 100 shares
6		Pay for 200 shares and get the shares
7		Deliver 100 shares and get paid for them
14	Pay the net price for 100 shares	
15	Get 100 shares	

Note: The functioning of a market with rolling settlement is contrasted with that of a market with futures style settlement, by enumerating the actions which derive from buying 200 shares on the first day of the settlement period and selling off 100 shares one day later. In both cases, the details are based on practices at the NSE. In the case of futures style settlement at the NSE, the settlement period runs from day 1 to 5. On the BSE, trading takes place from days 1 to 5. Sellers bring in the securities on day 11 and 12. Funds are brought in on day 12. Funds and securities are paid out three days later, on day 15.

Rolling settlement in India is often considered an impractical idea, partly owing to the unsuccessful experience of Over the Trading Counter Exchange of India (OTCEI), which used rolling settlement. There were many *other* elements of the market mechanisms adopted at the OTCEI which were responsible for its poor success; it is not correct to indict rolling settlement.[17]

---

[16]Rolling settlement and futures style settlement coexist on the Paris Stock Exchange as of today. However, the bulk of the trading takes place using monthly settlement.

[17]One of the basic features which is essential for rolling settlement to work is 'margin trading' facilities (Section 3.1) for borrowing funds or shares. The OTCEI attempted to introduce rolling settlement without having margin trading in place. Similarly, the OTCEI attempted the creation of a trading facility for the smallest

The difficulty in introducing rolling settlement into India lies in the widespread use of the cash market, with futures style settlement, for leveraged speculative trading. The network externality character of market liquidity (Section 3.1) will make it difficult for liquidity to get established in any new trading system, especially one which does not support leveraged trading.

In a $T + x$ rolling settlement market, the use of a small x requires a strong banking system and a depository. Hence most markets do not directly start with $T + 3$ settlement; rolling settlement typically starts off with $T + 5$ or even longer delays. The NSE today uses $T + 5$ in the rolling settlement that is available with electronic settlement.

Margin Trading:

Access to borrowed shares and funds can be safely got using the institution of 'margin trading' which is present in the US. With margin trading, a buy position who does not want to put up the full funds goes through the following steps:

1. The buyer puts up 40 per cent of the funds.
2. The moneylender brings in 60 per cent.
3. Shares are purchased, and immediately pledged to the lender through the depository.[18]
4. 'Mark to market' is done regularly to collect all losses made on the position, and to ensure that the funds put up by the buyer do not drop below 40 per cent.

Margin trading is a relationship between a financier (e.g. a bank) and the customer.[19] A beautiful feature of margin trading is that the cash market remains a cash market—all open positions turn into delivery and payment. Margin trading is different from *badla* in the absence of netting *at the clearinghouse* between long and short positions. All longs who

---

stocks of the country, and (naturally) obtained low trading volumes. That does not accurately convey the liquidity which could be obtained if the largest stocks of the country were trading using rolling settlement.

[18]Market participants in India are often used to securities lending or moneylending based on physical certificates. This is a procedure which is fraught with danger owing to the apparent ease with which share certificates are forged in India. Margin trading in India would only function safely through the depository.

[19]The clearing corporation can perform its credit enhancement function here also, in order to reduce the risks faced by the bank.

are unable to take delivery borrow funds, and all shorts who lack securities borrow securities. As far as the clearing corporation is concerned, every open position turns into delivery and payment. Through margin trading, leveraged positions become available without generating credit risk for the lender, though they involve a lot less leverage than is presently observed with *badla*.

The Network Externality Aspect of Market Liquidity

A market derives liquidity (low impact cost) by virtue of the order flow that it has. A new market starts out with no orders and no liquidity; this can be a vicious cycle where illiquidity deters order placement, which perpetuates illiquidity.

This network externality problem inhibits institutional evolution. Indeed, this network externality is a major justification for a role for government in influencing the development of markets. Every new market mechanism, no matter how attractive, finds it difficult to displace the entrenched form of market organization. Individual economic agents might understand that a new market mechanism offers reduced transactions costs, but they would be deterred by the high *market impact cost* which is involved in participating in a market which lacks other users.

The clearest example of this in India is seen at the NSE in the contrast between the liquidity of trading for physical delivery (EQ) and illiquidity of trading for settlement at the depository (BE). For users of the NSE who do intra-day or intra-settlement trading, EQ trading is no different from BE trading. Yet as long as most orders go to the EQ limit order book, the BE market will be illiquid, a vicious cycle which perpetuates itself.

The NSE's success, in 1995, in displacing the BSE as the leading market of the country is unique by world standards. In most countries, once liquidity is established in one kind of market, the second market fails to attract away the liquidity. The NSE's success has to be explained by the drastic fall in transactions costs *other* than market impact cost as compared with the BSE—denial of access, transparency of liquidity, elimination of *gala*, elimination of delays in payment, etc.—which was able to attract away a minimal critical mass of users in the early days of the market.

3.2 POLICY ISSUES IN INDIA'S CASH MARKET

Using this backdrop, we can now approach the specific questions which policy makers face in the context of the cash market.[20]

How Should the Cash Market be Organized?

The cash market would function best if it used the following practices:

1. trading through the open electronic limit order book,
2. novation at the clearing corporation,
3. rolling settlement, coupled with margin trading,
4. all settlement through the depository.

The exclusive use of the depository would generate a sharp drop in the transactions costs in settlement seen in Table 7.3. The institution of the clearing corporation which does novation would eliminate counter-party risk. The use of rolling settlement, coupled with margin trading, would remove pricing discrepancies on the market that derive from the use of futures style settlement.

The first objective listed here has already been fully met. Novation at the clearing corporation is taking place on the largest market (NSE) though not at other exchanges. Margin trading and rolling settlement do not exist; instead we have a mixture of futures style settlement and *badla*. The depository exists, but most settlement still takes place using physical certificates.

One consequence of all exchanges in India using rolling settlement would be the elimination of the 'cycling of positions' which is currently taking place through multiple exchanges with different settlement schedules.

Can Exchanges Drive the Transition into Rolling Settlement?

In India today, speculators look to the cash market to provide facilities for leveraged trading. Any exchange which makes the transition to rolling settlement and margin trading, which offer reduced leverage, runs the risk of losing volumes as a consequence.

If an exchange tries to run rolling settlement and futures style settlement in parallel, it would come up against the network externality problem of market liquidity (Section 3.1).

In this situation, the presence of multiple exchanges competing for

[20]Related issues are addressed in Shah 1998a and http://www.igidr.ac.in/~ajay-shah.

speculative order flow implies that any one exchange cannot reform the cash market in isolation.

What is a Strategy for Reaching a T+3 Cash Market?

The steps through which India's cash market can make the transition to T + 3 rolling settlement might be outlined as follows:

1. Introduction of margin trading, with the cooperation of the Reserve Bank (and hence the banking system), clearing entities (which must perform novation), and the depository (which will make stocklending facilities available to all its customers, and will support margin trading through pledging facilities).

2. Introduction of equity derivatives, which might be an alternative outlet for individuals in the economy who have skills in leveraged trading. This would help diminish the political opposition that would otherwise be encountered in reducing the leverage that is available in cash market trading. Equity derivatives would also help augment the liquidity of the cash market.

3. On one date, conversion of all exchanges in the country into T+5 markets for a designated set of stocks (where electronic settlement is commonplace). This set of stocks could grow to gradually cover all stocks in the country; however, 95 per cent of trading volume is concentrated in the most liquid fifty stocks of the country, so it is easy to obtain dramatic progress in the transition to rolling settlement.

From this perspective, the efforts which have been under way since 1996 to weaken the restrictions upon *badla* and make it an important part of the securities industry are steps in the wrong direction. If migration of the cash market into a true spot market with rolling settlement is the objective, a reversion towards *badla* marks a step in the opposite direction.

What is the Role for Equity Derivatives in Improving the Cash Market?

Equity index derivatives are important in their own right, in so far as they offer hedging mechanisms to all equity portfolios in the country. From the viewpoint of the market microstructure of the cash market, equity derivatives have three implications:

1. Derivatives trading will offer employment for those individuals

in the economy who possess human capital for leveraged speculation, and thus reduce the political opposition faced by reforms
on the cash market.

2. The index futures market will diminish market impact cost on
the cash market, by reducing the risks faced by traders who temporarily hold inventories of shares as part of their cash market
trading.

3. The activities of index arbitrageurs will generate a strong order
flow on the cash market, thus enhancing the liquidity of the cash
market.

In these ways, the creation of equity index derivatives fits into the
objective of reducing transactions costs on the cash market.

If Badla must Exist in the Short Run, How should It Function?

The dangers that we face with a resumption of traditional *badla* are
enhanced levels of systemic risk and market manipulation. The payments crisis of early 1998 vividly illustrated the inadequate risk containment systems of the BSE. If *badla* must exist, the protection of systemic
integrity requires four principles:

1. Novation should take place at the clearing house. The clearing
house must become legal counterparty to both legs of every
trade, and to the financier, thus eliminating the risk of default on
the part of the borrower.

2. Initial margin should be charged upfront, with exposure limits
operating in realtime, and the daily mark to market margin
should be strictly enforced. The initial margin should be large
enough to pay for the (large) movements that prices of individual
stocks can experience over the time that is required for effecting
the mark to market margin payments. The calculations in Table
7.8 illustrate the insecurities of the present approach towards
margins.

3. Price and position limits should be used to contain market manipulation. The open interest of the market should be capped at
a conservative estimate of the floating stock, and no individual
member should be allowed to have above 5 per cent of the open
interest.

4. *Badla* trading should only be allowed to take place for the fifty
most liquid stocks of the country.

*How can Exchanges be Prevented from Competing by
Reducing Margin Requirements?*

One of the problems faced by regulators in the competition between
stock exchanges in India is the effort by exchanges to dilute margin
requirements (either in precept or in practice) in the hope of attracting
increased volumes. Conversely, exchanges with weak margin requirements face a loss of volume when margin requirements are made
stronger. This sort of competition was essential in enabling the payments
crisis of early 1998.

What policy changes can help diminish this problem?

1. The minimum standard should be a clearing corporation performing novation: The use of clearing corporations performing
novation would yield entities which have objectives that are
somewhat closer to those of regulators. If the clearing corporation becomes the legal counterparty' to both legs of every trade,
this generates pressures upon the clearing corporation to improve
the risk containment procedures so as to reduce the probability
of bankruptcy.

2. There should be fewer clearing corporations than exchanges:
If clearing corporations arise which clear trades on multiple markets (e.g. the NSCC, which clears for the NSE and OTCEI), then
the dangers of diluting margin requirements are diminished. If an
exchange lacks a clearing corporation controlled by it, then competing for volumes by diluting margin requirements is not feasible. NSCC employees have few incentives to endanger the
NSCC in order to foster volumes at the OTCEI. There need only
be a few clearing corporations in the country, even though there
are twenty-four stock exchanges. Such a strategy will assist the
skills development at clearing corporations, which is probably
the slowest part of the development of India's markets.

3. Information disclosure: Every clearing corporation should disclose, on a daily basis, the basic facts about its position: the open
interest of the entire market and of the top five members, and the
funds in hand.

4. Annual 'stress testing' of clearing corporation: Once clearing
corporations exist, modern methods of risk measurement and
risk containment are the essence of their survival (Gemmill,
1994; Longin, 1996; Jorion, 1997; Shah, 1998c; Thomas,
1998b). Regulators can help this process along by requiring that

each clearing corporation have an external agency conduct a 'stress testing' of the clearing corporation every year. The report of this stress testing should be made public, and should generate a dialogue between the regulator and the clearing corporation about remedying the deficiencies.[21]

5. Skills development at the Securities and Exchange Board of India (SEBI): Finally, a strong effort towards skills development at SEBI is vital for meaningful regulation. When facing problems like understanding the risks of *badla*, or comprehending the widely different margin requirements between the BSE and NSE, regulators need to have clarity on fairly technical questions, i.e. how portfolio risk is measured, and how strength in clearing is obtained.

How should the Institutional 'Phone Market' Function?

One of the weaknesses of India's equity market is the complete delinking of the 'upstairs' market, where institutions directly negotiate trades with each other, and the main trading screen where the bulk of trading takes place.

There is a simple procedure through which the two markets can be integrated; this requires every negotiated trade to be 'put through the screen' to the extent of matching all limit orders which are compatible with the price of the limit order. If a pair of institutions agree to do a trade for Rs 1 billion at Rs 200, then the buyer should first put a buy limit order on the screen for Rs 1 billion, and the seller should then put a sell limit order on the screen at Rs 200.[22] This ensures that if there are any buyers or sellers on the trading screen who are willing to transact

---

[21]In the US, the Commodity Futures Trading Commission (CFTC) has conducted such stress-testing exercises and used the results to initiate dialogue with clearing corporations about how procedures should be modified to increase the integrity of the clearing corporation. In India, the three disaster scenarios which should be explored in a stress-testing exercise are: (a) a change in Nifty of 10 per cent in one day (a 7σ event); (b) simultaneous failure of the five largest members; and (c) failure of the UTI. A clearing corporation which survives these three shocks well should be considered strong enough.

[22]A similar procedure is presently used at the NYSE. Prior to the depository, such requirements could not be implemented because institutions were unwilling to buy physical securities from the retail market, believing that institutional sellers were more likely to be free of fake paper. This procedure can be readily implemented in trading for electronic settlement.

at a price *better* than Rs 200, their orders receive precedence over the opposite institution.

The principle here is not unlike that used in the takeover code, where small shareholders get an opportunity to participate in the price which is negotiated behind closed doors. This procedure also produces superior price discovery by integrating the order flow of the screen with the institutional market. This will serve to improve the liquidity and price discovery for both retail and institutional users of markets.

3.3 ADOPTION OF THE DEPOSITORY

The *Emerging Markets Factbook* produced by the IFC gives evidence about settlement procedures in emerging markets. Their evidence about India is summarized in Table 7.5. These data suggest that settlement procedures in India have improved in 1995 and 1996 as compared with 1994, but India remains close to the lowest ranked emerging market. In a world which is rapidly converging towards T+3 settlement through a depository, the Indian market continues to lag behind the minimum standards used internationally.

TABLE 7.5
SETTLEMENT IN INDIA, COMPARED WITH OTHER EMERGING MARKETS

	India's score	Median Score	India's Rank
1994	71.8	91.9	11/11
1995	75.0	90.6	12/14
1996	76.6	90.7	14/15

Note: Global Securities Consulting Services (GSCS) Safekeeping Benchmark, derived from the IFC's *Emerging Markets Factbook*, 1996 and 1997 editions. This tries to measure the cost to market participants of failed trades, and is based on data for (a) average trade size, (b) local market interest rates, (c) the proportion of trades that fail, and (d) the length of time for which they fail. The scores range from 0 to 100. The highest score among emerging markets for 1996 was Portugal, at 94.4.

The median is calculated with respect to the emerging markets for which data was available; e.g. in 1994, the median is the score obtained by the sixth ranking country.

Viewed from a purely Indian perspective, the evidence presented earlier in Table 7.3 suggests that transactions costs *at the trade* have come down sharply in India as compared with the status as of 1993. However, the costs faced in settlement have actually worsened. These costs are a major impediment for households to route their investments through the equity market. As observed in Section 2.4, the criticism about low delivery ratios in India is partly a reflection of the asymmetry between some of the lowest transactions costs in the world when it comes to trading, coupled with some of the highest transactions costs in the world when it comes to settlement.

The depository was inaugurated in November 1996. It has made significant progress: it has established systems,[23] signed agreements with 250 firms, obtained 50,000 investor accounts, and dematerialized Rs 40,000 crore of paper.[24] However, the bulk of the trading volume continues to take place on the NSE's EQ market, for physical settlment.

This is the example cited in Section 3.1 earlier, where the order flow coming into the EQ market is hard to dislodge owing to network externality. Use of the depository is in the best interest of everyone, provided everyone uses the depository and thus provides liquidity to depository-based trading.

There are three policy initiatives which can accelerate the adoption of the depository:

1. The NSE can phase out EQ trading on stocks, thus forcing its order flow to go to the BE market. In doing this, the NSE risks losing market share if users of the market prefer to continue with physical certificates and take their order flow to alternative exchanges.

2. SEBI can use a variety of policy instruments aimed at phasing out the use of physical certificates. Specific alternatives amongst these are accelerating the introduction of margin trading (Section 3.1), requiring institutional users to only settle through the depository, and putting an end to any new physical certificates being created through public issues.

3. The banking system (including the development financial institutions) can phase out the use of physical certificates which are pledged with them, in favour of pledging through the depository.

---

[23]One of the biggest constraints faced in making depository services available at myriad locations all over the country is DOT's 'Closed User Group' policy, which is discussed in Section 6.5.

[24]Two major capabilities which have yet to appear at the NSDL are: (a) routing of dividend payments from firms to bank accounts of investors, and (b) interfacing with clearing corporations for margin trading.

The existing certificates which have been pledged should all be dematerialized on a cutoff date, and no new physical certificates should be accepted as collateral. This is in the interests of the banking system, in so far as it avoids the risk of the pledged certificates being fake.

A remarkable consequence of the network externality aspect of market liquidity is that *gradual change is likely to be more painful than complete change.* If most of the market uses physical settlement, and if policy makers try to force 10 per cent of the users to work through the depository, it will inflict costs upon the pioneers, generate strong political opposition, and reduce the possibility that policy makers will try to push the next 10 per cent of users into settlement through the depository. Hence there is a case for coordinated action between the SEBI, the RBI, and the NSE designed to decisively create a critical mass of users on the BE market, after which a virtuous cycle will take over to increase order flow and generate a complete phase out of physical certificates in the country.

4. DERIVATIVES

The enhanced price volatility in the liberalized economic environment, coupled with the manifest advantages of markets where risk could be transferred among economic agents in the economy, has inspired many independant initiatives aiming to create derivatives markets in the country. In the equity, foreign exchange, fixed income, and commodity markets, various stages of progress have been made towards the creation of markets for derivatives instruments, such as futures and options.

One fundamental objective of the financial system is to enable welfare improvement through the reallocation of risk. Derivatives markets are a highly effective way through which this risk transfer can be achieved.

In Section 4.1 we describe the role of derivatives in the modern economy. One of the major debates which perenially rages in the worldwide derivatives industry concerns the benefits of derivatives which trade on exchanges versus privately negotiated (OTC) derivatives. An Indian perspective on this debate is in Section 4.2. The building blocks required to build a derivatives exchange are outlined in Section 4.3. This leads us to Section 4.4, which directly addresses some major policy issues about derivatives markets in India.

4.1 The Role for Derivatives

Risk owing to price volatility is pervasive in the modern market economy. Drawing upon Mason (1995), we can employ a functional classification of the three major 'technologies' which the financial system offers for the reduction of risk:

1. *Diversification* reduces risk through combining less than perfectly correlated assets.
2. *Insurance* refers to securities or contracts which limit risk in exchange for the payment of a premium.
3. *Hedging* refers to offsetting a risk exposure using a financial transaction.

Financial derivatives, such as futures and options, can be used for hedging and insurance, and hence help economic agents obtain better control over the risks that they encounter.

4.2 Exchange Traded versus OTC Derivatives

There are two basic approaches through which derivatives can function: exchange-traded or over the counter (OTC) derivatives (Houthakker and Williamson, 1996; Culp, 1995).

OTC derivatives function in an institutional vacuum; any two agents in the economy could enter into derivative contracts with each other. The contracts which can be entered into, the prices agreed upon, and the consequent credit risk are negotiated between the two parties involved in the trade. India's dollar–rupee forward market is an OTC derivative market, operating without the institutions of an exchange and a clearing corporation. In contrast, exchange-traded derivatives operate in a rich institutional environment. The differences between OTC and exchange-traded derivatives are summarized in Table 7.6. These issues are relevant not only in the policy issues concerning derivatives, but also for thinking about the *spot market* in fixed income and currencies (see Table 7.2).

The comparison between exchange-traded and OTC derivatives is a perenially debated topic in the worldwide derivatives industry. Market intermediaries have a strong preference for selling OTC derivatives owing to the tight margins that accompany the 'commoditization' of standardized, exchange-traded products. In contrast, the OTC derivatives markets typically deal with custom-configured contracts, where competition is much diminished. This supports higher profit rates. On the other hand, the liquidity and transparency obtained in exchange-traded derivatives is unique, through the combination of centralized trading, with anonymity, on a few standardized contracts, without intervening credit risk.

TABLE 7.6
EXCHANGE-TRADED VERSUS OTC DERIVATIVES

Exchange-traded	OTC	Consequences
Trading		
Centralized at exchange.	Distributed over economy.	Exchange traded derivatives obtains greater liquidity through centralization of order flow.
Contracts Traded		
A few defined, standardized contracts.	Anything that the buyer and seller agree upon.	Exchange traded derivatives obtains greater liquidity through trading a *few* standardized objects, while liquidity in OTC derivatives gets fragmented. OTC derivatives are better at coping with heterogenous needs of customers.
Credit Risk		
Absent, through novation at clearing corporation.	Present. Clear capital adequacy norms do not exist in the OTC derivatives industry.	The credit risk in OTC derivatives can get amplified into 'systemic risk' if several large dealers fail (GAO, 1994).
Entry Barriers into Trading		
None.	Credit risk generates entry barriers; large OTC dealers would require a risk premium to deal with weaker entities thus further destandardizing the market.	Exchange-traded derivatives generate greater participation and hence liquidity.
Transparency		
Full transparency of liquidity and prices. No possibility of trades at off-market prices owing to price–time priority at the exchange.	Non-transparent.	Exchange-traded derivatives are more transparent, and reveal useful prices to the economy.

Exchange-traded	OTC	Consequences
Intermediation Costs		
Low, owing to 'commoditization' i.e. severe competition through standardization of contracts and low entry barriers into brokerage	High, owing to 'customized' contracts, with entry barriers.	Exchange-traded derivatives are less profitable for intermediaries.
Potential for Ethics Lapses		
Minimal, through anonymity at trading, and standardized procedures of clearing corporation.	Greater risk through trading between dealers who know each other.	OTC derivatives require strong regulatory supervision *at each dealer*. Exchange-traded derivatives require strong regulatory supervision at *exchanges and clearing corporations*.

Note: This table summarizes the differences between exchange-traded and OTC derivatives, and the implications of these differences.

As is the case in the apparent competition between banks and markets, there are significant synergies between exchange-traded and OTC derivatives:

1. Dealers who sell products on the OTC derivatives markets would typically turn around and hedge away their exposure using exchange-traded derivatives. In this fashion, the OTC derivatives dealers benefit from liquid exchange-traded derivatives.

2. When users want risk management services which are not directly met using the (limited) range of standardized products which are traded on a derivatives exchange, OTC dealers can add value by customizing products specially for them. Standard examples of this are users who desire expiration dates which are different from the expiration dates used on the exchange, or the synthetic creation of options using dynamic hedging on a futures market. These services could alternatively be performed by financial consultants directing users in their use of exchange-traded derivatives.

In an Indian perspective, the appealing features of exchange-traded derivatives are transparency, anonymity, and the elimination of credit risk. OTC derivatives transactions take place behind closed doors, exchange-traded derivatives yield reliable quotes and prices in realtime. The OTC derivatives industry lacks anonymity; dealers can form cartels, and a variety of ethics lapses can develop, e.g. trades at off-market prices.[25] Exchange-traded derivatives avoid this by trading in complete anonymity, with strict price–time priority (i.e. every order is matched at the best price available).

Finally, India's financial system contains numerous relatively weak entities who would generate credit risk in OTC derivatives transactions. One possibility which might arise here is that of a 'club market' of a few large entities, who have homogeneous credit risk, who trade against each other, and dislike trading against entities with weak credit risk. Such a scenario would generate inferior liquidity and elevated fees for users of the market. It would effectively throw up entry barriers against the growth of myriad small financial companies in the country and fail to harness the contribution which these firms can make towards liquidity, price discovery, and the healthy commoditization of the derivatives industry.[26]

These considerations suggest that the development of India's derivatives industry should be channeled into exchange-traded derivatives wherever feasible. Existing markets which have developed in an OTC direction, like the dollar–rupee forward market, should be gradually converted into exchange-traded futures markets. OTC derivatives are the natural offshoots of these markets, to the extent that they are better customized for client needs.

[25]The abuses of the Scam of 1991 may be categorized as follows:
1. dangerous leverage,
2. transfer pricing using trades at prices different from normal market prices,
3. strategic gaming by cartels controlled by major indian and foreign banks,
4. dangerous forms of netting with absurd settlement procedures, and
5. credit risk.

Each of these abuses is more feasible on an OTC derivatives market, in the absence of high quality supervision and a credible threat of punishment. The risk of each of these abuses is much diminished using exchange-traded derivatives.

[26]The experience of the NSE on the cash market, with 1000 small brokerage firms, many of which are firms which have never been in the brokerage industry before, is a prime example of the liquidity that can be obtained by pooling the order flow from myriad entities, each of which is small by itself. The credit enhancement service of the clearing corporation is a vital enabling factor in making this pooling of order flow possible.

4.3 COMPONENTS OF A DERIVATIVES EXCHANGE

A derivatives exchange is made up of four components: the definition of a traded product, a trading mechanism, a clearing facility, and settlement procedures.

1. Product: Derivatives exchanges trade completely standardizes products. The exchange defines the traded product, and traders have no flexibility in altering the terms. An example of such a product could be a futures contract on an index, or options on a security, or options on coffee, etc. All aspects of the traded contract would need to be specified, including the expiration date, date of making delivery, and the exact specification of the grade and quantity of the goods which will be delivered.

2. Trading: A derivatives exchange needs a trading system. The modern consensus in the securities industry is that liquidity is maximized using the *open electronic limit order book* market, where trading takes place in anonymity, where individuals all across the country have equal access to the trading floor, and prices and liquidity are transparent.

3. Clearing: Trading on a derivatives exchange takes place anonymously; the buyer does not know the identity of the seller, and *vice versa*. This would only be feasible if credit risk were eliminated. This is done through novation at the clearing corporation.[27]

4. Settlement: Derivatives can involve the exchange of funds and goods. For example, the holder of an option to buy coffee might choose to exercise the option, delivering funds and taking delivery of coffee. The derivatives exchange needs to establish smooth procedures for settlement.

4.4 POLICY ISSUES IN INDIA'S DERIVATIVES INDUSTRY

Is India Ready for Equity Derivatives?

As we approach the date when trading in exchange-traded derivatives commences, many observers are apprehensive about the potential for fraud, bankruptcy, or crises in this market. Hence the question 'Are we ready for derivatives?' is often voiced.

---

[27]The essential feature of importance in this context is novation. Novation can also be done by exchange clearinghouses, though most derivatives exchanges favour the use of a distinct entity, the clearing corporation.

The main effort towards building exchange-traded derivatives in India is that of the NSE. The milestones marking the completion of building blocks of the NSE's derivatives market are summarized in Table 7.7. The NSE's developmental effort was completed in December 1996. SEBI's L.C. Gupta Committee, which was constituted to draft a policy framework for exchange-traded derivatives, is expected to submit its report in early December 1997. It should be possible for trading to commence fairly soon after this.

TABLE 7.7
STATE OF PREPARATION OF NSE'S DERIVATIVES MARKET

Objective	Date Attained
Creation of NSE-50 index	April 1996
Design of index futures product	April 1996
Trading software for index futures	May 1996
Novation at clearing corporation	June 1996
Creation of market regulations	August 1996
Admission of members	November 1996
Training of traders	November/December 1996

Note: This table summarizes the dates by which NSE could be considered as possessing the critical capabilities that are required to create a derivatives exchange.

Some observers have advocated caution in the introduction of equity derivatives on the grounds that these are 'highly leveraged instruments'. However, given the use of futures-style settlement on the spot market for equity, a greater extent of leverage is already present on India's spot market for equity. As illustrated in Table 7.8, the danger of a payments crisis on the NSE's proposed index futures market is lower than that on the spot market on either the NSE or the BSE, which are the centres of highly leveraged trading in India. It is only when India's equity market moves into T + 3 rolling settlement that we will see greater leverage on the index futures market as compared with the cash market. In addition, India's cash market for equity is fraught with risk owing to the use of physical certificates, whereby forgery and theft are common. The index futures market will be less risky in this dimension in so far as cash settlement is used.

Another source of concern is market manipulation. Index-based derivatives are intrinsically safer than trading on the cash market, since it is much harder for manipulators to distort the level of an index as compared with the difficulties presently observed with illiquid securities on the cash market.

In summary, it appears that the risks with respect to clearing and market manipulation that derive from trading in index derivatives are lower than the risks presently observed with futures style settlement on the cash market.

TABLE 7.8
SAFETY AT CLEARING: SOME COMPARISONS

Feature	Index Futures		Individual Stocks	
	CME	NSE (proposed)	NSE	BSE
Novation at clearing	Yes	Yes	Yes	No
Volatility of underlying (%)[a]	0.9	1.3	2–4	2–4
Initial margin				
Level (%)	5	10	15	10
Of which upfront (%)		10	15	5
In standard deviations[b]	5.6	7.7	3.54	2.36
Days/year when < MTM	5.4×10^{-6}	3.4×10^{-12}	0.1	4.6[c]
Portfolio margining	Yes	Yes	No	No
EFT capabilities	Yes	Yes	Yes	No
Minimum deposit by members (Rs mn)		7.5	7.5[d]	1.5

Notes: The strength of clearing on four markets is compared here: index futures on the Chicago Mercantile Exchange, trading in individual stocks on the NSE and the BSE, and the proposed equity index futures market at the NSE.

The number of days per year when initial margin proves to be smaller than the mark-to-market margin is based on an assumption of normally distributed returns. For example, if initial margin was set at 1.96 standard deviations, then it would fail to be adequate for half of the open interest on 2.5 per cent of the days, i.e. on 6.25 trading days per year. In reality, returns deviate from normality in having 'fat tails', hence the level of safety reported here is somewhat *overstated*.

[a]Standard deviation of continuously compounded daily returns.

[b]For the cash market on the NSE and the BSE, two-day risk is assumed owing to the lack of EFT. For individual stocks, a daily \o of 3 per cent is assumed. The actual failure probabilities will be higher for more volatile stocks and lower for less volatile stocks.

[c]In the absence of EFT, it is only the upfront initial margin which helps protect against member losses. Using 5 per cent upfront initial margin on the cash market, as is presently the case on the BSE, this corresponds to 1.2 standard deviations, or around 57.5 trading days per year where the initial margin is not able to cover the MTM loss.

[d]The NSE requires minimum deposits of Rs 7.5 million from corporate members and Rs 5 million from individual members on the cash market. The NSE requires minimum deposits of Rs 7.5 million, additionally, for membership of the derivatives market. These deposits generate 'exposure limits' which are applied intra-day, and members desirous of taking larger positions enhance their deposits of liquid funds with the clearing corporation.

In clearing, it is only liquid funds which enable the reliable and timely movement of funds and securities. A fuller sense of the strength of the clearing corporation would include other factors like the ability of the clearing corporation to repossess the assets of the member, personal guarantees by directors, and proceeds from the sale of exchange membership, but none of these helps the clearing corporation meet its obligations at the time a default takes place.

What are the Prospects for Derivatives in Other Areas?

One of the simplest areas where exchange-traded derivatives could come about is the dollar–rupee market. An OTC version of this market, the dollar–rupee market, already exists. In response to the problems of OTC derivatives (e.g. Table 7.6), this market has remained a small inter-bank club market. The challenge that the RBI now faces is of institutionalizing this market in the form of a dollar–rupee futures' market. This would enable participation by a much greater mass of users in India, including numerous non-bank entities.[28]

In the fixed income area, futures on treasury bills, involving delivery of treasury bills at the expiration of the futures, are a viable product design which could be used.

Futures on commodities have the potential to revolutionize India's agricultural sector. Futures markets in commodities will energize private-sector initiatives in *sourcing* commodities from rural areas, *transporting* them within the country, and *storing* them in order to transport them across time (Faruquee, Coleman, and Scott, 1997). Futures markets will also induce heightened supply and demand responses to future fluctuations in availability. The combination of improved storage and improved responsiveness of supply and demand will help produce better prices and cropping patterns in the agricultural sector. The development of futures markets in agricultural commodities complements, and enables, the phase out of the myriad state interventions in the agricultural sector.

The government has permitted the growth of commodity futures in certain small commodities, e.g. pepper, castor seed, and turmeric. The first large commodity where futures trading will soon commence is cotton (Balasundaram, 1998). A major flaw in the organization of commodity futures in India is the notion that contracts based on each commodity should trade at a distinct exchange. The volumes available in each of the small commodities where futures trading has been

[28]One hurdle which is present in the short run is that of effecting multi-currency settlement. An interim solution, which fully meets the needs of users of the market, is to commence trading on this market using purely rupee-settled contracts.

permitted do not allow for the large investments which are required to create a derivatives exchange. In the absence of such investments, the functioning of India's commodity derivatives industry will appear to be inadequate, and progress towards the really important commodities— wheat, rice, sugar, and edible oils—will not take place.

Should Distinct Derivatives Exchanges Exist for Each Product Class?

The functioning of the derivatives industry emphasizes the notion that a futures is a futures, regardless of the underlying from which it derives value. This suggests that there are enormous economies of scale in having exchanges which trade on a whole range of derivative contracts. This is consistent with the functioning of every important derivatives exchange in the world.

An extreme contrast with this was mentioned in the previous section, where separate exchanges are being built to trade futures on each commodity. This might perhaps be likened to having one stock exchange to trade shares in Reliance, another stock exchange to trade shares in State Bank, etc. If such a system were employed, none of the exchanges would be able to put in the investment, of around Rs 150 crore, which is required to build an exchange like the NSE.

This same reasoning holds across product classes also. The trading software, clearing corporation expertise, portfolio margining software, member training, surveillance procedures, and underlying computer and communications hardware are common across all futures contracts.

For example, it would be fairly easy to use the NSE's systems for trading futures and options on the NSE-50 index in order to trade futures on the dollar. It would be inefficient to attempt the creation of a new derivatives exchange to trade currency futures. An initiative to start such an exchange would also be more risky in so far as it would not be able to harness the human skills developed at the NSE and NSCC.

In conclusion, India's derivatives industry, across all product classes, should develop around a small number of derivatives exchanges. In the East Asian countries, the number of derivatives exchanges observed is quite small (Gorham, 1994). This will help harness economies of scale and focus the attention of regulation and supervision on a few clearly defined entities.

5. THE PRIMARY MARKET

The problem of resource allocation in the economy is not directly addressed by the secondary market. Secondary market trading generates liquidity and prices, which enable and guide the sale of securities on the primary market. The primary market is where firms actually obtain resources to finance investment projects.

We can classify the primary market into two parts: the Initial Public Offering (IPO) market, where firms go public for the first time, and the Seasoned Equity Offering (SEO) market. The informational asymmetry, and hence the complexity of pricing, is much greater in the IPO market, where the valuation of a new firm is not easily known. Once trading commences, subsequent issues (seasoned issues) are intrinsically simpler through the continuous valuation services of the secondary market which are freely available.

5.1 IPO UNDERPRICING

An ideal IPO market would be one which was able to accurately determine the fair value of a company going public, and place shares at this price. Such a primary market would accurately distinguish good IPOs from poor IPOs, awarding high valuations to the former and low valuations to the latter.

India's IPO market performs poorly as compared with this ideal. A great deal of media attention has focused on the frauds which have taken place through the IPO market. However, the IPO market can only be at equilibrium if the returns obtained by uninformed investors through IPOs *on average* are large enough to pay for these losses and the attendant risks. This generates a phenomenon known as IPO underpricing, where the IPO market awards lower issue proceeds as compared with the valuation of the secondary market—i.e. the average returns from buying at the IPO and selling at first listing.

IPO underpricing is a feature of every IPO market in the world, with varying degrees of severity (Ibbotson and Ritter, 1995). Economists view underpricing, on average, as a blemish of an IPO market: the ideal market would have zero underpricing. IPO underpricing *on average* is generally associated with some firms obtaining valuations above fair value coupled with most firms obtaining valuations below their fair value; these variations are pricing errors of the market. From the viewpoint of a firm, an IPO market which underprices IPOs, on average, gives them inferior proceeds at the IPO. This generates diminished incentives to go public, and inferior access to funds for expansion.

India's IPO market suffers from an extreme degree of IPOs underpricing (Shah, 1995a). Around 15 per cent of the 2056 IPO where trading commenced over the period from 1 January 1991 to 15 May

1995 obtained issue prices which were in excess of the listing price. The remaining 85 per cent of issues were underpriced. The median annualized returns on IPOs were 50 per cent.

5.2 INSTITUTIONAL DEVELOPMENT OF THE IPO MARKET

The level of IPO underpricing in the country is a product of the mechanism through which IPOs take place. Conversely, the elimination of IPO underpricing requires the development of new mechanisms in the IPO market. The IPO can be viewed as an informational problem where the firm, the merchant banker, and investors all possess important pieces of information, which each has incentive to not fully disclose. The challenge of the IPO market is to provide incentives to each to maximize the pooling of information.

The method of issue mainly prevalent in India is called the 'fixed price offering', where the firm and the merchant banker choose an offer price, and feedback from investors cannot influence the offer price. This is a poor mechanism in so far as the information elicited from investors is limited. The problems of India's IPO market are exacerbated by the fact that these fixed price offerings are offered to uninformed retail investors. The resulting market is reminiscent of George Akerlof's 'lemons model' where buyers cannot discriminate good cars from bad cars, thus forcing sellers to underprice cars. An additional peculiarity of fixed price offerings in India is the long timelags between the date of pricing, the date the issue opens, and the date on which trading commences. The possibility of price fluctuations in the intervening period, coupled with the inability of investors to trade immediately after the issue date, generates heightened risks in the IPO process.[29]

There are two directions in which India's IPO market can evolve away from fixed-price offerings: bookbuilding (Benveniste and Wilhelm 1997) and auctions (Pettway and Kaneko 1994). In both these modes of functioning, the issuer and merchant banker approach the IPO market

---

[29]It is estimated that four months elapse between the date on which the offer price is finalized and the date on which the issue opens. An average of 70 days elapses between the date the issue opens and the date of first trading. In all, there are 190 days between the date on which the price is set and the date on which trading commences. For the typical small stock, the standard deviation of returns over 190 days is over 60 per cent. Hence the risks introduced by these delays are extremely significant.

without a clearly defined price. The only investors who can participate in such a market are investors who can consume an offer document and emerge with a view on the price that they are willing to pay for the shares. In this sense, the large-scale distribution of IPOs to retail investors across the country is unlikely to play a role in the future development of India's IPO market.

5.3 BOOKBUILDING

Bookbuilding is a complex institutional mechanism through which the firm, the merchant banker, and investors interact in determining the offer price. Bookbuilding offers checks and balances through which each of the three participants has incentives to play fair in his/her information revelation. A detailed description of the bookbuilding process as it operates in the US may be found in Shah and Thomas (1997, p. 187); it differs substantially from the 'bookbuilding' efforts which have taken place in India to date. Benveniste and Wilhelm (1997) summarize a body of research which suggests that this procedure effectively elicits the required information flows, thus obtaining low IPO underpricing.

From a policy perspective, the problem with bookbuilding is the difficulty of transplanting it into India. Bookbuilding relies on a rich set of interactions between firms, merchant bankers, and investors. Some aspects of bookbuilding rely on optimal punishment of investors by merchant bankers which have the nature of a repeated game across multiple IPOs. The learning of equilibrium strategies in India's financial sector might not be achieved over a short time period. The lack of transparency at crucial steps of the bookbuilding process is an additional source of concern; in the absence of strong regulation and the threat of punishment, ethics lapses could take place.

5.4 AUCTIONS

In contrast, auctions are a highly practical alternative, which can commence functioning in India in a short time (Shah, 1995b). One possible design of an auction-based IPO market is offered in Table 7.9.

Such an IPO market appears to substantially address the problems faced in India's IPO market. The absence of an offer price enables price discovery through competition between investors, spread all over the country, at the computerized auction. The sequence of events outlined here require seven days for the entire IPO process. The delays observed in the present IPO mechanism are eliminated, as are the costs and dangers of printing and posting physical certificates.

TABLE 7.9
AN IPO MARKET BASED ON AUCTIONS: AN EXAMPLE

Date	Day	Action
0	Monday	An offer document would be released to investors. This distribution could be done over the Internet (Section 6.6) or in full-page advertisements in newspapers, thus eliminating delays in postage. The offer document would specify the number of shares being sold, but not an offer price.
4	Friday	On a market like the NSE, a uniform price auction (Feldman and Mehra, 1993) would take place where investors could bid for the shares. This auction would be computerized, redisplaying all bids and the equilibrium price each second, and allowing agents to revise their bids. This flexibility and instantaneity of updating bids is absent with tender offers implemented without computers. At the end of the day, the auction would be complete. Over the weekend, funds would be transferred (Section 6.3), and shares allocated at the depository (Section 3.3).
7	Monday	Trading would commence.

Note: IPOs can take place without a defined offer price through auctions, where a fixed number of shares are sold at a price that is determined by bids made by investors at an auction. One concrete example of how such a market could function in India is offered here. In this market, the IPO process begins with the release of an offer document on day 0 and ends with the start of trading on day 7. The computer runs a uniform price auction, i.e. an auction where all winning bids are charged the same price. In addition to placing bids at a stated price, users would be able to place 'market orders', or 'non-competitive bids' which offer to buy securities at the market equilibrium price, whatever it be.

An IPO market organized around such an auction would be likely to experience substantially smaller underpricing as compared with what is observed today. It is also practical to think that such an IPO market could be made to commence functioning in India within a matter of months.

The main argument here is not to suggest that auctions produce superior price discovery as compared with bookbuilding. The possibility that a bookbuilding process could generate even lower underpricing remains; however, it is unlikely that bookbuilding could establish itself within a short time span. Additionally, the transition from fixed price offerings to auctions is likely to sharply reduce the extent of underpricing as compared with present levels. Bookbuilding might well be a way to evolve the markets further, to further reduce underpricing, but it would yield second order gains as compared with what is readily attainable using auctions.

5.5 SEASONED EQUITY OFFERINGS

From an economic perspective, the Seasoned Equity Offerings (SEO) market must also satisfy the zero—underpricing objective. Additional notions of market quality in the SEO market relate to abnormal fluctuations of the secondary market price prior to, and after, the SEO.

There are three major mechanisms which are used in India's SEO market: rights issues, public issues, and private placements. An interesting aspect, which is related to the discussion about the IPO market above, concerns private placements as compared with the other two alternatives: rights and public issues are fixed price offerings which are fraught with delays as with IPOs, while private placements are not. The asymmetric information that is intrinsic in selling shares to uninformed investors is minimized with private placements.

Thomas and Shah (1996) offer evidence about returns on the secondary market in a window of time around the date of an SEO. Their results, which are based on 2273 SEOs over the period 1990–5, are summarized in Figure 7.1. The main pattern observed here is that the average SEO is preceded by positive stock market returns, and followed by poor stock market returns. Returns (in excess of market index returns) over the 200 days following the SEO average –11.4 per cent for rights issues, –25.4 per cent for public issues, and –5 per cent for private placements.

The unusual post-issue negative returns following rights and public issues might reflect phenomena like 'opportunistic firms' which raise capital at a time when their track record *looks* impressive to an external observer. There may also be a possibility of market manipulation playing some role in the pre-issue gains in prices. Thomas and Shah (1996) also find substantially worse post–SEO returns for companies where the secondary market for equity is less illiquid. This serves as an example of the role of market liquidity in producing superior market efficiency and improved allocative efficiency (see Section 2).

The minimal abnormal price fluctuations with private placements conform to the difficulties with fixed-price offerings to uninformed investors which have been emphasized above. Private placements do not involve a fixed price offering, and the purchaser of shares at the private

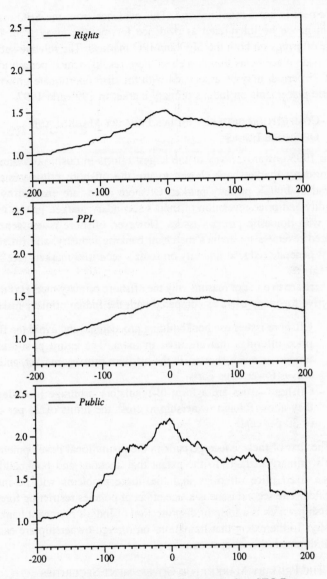

Figure 7.1   Stock Price Movements Surrounding SEO Date

Note: Average cumulative abnormal returns around SEO date in each of the three issue types, in excess of returns on the market index. The y-axis shows the market value of a portfolio valued at Re 1 initially. On average, the market traded for 230 days per year over the estimation period.

placement is not a retail investor. This evidence from the SEO market might hence be interpreted as evidence for moving away from fixed price offerings on both the SEO and IPO markets. The relative success of private placements that is seen in these results, which pertain to the 1990–5 period, may be associated with the disproportionate growth of private placements on India's primary market in 1996 and 1997.

5.6 COMPETITION BETWEEN INDIA'S PRIMARY MARKET AND OFFSHORE ISSUES

From 1993 onwards, many of the largest efforts in raising resources at the primary market have chosen to use the offshore primary market instead of India's primary market. Offshore issues are enabled by the liquidity and price revelation of India's secondary market, just as is the case with domestic primary issues. However, offshore issues generate reduced revenues for India's merchant banking industry, and (in some cases) generate reduced liquidity on India's securities markets (see Section 1.4).

There are two major reasons why the offshore primary market is more attractive for many users as compared with the Indian primary market:

1. Offshore issues use bookbuilding procedures, and avoid the fixed price offerings that are used in India. The entire public issue process is much shorter on the offshore primary market, and involves lower issue costs.
2. Offshore issues are a form of regulatory arbitrage in so far as they allow foreign ownership to cross the limits of 24 per cent or 30 per cent.

The first of these issues pertains to the institutional development of India's primary market. To the extent that auctions and bookbuilding replace fixed price offerings in India, these problems will be much mitigated. The second issue is a side effect of policies restricting foreign ownership which is a form of disprotection of India's merchant banking industry. To the extent that limitations on foreign ownership are eased, it will diminish this disprotection.

5.7 THE PRIMARY MARKET FOR GOVERNMENT SECURITIES

Auction of government securities is an important problem influencing public finance and the fixed income markets (Chari and Weber, 1992). The procedure shown in Table 7.9 is equally applicable for primary issues of government securities as it is for IPOs. Apart from the discussion about this auction procedure above, there are two specific benefits that apply in the case of auctions of government securities:

1. The auction format used here is compatible with a large mass of buyers of government securities, spread all over the country. This is in contrast with the present functioning of the primary market for government securities, which is dominated by banks operating in Bombay.

   Access to this pool of investors will help the Reserve Bank reduce its dependance on reserve ratios in primary market offerings of government paper, and contribute to liquidity on the fixed income market in so far as these new buyers are likely to trade their portfolios more actively than banks.

2. For banks that plan to buy securities owing to reserve requirements, participation in a transparent computerized auction is superior to the present tendering process, in that the bank can observe the market equilibrium price while the auction is going on, and revise the bid before the auction closes. This would eliminate the guesswork that is required in bidding at the auction.

6. INFRASTRUCTURE FOR CAPITAL MARKETS[30]

The term 'infrastructure' here refers to the public goods which generally lie outside the focus of short-term priorities for public policy even though they are vital to the functioning of the financial system (Merton and Bodie, 1995 b).

6.1 HARMONIZATION AND REDRAFTING OF LAW

The major laws which govern the financial sector are:

1. The SEBI Act 1992
2. SCRA 1956 and the rules/regulations
3. FERA 1973
4. The Depositories Act
5. The Debt Recovery Act (Bank and Financial Institutions Recovery of Dues Act 1993)

---

[30]The treatment of this section is substantially based on the AMBI *Committee on Infrastructure for the Capital Markets*, led by S.A. Dave, which produced a report on these issues on 30 June 1997.

6. The Benami Prohibition Act
7. The Arbitration and Conciliation Act 1996
8. The Indian Penal Code
9. The Banking Regulation Act
10. The Indian Evidence Act, 1872
11. The Indian Telegraph Act, 1885

Many of these Acts and the associated rules, regulations, and guidelines suffer from inconsistencies and contradictions with respect to each other. They are often out of touch with contemporary institutions, technology, and the modern approach towards economic policy. Glaring examples of this are the Evidence Act of 1872 and the Indian Telegraph Act of 1885.

The present legal structure hampers and distorts the development of capital markets in a pervasive manner. Some examples of these distortions may be cited here:

- The healthy growth of the derivatives industry requires modifications to the Indian Contracts Act.
- In a situation where economic policy reforms work towards obtaining markets with *reduced* transactions costs, stamp duty laws are directly distortionary since they work towards raising transactions costs. Stamp duty laws also inhibit asset securitization.
- Electronic funds transfer and internet commerce require changes to the Indian Evidence Act.
- The takeover market is an important check upon poor management, and a vital part of obtaining efficient resource allocation in the country. Many provisions of the Income Tax Act, Industrial Disputes Act, Stamp Laws, and ULCRA impede smooth takeovers.

Some efforts at overhauling company law and income tax law have begun. Ideally, a comprehensive and internally consistent redrafting effort should be undertaken on this full set of laws from the perspective of the entire financial sector.

6.2 SWIFT DISPUTE RESOLUTION

A legal system which acts in a swift and fair manner in upholding financial contracts is a vital part of a well-functioning financial sector. In India, as of today, contract enforcement is weak. This generates a reduced richness of contractual relationships, and reduced specialization, in the economy. It encourages contracting based on feudal ties rather than on economic merit. It throws up entry barriers against new companies by favouring established and well-trusted companies that have a reputation for upholding contracts; in contrast, if the legal system enabled effective contract enforcement, then young companies could compete with established companies on an equal footing.

Regardless of the state of the underlying laws, swift dispute resolution is an administrative problem where progress is urgently required. If the existing structures cannot be radically improved, a special tribunal for capital markets could be created. A greater role for arbitration would reduce the number of cases coming to court.

6.3 THE PAYMENTS SYSTEM

The payments system essentially is the telecommunications system for funds transfer. Traditionally, the payments system is viewed as part of the banking system. However, it can be viewed more generally as being an electronic highway through which funds will move between the various entities of the financial sector and connect them up into international payments networks (Folkerts-Landau, Garber and Schoenmaker, 1997). Electronic funds transfer (EFT) is obviously important in a mundane fashion for problems like the direct payment of dividends into bank accounts and bypassing the postal system. Less apparent, but perhaps far more important, is the fundamental and irreplaceable role that the EFT plays in the elimination of counterparty risk (Perold, 1995).

The daily mark-to-market margin is a key instrument through which clearing corporations eliminate counterparty risk. If a member fails to post margin, the clearinghouse has to close out the position and prevent any further losses from accumulating. If the payments system is slow, it is impossible for the clearinghouse to know whether the funds put up by the member are sound or not. The response of clearinghouses is to increase the initial margin requirements (see Section 3.1). This reduces the efficiency of the financial industry, by demanding a larger working capital per unit trading volume.

Many markets worldwide now use an additional margin call at 11:30 AM on days with high volatility. The very existence of this capability further reduces the initial deposits (i.e. working capital) required to safely get the same levels of trading.

Once reliable EFT and well-functioning depositories come about, markets in India can begin the transition into realtime gross settlement, a superior approach which cuts through the complexity of clearing.

A related difficulty concerns incompatible time zones. The lack of EFT, coupled with the days lost owing to incompatible time zones has generated long lags in many routine activities of FIIs. FIIs have found it difficult to work even with seven-day settlement in India owing to these problems, as compared with their routinely working with T+3 settlements in most other countries. While EFT and the depository are obviously parts of the solution, incompatible time zones continue to be a hurdle.

In order to overcome this, the central bank should extend the operating hours of the payment system to reduce the time gap between payments in different time zones (Steil, 1994). This would reduce transactions costs faced by international investors dealing with India, and improve India's integration within the worldwide financial system.

6.4 ENHANCING THE QUALITY OF ACCOUNTING DATA

Accounting data in India is the lifeblood of the process of markets consuming information and emerging with valuation of securities. As of today, accounting data in India is weak on quality, quantity, and frequency. Two initiatives are needed in this regard:

1. Accounting standards in India should be upgraded to international levels. Specific areas where Indian accounting practice is deficient are consolidation of group accounts, segment reporting, and standards on deferred tax liability.
2. The full audited results should be available on a quarterly basis, as is the case internationally.

Going beyond accounting data, there is the question of disclosure in the aftermath of substantive events. Companies have a responsibility to reveal information to markets, and reveal information in a manner which does not favour some market participants over others. As of today, firms in India release information into markets in an unsystematic manner. Information is often leaked to analysts or journalists first. In many other countries, such behaviour would be considered criminal on the part of management, analysts, and journalists.

SEBI has constituted the Bhave committee (Bhave, 1997) on continuing disclosure standards by companies to address some of these questions. This committee is working on the problems of consolidation of accounts, segment reporting, handling of deferred tax liabilities, and ground rules to govern disclosure to markets about 'material events affecting a company's performance'.

These policy initiatives will generate more informative accounting data as well as lead to more informative market prices, reduced asymmetric information on financial markets, and increased market liquidity.

6.5 DEPARTMENT OF TELECOMMUNICATIONS' (DOT) CLOSED USER GROUP POLICY

As of today, DOT controls the basic infrastructure through which 'wide area computer networking' takes place. Connecting up computers within one office can be done easily, but connecting up computers that span a large distance requires either very smalll aperture terminal (VSAT) or leased lines or some form of long distance communications. Today, DOT is the monopoly provider of long-distance communications (Shah, 1997).

In terms of the basic economic rationale, DOT should be a pure telecom service provider, and have no *locus standi* on how users use these telecom services. An analogy here may be a bridge; the provider of this facility has a right to charge fees for the use of these facilities, but has no *locus standi* in controlling what goods are carried across the bridge.

In violation of this principle, DOT has adopted a 'Closed User Group (CUG)' policy which says that any one CUG can establish wide-area networking, but no two networks can connect with each other. In other words, when people purchase telecom bandwidth from DOT, they are not allowed to use it to carry traffic from site to site in response to their needs: they are forced to keep distinct networks isolated.

For example, the NSE is one CUG—all NSE VSATs are part of one CUG. With 'Build, Operate, Lease, Transfer' (BOLT) expansion, the BSE is also a CUG—all BOLT VSATs are one CUG. Under the terms of DOT's CUG policy, the two networks would be forbidden from connecting up for any purpose. Similarly, if all offices of SEBI are connected up into a nationwide network, then DOT would prohibit SEBI from being connected to the BSE or NSE.

Implications for the Financial Industry

The CUG policy cripples the growth of computer networking in the country in a variety of areas. The financial industry, being highly dependent upon modern telecom, is especially affected. Examples of sophisticated activities which are rendered infeasible owing to the CUG policy are:

1. Consider the problem of setting up a brokerage company which has nationwide outreach. Merill Lynch in the US is an example of such an operation.

In India, this comes into conflict with the CUG policy. The brokerage firm would need to set up one wide area network connecting up its branch offices around the country. It would need at least one exchange membership which would connect it into another CUG. This is rendered infeasible thanks to DOT's CUG policy. Several large firms like UTI Securities, and Karvy Securities are all confronted with this constraint.

2. Arbitrage between exchanges is a key mechanism through which prices on different exchanges stay in synch, and for smaller exchanges, arbitrage is essential in order to compete with the bigger exchanges.

Traditionally, arbitrage has been done in a labour-intensive way. Employees at financial firms watch both screens, isolate mispricings, and trade on both sides. This is inefficient and incomplete. Given the large number of stocks and small number of traders, the effectiveness of this arbitrage will be limited.

The way forward is to implement computer software which does arbitrage. Instead of a human being watching prices on both markets, a computer would do that. A single computer could work hundreds of stocks. A few dozen large finance companies in this business could produce a substantially smaller rate of mispricing in India's exchanges, and improve the retail order flow obtained by smaller exchanges.

What we need here is a trading firm which connects up into the computer network of two exchanges. Today, this cannot be done because it violates DOT's CUG policy.

3. If a bank establishes its own wide area network connecting up branch offices all over the country, and if the bank becomes a depository participant (DP), then the simplest connectivity imaginable is for the bank to obtain one leased line connection to the depository, and for all the branches to offer DP services over the interlinked network. This is forbidden under the CUG policy. Hence the only alternative possible which is consistent with the CUG policy is for each of the branch offices to get an independent connection with the depository, which completely defeats the purpose of computer networking in the first place.

This constraint has crippled the process through which the NSDL is able to reach out to investors all over the country.

4. A variety of more complex applications involve interconnections between markets, banks, mutual funds, NBFCs, etc. Today, firms

in India do not even plan or research such applications because of DOT's CUG policy.

The technological progress of India's financial sector would be speeded up if DOT's closed user group policy were eliminated. More generally, all service providers should have no powers over the content that is carried over their wires. Whether a line carries voice or data or fax, or is used for some kind of computer networking, the service provider should charge a price for bandwidth, and then have no *locus standi* in dictating how bandwidth can (or cannot) be used.

6.6 THE NATIONAL INFORMATION INFRASTRUCTURE

There are three classes of participants on capital market:

1. Issuers: the ultimate users of capital.
2. Households: the ultimate sources of savings.
3. Intermediaries: markets, brokerage firms, mutual funds, insurance companies, banks, etc.

The proposed 'national information infrastructure' (Shah and Misra, 1997), which would offer computer connectivity using Internet protocol, has a tremendous potential in being a common computer communications facility which interlinks all these participants. This would generate great efficiencies, improve information transmission and dissemination, and reduce rigidities in the markets. Examples of the applications of Internet to the financial sector are:

1. Companies could keep up steady channels of communication with bondholders and shareholders, using both broadcast methods and individual email.
2. Information dissemination for primary market offerings could be done over Internet (e.g. that called for in the auction process of Table 7.9).
3. Shareholders could vote on an AGM over Internet, thus producing a revolution in corporate governance.
4. Exchanges could put price feeds on realtime on Internet, whereby people could observe the markets in their homes and offices.
5. Analytical tools and information would be disseminated over Internet on a pay-per-use basis, which would reach far more people than the clumsy methods of distributing analytics and information that are used today.

6. Users could visit banks and NSDL over Internet and find out their account balance.
7. The duplication of costly telecommunications infrastructure by OTCEI, NSE, NSDL, BSE, etc. could be eliminated if all exchanges and brokerage firms shared a common high speed Internet connectivity.
8. As India's financial system gets plugged into Internet, the special locational advantage of Bombay would be diminished, and the financial industry would be better able to spread all over the country.

In India, the growth and spread of Internet has been crippled by high prices and the CUG policy (mentioned in Section 6.5). The most important instance of these high prices is the price for Internet connectivity that a corporate office requires, i.e. a leased line to Internet running at 1.5 to 2 million bits/second. In the US, this line costs around Rs 6 lakh a year (all inclusive) and comes with no restrictions on use. In India, a comparable facility purchased from VSNL would cost around Rs 2 crore a year (all inclusive) and comes with serious restrictions on use. Even ignoring the restrictions on usage, the price in India is around thirty times higher.

Growth of Internet, a reduction of costs for Internet access to international standards, and complete connectivity for all parts of the financial industry should be viewed as important infrastructure developments for capital markets.

REFERENCES

Akerlof, G.A. (1970). 'The Market for "Lemons": Quality Uncertainty and the Market Mechanism'. *Quarterly Journal of Economics*, vol. 84, pp. 488–500.

Amihud, Y. and H. Mendelson. (1986). 'Asset Pricing and the Bid-ask Spread'. *Journal of Financial Economics*, vol. 17, pp. 223–49.

Balasundaram, D. (1998). 'Prospects for Cotton Futures in India'. In Thomas (ed.) (1998c), Ch. 13, pp. 113–34.

Basu, D. and S. Dalal. (1993). *The Scam: Who Won, Who Lost, Who Got Away*. New Delhi: UBS Publishers.

Benveniste, L.M. and W.J. Wilhelm. (1997). 'Initial Public Offerings: Going by the Book. *Journal of Applied Corporate Finance*, vol. 10, no. 1, pp. 98–108.

Bhave, C.B. (1997). 'Report of the Committee on Continuing Disclosure Standards by Companies'. Committee Report, SEBI, Mumbai.

Black, F. (1971). 'Towards a Fully Automated Exchange, Part I and II'. *Financial Analysts Journal*.

Chari, V.V. and R.J. Weber. (1992). 'How the U.S. Treasury Should Auction Its Debt'. *Federal Reserve Bank of Minneapolis Quarterly Review*, vol. 16, no. 4 (Fall), pp. 3–12.

Crane, D.B., R.C. Merton, K.A. Froot, Z. Bodie, S.P. Mason, E.R. Sirri, A.F. Perold, and P. Tufano (1995). *The Global Financial System: A Functional Perspective*. Cambridge, MA: Harvard Business School Books.

Culp, C.L. (1995). 'A Primer on Derivatives: Their Mechanics, Uses, Risks and Regulation'. Technical Report, Competitive Enterprise Institute, Washington, D.C.

Dave, S.A. (1997). 'Report of the Committee on Infrastructure for the Capital Markets'. Committee Report, Association of Merchant Bankers of India, Mumbai.

Demirguc–Kunt, A. and V. Maksimovic. (1996). 'Stock Market Development and Financing Choices of Firms', *The World Bank Economic Review*, vol. 10, no. 2, pp. 341–69.

Domowitz, I. (1990). 'The Mechanics of Automated Trade Execution Systems'. *Journal of Financial Intermediation*, vol. 1, pp. 167–94.

Faruquee, R., J.R. Coleman and T. Scott. (1997). 'Managing Price Risk in the Pakistan Wheat Market'. *The World Bank Economic Review*, vol. 11, no. 2, pp. 263–92.

Feldman, R.A. and R. Mehra. (1993). 'Auctions: Theory and Applications', *IMF Staff Papers*, vol. 40, no. 3, pp. 485–511.

Folkerts-Landau, D., P. Garber and D. Schoenmaker. (1997). 'The Reform of Wholesale Payment Systems'. *Finance and Development*, vol. 34, no. 2 (June), pp. 25–8.

GAO. (1994). 'Financial Derivatives: Actions Needed to Protect the Financial System'. Technical Report, United States General Accounting Office.

Gemmill, G. (1994). 'Margins and the Safety of Clearing Houses'. *Journal of Banking and Finance* vol. 18, no. 5 (October), pp 979–960.

Glosten, L.R. (1994). 'Is the Electronic Open Limit Order Book Inevitable?'. *Journal of Finance*, vol. 49, pp. 1127–61.

Glosten, L.R. and P.R. Milgrom. (1985). 'Bid, Ask and Transaction Prices in a Specialist Market with Heterogeneously Informed Traders', *Journal of Financial Economics*, vol. 14, pp. 71–100.

Gorham, M. (1994). 'Stock Index Futures: A 12-year Review'. Technical Report, Chicago Mercantile Exchange.

Houthakker, H.S. and P.J. Williamson. (1996). *The Economics of Financial Markets*. Oxford: Oxford University Press.

Ibbotson, R.G. and J.R. Ritter. (1995). 'Initial Public Offerings'. In R.A. Jarrow,

V. Maksimovic, and W.T. Ziemba (eds), *Finance: North-Holland Handbooks of Operations Research and Management Science'*, 1st edn, vol. 9. Amsterdam: North-Holland, Ch. 30, pp. 995–1018.

Jorion, P. (1997). *Value at Risk: The New Benchmark for Controlling Market Risk*. Chicago: Irwin Professional Publishing.

Levine, R. and S. Zervos. (1996). 'Stock Market Development and Long-run Growth'. *The World Bank Economic Review*, vol. 10, no. 2, pp. 323–40.

Longin, F.M. (1996). 'The Asymptotic Distribution of Extreme Stock Market Returns'. *Journal of Business*, vol. 69, no. 3, pp. 383–408.

Mason, S.P. (1995). 'The allocation of Risk'. In Crane et al., Ch. 5, pp. 153–96.

Melamed, L. and B. Tamarkin (1996). *Escape to the Futures*. John Wiley.

Merton, R.C. and Z. Bodie (1995a). 'A Conceptual Framework for Analyzing the Financial Environment', In Crane et al., Ch. 1, pp. 3–32.

——— . (1995b). 'Financial Infrastructure and Public Policy: A Functional Perspective'. In Crane et al., Ch. 8, pp. 263–82.

Neuberger, A. (1995). 'the Peter Pan Contract: A Futures Contract that Never Matures'. Technical Report, London Business School.

Parikh, K.S. (ed.). (1997). *India Development Report 1997*. New Delhi: Oxford University Press.

Perold A.F. (1995). 'The Payment System and Derivative Instruments'. In Crane et al., Ch. 2, pp. 33–80.

Pettway, R.H. and T. Kaneko (1994). 'The Effects of Removing Price Limits and Introducing Auctions upon Short-term IPO Returns: The Case of Japanese IPOs'. Technical Report 52794, Financial Research Institute, University of Missouri, Columbia.

Sarkar, J. and P. Agrawal. (1997). Banking. In Parikh (ed.), Ch. 11, pp. 193–218.

Shah, A. (1995a). 'The Indian IPO Market: Empirical Facts'. Technical Report, Centre for Monitoring Indian Economy, Mumbai.

——— . (1995b). 'The Indian IPO Market: Suggestions for Institutional Arrangements'. Technical Report, Centre for Monitoring Indian Economy, Mumbai.

——— . (1997). 'Telecommunications'. In Parikh (ed.), Ch. 13, pp. 239–50.

——— . (1998a). 'The Institutional Development of India's Financial Markets'. In T. Waghmare (ed.), *The Future of India's Stock Markets*. Invest India–Tata McGraw-Hill Series. New Delhi: Tata McGraw-Hill, Ch. 3, pp. 21–39.

——— . (1998b). 'Securities Markets. In B. Debroy and P.J. Shah (eds), *Agenda for Change*. New Delhi: Rajiv Gandhi Institute for Contemporary Studies, pp. 1–10.

——— . (1998c). 'Value at Risk: A Conceptual Examination'. In Thomas (ed.), (1998c), Ch. 23, pp. 215–24.

———. (1998d), 'What Ails Active Fund Management?'. In Waghmare (ed.), Ch. 1, pp. 3–14.

Shah, A. and S. Misra. (1997). 'Building India's National Information Infrastructure'. *Economic and Political Weekly*, vol. 32, nos. 44–5, pp. 2880–4.

Shah, A. and S. Thomas. (1994). 'Performance Evaluation of Professional Portfolio Managers in India'. Technical Report, Centre for Monitoring Indian Economy, Mumbai.

———. (1996). 'How Automation and Competition have Changed the BSE'. Technical Report, Centre for Monitoring Indian Economy, Mumbai.

———. (1997). 'Securities Markets'. In Parikh (ed.), Ch. 10, pp. 167–92.

Singh, A. (1997). 'Financial Liberalisation Stock Markets and Economic Development'. *The Economic Journal*, vol. 107, pp. 771–82.

Solnik, B. (1990). 'The Distribution of Daily Stock Returns and Settlement Procedures: The Paris Bourse'. *Journal of Finance*, vol. 45, no. 5, pp. 1601–9.

Steil, B. (ed.) (1994). *International Financial Market Regulation*. New York: John Wiley and Sons.

Tarapore, S.S. (1997). *Report of the Committee on Capital Account Convertibility*. Reserve Bank of India, Mumbai.

Thomas, S. (1995). 'An Empirical Characterisation of the Bombay Stock Exchange'. Ph.D. thesis, University of Southern California, Los Angeles, California.

———. (1998a). 'Performance Evaluation of Indian Funds'. In Waghmare (ed.), Ch. 4, pp. 23–32.

———. (1998b). 'Volatility Forecasting in Indian Financial Markets'. In Thomas (ed.), (1998c), Ch. 24, pp. 225–33.

———. (ed.) (1998c). *Derivatives Markets in India*. Invest India–Tata McGraw-Hill Series, Tata McGraw-Hill.

Thomas, S. and A. Shah. (1996). 'Post-issue Underperformance of Seasoned Equity Offerings in India'. Technical Report, CMIE, Mumbai.

Waghmare, T. (ed.) (1998). *The future of Fund Management in India—1997*. Invest India–Tata McGraw-Hill Series, Tata McGraw-Hill.

Warburg, S.B.C. (1996). 'India Funds'. Technical Report, SBC Warburg.

Williams, J. and E. Barone. (1991). 'Lending of Money and Shares through the *riporti* Market of the Milan Stock Exchange'. Technical Report, Stanford University and IMI.

Regulation and Market Microstructure

P. JAYENDRA NAYAK*

L51

G10 076

This chapter examines the relationship between market microstructure and regulation in the context of India's securities markets. Microstructure—the manner in which a market is organized, the trading and post-trading technology which it adopts, and the information structure and transactions costs confronting it—determines several market characteristics such as price discovery, trading liquidity, and opportunities for risk management, as also the ease with which restrictive and unfair trade practices can occur. It also inevitably influences the design of regulation and the style and content of supervision. With an impressive corpus of regulatory law having been laid out since 1992, a broad framework of regulation of the Indian securities markets is clearly in place. This chapter suggests that as regulatory law becomes increasingly layered, certain regulatory objectives are difficult to realize through further additions to regulatory law where sharply diminishing marginal returns might set in, and that these objectives are instead better approached through changes in microstructure. While the regulatory design phase typically operates on existing institutions, the focus on market microstructure brings in newer institutions which perform functions that are critical to enhancing market order flow, often in a different manner, while preserving market integrity. While the process begins by introducing new *mechanisms* for trading, over time it also alters the *quality* of the market.

Market microstructure clearly matters. A market for equities trading consisting largely of institutional players whose securities are held in a depository, and whose trades are based on a limit order book and

*I would like to thank Ajay Shah for very helpful discussions and Rajesh Tiwari for comments on an earlier version. The views expressed are my own and not necessarily of the UTI, and have drawn upon earlier work, particularly Nayak (1996, 1997).

guaranteed by a clearing corporation will possess characteristics markedly different from a predominantly retail market where brokers trade paper securities and confront each other for counterparty risks. Similarly, a market without exchange-traded derivatives must make the trading strategies of fund managers more conservative and passive[1], as it exposes them to risks which can be traded at finer prices in those markets where derivatives contracts can be written. Or again, the issuance of securities by firms is likely to be more attractive to investors if a price discovery in a *premarket* can occur, thereby providing evidence of what constitutes a fair price. And, finally, markets where trading liquidity is concentrated in half a dozen stocks are likely to possess compulsions for trading which are different from those in markets having a more uniform distribution of liquidity.

An alternative perspective arises from the need for risk diversification by recognizing that regulation would be more effective if it were better focused on facilitating the emergence of market processes and institutions which enable participants to better manage the risks of their transactions. Moral hazard and adverse selection, ubiquitous foes of regulators and participants alike, are more likely to be contained by encouraging risk sharing between participants rather than through a legal curtailment of risk taking.[2]

1. WHAT HAS REGULATION BEEN UNABLE TO ACHIEVE?

The formal regulation of the Indian capital market began in 1992 when a four-year old market regulator, the Securities and Exchange Board of India (SEBI), was statutorily empowered to regulate market intermediaries so as to better protect the integrity of transactions and thereby create investor confidence. SEBI's powers were further reinforced in

[1]Conservatism relates to the zone of preference in the risk–return spectrum; passiveness to shifts across the spectrum. Derivatives permit fund managers to make these shifts by pricing risks and making them tradeable.

[2]The National Stock Exchange (NSE) is a good example of this proposition. By creating a new microstructure for equities trading in 1994, it also brought in modern risk containment mechanisms, reduced transactions costs for investors by introducing price transparency, raised the average level of broker confidence in the trading and settlement system (particularly for brokers outside of Mumbai), and virtually carved out for itself a new market. It achieved several objectives which regulation for the secondary market was unsuccessfully grappling with.

1995, transferring to it virtually all substantive powers earlier vested in the Finance Ministry of the government. Prior to that, while the market had developed into a powerful allocator of financial resources for corporates, and rated impressively in terms of the many institutions which had grown around it, it was increasingly felt to be underregulated. Major irregularities were detected during 1991 which enabled one broker to illegally divert funds from commercial banks to the stock market, raising the market capitalization on the Bombay Stock Exchange (BSE) by 130 per cent within seven months, until the bubble eventually burst. The episode soon snowballed into a major indictment of financial market practices, as other kinds of banking and securities market irregularities were unearthed, raising crucial questions about the design and enforcement of financial market regulation.

In 1992 companies were provided with two new channels of resource mobilization: they could issue global depository receipts (GDRs), and overseas portfolio investment in their stocks was permitted. These limited measures of cross-border financial integration led to trading volumes increasing sharply and revealing the inadequacies of existing institutional arrangements for trade, while also casting doubts on the compatibility with fair trading practices of several market practices and stock exchange procedures, which had evolved when trading volumes were much lower and investors less institutionalized. Gaps in stock exchange surveillance were also visible, leading to periodic settlement problems. The phase of building a suitable regulatory law and of strengthening enforcement could be said to have begun in 1992 and lasted about five years.

This has altered significantly the character of the market. A new exchange, the NSE, captured the highest order flow among exchanges within a year of its commencing equities trading in late 1994, and the aggregate order flow on the two dominant exchanges has risen sharply. The structure of the brokerage industry has been transformed, in large measure on account of the entry of overseas brokerage firms, and brokerage fees have dropped sharply. Foreign Institutional Investors (FIIs) have become dominant players in the secondary market, with an aggregate net investment of over US $9 billion since 1993. Nevertheless several problems remain and appear to resist a regulatory solution. They include the following:

(a) *Allocation Problems*

• The market is not performing its allocative function as firms are unable to raise capital from the market on terms which they consider fair. Price discovery in this market is compromised.

- *Very* long-term financial savings are not being intermediated through the market, leading to a paucity of private domestic equity and debt for infrastructure investment.

(b) *Liquidity Problems*

- Trading liquidity is poor in all but a handful of listed stocks.
- Leveraging in the market is problematic. Formal markets do not exist for borrowing stock or for borrowing cash against stock, and such markets appear unlikely to grow rapidly.
- Similarly, while changes in regulatory law during 1997 have created a visible market for corporate control, domestic banks do not finance takeovers or the prevention by incumbent managements of takeovers, making domestic firms particularly vulnerable to takeovers by firms *overseas.*
- Closed end equity mutual funds typically trade at a very high discount to net asset value, leading to investments in these products being extremely illiquid.

(c) *Risk Management Problems*

- Trading for settlement in electronic book entry is rising very slowly, notwithstanding a depository commencing operation in late 1996. Meanwhile fake, forged, and stolen securities continue to be offered during stock exchange settlement, get categorized as bad delivery, and require to be replaced by brokers who sold them, thereby introducing sand in the wheels of the trading system.
- Risk management opportunites for mutual funds and other institutional investors are slender in the absence of derivatives.
- The market is vulnerable to a run if foreign investors have a pessimistic view on the currency, with domestic investors constituting a weak counterveiling force.
- Investors face the risk of price manipulation on illiquid stocks, which is often difficult to detect.

(d) *Corporate Governance Problems*

- Information disclosures by companies are still poor by international standards, and not conducive to the creation of market efficiency. Information traders are consequently disadvantaged, with swings in the market being controlled by noise traders.

- Corporate governance standards are weak, and neither regulation nor large institutional shareholders have succeeded in rapidly strengthening them.

This chapter examines how changes in market microstructure could address some of these problems. The discussion is grouped separately around the primary and the secondary markets for equity, mutual funds, and the debt market. A final section examines the impact on the capital market of the rupee becoming more fully convertible.

2. THE MARKET FOR EQUITY ISSUANCE

Three consequences flow from the existing microstructure of the market for equity issuance. First, incentives have been created for equity offerings to be inefficiently priced, leading investors to question the fairness of offer prices. Second, full disclosure of relevant information by firms is not a sufficient condition for fair pricing. Indeed, in the absence of strong investment banking institutions the validity of the *full disclosure regulatory model*, which India has borrowed from other markets, is contestable. And third, the primary market for equity has consequently been *exported*, aided by higher transactions costs to firms of placing equity domestically, though since 1996 overseas investors have become equally discriminate. All three propositions stem from the prevailing market microstructure, have implications for regulatory design, and will be defended after a brief overview of the history of primary market regulation.

2.1 HISTORY: REGULATING THE PRIMARY MARKET

Equity issuance until 1992 was directly regulated by the government, with the issue price computed on the basis of an accounting formula rather than what the market might bear, so as to signal the notion of 'fair value' to investors. In practice, however, initial public offerings (IPOs) of equity were typically severely underpriced in relation to the price upon listing, and where a listed company sought to make a fresh issue it was priced at a substantial discount to the existing share price. In 1992 regulatory powers were transferred from the government to SEBI, resulting in firms being permitted to raise capital from the public without regulatory price controls. The exception to this pricing freedom arises in the case of IPOs, which are required to price at the face value of the share unless the issuer has a consistent three-year record of profitability (subsequently amended to require a suitable track record of dividend payment) or has been promoted by a company with a similar record. SEBI's role was until recently confined to vetting the disclosures made by issuers in accordance with guidelines for disclosure and investor protection, but formal vetting has now been dispensed with. These guidelines require issuers to assess 'risk factors' arising in the investment of issue proceeds and to make other elaborate disclosures. Regulatory controls over the issue of rights and over making bonus issues (or stock splits) have also been removed. The mobilization of equity from the capital market consequently received considerable boost in the initial years of pricing freedom, as Table 8.1 indicates, though the number of companies able to raise equity fell sharply from 1996–7. Together with GDR issues and preferential allotments, it has led to a healthier capital structure for firms by making them less leveraged, enabling them to substitute long-term debt, raised largely from financial institutions, with equity.[3]

TABLE 8.1
THE SIZE OF THE DOMESTIC PRIMARY CAPITAL MARKET

Rs billion

Nature of offering	1992–3		1993–4		1994–5	
	No.	Amt.	No.	Amt.	No.	Amt.
Public	546	107	773	155	1342	210
Rights	488	60	370	89	324	66
Total	1034	167	1143	244	1666	276

Nature of offering	1995–6		1996–7		1997–8
	No.	Amt.	No.	Amt.	Amt.
Public	1426	142	773	130	14
Rights	299	66	208	92	17
Total	1725	208	981	222	31

Note: Till September 1997, as estimated from market reports.

Source: Government of India, *Economic Survey*, various issues, and CMIE. Private placements are excluded.

Despite liberalization in equity issuance, the primary market in India retains one facet of its earlier distinctive character, its predominantly retail nature, in view of the regulatory insistence that all public issues be (at least partially) retailed in the form of fixed price offers. SEBI's stipulation that at least 25 per cent of the issue be widely retailed, with

---

[3]There could, however, be higher agency costs (viz. costs of moral hazard) associated with lower leveraging. It has sometimes been argued, for instance, that the impetus for higher equity mobilizations by firms since 1993 was at least partly related to the desire by incumbent managements to escape from a tightening of standards of corporate governance.

half of the retail offer being allotted to small investors, has increased the possibility of IPOs being mispriced, for a combination of reasons, First, the need for a fixed price offer leads to weak price discovery as institutional investors are unable to access informational *premarkets* which enable more informed assessments of likely prices upon listing to be made; retail investors cannot consequently free-ride on pricing decisions of institutional investors; and there are pervasive uncertainties for the issuer about whether the issue will be fully subscribed.

Company law in India permits firms to issue both equity and preference shares. Barring warrants, there has been no share derivatives issuance, and the trading of derivatives is still not permitted under regulatory law although the NSE has been in readiness for it since late 1996. Equity shares necessarily have voting rights, though company law is proposed to be amended to permit non-voting shares to be issued.

2.2 PRICE DISCOVERY: WHERE IS THY STING?

International practice is more supportive of the benefits of price discovery. Thus firm commitment underwriting in more developed capital markets, akin to bought-out deals in India, involves pre-selling the issue to one or more investment bankers, who in turn resell the issue to other investors.[4] Similarly, cross-border equity flotation, such as of GDRs, typically involves building an order book, which creates the information premarket enabling the firm to construct each institutional investor's demand curve for the shares being offered.[5] Some countries permit more specialized

---

[4]This needs to be distinguished from *best effort* underwriting, in which the underwriter advises and markets the issue and bears the risk during the offer, and *standby* underwriting, in which the underwriter guarantees the unsubscribed portion of the issue at the issue price. An underwritten issue in India resembles standby underwriting.

[5]It is easy to demonstrate that if the investor is not to falsely undervalue the offer in the information premarket, the firm would need to assure a quantity allocation in the postmarket which increases with the offer valuation as conveyed by the investor in the information premarket. This is not feasible under a system of proportionate allocation of shares of the kind that SEBI has been insisting upon for Indian equity issues. For example, when an order book is built and investors have incentives to respond strategically by deliberately undervaluing the offer in the information premarket in order to induce the firm to lower the offer price, an *incentive compatibility* problem arises in the sense of Hurwicz (1972). Such problems characterize several two-stage games: in the present context, price bids

mechanisms for offering equity which recognize the logic of price discovery as an aid to reducing the mispricing of the offer.[6] In contrast, the direct retailing of a fixed price issue, without regulatory legitimacy for premarket informational exchanges, aggravates mispricing. The importance of the information premarket, which feeds demand curves of potential investors into pricing and share allocation decisions of the firm, has gone largely unrecognized by SEBI and has resulted in a primary market microstructure which exacerbates uncertainty about whether offerings are fairly priced, and thus about whether they will be fully subscribed.

In November 1995, SEBI announced its preparedness to consider corporates adopting the book building mechanism for issue sizes exceeding Rs 1 billion, but only as an alternative to selling that portion of the issue which is not being retailed. Companies have hitherto not adopted this mechanism. Even as the information premarket wins regulatory legitimacy, however, there are other barriers to efficient pricing which would need dismantling. First, listing occurs several weeks after the issue is priced, and meanwhile the investors' offer valuations may alter in response to new information entering the market, thereby militating against efficient offer pricing.[7] The problem is further aggravated by the issue price having to be set well before the issue pricing date.[8] Second,

---

are transmitted by investors in the first stage and an issue price announced by the firm in the second stage. Benveniste and Spindt (1989) and Nayak (1997) examine aspects of this game-theoretic problem, and demonstrate that efficient price outcomes under book building are not reconcilable with proportionate share allocation.

[6]Japan allows companies to partly auction a proposed flotation and to sell the rest through a fixed price offer, where the price is derived from the results of the auction, while France and the Netherlands have public issue mechanisms which closely resemble explicit auctions.

[7]Shah (1995) estimates the average period between offer pricing and listing of 2056 new listings on the BSE between 1 January 1991 and 15 May 1995 as eleven weeks, though he reports reduced delays from 1994 onwards. In more developed capital markets the average period does not exceed a few days, and for bought-out deals could be as low as one day.

[8]Until 1966, SEBI permitted the draft prospectus, which it vetted, to contain a price band (where the maximum is not more than 20 per cent higher than the minimum) within which the eventual price would have to be set. The draft prospectus could take several weeks for SEBI to clear, though in July 1996 SEBI dispensed with the explicit vetting of prospectuses in a large category of public

the regulatory insistence that issues be mandatorily retailed sharply jacks up transactions costs. And third, as discussed earlier, there continue to be regulatory price controls on IPOs.

2.3 THE SIGNIFICANCE OF REPUTATION

In 1997, SEBI removed all shackles on book building. Will this lead to fairer issue pricing? Here again, market microstructure characterized by weak investment banking institutions, is likely to be an impediment. In more developed capital markets investment bankers—who go periodically to the same group of institutional investors—are judged by the returns the investors earn, and this encourages due diligence by the bankers whose reputation is enhanced by proper issue pricing. An investment banker must, while certifying an issue, necessarily protect his reputation capital which is at stake if the next issue is overpriced.

The contrast with India rests essentially on the importance the market attaches to reputation, and the economic argument runs as follows. First, the investment banker's reputation must far exceed that of the issuer, with a part of the reputation being 'leased out' for each issue. For the issuer as also the investment banker, the marginal benefits of doing so must exceed the marginal costs. Second, if an investment banker leads an overpriced issue, his reputation capital must fall sharply.[9] And finally, a reputed investment banker must not consistently lead underpriced issues in order to maintain his reputation as he will then lose market share with issuers. These behavioural assumptions are very weakly, if at all, applicable to India where regulation has underestimated the significance of strong merchant banking institutions. The recent SEBI directive requiring merchant bankers to separate fund business from their commissions business can be expected to further weaken the investment banking industry.[10] Resource raising by firms in the primary equities

---

equity offerings. Further, company law requires the Registrar of Companies to be informed of the issue price three weeks before the issue opens.

[9]Tinic (1988) argues that this is contingent on a supportive legal system, as the erosion of reputation capital depends on the ease with which investors can claim damages against investment bankers for overpricing issues based on inadequate information disclosure. Changes in legal jurisprudence (class action suits) and rapid legal enforcement are prerequisites to this becoming applicable to India.

[10]The directive appears to stem from the need to avoid regulatory overlap, with the funds business being regulated by the RBI, while SEBI regulates the merchant banking business.

market will continue to be uncertain as long as the market is characterized by a fragile microstructure.

2.4 UNDERPRICING AND THE IPO PUZZLE

With the microstructure of the primary market not being conducive to efficient pricing, how have firms priced their offerings? Empirical evidence supports the view that asymmetric information between an issuer and its investors generates adverse selection in the investors' choice of IPOs to invest in, with firms consequently needing to underprice issues in order to attract investors.[11] Thus one empirical study on Indian IPO pricing analyses all the 2056 new listings on the BSE between 1 January 1991 and 15 May 1995[12] and concludes that the mean issue underpricing (measured as the return from issue date to listing date) exceeds 100 per cent.[13]

If IPOs are underpriced, the rejection by investors of primary offerings since 1996 is a puzzle. One explanation is that 1996 saw an appreciable enough erosion of share value to invalidate these findings from 1995 onward, and there were certainly some large primary offerings in 1995 which by hindsight appear to have been overpriced. A related explanation hinges on price manipulation: promoters of these companies provide the initial contributions to the IPOs, then organize collusively with others to ramp prices in order to attract other investors, and finally sell out with a capital gain.[14] There is considerable impres-

---

[11]The argument is a straightforward application of Akerlof's (1970) market for 'lemons' and is based on a proposition first formalized by Rock (1986): if investors are either fully informed about the likely price upon listing, or else completely uninformed, the uninformed must either withdraw from investing repeatedly in IPOs on account of losses incurred, or else the proportion of overpriced issues must fall and the proportion of underpriced issues rise. For the investor, the overpriced issue is a lemon. While it is clear that there was significant underpricing till early 1995, empirical studies do not exist for the subsequent period, and do not throw light on whether the withdrawal of uninformed retail investors after 1995 was on account of overpriced issues.

[12]Shah (1995). A more recent study by Madhusoodanan and Thiripalraju (1997), encompassing 1922 issues listed on the BSE from 1922 to 1995, corroborates this view.

[13]The mean underpricing falls marginally if outliers from this dataset (the highest 2 per cent and lowest 2 per cent of underpricing) are rejected, but more strikingly the standard deviation of underpricing almost halves.

[14] Shah (1995) computes the average *excess* weekly return to be high at 3.9 per

sionistic evidence to support the view that with the dismantling of entry barriers in the IPO market, many companies which constitute poor value in the medium term have been able to fluently raise capital from the public. Uninformed retail investors, victims of such practices, have therefore chosen to stay out of the primary market. Yet another explanation is that as firms have become familiar with the placing of GDRs overseas, they have preferred that route.

2.5 EXPORTING THE PRIMARY MARKET

Equity offerings are more expensive to place domestically than overseas, a consequence also of differences in microstructure. The average transactions cost of GDR flotations was estimated by SEBI in 1994 at 4 per cent for an issue size of $50 million, while it was 9.6 per cent for an equivalent size domestic offering which is sought to be retailed. Of the 9.6 per cent, 4.9 per cent comprises expenses on advertising, registrars' expenses, postal and bankers' charges, and printing; the comparable average transactions cost for a GDR issue is 0.1 per cent[15].

In addition, the government has also recently permitted firms to freely borrow overseas to an extent equal to GDR funds raised, and this ability to leverage GDR funds will make overseas equity offerings even more attractive. Finally, as GDRs are tantamount to non-voting shares, GDR funds can be raised without diluting incumbent management control. For all these reasons companies will prefer to raise equity capital abroad, and in this manner a combination of government policy and microstructure has effectively exported the primary capital market.

2.6 THE DISCLOSURE-BASED REGULATORY MODEL

To these limitations of the disclosure-based regulatory model for the primary market must be added the implications arising from inadequately rigorous accounting standards and the fledgling nature of the market for corporate control. Both make it difficult for the stock market

---

cent, with a standard deviation of 3.5 per cent. Further, the average excess return in the first 200 trading days is 40 per cent, while in the first 400 trading days the excess return is zero. Subsequently, average IPO pricing resembles that of the market index. While supporting the price manipulation hypothesis, Shah observes that excess returns are most pronounced for small issue sizes between Rs 45 and 75 million, and are reversed within a period shorter than the period during which they rose (suggesting that excess returns vary directly with ease of manipulation).

[15]Securities and Exchange Board of India (1994).

to accurately calibrate the value of a firm. To respond to these problems, a new microstructure for the primary market would need to be created, incorporating reliable equities research, well-capitalized investment banks, an active premarket before equity offerings are priced, and encouragement to book running based on prices acceptable to institutional investors. These are more likely to lead to smoother price discovery and to proper pricing of equity issues.

2.7 QUALIFIED INSTITUTIONAL INVESTORS

Price discovery would be further enhanced if regulation were to recognize the importance of a qualified institutional investors (QII) category in the context of the understandable concern with whether preconditions for unlisted firms going public should be made more stringent. One proposal, currently deemed unfashionable, is to restrict the investor group for such firms to QIIs, and to prevent other (retail) investors from subscribing to such IPOs unless there is a proven record of profitability. SEBI's present stance permits such firms to reach out liberally to all investors but puts fetters on the issue price, thereby risking underpricing and oversubscription for some issues and investor losses for other issues. In such a market characterized by adverse selection, unfettered pricing and (restricted) access solely to QIIs would lead to superior price discovery and eventually better protect the retail investor.

3. THE SECONDARY EQUITIES MARKET

The prevailing microstructure for equities trading has had the following consequences: First, although institutions for handling stock exchange clearing and settlement risk are in place, several other processes for risk containment are absent, but could be readily introduced. Crucial to the ability to do so is the role of the *clearing corporation*. Second, despite a surge in aggregate trading volumes in the last two years, liquidity is generally poor in all but a few stocks, and is likely to be asymmetrically distributed across stocks until a separation between cash and futures markets occurs. Third, the liquidity risk on depository trades is very high, unless the borrowing and lending of securities and funds is possible or unless trades over a certain size are *mandated* to be depository settled. Fourth, mutual funds managing large-sized portfolios face a combination of illiquidity and the absence of risk containment through derivatives, making the funds vulnerable to rapid changes in market conditions. And finally, while price discovery based on trading on the limit order book is rapid, 'block deals' between institutions are inadequately integrated with the book, as price realization for such deals is typically sub-optimal. These propositions are discussed after a brief review of regulation and its impact on market efficiency.

3.1 HISTORY: REGULATING THE SECONDARY MARKET

Regulation of the secondary market since 1992 has led to the following broad strategic interventions: stock exchanges have been induced, and sometimes coerced, into reforming their trading, clearing, and settlement practices; a large category of market intermediaries has been brought within SEBI's ambit, with increasing regulatory intolerance and punishment of market manipulation and unfair trade practices; and a new microstructure based on a different technology has been designed which has been conducive to improving operating practices and enhancing market efficiency.

The reform of stock exchange practices proved to be the most contentious part of the initial regulatory thrust, but with the NSE constituting government's strategic institutional intervention, it may also be the most durable. The NSE commenced equities trading in November 1994 and in just over a year its average daily trading volumes began exceeding those of the BSE, an exchange which in 1993 had an 80 per cent trading share across the country. The NSE has brought to the Indian stock market a new microstructure in the form of automated screen trading based on an open electronic limit order book, a one week trading and settlement cycle, prudential margining and capital adequacy for brokers and strict surveillance of trading positions on individual shares, and has emphasized the importance of managing the risk of clearing and settlement by setting up a clearing corporation and a depository. The NSE has indeed provided the critical competitive spur to the reform of other exchanges, including the BSE, which earlier often appeared resistant to regulatory pressure for reform.[16]

3.2 MARKET EFFICIENCY AND TRANSACTIONS COSTS

Have changes in the stock market during the 1990s enhanced the efficiency of the secondary market? One analytically precise response to this is to check whether the Efficient Markets Hypothesis (EMH)

---

[16]It is the cross-country experience that an incumbent dominant stock exchange has characteristics of a 'natural monopoly', with economies of scope creating formidable barriers to entry for other exchanges. The NSE is a rare counter-example to this.

holds.[17] Tests of two variants of market efficiency are discussed below, and a third in connection with mutual funds.[18] The tests generally do not validate the hypothesis. Yet another way of responding to the question is to examine whether transactions costs in trading have diminished. The evidence here is more supportive of increased efficiency.

(a) *Empirical Evidence of Weak-form Efficiency*

Tests of weak-form market efficiency assume that the information set consists of current and past prices of securities, and that trading based on stock market returns cannot provide for systematic arbitrage gains. Typical statistical tests look for serial correlation of returns and conduct 'runs tests'. Studies which have used *weekly* or *monthly* trading data on the BSE during the 1980s have generally rejected evidence of serial dependence,[19] but such a conclusion also typically emerges from other

[17]EMH distinguishes between weak-form, semi-strong form and strong-form market efficiency, each based on a different characterization of the information set used by traders to arbitrage away excess returns from trading.

[18]The hypothesis (EMH) is akin to a statement of rationality, and asserts the no-arbitrage principle which denies the existence of arbitrage possibilities when profit maximizing agents trade financial assets based on commonly available information. Thereby, the basis of profitable trading rules cannot be commonly known information, but rather *differences* in information between agents ('information not fully reflected in prices'). Tests of the hypothesis therefore amount to tests of whether the use of commonly available information can lead to sustained trading profits. When the hypothesis is applied to a particular financial asset pricing model (such as CAPM), an econometric rejection of the model constitutes a rejection of a joint hypothesis (such as of EMH + CAPM), which cannot constitute the basis of a rejection of the EMH. Tests of the EMH, such as those contained in the influential work of Fama (1965), have therefore often tended to be purely statistical without grafting an asset pricing model, but being shorn of economic theory have integrated unsatisfactorily with notions of efficiency arising out of general equilibrium models. One question which generates unease is how the EMH is reconcilable with substantial investments in equities research. A better integration, with newer theoretical perspectives for the stock market, has emerged from the application of rational expectations equilibrium to asset pricing, resulting in a more coherent understanding of how well financial markets transmit information and of the role of prices in doing so. Early theoretical work was by Grossman and Stiglitz (1980) and Stiglitz (1982). Bray (1989) provides a good interpretation of the significance of this literature.

[19]Studies include Obaidullah (1990), who examined weekly prices of thirty-six

more developed capital markets. Evidence of serial dependence has, however, been detected when *daily* prices on the BSE are used.[20] Thus an analysis for the period January 1990–December 1994 reveals a strongly significant serial dependence between values of the BSE Sensex and one-day lagged values of the Sensex (though not when the lags are longer), as also a similar one-day lagged serial dependence in the prices of a larger set of 250 companies, conclusions indicative of departures from market efficiency.[21] The same study demonstrates that there is also a 'size' effect on returns,[22] with the performance of 'small' companies that constitute the 'A' group having been distinctly superior. These results suggest that during 1990–4 the market was not characterized by weak-form efficiency.

(b) *Empirical Evidence of Semi-strong Form Efficiency:*

By also including company-specific information which is publicly

---

active shares during 1985–8, Rao (1988), who investigated weekly prices of ten blue chip shares during 1982–7, and Yalawar (1986), who examined the monthly prices of 122 shares during a longer 1963–82 duration. The results of these studies are summarized in Obaidullah (1994).

[20]Chowdhury (1991), who examined daily prices of ninety three shares between January 1988 and April 1990. Srinivasan, Mohapatra, and Sahu (1988), however, find no evidence of statistical dependence in the daily prices of thirty active shares, but the study examines a brief two-month period during 1987, diminishing its relevance for weak-form efficiency over longer periods.

[21]Thomas (1995) examined serial correlation with eight one-day period lags, and derived the following autocorrelation function (ACF) for the BSE Sensex:

Lag days	1	2	3	4	5	6	7	8
ACF value	0.114	−0.039	0.001	0.008	−0.014	0.003	0.001	0.010

As the asymptotic bounds can be shown to be ±0.0347, sizable departures from market efficiency occur only with a one day lag.

[22]If 'A' group companies are sorted each quarter on the basis of market capitalization into four quartile portfolios of small, q2, q3 and big, with each of the quartile portfolios held constant for the duration of the quarter, the cumulative yields on the portfolios are 735 per cent for small, 457 per cent for q2, 458 per cent for q3 and 297 per cent for big. The cumulative yield on the BSE Sensex during the same five-year period was 328 per cent. Yields of 'small' companies within the 'A' group have clearly been the highest, implying a 'size' effect on returns.

released, semi-strong form efficiency admits a wider information set. These information releases constitute *events*, and event studies evaluate the speed and accuracy of the company's share price adjustment to such events. Announcements of bonus issues (stock splits) and of company earnings, as also the impact of political and economic events, are some of the events which have been studied for price adjustments on the BSE. Bonus issue announcements have an upward price impact as Indian companies are perceived as wanting to maintain their dividend rates irrespective of the number of shares they issue, and are therefore viewed as signalling strong excess returns. The studies do not, on balance, validate semi-strong form efficiency as there is common knowledge about the dates on which the shares go ex-bonus, and yet there are excess returns arising out of the declaration of bonus; and less liquid stocks, which are traded less frequently, are prone to display an overreaction in their returns.[23] The impact of earnings announcements on share prices also does not support semi-strong form efficiency.[24]

(c) *Transactions Costs*

These comprise costs for trading, clearing, and settlement. In turn, trading costs can be divided into brokerage costs and costs of market impact. A recent study estimates that aggregate transactions costs have halved

---

[23]Ramachandran (1988) studied forty bonus issues during a six-year period, and identified two distinct clusters among the firms, representing short and longer adjustment periods respectively. The evidence on semi-strong form efficiency was thus mixed. In a later study, Obaidullah (1992) investigated seventy-five bonus issue announcements during 1987–8, for the period six months before to six months after each announcement date, and detected an upward drift in returns four months before the date, which continued till two weeks after the date, followed by a subsequent marginal decline and a final increase when the shares went ex-bonus. Thomas (1995) reports broadly similar trends for 196 firms whose shares went ex-bonus between January 1990 and July 1995.

[24]Obaidullah (1991) examined returns during the periods surrounding the annual announcements of earnings of a sample of 125 firms during 1987–90. Where unexpected earnings were positive, prices moved upwards within a period of two months before the announcement, though when unexpected earnings were negative prices moved downwards five months before the event. Further, the returns–earnings correlation was extremely low. Obaidullah concluded that inaccurate and inappropriate price adjustments are not consistent with semi-strong form efficiency.

from mid-1993 to 1997, and could in a few years be substantially lower than in the US.[25] The cost details are included in Table 8.2 and are suggestive of increased market efficiency since 1993.

TABLE 8.2
TRANSACTIONS COSTS ON INDIA'S EQUITY MARKET

(per cent)

Component	Mid-1993	India Today	Future	New York Today
Trading	3.75	0.75	0.40	1.23
Brokerage	3.00	0.50	0.25	1.00
Market impact cost	0.75	0.25	0.15	0.23
Clearing				
Counterparty risk	Present	In part	0.00	0.00
Settlement	1.25	1.75	0.10	0.05
Paperwork cost	0.75	0.75	0.10	0.05
Bad paper risk	0.50	1.00	0.00	0.00
Total	5.00	2.50	0.50	1.28
	(+ risk)			

Source: Shah and Thomas (1997).

3.3 THE WAY AHEAD: FURTHER CHANGES IN MICROSTRUCTURE

The microstructure for secondary market trading has undergone visibly dramatic changes since 1994. Nevertheless, the capabilities for risk bearing and risk assessment are poor, the market continues to be illiquid, and depository trading is very thin. Market microstructure would need to further alter in order to accommodate the following requirements, and the process could be speeded up through regulatory support.

(a) *The Clearing Corporation and Risk Assessment*

While the NSE has set up an independent clearing corporation, the BSE has constituted a Trade Guarantee Fund (TGF). Several other exchanges are also proposing to set up TGFs. Both kinds of institutional mechanisms cover brokers against other brokers' defaults. Risk assessment of brokers, however, operates differently in the two mechanisms. As the

---

[25]Shah and Thomas (1997). The cost comparison pertains to retail trading. For institutional trading, custodial costs would need to be included, and these costs are typically still high in India though they can be expected to fall as depository trading occurs.

clearing corporation is the counterparty to all market orders on the NSE executed by brokers, it has to continually form assessments of each trading broker's creditworthiness: the gross and net positions taken, the extent of leveraging in relation to net worth, and capabilities in delivering on margins as prices turn volatile, as also replacing fake and forged shares if they are delivered into the market by the broker. The NSE clearing corporation is rapidly developing into the first and only organization which can *credit rate brokers*.[26] The BSE's TGF will lack such skills, as the TGF is invoked only when a broker defaults. The continual ability to assess a broker's creditworthiness should find several applications which are discussed below.

(b) *Credit to Brokers*

Banks will continue in the foreseeable future to be extremely cautious about lending to brokers as they do not possess the information and skills to assess broker creditworthiness. The clearing corporation can provide credit enhancement to banks in the form of guarantees or other forms of comfort. It can use its risk assessment skills to open a sustainable channel of bank credit to brokers.

(c) *Stock Lending to Brokers*

SEBI's stock lending guidelines specify that stock borrowing and lending should be through a designated intermediary which will act as counterparty for all such transactions. Here again, it is unclear how the intermediary will assess a broker's borrowing capacity; the clearing corporation can create value by providing such an assessment. Stock borrowing would also enable exchanges to move to a shorter trading cycle (either fixed or rolling) without affecting trading liquidity.

The contrast with the *badla* system (which is a contango mechanism for borrowing funds or stock, recently reintroduced on the BSE) captures key differences in risk assessment. Analogous to the clearing corporation, it is the *badla* broker who undertakes the risk assessment of the

[26]Among the several risk containment techniques deployed by the NSE are the introduction of real time monitoring (which enables risk assessment to be made at the point of a broker's trade and ahead of his margin payments), using delays on margin payments as an early warning system, disenablement and enablement for trading in order to prevent positions building up, declaration of default as soon as a broker's inability to pay his dues is apparent, and speedy resolution of objection cases arising out of stolen, fake and forged certificates.

broker who does not wish to deliver, and it is this assessment which enables the *badla* broker to access funds or securities. A mechanism which leads to a select group of *badla* brokers assessing the creditworthiness of all other brokers on an exchange must necessarily be based on familiarity and trust, and resembles 'club' deals; it works better when the number of brokers and the positions taken are small, and when the broking fraternity is relatively homogeneous. When the structure, capital requirements, and style of the brokerage business are changing rapidly, as they have been since 1995, an external agency in the form of a clearing corporation is likely to assess broker risk more rigorously and prudently.

(d) *Hedging and Leveraging of Positions*

The absence of derivatives has been particularly disadvantageous to fund managers when either markets or portfolio sizes turn volatile. Thus in 1995–6 the largest mutual fund scheme, UTI's Unit Scheme 64, had to cope with large-sized redemptions and had to sell equity, often with uncomfortably high impact costs. Had derivatives existed, the UTI could have 'shorted' the portfolio by selling index futures, and gradually unwound the short as it sold equity, thereby maintaining the value of the portfolio. Alternatively, in the falling market of that year, the UTI could have bought an index put option and then sold equity from the scheme's portfolio. The introduction of derivatives is critical to enhancing the risk-bearing capabilities of investors and stock exchange traders, as also providing a stimulus to liquidity in equity markets. Investors would be prepared to hold more equity if index futures and options on equities were to exist.[27]

[27]The delay in the introduction of derivatives, or inappropriate regulatory or tax regimes governing them, could well drive the market overseas, as cross-border trading increases. The example of trading in the Nikkei 225 futures moving from Osaka to Singapore is an example often quoted, arising on account of an inappropriate trading tick size being imposed by Japan's Ministry of Finance, and demonstrating the powerful impact on trading which market microstructure can have. As another example, trading in Swedish interest rate derivatives moved to London consequent to a transactions tax being levied on fixed income securities and associated derivatives on 1 January 1989. In the first week of the tax, trading volumes for bonds fell by 85 per cent, for futures on bonds and bills by 98 per cent, and trading for fixed income derivatives virtually disappeared. The tax was removed fifteen months later.

(e) *Enhancing Liquidity*

Illiquidity affects all but a few stocks in an appreciably sized portfolio of a fund manager, and between 50 and 80 per cent of daily trading on the BSE and NSE is often accounted for by just five stocks. Illiquidity manifests itself through high impact costs of trading, as Table 8.3 demonstrates. The impact cost differences between the most and the least liquid of the NSE-50 stocks are staggeringly high, demonstrating that liquidity tapers off rapidly. At present liquidity arises through opportunities to arbitrage[28] between the BSE and NSE on account of their weekly trading cycles being non-synchronous, through offsetting trades being conducted during the same trading cycle ('squaring up'), and through *badla* finance now available on the BSE. As in capital markets elsewhere, liquidity is likely to rise sharply and become less skewed when opportunities for arbitrage between separate but related markets become available, and the absence of exchange traded derivatives has thus constrained the broadbasing of liquidity across stocks.

---

[28]These trading volumes arising out of arbitrage are often contrasted with the much lower volumes for delivery. Notwithstanding a popular perception, however, they are complements rather than substitutes for each other. Thus, the higher trading volumes on the NSE compared to the BSE have also resulted in higher proportionate deliveries, as the following Table demonstrates.

DELIVERIES IN STOCK EXCHANGES 1996–97

Stock Exchange	Turnover (Rs billion)	Delivery Value (Rs billion)	Delivery %	% Share in Total Delivery for 5 Exchanges
NSE	2945	358	12.2	72.6
BSE	1243	110	8.9	22.2
Calcutta	1057	16	1.5	3.2
Delhi	486	8	1.5	1.5
Ahmedabad	205	2	1.2	0.5
Total of 5 exchanges	5936	494		
Total of remaining 17 exchanges	525			
Total of 22 exchanges	6461			

TABLE 8.3
IMPACT COSTS ON NSE-50 STOCKS IN FEB–JULY 1997

(per cent)

Portfolio/ Scrip	Transaction Size		
	Rs 5 million	Rs 10 million	Rs 20 million
NSE-50	0.29	0.35	0.40
Lowest in NIFTY	0.13	0.15	0.18
Highest in NIFTY	1.30	1.61	2.20

Source: NSE.

The clearing corporation holds the key to the enhancement of liquidity through leveraging. As discussed earlier, it is the only institution in the market which can generate confidence that brokers are creditworthy. Its role in assessing the risks taken in derivatives trading and in ensuring proper margining will be crucial to activating arbitrage between the derivatives and the cash markets.[29]

(f) *Depository Settled Trading*

Trading in the sole depository, NSDL, which began operation in December 1996 has hitherto been low. FIIs are joining the depository cautiously, and a lower level of liquidity than in paper trading is perceived as a limitation. Liquidity being critical to fund managers and institutional investors, it is unlikely that they will barter it away in exchange for faster, cleaner and cheaper settlement. In the absence of compulsion, depository settled trading can be expected to grow slowly.

There are three good reasons for policy intervention. First, the incidence of fraud in paper securities is growing, and though still very low it could escalate suddenly; the most effective antidote to this is dematerialization. Second, if depository trading rises gradually, it will at a certain point fragment the market, and therefore shrink total trading liquidity. Third, stock lending—which is crucial for expanding liquidity—can only work within the book entry segment, as lenders would otherwise have a fear of receiving bad deliveries in return for good deliveries. The most effective way to handle this is for regulatory law to

---

[29]Liquidity in a stock is generally viewed as a function of the market's perception of the quality of the stock, the size of the float, and the availability of information about the company. The standard finance literature uses intertemporal models to price 'immediacy', an inherent characteristic of liquidity. O'Hara (1995) provides examples of how market microstructure can also influence liquidity through 'cross-section' models.

mandate that all trading above a certain modest level of trades should be depository settled; thereby all institutional trades will move to the book entry segment in one shot.[30]

(g) *The Problem of 'Block Deals'*

Despite the much faster price discovery on limit order books, large or 'block' deals continue to be transacted off the screen, for reasons of better price realization.(This is reminiscent of the 'upstairs market' on the New York Stock Exchange.[31]) A major reason is the assurance of good deliveries in directly negotiated purchases, and the wider integration of such trades with the limit order book would therefore require such trades to be depository settled and adequately liquid. Such a change in microstructure would greatly extend the reach of the limit order book.

(h) *Shakeout among the Exchanges*

With two exchanges having gone 'national', the future for several regional exchanges must appear bleak. Mergers and the close down of some exchanges appear likely.

4. THE DEBT MARKET

The microstructure of the debt market has, in recent years, changed much less than in equities, and has had the following consequences: first, the market has been fragmented on account of heterogeneous regulatory norms arising from competing regulators, as also from differential taxa-

---

[30]In October 1997 SEBI announced a move in this direction. In the first instance, as from 15 January 1998, all trading by institutional investors in eight stocks was to be mandatorily depository-settled. In subsequent modifications, and in order to assist institutions to cope with illiquidity, SEBI now permits institutions to also purchase paper shares, as also to sell dematerialized shares in the paper trading segment.

[31] In 1992, over 50 per cent of the total traded volume on the NYSE was accounted for by such block trades, defined as trades of at least 10,000 shares. A fundamental asymmetry exists in the way orders are submitted on that exchange, as 'blocks are sold, not bought'. It is of interest that most block trades in India during 1996 were 'bought, not sold', an asymmetry nonetheless. O'Hara (1995) argues that a separate market for block trades arises because of superior 'search' properties in locating counterparties to block deals, compared to screen trading. For market-making exchanges such as the NYSE, the limited risk-bearing capabilities of 'specialists' also induce a separate market for trading.

tion, and this has left it an essentially telephone market, often leading to poor price discovery. Second, the market will not provide for the accessing of *very* long-term debt (such as infrastructure finance) in the absence of insurance and pension fund reform. Third, the absence of interest rate derivatives results in an inability to manage the risk of holding fixed income portfolios. Fourth, even though the stock of debt issued is high, the secondary market is very illiquid and trading volumes will be low unless the number of investor classes is enlarged leading to investor expectations becoming adequately heterogeneous. And finally, trading volumes will also be restricted unless institutional investors acquire incentives to price debt more accurately. These propositions are discussed after a brief review of the debt market microstructure.[32]

4.1 DEBT MARKET MICROSTRUCTURE

Notwithstanding secondary market illiquidity, securitized debt issues have grown rapidly over the last decade and the outstanding issued stock is estimated to be the third largest in Asia, after Japan and Korea. It is dominated by government debt (bonds of the central and state governments, and treasury bills issued by the central government), amounting in March 1996 to 64 per cent of total outstanding securitized debt. Table 8.4 reveals the composition of outstanding debt, and demonstrates that it is central government bonds which constitute the most dominant instrument category. The RBI places central and state government debt in the market or, failing that, purchases the debt itself. While fiscal policy determines the size of aggregate government debt, it is RBI's debt management policy which shapes the composition of this debt. Public sector undertakings (PSUs) issue bonds, which are sometimes tax-free, and for some bonds the central government also guarantees repayments. Finally, outstanding private sector corporate debt is comparatively low, where the instruments include debentures, which can also be partly or fully converted into equity.

---

[32]Corporate debt instruments issued include bonds (known also as debentures, including convertibles), certificates of deposit (issued by banks and financial institutions), short-term commercial paper, and units of mutual funds. However, the fixed income securities market is dominated by the issuance of government securities (generally treasury bills of 14-day, 91-day and 364-day maturities, and longer dated securities with maturities between two and ten years).

TABLE 8.4
STOCK OF OUTSTANDING SECURITIZED DEBT

(Rs billion)

As at end-March:	1986	1989	1992	1995	1996
Total bond market instruments	643	1216	1825	2614	2941
Of which:					
Central government bonds	353	552	772	1305	1570
State government bonds	61	107	190	305	331
Govt. guaranteed bonds	205	238	341	–	270
PSU bonds	4	72	216	332	365
Corporate bonds (estimated)	100	280	330	300	405
Total money market instruments	260	143	160	321	531
Of which:					
Treasury bills	260	143	88	256	437
Certificates of deposit	–	–	70	35	59
Commercial paper	–	–	2	30	35
Total securitized debt	903	1359	1986	2935	3472

Source: World Bank (1995) and RBI, *Report on Currency and Finance*, 1996.

One reason for the low trading in debt is the limited number of well capitalized, institutional players, and in the case of government securities which are held by a large number of banks in pursuance of mandatory reserve requirements, trading is limited by the largely homogeneous nature of preferences which banks have at any point of time. Overseas investments in such instruments were, until recently, subject to stringent entry barriers, on the argument that they added to the stock of the country's external borrowings. Investment by an FII in corporate fixed income securities was permitted in 1996, and investment in government securities (excluding treasury bills) in 1997. In practice, FII investments continue to be made almost entirely in corporate equity.

Trading volumes in treasury bills make these instruments relatively liquid, though other securitized debt instruments are very illiquid as Table 8.5 demonstrates. Several recent studies have documented the reasons for the illiquidity of the secondary debt market, notwithstanding the government having moved rapidly from 1993 to borrow in the market by conducting auctions, and despite the NSE having commenced wholesale debt trading in 1994.[33] These measures, though conducive to developing greater activity in the debt market, are clearly not sufficient;

[33]Two recent studies are World Bank (1995) and NSE (1996).

with price controls on debt issuance having been largely eliminated, a significant upsurge in debt market trading can occur only with crucial changes in the regulatory regime and with an institutional reorientation which situates debt trading in a more active treasury and investment management strategy.

TABLE 8.5
TRADING VOLUME AND LIQUIDITY IN 1994

(Rs billion)

Instrument	Outstanding Amount at Year-end	Yearly Trading Volume	Turnover Ratio (%)
Commercial paper	30.0	36.0	120.0
Treasury bills*	150.0	120.0	80.0
Central government bonds	1305.0	72.0	5.5
PSU bonds	332.0	12.0	3.6
Corporate debentures	330.0	5.0	1.5
State government bonds	272.0	1.2	0.4
Government guaranteed bonds	388.0	0.6	0.1
Certificates of deposit	30.0	NA	NA

Note: * Refers only to auctioned bills.

Source: World Bank (1995).

(a) *Market Fragmentation*

The debt market is fragmented. Segmentation by maturity begins with the division in regulatory jurisdiction, with the RBI regulating the issuance of money market instruments and SEBI regulating the issuance of longer-term corporate debt instruments.[34] A synchronization of policy is sometimes impeded by this dichotomy, as disclosure and credit rating requirements differ, as do modalities for issuance which are stipulated by each regulator. Fragmentation also characterizes the money market, as the inter-bank market, the commercial paper market, and the certificates of deposit market are subject to dissimilar regulatory norms.

(b) *Compulsions to Hold till Maturity*

Accounting norms for banks, which are the main holders of government debt, are stipulated by the RBI, and they can value a portion of their

---

[34]With the caveat that, in the case of PSU bonds, the Ministry of Finance has been prescribing norms for issuance which are less stringent than those laid down by SEBI for the issuance of other corporate debt.

debt securities at their cost of acquisition.[35] A more rapid phasing in of the market valuation of securities will conflict with the pace of recapitalization of banks which the government is presently agreeable to, and which has been held back on fiscal grounds. A 'hold till maturity' approach to securities for a part of the portfolio will therefore continue to guide the perspective of banks, thereby reducing trading volumes. The position is worse with respect to insurance companies and provident funds. Under the Insurance Act, 1938, which is applicable to life and general insurance, all investments are to be valued at cost. This inevitably generates a 'buy and hold' perspective, without an active strategy for trading in debt so as to maximize the market value of the investment portfolio. Provident funds, too, are subject to identical guidelines.

(c) *Liquidity in the Money Market*

Liquidity varies inversely with the maturity of a bond[36], and a condition precedent to developing longer-term debt markets is therefore the enhancement of liquidity in the money market. For this the inter-bank market, which constitutes the core of the money market and thereby provides the key benchmark interest rates, needs to be developed.[37] Further, the RBI needs to allow a much wider range of repurchase offer agreements (or repos) between traders in securities than is currently permissible.[38]

---

[35]In 1992 RBI stipulated that at least 30 per cent of these securities be marked to market, the rest being valued at cost. This was increased to 40 per cent in 1994 and 50 per cent in 1996. The proportions correspond roughly to the government securities acquired by banks from 1991 onwards, and as this proportion rises in future it is expected that so will the proportion needed to be marked to market.

[36]Because price variance increases with maturity, and liquidity generally decreases with price volatility.

[37]A Cash Reserve Ratio (CRR) on the Net Demand and Time Liabilities (NDTL) of banks is pre-empted by the RBI and computed on a fortnightly basis, ending each 'Reporting Friday'. Banks therefore had an incentive to minimize their NDTL each Reporting Friday, by striving to reduce to zero their inter-bank borrowings, only to raise the levels soon thereafter. This hampered the development of inter-bank markets for maturities exceeding two weeks. In April 1997, the RBI withdrew inter-bank reserve requirements.

[38]Ninety-six per cent of global money market transactions are estimated to be in the form of repos. Further, about 90 per cent of transactions in India were through repos, before repos were severely curtailed by the RBI in 1992 (with only repos

(d) Broadening the Investor Base

The broadening of the investor and trader base has typically focused on providing participation for the overseas investor without dismantling barriers to domestic participation. However, FIIs have invested very little in fixed income paper, as falling domestic interest rates during 1997 have diminished the attractiveness of debt. Instead, reducing preemptions on the resources of insurance companies and provident funds, and a major broadbasing of the pension fund industry offer greater confidence that the trading of debt will rise rapidly.[39] Mutual funds, particularly the UTI, also have incentives to trade, and other trading categories are needed to create a microstructure which actively encourages trading.[40]

(e) Facilitating the Management of Interest Rate Risk

Interest rate swaps, bond futures, and repos are among the instruments which enable the risk of holding fixed-income portfolios to be managed. Such portfolios cannot grow unless SEBI facilitates the introduction of such instruments.

(f) Encouraging Debt Securitization

The securitization of existing debt will also broaden the class of debt

---

between commercial banks and the RBI in selected government securities being subsequently permitted). See NSE (1996). Repos on government securities (as also on PSU bonds and units of UTI) became a conduit for the siphoning of bank funds into the securities market during 1991 and 1992, facilitated by the absence of a delivery versus payment (DVP) mechanism for settling transactions in these instruments. Such a mechanism for government securities was introduced by the RBI in 1995, with the RBI maintaining the ownership register for banks and specified financial institutions in the form of a Subsidiary General Ledger (SGL). A restoration of repos under a DVP system could therefore avoid the emergence of earlier irregularities. A trader without an SGL account can trade by crediting either cash or securities to his bank, which in turn makes identical credit and debit entries in its SGL account.

[39]Resources are preempted to the extent of 75 per cent in the case of LIC and to the extent of 70 per cent in the case of the general insurance companies.

[40]Till early 1997, bond issues of financial institutions also provided confidence that *retail marketing* could result in handsome subscriptions, but the very illiquid secondary market appears to have created a situation of some debt fatigue. Provided trading opportunities can be created, the retail market—which has been a good source of equity funding and mutual fund resource mobilization since the early 1980s—could well be tapped to broaden the investor base for debt.

holders who wish to trade. Although sporadic attempts at securitization have taken place, the mechanisms proposed for securitization are necessarily contrived, involving securitizing the beneficial returns on the debt, rather than the debt itself, in view of the much higher stamp duty payable under the Transfer of Property Act when tangible assets are traded. As stamp duty under the Indian Stamp Act is akin to a turnover tax and therefore inefficient, a major rationalization of stamp duty provisions in its applicability to the securities market would be beneficial.

(g) *Regulating Private Debt Issuance*

Debenture issuance costs through private placements are a tenth of the public issue costs, as Table 8.6 demonstrates, acting as a disincentive to making public issues. However, disclosures for private issuance are often very poor, and regulation needs to tighten this before the quality of privately issued paper deteriorates, particularly as private debt issuance has become very popular in recent months. There are, for instance, no obligations on firms for post-issue reporting.

TABLE 8.6
AVERAGE ISSUANCE COST FOR A RS 1 BILLION CORPORATE DEBT ISSUE

(per cent)

Item of Cost	Public Issue	Private Placement
Trusteeship fees	0.02	–
Issue management fees	0.50	0.50
Rating agency fees	0.20	–
Stamp duties	0.02	0.02
Listing fees	–	–
Transfer registration	0.50	–
Brokerage fees	1.50	–
Postage, printing & other expenses	3.50	0.10
TOTAL	6.24	0.62

Source: NSE (1996).

(h) *Market Pricing of Bonds*

The accurate valuation of bonds is crucial to their enhanced tradeability. Bonds are mispriced because of tax-generated aberrations and the inadequately sophisticated techniques of valuation adopted by large holders of debt.[41] Differential tax rates (such as different interest tax rates payable by different categories of debt holders) lead to trades being priced bilaterally through the telephone market, and this forestalls the emergence of generalized market prices based on a process of price discovery on an order book.[42] Further, trading on an exchange is more expensive than bilaterally negotiated trading through the 'telephone market'. Brokers have to pay a 5 per cent turnover tax on income for trading, which banks are often unprepared to bear. Finally, although Indian debt portfolio managers have moved recently to computing yields to maturity rather than current yields, techniques of risk containment which emphasize portfolio duration and convexity are not deployed.[43] Consequently, bond portfolio valuation techniques adopted lead to the mispricing of securities. As trading in debt securities rises, commercial incentives in adopting more sophisticated valuation techniques can be expected to increase. Similarly, price calibration based on credit rating is still relatively coarse, and will improve only when the major institutional investors in debt begin to perceive the commercial benefits of finer calibration.

5. MUTUAL FUNDS

Although illiquidity in the equities market and the absence of derivatives have constrained the ability of fund managers to actively manage their portfolios (as discussed earlier in relation to the secondary market), it is regulatory law rather than market microstructure which has been more decisive in influencing fund industry practices. Recent relaxations in regulations open out the possibility of mutual funds offering new products which will help investors to understand, and choose more critically from, competing risk-return investment alternatives. Mutual funds have

---

[41]The debate in India on the reasons for the inadequate activity in the secondary debt market has tended to ignore the importance of proper valuation. NSE (1996) provides a discussion of issues.

[42]It has also induced debt holders to sell their debt just before interest payments are due, and to repurchase them after interest has been paid. This is known in the market as *voucher trading* and facilitates tax avoidance. Voucher trading in government securities has been eliminated after the removal of Tax Deduction at Source (TDS) on earnings on such debt in April 1997.

[43]Convexity is the second derivative of the price–yield relationship.

the opportunity therefore of *separating investors* according to their risk-bearing preferences, and of providing a superior understanding of different kinds of market risk. These ideas are developed after a discussion of mutual fund regulation and of the growth of the industry and its impact on market efficiency.

5.1 HISTORY: REGULATING MUTUAL FUNDS

The Mutual Funds regulations were first notified in 1993, indicating that the regulatory framework has evolved recently.[44] The regulations require mutual funds to be set up as trusts with distinct legal entities needed to be constituted in the management of funds, separating for each fund the board of trustees, the asset management company, and the custodian, with an independent division of functions between them.[45] The possibility is recognized of conflicts of interest with the sponsor, and constraints placed in order that asset management is not subordinated to the resource needs of the sponsor.[46] Such a management structure is clearly conducive to mutual funds discharging their fiduciary responsibilities to investors. Amendments to regulatory law in 1996 and 1997 have also provided flexibility to funds to adjust to fast changing market conditions which require the use of defensive fund management strategies to cope with unexpected

[44]Major amendments to the regulations were made in 1996, and again in 1997. Although the UTI now comes within SEBI's regulatory purview, the manner of its regulation is circumscribed by the UTI Act which invests fund management authority in the board of trustees and in its committees. SEBI has sought since 1994 to bring UTI's new schemes on a par with the discipline which other fund schemes are subject to.

[45]Trusts are constituted under the Indian Trusts Act, which was enacted in 1882 primarily to govern nineteenth-century charitable and religious organizations. The counterpart for corporate governance is more appropriately the Indian Companies Act, 1956, and unit holders would then be akin to shareholders in such a 'trustee company', while trustees would be akin to the Board of Directors. Internationally, mutual funds can be constituted under either form, though in India the trustee company form is not popular. The liabilities of trustees under the two Acts differ, and the issue needs to be addressed from the perspective of corporate governance when there are strong fiduciary obligations.

[46]This is sought to be achieved by stipulating that the Board of Trustees and of the asset management company (AMC) should contain an adequate number of directors who are independent of the sponsor; and by restricting the transactions which the mutual fund can conduct with the affiliate businesses of the sponsor.

market adversities.[47] There is also a much stronger emphasis on fuller disclosures with the design of a standardized offer document.

5.2 GROWTH OF THE INDUSTRY

The evolution of the Indian mutual funds industry can be telescoped into three distinct phases. The UTI was the only mutual fund in the country during the first phase from 1964 to 1987, with the monopoly being broken in the second phase when public sector banks and financial institutions were permitted to sponsor mutual funds. Finally, in 1993 a further liberalization occurred with private sector entry being allowed. Sponsors from overseas are also permitted to invest in domestic asset management companies (AMCs), typically on a joint venture basis, during this most recent phase. Table 8.7 reveals that the UTI's dominance in the industry continues, with an 83 per cent share of cumulative resources raised for asset management, while the private sector has achieved a 4 per cent market share. During 1995–6, which was a difficult year for resource mobilization by the mutual fund industry, the UTI had a share of 92 per cent of funds mobilized within the industry. In 1996–7, the UTI's share was 94 per cent.

Changes in the composition of household financial savings illustrate the pace of growth of the mutual fund industry. In 1985–6 a minute 0.3 per cent of gross household financial savings was invested in units of the UTI, but this had increased rapidly to 7 per cent in 1993–4. If investments in shares and debentures are added, this aggregate stock market investment rose from 3.7 per cent to 15.8 per cent of gross household financial savings during the same period. It is apparent from

---

[47]Earlier investment restrictions stipulated that not more than 5 per cent of a scheme's corpus or 10 per cent of a fund's corpus could be invested in the shares of a single company, and that not more than 5 per cent of the voting rights of a company could be held by all schemes in a fund. Schemes were also not permitted to borrow to meet unforeseen redemptions. Limits were also placed on the proportion of funds which could be deployed in cash or cash equivalents in a falling stock market in order to mitigate the fall in NAVs. Had regulatory constraints to doing so not existed, the fall in NAVs during 1995 could arguably have been better cushioned, and it can be argued that investor interests have therefore not been subserved by some of these regulatory norms. SEBI now permits the burden of risk management to be shifted from the regulator to the AMC by giving it wider autonomy in determining its asset structure, while requiring that adequate portfolio disclosures be made.

Table 8.8 that this increase over thirteen years has been largely at the expense of the share of bank deposits held by households. Further, there were 196 schemes operating at the end of July 1995, of which 159 were closed-end while 37 were open-end.

TABLE 8.7

MUTUAL FUND CUMULATIVE RESOURCE MOBILIZATION

(Rs billion)

Up to	UTI	Sponsor of Mutual Fund		Total Non-UTI	Total
		Public Sector	Private Sector		
June 1987	45.64				45.64
June 1988	67.39				67.39
June 1989	118.35	16.21		16.21	134.56
June 1990	176.51	14.60		14.60	191.11
June 1991	213.76	16.84		16.84	230.60
June 1992	318.06	56.74		56.74	374.80
June 1993	389.77	80.11		80.11	469.88
June 1994	519.78	84.07	9.16	93.23	613.01
June 1995	615.00	105.50	30.00	135.50	750.50
Dec 1995	667.00	106.67	32.23	138.90	805.90
%	83	13	4	17	100

Source: Securities and Exchange Board of India (1996)

TABLE 8.8

COMPOSITION OF HOUSEHOLD FINANCIAL SAVINGS

(per cent)

Financial Asset	1980–1	1985–6	1990–1	1993–4
Gross household financial savings	100.0	100.0	100.0	100.0
Of which:				
Currency	13.4	8.7	11.0	14.2
Bank deposits	45.8	41.0	29.2	37.3
Life insurance fund	7.5	7.0	9.8	8.9
Provident and pension fund	17.5	16.4	19.6	16.7
Shares and debentures	3.4	5.5	8.7	8.8
Units of UTI	0.3	2.3	6.0	7.0
Others	12.1	18.8	15.6	7.1
Gross household financial savings in Rs billion	121	256	569	935
Net household financial savings in Rs billion		186	463	810
Net household financial savings as % of net household savings		52	43	49

Source: RBI, *Report on Currency and Finance*, various issues.

The entry of privately sponsored mutual funds consequent to policy liberalization in 1993 also coincided with a rising stock market. Although this helped mutual funds in raising resources, the steady fall in the market index after it peaked around September 1994 led to an erosion in the BSE's market capitalization by over 30 per cent by the end of 1995. This led typically to a steep decline in the NAVs of funds which had invested strongly in equities as the market fell, while schemes listed on stock exchanges also began quoting at high discounts to their NAVs. For instance, during 1995 the average discount to NAV for closed-end schemes was in the range of 19–26 per cent, and has continued in that range even while the markets revived in 1997. Despite liberalization in this sector, it is evident that the gloss has worn off the newer mutual funds before the larger gains of enhanced competition have been realized, and it is only in 1997 that a limited reversal of this trend is visible. The limited gains for investors hitherto have come from superior disclosures and some product diversity in the design of fund schemes, though the greatest diversity continues to be in the varied menu of schemes offered by the UTI. Superior disclosures include daily computations of NAVs, voluntary half-yearly details of investment portfolios and periodic newsletters. Diversity in the characteristics of mutual funds includes greater variety in the maturity periods of closed-end schemes; switchover facilities between schemes of a fund to match changing investor preferences on risk-return trade-offs; and withdrawal plans in closed-end schemes so as to harmonize better with the investor's liquidity requirements.[48] The polarization between closed-end and open-end schemes has become fuzzier, with schemes having intermediate characteristics being launched. Regulatory changes have led to a standardization and more detailed listing of disclosures in offer documents, and investors and financial analysts now consequently receive better quality information about fund schemes than they did some years back.

5.3 EMPIRICAL EVIDENCE OF STRONG-FORM EFFICIENCY

How has the evolution of the mutual funds industry affected the efficiency of the capital market? If trading strategies are contingent on information available, mutual funds which can be expected to have

[48]Systematic withdrawal plans of closed-end funds at near-NAV prices provide considerable boost to liquidity, as these funds which need mandatorily to be listed under SEBI regulation typically trade at very high discounts to NAV.

additional information about companies into which they have invested would be expected to outperform other investors who do not have such information. It is possible to empirically evaluate this by investigating whether the capital market in India provides evidence of *strong-form efficiency*, an efficiency concept which admits a broader category of information which is relevant for price formation: both public and commonly available information as also *private information* which may be available exclusively to large institutional investors and corporates, including mutual funds. The market is characterized by strong-form efficiency if access to such private information cannot result in the generation of consistently superior returns. One test of strong-form efficiency is therefore determined by the returns earned by mutual funds.

There is no clear pattern emerging from the performance of schemes. Thus, one study has evaluated the performance of several schemes during periods extending up to April 1994 (Shah and Thomas, 1994). By utilizing weekly returns data, it computes for each scheme the expected value of cumulative excess returns (which are the returns in excess of the riskless rate of interest, compounded over the period). By comparing it with similar returns on the Sensex, it concludes that out of eleven schemes six schemes generated negative excess returns while only one (the UGS 2000 of UTI) outperformed the market.[49]

5.4 NEW PRODUCTS

As the markets become more efficient and exchange-traded derivative contracts get written, mutual funds can be expected to offer products whose risk bounds are defined at the outset and can be asset managed to keep within those bounds. Thus index funds, which are already available to offshore investors, will also begin attracting domestic investors. Index-plus funds, which will be *partially* actively managed, will enable investors to take higher (but bounded) risks in return for expected returns which are superior to market index returns. Money market funds, which were launched in 1997 and have shown early evidence of providing

[49]The study concludes that the schemes took on high levels of risk and that the variance of excess returns of mutual fund schemes resembles more closely the variance of excess returns of large listed companies, despite fund schemes being in a position to diversify and lower their risks in a manner which company shares cannot. This is non-intuitive and possibly explained by the caveat that estimates of diversifiable risk are derived from the capital asset pricing model (CAPM), whose validity for India has not as yet been supported by evidence.

appreciably higher returns than are earned from short-term bank deposits, can be expected to grow. Funds for private equity and infrastructure, hitherto largely mobilized overseas, can be expected to be raised domestically if the pension fund and insurance industry are liberalized. Investors will begin displaying varying appetites for risk, and for the containment of such risk.

6. BEYOND CAPITAL ACCOUNT CONVERTIBILITY

The limited financial integration hitherto with cross-border markets has spurred the development of an institutionalized network of capital market intermediaries, leading to a well-capitalized financial services industry. There have been several collaborations and strategic alliances since 1993 between domestic financial services companies and investment and merchant banks abroad. Overseas brokerage houses have also become members of the larger stock exchanges and thereby entered the Indian broking industry. The financial services industry has grown fast, is better capitalized than it was in 1991, and has witnessed rapid structural change with the emergence of some large finance companies. The manner of their regulation has, however, sometimes lacked definitiveness.

The convertibility of the rupee on the capital account will open new opportunities and expose existing weaknesses. In October 1997, the RBI signalled its intention to permit domestic mutual funds to invest in assets offshore, providing them with risk diversification opportunities hitherto denied to them. Overseas funds can also very soon be expected to seek approval to source an investor base in India. It is at this stage that financial product innovation will need to be nimble, if markets are not to move overseas. An exchange-traded derivatives market would need to be operational if it is not to move offshore where liquidity is higher, making a subsequent relocation back to India difficult; transactions costs for raising finance and for trading would need to be internationally competitive; and a conscious attempt would need to be made to adopt best international practices. The compulsions will be strong for regulators and market participants alike to be sensitive to the importance of market microstructure.

6.1 THE CURRENCY MARKET: A WILL O' THE WISP?

Currency market turmoils, which began in East Asia in 1997, rapidly spread to the stock markets in that region, and within days shaved appreciable value off stocks globally, raising new fears about capital account convertibility. If markets in East Asia were truly efficient, 'bad' news about burgeoning current account deficits and asset financing by banks (particularly in property loans) would have filtered into stock prices much earlier, rather than leading to episodic crashes. As currency and stock markets in India integrate with each other and with markets overseas, one imperative must be to make the domestic stock market more efficient. If the market is to trade more strongly on information, corporate disclosures would need to be faster and more accurate: tighter accounting standards including division-wise accounts for diversified companies, consolidation of accounts for multi-company groups, and faster changes in credit ratings, would assist the market in responding faster to corporate performance. But only if investors were to actively trade on this information.

This is unlikely to happen unless a diversified fund industry is in place. When there are fears among overseas institutional investors about the value of the currency, it is domestic fund managers (who do not face a currency risk) who can act as a bulwark against stock disinvestment from overseas. Such a domestic fund industry, underpinned by hetero-geneous expectations about the market, cannot emerge unless insurance and pension fund money is managed in a more diversified manner. While much of the recent policy focus has been on insurance, it is the transformation of the provident and pension fund industry which can result in short-term spread effects which will bring greater stability to the market.[50] By permitting long-term savings to enter the market, and bringing much needed trading liquidity to a substantially broader range of securities, it will widen the market; and by strengthening the trading sentiment based on price expectations devoid of the domestic currency risk, it will bring resilience and stability to the market.[51]

---

[50]The transformation of the insurance and pension fund sector has been inade-quately projected as an integral part of capital market reform. (Particularly in the case of insurance, this has concentrated the debate almost wholly on the issue of the ownership of companies in this sector.) The existing stock market cap is about Rs 4.5 trillion, while the floating stock is appreciably lower with government continuing to hold large majority stakes in almost forty listed public sector companies which constitute about half the market cap. As against this, the total size of retirement funds is about Rs 1.3 trillion, indicating how powerful an impact retirement funds entering the capital market would generate.

[51]This is in addition to other benefits which a diversified pension fund industry will provide: enhancing earnings at retirement, and so mitigating old-age financial

There are two broad ideas which need acceptance for this to occur. The first is the notion of 'contracting out', of encouraging such funds to be managed by other asset managers, and of allowing employers and employees of firms to contract out the management of their pension funds to such asset managers, as also to switch between asset managers at near-zero cost.[52] And the second is to permit diversification across asset classes, without which there can be no benefit to the capital market, implying that the current ban on investing in private corporate debt, mutual funds and equities would need relaxation. This also requires government expenditures to be managed without the existing excessive reliance on retirement fund preemptions.

REFERENCES

Akerlof, G.A. (1970). 'The Market for "lemons": Quality Uncertainty and the Market Mechanism'. *Quarterly Journal of Economics*, vol. 84, pp. 488–500.

Benveniste, L.M. and P.A. Spindt (1989). 'How Investment Bankers Determine the Offer Price and Allocation of New Issues'. *Journal of Financial Economics*, vol. 15, pp. 343–61.

Bray, M. (1989). 'Rational Expectations, Information and Asset Markets', in F.H. Hahn (ed.), *The Economics of Missing Markets*. Oxford: Clarendon Press.

---

distress; providing long-term funds for the development of infrastructure, which are raised today either from the government or from overseas, with domestic market-mediated long term savings being scarce; and thereby increasing the domestic savings rate. Very rarely in economic policy intervention is there an opportunity to reach out simultaneously for growth, market stabilization, and distributional equity. A well-structured reform of the pension fund market provides just such an opportunity.

[52]This is the device which Chile adopted in the early 1980s, and which several other South American countries have moved to: Argentina, Bolivia, Columbia, Mexico, Peru, and Uruguay. Contracting out was also the device which the UK adopted in the mid-1980s. The device has led in other countries to competitiveness between fund managers and to increased yields. As in Chile, the government could set a minimum yield which is linked to the average yield earned by all such asset managers. With a tight regulatory system in place, asset managers whc underperform would need to draw from reserves and (where these are inadequate) to bring in additional capital. These will therefore be fully funded pension arrangements. Patel (1997) contains a discussion of the relevance to India of pension fund models elsewhere.

Chowdhury, S.K. (1991). 'Short-run Share Price Behaviour: New Evidence on Weak-form Market Efficiency'. *Vikalpa*, vol. 16, no. 4, pp. 17–21.

Fama, E.F. (1965). 'The Behaviour of Stock Market Prices'. *Journal of Business*, vol. 38, no. 1, pp. 34–105.

Grossman, S.J. and J.E. Stiglitz. (1980). 'On the Impossibility of Informationally Efficient Markets'. *American Economic Review*, vol. 70, no. 3, pp. 393–408.

Hurwicz, L. (1972), 'On Informationally Decentralized Systems'. In R. Radner and C.B. McGuire (eds), *Decision And Organization: A Volume in Honour of Jacob Marschak*. Amsterdam: North-Holland.

Madhusoodanan, T.P. and M. Thiripalraju. (1997). 'Underpricing in Initial Public Offerings: The Indian Evidence'. *Vikalpa*, vol. 22, no. 4, pp. 17–30.

National Stock Exchange (NSE). (1996). *A Review of the Operational Impediments of the Debt Market in India*. Report prepared by Price Waterhouse LLP, Arlington, Virginia.

Nayak, P.J. (1996). *Information, Incentives and Regulation: The Microstructure of Financial Markets*. Policy Paper no. 8, LARGE. New Delhi: Allied Publishers Limited.

————. (1997). 'The Inefficiency of Public Equity Issues'. In S. Gangopadhyay (ed.), *Institutions Governing Financial Markets*. New Delhi: Allied Publishers Limited.

Obaidullah, M. (1990). 'Stock Market Efficiency: A Statistical Inquiry'. *Chartered Financial Analyst*, vol. 5, no. 1 (July–August), pp. 10–14.

————. (1991). 'Earnings, Stock Prices and Market Efficiency: Indian Evidence'. *Securities Industries Review* (Singapore), October.

————. (1992). 'How Do Stock Prices React to Bonus Issues?'. *Vikalpa*, vol. 17, no. 1, pp.17–22.

————. (1994). *Indian Stock Market: Theories and Evidence*. Hyderabad: The Institute of Chartered Financial Analysts of India.

O'Hara, M. (1995). *Market Microstructure Theory*. Oxford: Blackwell Publishers.

Patel, U. (1997). 'Aspects of Pension Fund Reform: Lessons for India'. *Economic and Political Weekly*, vol. 32, no. 38, pp. 2395–2402.

Ramachandran, J. (1988). 'Behaviour of Stock Market Prices, Information Assimilation and Market Efficiency'. Unpublished thesis, Indian Institute of Management, Ahmedabad.

Rao, N.K. (1988). *Stock Market Efficiency: The Indian Experience*. New Delhi: Anmol Publications.

Rock, K. (1986). 'Why New Issues are Underpriced'. *Journal of Financial Economics*, vol. 15, pp. 187–212.

Securities and Exchange Board of India (SEBI). (1994). *Indian Securities Market: Agenda for Development and Reform*. Mumbai: SEBI.

———. (1996). *Mutual Funds 2000 Report*. Mumbai: SEBI.

Shah, A. (1995). *The Indian IPO Market: Empirical Facts*. Mumbai: Centre for Monitoring the Indian Economy.

Shah, A. and S. Thomas (1994). *Performance Evaluation of Professional Portfolio Managers in India*. Mumbai: Centre for Monitoring the Indian Economy.

———. (1997). 'Securities Markets: Towards Greater Efficiency'. In K.S. Parikh (ed.), *India Development Report 1997*. Delhi: Oxford University Press.

Srinivasan, S., P. Mohapatra, and K. Sahu. (1988). 'Weak-form Efficiency in Indian Stock Market: No Excess Return for Investors'. *Modern Management*, vol 5, no. 2.

Stiglitz, J.E. (1982). 'Information and Capital Markets'. In W.E. Sharpe and C.M. Cootner (eds), *Financial Economics: Essays in Honour of Paul Cootner*. London: Prentice-Hall.

Thomas, S. (1995). 'An Empirical Characterization of the Bombay Stock Exchange'. Unpublished Ph.D Thesis, University of Southern California, Los Angeles, California.

Tinic, S.M. (1988). 'Anatomy of Initial Public Offerings of Common Stock'. *Journal of Finance*, vol. 43, pp. 789–822.

World Bank. (1995). *The Emerging Asian Bond Market: India*. Mumbai: Report prepared by ICICI Securities and Finance Company Ltd.

Yalawar, Y.B. (1986). 'Rates of Return and Efficiency on Bombay Stock Exchange'. Research Monograph, Indian Institute of Management, Bangalore.

Restructuring Pensions for the Twenty-first Century

S.A. DAVE*

(India) 015016
H55
623

The world over, the percentage of population above the age of 60 is on the increase. According to estimates by the World Bank, this percentage will be on the rise throughout the twenty-first century and reach between 25 and 31 per cent by the year 2100. The level of this aging population was as high as 18.2 per cent in the OECD countries in 1990 and is expected to reach 27 per cent by the year 2020. In India, this percentage, which was 6.9 in 1990 is expected to increase to 10.3 by the year 2020 and 27.9 by the year 2100 (World Bank, 1994).

Care of this section of the population, the aged, is an area of serious concern for all societies. Many countries have evolved social security systems in the form of pension funds or provident funds with the state assuming considerable responsibility in making these payments or guaranteeing them. The resources required are increasing and in several countries posing a threat to government finances. Solutions are being sought to reasonably meet the responsibility without hampering economic growth. Ideally it should be a solution that, while taking care of the aged, simultaneously supports processes of economic growth. Experiences in Chile and Singapore give hope that the pursuit of these twin objectives can be reconciled.[1]

In India, aged people have traditionally been supported by the younger generation in a joint family or integrated family system. This

*I am grateful to the World Bank for providing financial support for preparation of this chapter. Information on the Indian pension fund industry is widely scattered and not easily available. I have benefited immensely from discussions with various individuals associated with the industry and working in the financial services sector. My special thanks to Nalin Thakore, Urjit Patel, Ajay Shah, and Kaushik, Central Provident Fund Commissioner.
[1]For a good discussion *see* Sebastian (1996); Julio (1996); Kenneth (1995).

has been the largest and the most pervasive security system for the aged. Nevertheless, the Indian provident fund system is one of the oldest, and today, the largest social security system in the world serving about 25 million subscribers. It has become quite a complex system governed by several Acts. Provident fund is one of the benefit schemes payable to retired employees who have put in certain minimum years of service with the employer. This benefit is extended to the employees pursuant to the provisions contained in the Provident Fund Act, 1925, the Constitution of India, Employees Provident Fund and Miscellaneous Provisions Act, 1952 (EPFMF Act), the Income Tax Act 1961, the Public Provident Fund Act 1968, and other specified enactments.

With over 20 million subscribers to the Employees Provident Fund Scheme, plus direct government employees estimated at about 3 million and other public sector employees at about 1.5 million, the provident fund system covers hardly 6 per cent of the population within the age group 20–59 and 10 per cent of the labour force in the country. It is a mandatory scheme for all establishments employing more than twenty workers. There are about 300 million workers employed in the informal and unorganized sector. These workers and self-employed people are outside the ambit of the Employees Provident Fund Scheme. They can all be covered under a voluntary scheme: the Public Provident Fund Scheme, with similar tax benefits and similar rate of return but more generous withdrawal facilities. In terms of net growth rate, its performance is not very impressive. Somehow, it has not picked up well despite several attractive features.

Section 1 of the chapter describes broad features of provident fund schemes and pension funds prevalent in India, and offers an assessment of their performance. Section 2 briefly presents the features and achievements of the pension scheme in Chile and provident fund scheme in Singapore. Section 3 presents the needs of a social security system that is relevant for twenty-first-century India.

1. PENSION SCHEMES: FEATURES AND PERFORMANCE

The EPFMF Act, 1952, is the principal Act under which social security schemes for employees are provided. Today, this Act provides for (i) contributory provident fund; (ii) pension; and (iii) deposit linked insurance scheme.

The Employees' Provident Fund Scheme, 1952, is a defined contribution plan whereby employees contribute 8.33 per cent or 10 per cent of their wages to provident fund with a matching contribution by employers. (These figures were revised to 10 and 12 per cent with effect from September, 1997.)

The Employees' Pension Scheme, 1995, which incorporates the erstwhile Employees' Family Pension Scheme, 1971, has a much wider scope and provides for monthly pension. Employers' contribution towards the provident fund scheme is now diverted to this scheme. In addition, government contributes to it at the rate of 1.16 per cent of employees' wages. Employees do not contribute to the 1995 scheme, though they contributed to the 1971 scheme. This is a defined contribution cum defined benefit plan cum pay-as-you-go system. It provides for superannuation pension and survivor pension, but does not have withdrawal facilities for housing, medical needs, etc.

The Employees' Deposit Linked Insurance Scheme, 1976, provides an insurance cover in the unfortunate event of an employee's death. The employee does not contribute towards the insurance fund. The employer contributes at the rate of 0.5 per cent of wages, while government contributes at the rate of 0.25 per cent of the wages of the covered employee. In the event of the death of the employee (while in service), the person entitled to receive provident fund contributions would receive an additional amount equal to average balance in the account of the deceased during the preceding twelve months with a maximum of Rs 35,000.

The three schemes together provide a fairly comprehensive social security cover for those workers fortunate enough to be working in industrial and service establishments employing more than twenty workers.

The Employees Provident Fund Organization (EPFO) has been vested with the responsibility of implementing these three schemes. The Organization runs under the overall superintendence of the Central Board of Trustees, a tripartite body of the government, employees, and employers with the Union Minister of Labour as Chairman. The Chief Executive Officer is the Central Provident Fund Commissioner.

1.1 THE EMPLOYEES' PROVIDENT FUND SCHEME

This is the largest of the schemes with 278,000 establishments covered by it. The employers of these establishments have two options available to them: either to manage the provident funds themselves and get qualified as exempt funds or let the EPFO manage the funds and be classified as non-exempt funds. Those seeking exemptions have to satisfy certain criteria. The exempted companies are generally large companies. The number of exempt establishments at the end of March 1997 was 2970 compared to 274,583 non-exempt companies (Table 9.1).

TABLE 9.1
EMPLOYEES' PROVIDENT FUND SCHEME
(NO. OF COVERED ESTABLISHMENTS)

As on	Exempted	Unexempted	Total
31-3-1986	2790	155,073	157,863
31-3-1987	2797	163,243	166,040
31-3-1988	2830	167,595	170,425
31-3-1989	2882	178,761	181,643
31-3-1990	2907	192,054	194,961
31-3-1991	2933	204,053	206,986
31-3-1992	2956	208,503	211,459
31-3-1993	3041	220,549	223,590
31-3-1994	3109	233,772	236,881
31-3-1995	3143	247,870	251,013
31-3-1996	2934	263,711	266,645
31-3-1997	2970	274,585	277,555
CAGR	0.53	5.33	5.27

Note: CAGR–Compounded Annual Growth Rate
Source: EPFO, *Annual Reports*.

There were 20.3 million subscribers to the scheme at the end of March 1997 of which 4.6 million were to the exempt funds and 15.7 million to the non-exempt funds. With a share of just 1.1 per cent in total establishments, exempt funds command a share of 22.4 per cent in number of subscribers, indicating that exempted enterprises are large-sized enterprises (Table 9.2).

TABLE 9.2
EMPLOYEES' PROVIDENT FUND SCHEME (NO. OF SUBSCRIBERS)
(in thousands)

As on	Exempted	Unexempted	Total
31-3-1986	4025	9184	13,209
31-3-1987	4108	9500	13,609
31-3-1988	4179	9660	13,839
31-3-1989	4199	10,099	14,298
31-3-1990	4133	10,531	14,664
31-3-1991	4377	11,330	15,707
31-3-1992	4537	12,078	16,615
31-3-1993	4544	12,767	17,311
31-3-1994	4546	13,444	17,990
31-3-1995	4558	14,166	18,724
31-3-1996	4579	14,906	19,485
31-3-1997	4536	15,753	20,289
CAGR	1.12	5.05	4.00

Source: EPFO, *Annual Reports*.

The annual contributions to exempt and non-exempt funds also show a similar pattern with non-exempt funds demonstrating faster growth in the last ten years. This reflects the wider coverage of establishments under the non-exempt category (Table 9.3).

TABLE 9.3
EMPLOYEES' PROVIDENT FUND SCHEME
(CONTRIBUTIONS RECEIVED DURING THE YEAR)

(Rs Millions)

Year	Exempted	Unexempted	Total
1985–6	8600	6880	15,480
1986–7	10,240	7710	17,950
1987–8	11,510	8510	20,020
1988–9	13,870	10,370	24,250
1989–90	18,450	13,130	31,590
1990–1	20,410	16,250	36,670
1991–2	21,070	19,230	40,300
1992–3	24,580	22,080	46,660
1993–4	24,140	25,410	49,550
1994–5	22,810	27,960	50,770
1995–6	25,630	32,030	57,660
1996–7	30,560	29,150	59,710
CAGR	12.21	14.05	13.06

Source: EPFO, *Annual Reports*.

The cumulative contributions received under provident funds at the end of March 1997 were Rs 509,090 million with contributions from the exempt funds at Rs 274,960 million (54.01 per cent). This share of exempt funds, however, may be expected to diminish with an increasing number of smaller establishments coming under the fold of the EPFO (Table 9.4).

It is possible for subscribers to the Employees' Provident Fund Scheme, 1952, to make partial withdrawals for the purposes of house construction, illness, higher education of children, or marriage of brother, sister, etc. During the year 1995–6 there were 364,000 cases of withdrawals and the amount disbursed was Rs 5538 million which works out to about 2 per cent of the total funds in the non-exempt sector as on 31 March 1996. About 60 per cent of the withdrawals were for the purpose of house construction. Another 18 per cent was withdrawn for the purpose of one's own marriage or marriage of family members and for higher education of children. But overall, the withdrawals have not been significant. The figures for exempt funds are not readily available but they are unlikely to be very different from those for non-exempt funds.[2]

TABLE 9.4

EMPLOYEES' PROVIDENT FUND ORGANIZATION

(CUMULATIVE COLLECTIONS)

(Rs millions)

Year	Employees' Provident Fund	Family Pension	Employees' Deposit Linked Insurance Fund	Total
1985–6	131,630	11,310	2750	145,690
1986–7	–	–	–	–
1987–8	169,600	16,610	3790	190,000
1988–9	193,850	20,420	4320	218,590
1989–90	225,430	23,110	4650	253,190
1990–1	262,100	27,400	5270	294,770
1991–2	302,400	33,150	6000	341,550
1992–3	349,070	42,940	6780	398,790
1993–4	398,610	48,970	7800	455,380
1994–5	449,380	59,420	8610	517,410
1995–6	507,040	72,150	9810	589,000
1996–7	509,090	87,340	9530	605,960
CAGR	13.09	20.4	12.03	13.80

Source: EPFO, *Annual Reports*.

1.2 THE EMPLOYEES' PENSION SCHEME (EPS), 1995

The EPS, 1995 has replaced (with substantial modifications) the erstwhile Employees' Family Pension Scheme (EFPS), 1971. The EFPS had come into effect on March 1971 and was compulsorily applicable to all employees who became subscribers to the Provident Fund Scheme on or after March 1971. Those who were members of the Provident Fund Scheme prior to this date were given the option to join the new scheme.

The EFPS, 1971, was a contributory scheme and was financed by diverting a part of contributions ($1\frac{1}{6}$ per cent of wages) to provident fund of employees. In addition, the government also contributed an identical amount to the Family Pension Fund. It was a monthly pension scheme with benefits to survivors in the event of early death of the member.

[2]Compare this with Singapore where withdrawals in recent years have been more liberal. The corresponding percentage was nine per cent during 1976–83, 3.5 per cent during 1984–8 and 10 per cent during 1988–92. More than half of the withdrawals were for housing.

The EPS, 1995, is a more comprehensive scheme and provides for benefits to the member and his/her family in the following contingencies:

(I) Monthly pension to a member
   (a) on superannuation/retirement, and
   (b) on permanent/total disablement
(II) Family pension to spouse and two dependent children (below the age of 25) at a time on
   (1) death of a member while in service
   (2) death of a member as pensioner after superannuation or on permanent/total disablement
(III) Facility also exists for payment of pension to nominee of unmarried member and those having no family.

The quantum of pension will depend on the average of twelve months' salary prior to the retirement in accordance with applicable pension factor.

As mentioned earlier, employer's contribution to the provident fund of an employee is diverted to this scheme and government contributes at the rate of 1.16 per cent of wages of an employee.

The contributions received under the EFPS, 1971, were credited to the Public Account and earned an interest of 8.50 per cent from 1988. Contributions to the EPS from November 1995 onwards will be as per investment regulations of Employees' Provident Fund Scheme and will be managed by the EPFO, though government contributions of about Rs 90 billion till that date, to the EFPS, 1971, will continue to remain in the Public Account.

Exemption from the EPS, 1995, is possible, but in that event the government's contribution of 1.16 per cent will not be available and the employer may make good this contribution. So far not a single company has been granted such exemption by the EPFS.

The cumulative collections till 31 March 1997 were Rs 87 billion and have been growing at the annual rate of 20.4 per cent during the last ten years.

1.3 THE EMPLOYEES' DEPOSIT LINKED INSURANCE SCHEME (EDLIS), 1976

Contributions received under the EDLIS are credited to the Public Account and receive an interest of 8.5 per cent per annum. Total collections as on 31 March 1997 were Rs 9.5 billion.

1.4 LIFE INSURANCE CORPORATION OF INDIA (LIC)

Pension business is considered a part of the life insurance business, and under Section 2(11) of the Insurance Act, 1938, and Section 30 of the LIC Act, 1956, only the LIC can conduct pension business in India. The pension business, therefore, is an exclusive monopoly of the LIC in India. The pension business did not pick up in India until 1965 when the Payment of Bonus Act, 1965, was passed. Under this Act while bonus is compulsory for all workmen staff, officers above a certain level of income are not eligible for it. This prompted many companies to set up a superannuation scheme for their senior and high salaried officers who were not eligible for payment of bonus. But the growth has remained slow. During 1995–6, the LIC was administering 3305 group superannuation schemes covering 252,000 employees and with an annuity per annum of Rs 2.9 billion.

It is also possible for companies to accumulate funds till employees retire and buy an immediate annuity from the LIC. Under this the LIC had 672 schemes covering 167,000 employees and with an annuity of Rs 1.9 billion. But any company going to the LIC directly is not eligible for the government's contribution to pension scheme.

Pension funds, from the perspective of subscribers, suffer from the handicap that they do not offer withdrawal facilities which provident fund contributions offer. Moreover, pension funds also have the disadvantage that they are taxable when received in hand by subscribers whereas provident funds are tax exempt. Because of these factors, according to some officials of the LIC, pension schemes are less popular among Indian subscribers.

1.5 OTHER SCHEMES

Apart from the LIC's pension schemes, there is the government's pension scheme for central government employees. These funds are in the nature of a pay-as-you-go system. Similar schemes also exist for state government employees.

The is another scheme, a voluntary one, for self-employed people and all individuals called the Public Provident Fund (PPF), with tax concessions and return identical to the EPFO's provident fund scheme. It is in the nature of a voluntary, supplementary scheme for all those for whom the providend fund scheme is mandatory. The withdrawal facilities are liberal and up to 50 per cent of the funds subscribed can be withdrawn after four years. Total collections up to the end of March 1996 were

Rs 118 billion. The growth in net collections, however, has been slower. The scheme is not well marketed and has so far failed to pick up to the expected level despite very attractive features.

Besides, there are some occupational funds such as Army Group Funds, Coal Miners' Fund, and Seamens' Fund which are managed by different trusts with the help of fund managers. But they all broadly follow the investment regulations and return as prescribed for EPFO schemes.

Recently, the Reserve Bank of India, IDBI, UTI, State Bank of India, public sector banks, and insurance companies have set up their own pension schemes. Contributions are made out of employer's contribution to provident funds and have provision for both monthly and survivor pension. Pension is payable at the rate of the average of the last twelve months salary adjusted by a pension factor. No contribution is made by the government towards them. These schemes, therefore, are fully funded by employers.

It is not easy to collect information from all these sources and come to an aggregate figure for the provident funds and pension scheme in India. But it could be in the vicinity of Rs 1700 billion at the end of March 1998. The funds are not very large and may constitute about 12 per cent of GDP in 1997–8.

Contributions by employees to provident funds enjoy tax rebate up to a ceiling of Rs 60,000 (along with some other saving instruments). Employers can contribute up to 25 per cent of wages of an employee to provident funds or other employee benefit plans and claim tax exemption. Returns on these contributions also do not invite any tax, without any ceiling. But pension when received is taxable as income of the year. Provident funds enjoy withdrawal facilities for specified objectives such as housing, medical expenditure, and expenditure on higher education of children. No such facilities exist for pension funds. These tax concessions and withdrawal facilities would appear to be on a par with similar facilities in social security schemes in other countries.

1.6 INVESTMENT GUIDELINES

The funds collected by the EPFO have to be invested as per the investment guidelines the central government issues from time to time. Both non-exempt and exempt funds have to be invested subject to these guidelines. The guidelines have been periodically revised but one common feature has been that they require predominant share of investment in government paper. Till 1993, the entire corpus of funds had to be invested in government securities or government guaranteed securities or special deposits with the government. Since 1993, however, it has been permitted that a part of the funds be invested in bonds and securities of public sector undertakings (PSUs) and financial institutions. During 1993–4, 15 per cent of collections could be in bonds of PSUs or financial institutions. This percentage has since then been progressively raised and has reached 40 per cent in 1997–8 and could reach even 60 per cent with the permission of the Central Board of Trustees. In practice, however, the bulk of the funds, between 85 and 92 per cent, has been invested in special deposits with the government, which has provided a yield of 12 per cent since 1986. It is only since 1995–6 that the percentage of special deposits has come down. Not only has the rate of return on special deposits been attractive but they have been available on tap. Hence they have remained a preferred instrument (Table 9.5).

TABLE 9.5
PRESCRIBED INVESTMENT PATTERN FOR EPF[a]

	1986–93	1993–4	1994–5	1995–6	1996–7	1997–8[c]	1998–9[d]
Government and government guaranteed securities[b]	Not less than 15	15	15	40	40	40	40
Special deposit scheme of Government of India	Not exceeding 85	70	55	30	20	–	–
Public sector undertakings' bonds and securities of public financial institutions	–	15	30	30	40	40	40

[a]The pattern is for collections during the year and not for outstanding balances. There are some qualifications regarding investment of interest earned during the year and redemptions during the year.
[b]Central government, state government, and central and state government guaranteed securities.
[c]Twenty per cent can be invested in either government securities or public sector undertakings bonds and securities, as decided by the Central Board of Trustees.
[d]Twenty per cent can be invested in either government securities or PSU's bonds and securities as decided by the Board of Trustees. Of this up to 10 per cent can be invested in private secured bonds/securities which are rated investment grade by at least two rating agencies.

The instrument of special deposits was introduced in 1975 for a period of ten years, but was extended for another ten years in 1985. In 1995, through a government notification, its validity was extended for an indefinite period. From April 1997 onwards, however, the investment guidelines do not prescribe any investment in special deposits out of new subscriptions. No investment in special deposits can be made from fresh accruals but interest earned on special deposits till that date has to be mandatorily reinvested in special deposits only. They continue to be sufficiently attractive as return on government paper has come down to less than 12 per cent. Second, as mentioned earlier, they are available on tap. Third, there is just not adequate supply of highly rated bonds of PSUs and FIs to invest in without creating excessive exposure for a few companies. So far there have been only thirteen PSUs and FIs which have been rated Triple A by the credit-rating agencies in the country. The fund managers, in order to earn high return, will have no option but to invest in special deposits or lower the return below 12 per cent. Also, the corpus of provident funds is invested in special deposits. The cumulative investment was as high as 89 per cent at the end of March 1996. It will be impossible for fund managers to divest their portfolio of special deposits in a year or two unless the choice available to them for diversification is significantly widened to include investment grade securities of private sector companies (this has since been done from 1998). This diversification would also be necessary for maintaining or improving upon the yield provided on provident funds so far, when the yield on government paper is declining.

1.7 MANAGEMENT OF FUNDS

Non-exempt funds have been managed since the inception of the EPFO, by the Reserve Bank of India (RBI) (till 31 March 1995) and by State Bank of India (SBI) (since 1 April 1995). The investment pattern has been fairly simple, and very little discretion has been left to fund managers. The funds have been overwhelmingly invested in safe, easy, and sufficiently attractive avenues of special deposits. The skills of fund managers have never been tested. To put it differently, the investment pattern that is prescribed never allowed fund management skills to develop. The trustees are concerned, to the exclusion of all else, with the safety of funds of workers and will not allow any risk-taking by way of secondary market sale transactions in government securities. Fund managers, at the most, can buy government securities from the secondary market if it is profitable, and hold on to them till maturity. But they never sell. The RBI did not charge any fees for fund management, and the SBI has managed them at an exceptionally low cost, as low as .025 per cent on assets managed. But there has been hardly any discretionary management of funds.[3]

Exempted funds have also been subject to the same investment guidelines and followed almost similar practices. Any deviations from them have to go through time consuming and disadvantageous procedures. Provident Fund Commissioners expect them to hold all investments till maturity and require an exempted fund to obtain prior approval before any disinvestments are to be made. While the Ministry of Finance seems to have no objection to improving yield through secondary market transactions, the RBI requires a trustee resolution justifying reasons if any withdrawals are to be made from special deposit scheme. The consequence has been that provident funds have not been able to maximize the yield on investments they manage within the prescribed investment guidelines, by entering into secondary market transactions.

The interest rate on provident funds is declared by the EPFO on a year to year basis in advance at the time of preparation of the budget. This is a tax-free yield. Exempted funds have to declare a return not lower than that on non-exempt funds. If they declare a return higher than this, a higher portion of income is treated as income, and is subject to income tax. If the employer, in any year, has not earned sufficient income to declare the same return as on non-exempt funds, he/she has to meet the shortfall out of other income. It has been reported that a large number of exempt funds have been earning a higher rate of return than non-exempt funds. For 1996–7, out of 2987 exempt establishments for which information is available, 164 had declared interest higher than the statutory requirement of 12 per cent and 2129 had declared 12 per cent. Some of them might have earned higher returns but declared only what is required statutorily. The remaining had declared less than 12 per cent (229 units) or not declared (450 units). This indicates that over 30 per cent of units had not earned sufficient income to declare statutorily required return. This gives an idea of implicit subsidies that are given on funds managed by the EPFO (Table 9.6).

[3]The Bank of India which was managing the Coal Miners' Fund (Rs 117 billion) till 1998 has been at the fee of about 0.04 basic points for the year 1995–6.

TABLE 9.6
INTEREST DECLARED ON PROVIDENT FUNDS (A), GROWTH RATE IN
CONSUMER PRICE INDEX (B), AND REAL RATE OF RETURN (C)

Year	A	B	C
1985–6	10.15	6.8	3.35
1986–7	11.00	8.7	2.30
1987–8	11.50	8.8	2.70
1988–9	11.80	11.4	0.40
1989–90	12.00	4.2	7.80
1990–1	12.00	11.6	0.40
1991–2	12.00	13.5	1.50
1992–3	12.00	9.6	2.40
1993–4	12.00	7.5	4.50
1994–5	12.00	10.0	2.00
1995–6	12.00	10.0	2.00
1996–7	12.00	9.4	2.60
1997–8	12.00	6.8	5.20
Average	11.73	9.11	2.62

Source: EPFO, *Annual Reports*, and CMIE.

The yield, since inception, has always moved in an upward direction, and has been 12 per cent for the last eight years (since 1989–90). Over the last thirteen years, on an average, the real rate of return on provident funds has been 2.62 per cent. It has been negative in some years. It cannot be considered very satisfactory, but it just cannot be otherwise in the absence of freedom to invest in equity or even in good quality private debt. A beginning has been made towards liberalization and flexibility in investment pattern since 1993, but it has not been adequate and its implementation has been even less satisfactory. Investment in PSU bonds, where returns could possibly be the highest was only 10 per cent in 1995–6 and 8 per cent in 1996–7 for funds managed by the EPFO and 17 and 32 per cent respectively for exempt funds (Tables 9.7 and 9.8). This is a serious issue which the trustees must immediately look into.

There is good evidence, within the country, that if freedom were to be given to invest in equity, the yield could improve. The investment pattern for the LIC, which manages pension and other group schemes, permits investment in private equity and debentures up to a certain amount. The yield on the LIC's portfolio has been consistently higher, even when the Indian capital market has been passing through a bearish phase. Of course, world over, equity has yielded a higher rate of return than any other instrument over a longer period of time. And pension funds have been significant investors in equity in developed countries for many years.

TABLE 9.7
INVESTMENT PATTERN OF COLLECTIONS DURING THE YEAR
(NON-EXEMPT FUNDS)

(in percentage)

	1990–1	1991–2	1992–3	1993–4	1994–5	1995–6	1996–7
Government and government-guaranteed securities	5.5	7.5	7.0	10.2	5.1	16.8	12.20
Special deposit scheme	94.5	92.5	93.0	88.1	86.3	73.2	79.83
Public sector undertakings' bonds and securities	–	–	–	1.7	8.6	10.0	7.97

TABLE 9.8
INVESTMENT PATTERN OF COLLECTIONS DURING THE YEAR
(EXEMPT FUNDS)

(in percentage)

	1990–1	1991–2	1992–3	1993–4	1994–5	1995–6	1996–7
Government and government-guaranteed securities	12.9	12.6	14.6	14.5	17.6	38.5	33.0
Special deposit scheme	87.1	87.4	85.4	85.5	82.4	44.5	35.01
Public sector undertakings' bonds and securities	–	–	–	–	–	17.0	31.94

The investment pattern prescribed by the EPFO has given very limited, if any, freedom to fund managers and has not put to test their fund management skills. They have been given very limited freedom even in carrying out secondary market transactions in government securities. They only buy but do not normally sell in the secondary market. They have been highly risk averse. Also, given the predominance of special deposits with the government, there is a very small quantum left for discretionary management. It is not surprising, therefore, that the funds are managed at exceptionally low cost and have been 100 per cent safe. The obvious corollary is that the yield has been low.

Given a virtual absence of freedom in investing and transacting in the capital market, the question of pension funds contributing to development of the Indian capital market does not arise. Indian provident funds are quite large, one and half times the size of life insurance funds and more than twice the size of Indian mutual funds. They can contribute significantly to development of the capital market, debt market, corporate governance, and provide invaluable resources for the development of infrastructure market. But that has so far not happened. Therein lies vast potential and promise for future development in all these areas.

With an increase in the rate of provident fund contribution, savings under provident funds are bound to increase. Whether the overall long-term savings rate in the economy, will go up as a consequence of this depends on many factors—overall investment rate, income growth rate, public sector savings, etc. There will always be some substitution among saving instruments, the share of one picking up at the cost of some other. With growing awareness about the rise in life expectancy, tax incentives available on pension instruments, and hopefully better pension fund management, popularity of this instrument, as experiences in many countries show, is bound to increase. In fact, the government should aim at enhancing the popularity of this instrument in view of both the security it provides in old age and the economy's need for long-term resources.

The experiences of Chile and Singapore are worth studying before any suggestions for improvements in Indian social securities are made.

2. EXPERIENCES OF CHILE AND SINGAPORE

2.1 PENSION REFORM IN CHILE

Any discussion on pension reform would remain incomplete without examining the experience of Chile in this area over the last sixteen years. It has been unique, successful, and of considerable value to any country planning to undertake pension fund reforms. As an enthusiastic writer wrote about their 'Retirement Revolution', Santiago has become something of a Mecca for economists. It is no wonder that Argentina, Peru, Colombia, Mexico, Bolivia, and Uruguay have already adapted the Chilean version to suit their needs (Richard, 1996). Several East European countries are also studying the Chilean experience. There are advocates who would strongly recommend Chilean type pension reform even for the United States. It is an experience which cannot be ignored in any serious discussion on pension reforms (see Carter and Shipman, 1996).

Chile was the first Latin American country to introduce a social security programme as early as 1924. The spread was not nation-wide but began by covering major occupations. There were separate schemes for salaried workers, manual workers and for government employees, and smaller schemes for other employment categories. The benefits differed from scheme to scheme, but groups with political power or clout invariably ended up with larger benefits. The funds were not properly managed, and benefits to favoured groups were escalating. The result, as would be expected, was that the system ran into serious financial difficulties and had to rely on the government to fulfil the obligations. By the end of the 1970s the system had become an insolvent pay-as-you-go system. 'By 1980, about 28 per cent of the outgo of all the systems combined came from the deficit payments by the government. It was estimated that this proportion would rise greatly over future years' (Myers, 1992).

Apart from financial insolvency, the system was far from uniform and more than 100 different retirement systems had cropped up. 'While some workers could retire with a very high pension at 42 years of age, blue collar workers could only retire once they turned 65, and yet others could retire at 55 years with a full pension' (Sebastian, 1996). The system had become highly unfair with upper and middle class workers reaping substantial pension benefits, while poor workers were facing erosion of their pensions. To quote Jose Pinera, an architect of the reforms, 'By pressuring congress, each group of workers tried to minimize what it put in and maximize what it took out' (quoted in Carter and Shipman, 1996, p. 118). As a consequence of inflation and mismanagement, between 1962 and 1980, the average pension paid to blue collar workers had declined by 41 per cent (Sebastian, 1996).

Pension reform was introduced in response to four major considerations: (i) explosive fiscal consequences of the old regime; (ii) high degree of inequality of the old system; (iii) implied efficiency distortions; and (iv) an ideological desire to drastically reduce the role of the public sector in the economy.

The new system that was introduced is a defined contribution plan with a mandatory contribution of 10 per cent of wages by employees. In addition, workers make a contribution of approximately 3 per cent of wages as premium towards life and disability insurance. Employers do not contribute anything. To make this more acceptable to employees, the government mandated an increase of about 18 per cent in wages and salaries when the new system was introduced. In fact, those who opted for the new system experienced, on an average, 11 per cent increase in take-home pay (Sebastian 1996)

Under the new system, the amount of pension depends upon the funds accumulated. Fund management was handed over to private fund management firms called AFPs. Initially, there were 12 such firms but the number had increased to 21 by 1995.

Those who subscribe to the new system can be classified into those who are *affiliated* to the system and those who are *active contributors*. Those who are affiliated have at one time or another enrolled with an AFP. The active contributors, as the name suggests, contribute regularly to an AFP. The number of affiliates constitutes about 99 per cent of the labour force. But the active contributors are about 58 per cent of those employed. However, this figure underestimates the number of beneficiaries because if an affiliate has not contributed in one specific month, it does not mean he/she would not be able to enjoy a pension in future. The relatively lower level of active contributors is due to the fact that it is not mandatory for self-employed persons to participate (Julio, 1996).

The value of pension funds has increased remarkably during these sixteen years and constituted about 40 per cent of GDP in 1995 (Table 9.9).

TABLE 9.9
CHILE
GROWTH OF PENSION FUNDS (SEPTEMBER 1996)

		(US $ million)
Year	Amount of Pension Funds	Annual Rate of Growth
1981[a]	302	–
1982	951	214.9
1983	1728	81.7
1984	2253	30.4
1985	3147	39.7
1986	4124	31.0
1987	5052	22.5
1988	6160	21.9
1989	7614	23.6
1990	10,096	32.6
1991	14,289	41.5
1992	15,933	11.5
1993	20,474	28.5
1994	24,755	20.9
1995	26,314	6.3
1996[b]	28,130	9.2[c]

Notes: [a]July–December 1981.   [b]January–September 1996   [c]Annualized.

Source: Julio (1996).

The AFPs have performed quite well and over fifteen years have given a real rate of return of over 12 per cent. The real rate of return comes to 8.9 per cent during the least performing five-year period from 1992 to 1996 (Table 9.10).

TABLE 9.10
CHILE
REAL RATE OF RETURN ON PENSION FUNDS

Year	Annual Rate of Return[a]
1981[b]	12.6
1982	23.3
1983	21.3
1984	3.5
1985	13.4
1986	12.3
1987	5.4
1988	6.4
1989	6.9
1990	15.5
1991	29.7
1992	3.1
1993	16.2
1994	18.2
1995	2.5
1996[c]	4.6
Average annual return (July 1981–September 1996)	12.5
(1992–September 1996)	8.9

Notes: [a]Weighted average of returns of AFP.
[b]July–December 1981.
[c]January–September 1996.

Source: Julio (1996).

Since both the old and new systems have been co-existing, it is easy to compare the performance of the new system with the old. Till December 1994, the average pension under the new system were 42 per cent higher than under the old system. Also, in case of disability, pensions under the new system were 61 per cent higher than under the old one. (Sebastian, 1996).

The AFPs are under the supervision of the Pension Fund Superintendence (SAFP). It evolves investment guidelines for the AFPs and regularly monitors their performance. The SAFP prescribes the minimum
return each AFP has to pay to its members. The minimum is either 50
per cent of the average returns of AFPs, or 2 per cent below the average,
whichever is higher. If they have not earned this minimum rate, they can
make it up by drawing from 'investment reserve' funds they may create
during good times. If an AFP cannot meet this shortfall out of its
reserves, it will be liquidated; the state will make good the difference
and transfer the management of funds to some other AFP.

The AFPs have been investing as per the investment guidelines
prescribed by the SAFP. Initially funds were largely restricted to
government securities and no investment in private equity was permitted.
Investment in equity was permitted in 1985 up to 5 per cent of funds to
begin with. Progressively, this limit was liberalized. During the second
half of the 1980s, most AFPs invested in the equity of firms that were
privatized and benefited substantially as these were offered at good
discount. In 1992 they were permitted to invest 9 per cent of fund in
foreign securities with no more than half of it to be invested in equity.
But not even 1 per cent has been invested abroad. The domestic market
has appeared quite attractive during this period, with investment in
domestic equity around 28 per cent.

Though the AFPs have given an outstanding performance, the government has played an important role in popularizing the new system by
providing guarantee of returns. First, the government has given guarantee of minimum pension. Second, the government has given guarantee
for minimum return on funds managed by the AFPs. Third, the government has also given guarantee of pension payments (up to a limit) should
an insurance company go bankrupt. These government guarantees have
imparted tremendous confidence in the minds of workers towards the
new system. At the same time the regulatory system, though tight, has
provided ample freedom and opportunities to the AFPs in fund management.

The period of pension reform coincides with the period of general
economic reform and opening up of the economy. There was a remarkable increase in the saving rate of the economy, from less than 10 per
cent till 1986 to around 29 per cent in 1996. Public sector savings
increased by 5 percentage points during this period. Whether pension
funds themselves were responsible for increasing the private saving rate
is not a relevant question. Academicians have examined this issue and

find no conclusive answer.[4] But the fact remains that pension funds brought these savings to the capital market, provided funds to power and other infrastructure projects, and facilitated growth. The vast funds at the disposal of the AFPs helped build up a dynamic and modern capital market, developed and strengthened credit rating institutions, contributed to the growth of the insurance sector, and provided long-term finance to investment and infrastructure projects. And above all, it has contributed to enhancement of pension funds in the hands of those who need them the most—the aged, without any financial support from the government.

2.2 SINGAPORE'S CENTRAL PROVIDENT FUND (CPF)

A dissaver in the early 1960s, Singapore today boasts the highest saving rate in the world, at around 45 per cent. About three-fourths of these savings are in the form of private savings. And the single largest component (about 40 per cent) of these private savings is provident funds.

Provident funds were initiated in 1955, as a compulsory saving scheme. Both employees and employer contribute towards it. It started as a mandatory contribution of 5 per cent of wages by the employee, equally matched by the employer. These were gradually increased and touched a peak of 25 per cent each by employee and employer in 1984. Today these contributions are at the level of 20 per cent each by both the parties. Both contributions to provident funds and withdrawals from them are tax exempt, so also are earnings on these funds.

The CPF embraces employees as well as self-employed persons. Assets under the CPF constituted 57 per cent of GDP in 1995 and are growing.

Assets of the CPF are invested in government bonds or in advance deposits pending issue of such bonds. The funds are not required by the government as budget finance but are invested on behalf of the CPF by the Government of Singapore Investment Corporation (GSIC).

At the time of retirement, members are encouraged to buy life annuities, or they may deposit their savings with approved banks, or continue to keep them with the CPF Board.

Members are free to withdraw their contributions for approved purposes such as housing, education of dependents, investment scheme

---

[4] Richard (1996). According to Holzmann's findings, 'The direct contribution of financial market developments to private savings was negative.'

or medical treatment. Home ownership by workers in Singapore has now become universal, as a consequence. After building up a minimum reserve of S$ 40,000 or 50,000, a member is free to withdraw for the purpose of investing in equity, government bonds, or in fund management accounts.

Provident funds have become such a comprehensive saving plan that it has reduced the need for saving in other forms. Several studies have been made to evaluate the impact of provident funds on private savings. It is very difficult to conclude whether provident fund had any positive impact on private saving. High savings rates, through high investment rates, leads to high growth rates. High growth rates have all pervasive impact on savings rates basically through increase in labour participation rate and higher income for each participant. The total impact of high rates of growth is to encourage savings. Provident funds, therefore, became an intrinsic part of a virtuous circle where income growth and savings reinforce each other.

3. TASK FOR THE FUTURE

The preceding discussion reveals that the government in India has been keenly aware of the need for a sound security system for workers during their retirement and old age. It started a social security scheme about seventy years ago, and has been moving towards a fuller and more comprehensive system in recent years.

The implementation, however, has lagged behind intentions, and its coverage has touched only a fringe. A good social security system should cover all citizens during their retirement and old age, and not only select employees and self-employed people. It should cover all people irrespective of what income groups they belong to, high, medium, or low. And the benefits should flow to them in a manner that low income groups do not suffer because they could contribute relatively less as compared to their needs during old age. In addition to coverage, the pension should be reasonably adequate for all income groups.

It is, no doubt, true that it is the primary responsibility of an individual to make provision for his old age, his survivors, premature death, ill health, disability, etc. He will do this to the best of his abilities given his level of income. His best efforts, however, may fall short of what his needs would be when he gets old. A certain degree of redistribution of income has to be a necessary part of a good social security system, and the state has to play a crucial role in bringing it about.

The employer and the state have to play an important role through education, communication, facilitation, creation of appropriate incentives and savings schemes, and contribution (for employers) in ensuring that individuals effectively plan for these contingencies themselves. Social security has come to be regarded as a joint responsibility of employee, employer, and the state. Each one contributes, in one form or another, but the welfare state is ultimately expected to bear residual or contingent responsibility for shortfalls in contributions towards social security by the beneficiaries. The fairness of the system depends on whether it is comprehensive enough to include within it all citizens who are in need of help.

Also, social security should be sufficient and adequate to cover the basic needs of citizens. Ideally, the system should be fully funded and should impose very little burden on the state. But the state support should be forthcoming if required.

The Indian provident fund and pension system, so far, covers only some, not all, employees and leaves a large part of the old population outside its purview. Hardly 6 per cent of the population in the working age is covered by it. If one were to include the labour force in the informal sector, the agricultural sector, and self-employed persons, then not even 10 per cent of workers are covered by the social security system. This is inadequate and the coverage needs to be substantially increased, no doubt a mammoth task before the country.

For those who contribute towards the system, contributions are at a fairly high rate. The employee puts in 10 or 12 per cent of his wages, matched by a similar contribution by the employer. The state contributes 1.16 per cent towards the pension scheme and 0.25 per cent towards the Deposit Linked Insurance Scheme. Overall above 21.5 to 25.5 per cent of employee's wages are contributed towards the social security system. In addition to these, the employer contributes in the form of gratuity one-half month's salary for every one year's work, i.e. at the rate of 4.16 per cent of a worker's salary for every year. There is no return on it, and hence it is not compounded. There is an overall ceiling on gratuity payable to a worker, and is paid in a lumpsum at the time of retirement. By international standards, India would be among the countries which contribute very highly to the old age security system.

In terms of coverage, India has to go a long way in having a comprehensive social security system. It will have to grow multifold, resources for which are just not available with the government. To begin with, efforts will have to be concentrated towards bringing workers employed in the informal sector and self-employed persons within the fold of provident and pension funds. The existing PPF Scheme, eventually, should be merged with the Employees' Provident Fund Scheme, 1952, and the Employees' Pension Scheme, 1995. Further progress in the immediate future will have to be on the basis of defined contribution plans and fully funded schemes.

The rate of contribution is already high and there appears to be little scope for any further increase. Growing competition is already reducing profit margins of companies. As in the case of Singapore, it should be possible to step up provident fund contribution to 15 per cent of wages of employees without any obligation on the employer. This may help step up the long-term saving rate and provide resources for infrastructure investment. This should be achieved in rapid phases. If necessary, tax incentives should be enhanced and the current ceiling of tax exemption of Rs 60,000 should be raised, in phases, to Rs 100,000. Chile has a contribution rate of only 10 per cent of wages plus another 3 per cent for insurance and disability. It is making up the lower rate of contribution by earning a higher rate of return on it.

India can achieve the 'Chilean miracle' if its investment pattern can be freed, and progressively greater freedom is given, in regulated manner, to invest in private sector securities. In India, the contribution rate is over 21 per cent, but the rate of return (in real terms) is very low, only 2.62 per cent compared to over 12 per cent in Chile. As interest rates decline in the economy, the EPFO will find it difficult even to maintain the current 12 per cent. Investment regulations will have to be altered to step up the rate of return or even to maintain the existing rate of return. One per cent increase in the rate of return can result in 20 per cent additional accumulation in provident funds assuming a thirty-year period of service and contributions by a worker. India has to aim at a higher rate of return, so that provident fund accumulations are higher and ultimately pension becomes higher.

Having raised the yield on provident funds to 12 per cent for the last eight years, the EPFO would face considerable difficulty and loss of credibility if it were to be lowered. Any change in investment guidelines at this stage will have to face this reality and be undertaken only if the EPFO is confident that it can improve upon 12 per cent or, at least, maintain the current level. While not impossible, it will be far from easy.

Any change in investment guidelines will have to be made in phases, rapid enough to be acceptable and also flexible enough to meet the challenge of yield. The investment guidelines may be modified, for instance, according to the phasing schedule suggested below. All the three suggested phases should be implemented in a maximum period of not more than seven years.

PHASE I

(i)	Investment in government and government-guaranteed securities.	Not less than 40 per cent
(ii)	Investment in investment grade bonds and securities of PSUs and financial institutions.	Not less than 25 per cent
(iii)	Investment in investment grade private sector bonds and debentures and income schemes of mutual funds.	Not more than 25 per cent
(iv)	Investment in equity or growth schemes of mutual funds.	Not more than 5 per cent

PHASE II

(i)	Investment in government and government-guaranteed securities.	Not less than 40 per cent
(ii)	Investment in investment grade bonds and securities of public sector and private sector companies and of financial institutions. Investment in income schemes of mutual funds.	Not less than 40 per cent
(iii)	Investment in equity or growth schemes of mutual funds.	Not more than 10 per cent

PHASE III

(i)	Investment in government or government-guaranteed securities.	Not less than 40 per cent
(ii)	Investment in investment grade bonds and debentures of public and private sector companies and of financial institutions. Investment in income schemes of mutual funds.	Not less than 30 per cent
(iii)	Investment in equity or in growth schemes of mutual funds.	Not more than 30 per cent

It may be mentioned that even today the LIC, under its superannuation and group insurance schemes, is permitted to invest up to 60 per cent in 'approved securities' which include equity and debentures of private sector companies—as a consequence, the LIC has been able to earn a higher yield on these schemes compared to return on provident funds. This freedom was given to the LIC in 1995 and it has been exercising due diligence and prudence while investing in equity. As in March-end 1997, its investment in equity has been no more than 5 per cent (Table 9.11).

TABLE 9.11
LIFE INSURANCE CORPORATION
(GROSS YIELD)

(in percentage)

Particulars	1989–90	1990–1	1991–2	1992–3	1993–4	1994–5	1995–6	1996–7
(i) Individual fund	NA	11.34	11.87	11.80	11.95	12.08	12.08	12.23
(ii) Pension and group schemes	NA	12.10	12.27	12.61	12.42	13.09	13.65	13.77
(iii) Life annuities fund	NA	11.11	14.33	16.34	13.90	14.20	14.73	11.52
(iv) Total fund	11.13	11.44	11.96	11.56	12.42	12.22	12.30	12.39

Source: Life Insurance Corporation.

The EPFO should appoint more than one fund manager to manage the funds, in public or private sector, so that there is competition among them.

As far as possible, these fund managers should not invest in other mutual funds since there will be 'pyramiding' or duplication of management fees, first to fund managers of provident funds, and then fund managers of mutual funds. Unless higher returns justify this, such investments in mutual funds cannot be favourably looked upon. These have to be closely monitored by trustees. It would be imprudent to put a blanket ban on such investments, since closed-end funds are sometimes traded at such discount that they may provide excellent investment opportunities to medium-term investors.

There is a role for government guarantees in the transition, as was seen in Chile, and the Indian government should not hesitate to provide minimum performance guarantees.

As there will be more than one fund manager, it would be necessary to provide freedom to provident funds and pension funds of various companies to change fund managers. This freedom may be limited to just once in a year, so as to minimize the fund management cost. It is not necessary, in the initial stage, to give this freedom to individual subscribers. This would keep shifting to other funds at minimum desirable level and would keep the costs down.

TABLE 9.12
SELECTED OECD COUNTRIES
CHARACTERISTICS OF REAL TOTAL RETURNS 1971–90
Mean (standard deviation) of Real Total/Holding Period Return (domestic currency)

(per cent)

	USA	UK	Germany	Japan	Canada	Netherlands	Sweden	Denmark	Switzerland	France
Loans	3.9 (2.6)	1.2 (5.4)	5.2 (2.3)	0.9 (4.7)	4.2 (3.3)	3.9 (3.9)	3.0 (3.3)	6.5 (3.5)	2.4 (2.1)	2.4 (3.5)
Mortgages	3.1	1.8	4.5	2.7	3.4	4.3	2.4	6.3	1.2	3.3
Equities	5.9 (14.9)	10.8 (31.8)	9.3 (20.4)	11.2 (21.0)	5.0 (13.2)	8.6 (30.1)	9.3 (23.7)	9.4 (29.4)	4.7 (22.2)	9.6 (28.8)
Bonds	1.2 (15.0)	1.6 (11.5)	2.6 (15.10)	0.0 (20.3)	1.1 (17.8)	1.8 (11.5)	0.6 (8.6)	4.5 (17.0)	1.7 (18.7)	1.3 (13.9)
Short-term assets	2.1 (2.7)	1.5 (5.3)	2.9 (2.3)	0.7 (5.0)	2.6 (12.8)	1.7 (4.3)	0.9 (3.7)	1.7 (1.6)	1.1 (2.3)	1.9 (3.4)
Property	3.9 (5.5)	5.7 (13.0)	4.5 (2.8)	6.6 (7.2)	5.2 (5.8)	4.6 (15.0)	—	—	—	—
Foreign bonds	2.2 (16.0)	0.4 (16.8)	3.8 (12.2)	2.9 (15.8)	1.2 (13.9)	0.1 (12.2)	0.6 (13.9)	1.0 (12.9)	1.6 (14.9)	0.4 (14.3)
Foreign equity	9.6 (18.2)	6.2 (17.1)	10.6 (16.0)	8.6 (20.5)	6.4 (15.9)	6.7 (14.9)	7.4 (14.5)	5.9 (14.7)	5.2 (17.1)	7.2 (14.2)
MEMORANDUM ITEMS:										
Inflation (CPI)	6.3 (3.2)	9.8 (5.4)	3.8 (2.2)	5.5 (5.8)	6.9 (3.0)	4.9 (3.3)	8.4 (2.6)	7.9 (3.4)	4.2 (2.6)	8.0 (4.0)
Redemption yield on government bonds	2.8 (3.4)	1.9 (4.3)	4.0 (1.4)	1.5 (4.7)	3.3 (3.1)	3.3 (2.9)	2.2 (3.0)	5.7 (2.2)	0.7 (1.9)	3.0 (3.0)
Real earning growth	0.5 (2.2)	2.4 (2.5)	3.6 (2.5)	3.0 (3.5)	1.1 (2.7)	1.4 (2.6)	1.1 (3.4)	2.5 (3.7)	1.6 (2.0)	—

Source: Davis (1993).

With these reforms it should be possible to introduce flexibility in portfolio selection and management, and improve the yield on funds.

Trustees of the EPFO have been very cautious and have resented any idea or move towards liberalization of investment regulations in favour of private bonds or equity or even mutual funds. They have put high premium on safety of precious savings of workers for their old age. They have ignored the international experience of pension funds and have been highly prejudiced against capital market and mutual funds because of adverse capital market conditions during 1992–7. The experience of mature, OECD countries shows that in the long run, equity gives the highest rate of return of all the instruments. (Davis, 1993) (Table 9.12). Some educative process through better communications is necessary. The trustees have to become more open-minded, take a long-term view, and trust the fund managers. They have to, of course, closely monitor the performance of fund managers and change them, if necessary.

Trustees need to be given the confidence that fund managers will be able to improve the yield and future income of workers by investing part of the funds in equity. To impart this confidence, the state may have to give a guarantee for a minimum rate of return on funds. In Chile, the government gave a guarantee for minimum rate of return on funds, minimum return by a fund manager, and minimum pension payments should an insurance company go bankrupt. These guarantees were very helpful during the transition from state-managed pension funds to privately managed pension funds. In view of the enormous task before the Indian social security system, the government will have to perform this vital role of guaranteeing minimum performance. India has a healthy growth of fund managers in the public sector, and in the system it needs to evolve, public sector fund managers can make an important contribution. In fact, it would be prudent to have 10–15 fund managers to begin with, and introduce an element of competition among them. So far, because of very restrictive investment regulations, and having only one fund manager, the system has failed to get the best out of fund managers. The focus has excessively and perhaps wrongly shifted towards reduction in management costs, and safety at every point of time, rather than on maximization of long-term yield.

Provident fund trustees have a very good role model in the Unit Trust's US 64 Scheme which manages about Rs 20,000 crore. It is a unique scheme with a portfolio which includes bonds, debentures, equity as well as government paper. It is an open-ended fund with an equity component of over 40 per cent. The scheme has declared dividend, year after year and distributed it. In the last five years it has declared a dividend of over 20 per cent with a peak performance of 26 per cent. Over time it has built up a very strong portfolio. Unlike US 64, provident funds are long-term funds, with no obligation to distribute annual dividends. Potentially, they can build up much stronger portfolios for long-term maximization, and if US 64 can be seen as a benchmark, they can earn dividend no less than US 64 earns. In that case, the yield, over time, can be increased to much more than provident funds have so far earned and provided. With such a liberalized investment guideline and by utilizing the services of professional fund managers, it should be possible to significantly increase the yield and emulate what US 64 has done consistently for its unit holders for so many years in India.

The trustees will also have to consider and give limited freedom to fund managers to invest in equity in international markets. The RBI has recently permitted all mutual funds to invest abroad with a ceiling of US$ 50 million. This is a beginning. Many pension funds abroad have already started investing in Indian equity and deriving benefits from their investments. As India gradually moves towards full capital account convertibility, Indian Pension Funds should not lag behind. They should also start investing in bonds and equity abroad in a limited way.

The pension fund reforms that are proposed for India will work best only if there is a strong regulatory authority for pension funds in the nature of the Employees' Retirement Income Security Act, 1974 (ERISA) in the USA. The ERISA was adopted to protect the interests of subscribers to various employee benefit plans and their beneficiaries by mandating standards of conduct, obligations, and responsibilities for plan fiduciaries. India does not have any such framework and, as a consequence, the role and responsibilities of trustees and fund managers are not sharply defined. There are no disclosures to subscribers whatsoever except a statement of their account once in a year. Fund managers are not accountable for their due diligence, skill, or prudence. Some disclosures on portfolio are made in the EPFO's annual report. These are far from adequate. There is need to bring about greater transparency and better disclosures.

As funds are managed by only one fund manager, there is no portability for subscribers.

The Pension Scheme, 1995 is a recent one and it is too early to make a statement regarding its impact on the government's finances. Life expectancy of those who retire at the age of 58 is currently 75 in India, a post-retirement life of about seventeen years. Pension benefits are at the rate of average of last twelve months' salary multiplied by a pension factor. Today this may not work out to more than 50 per cent of last gross salary drawn. The survivor benefits are quite low. The pressures, soon, will mount to increase the quantum of pension. The finances of the government can come under serious strain unless return on pension funds improves. According to some actuaries, the government will have to earn a nominal return of at least 15 per cent to keep it fully funded. The government should be fully prepared for this before the situation worsens. It has taken up a challenge, and this should be satisfactorily met through immediate and comprehensive pension reforms.

REFERENCES

Carter, M.N. and W.C. Shipman. (1996). *Promises to Keep, Saving, Social Securities Dream*. Washington, D.C.: Regency Publishing.

Davis, E.P. (1993). 'The Structure, Regulation and Performance of Pension Funds in Nine Industrial Countries'. Policy Research Working Paper, World Bank Financial Sector Development Department, World Bank.

Julio, Bustamante. (1996). *Fifteen Years of Regulating and Supervising Chile's Pension System*. Washington, D.C.: World Bank.

Kenneth, Bercuson (ed.). (1995). 'Singapore: A Case Study of Rapid Development'. International Monetary Fund, Occasional Papers no. 119.

Myers, Robert J. (1992). 'Chile's Security Reform after 10 years'. *Benefits Quarterly*, vol. 8, no. 3 (3rd quarter), pp. 41–55.

Richard, Holzmann. (1996). 'Pension Reform, Financial Market Development and Economic Growth: Preliminary Evidence from Chile'. IMF Working Paper, WP/96/94. Later published in 1997 in IMF Staff Papers, vol. 44, no. 2, June.

Sebastian, Edwards. (1996). *The Chilean Pension Reform: A Pioneering Program*. Chicago: National Bureau of Economic Research.

World Bank. (1994). *Averting the Old Age Crisis*. New York: Oxford University Press.

Part IV

International Issues and Comparisons

Eureka: Capital Account Convertibility and the Laws of Flotation

SURJIT S. BHALLA*

F32

519

1. INTRODUCTION

The Asian crisis has heightened interest in capital account convertibility.[1] For some years the International Monetary Fund (IMF) has increased its emphasis on countries introducing KAC as well as CAC. Numerous studies have supported it (for example Hanson, 1994, and works cited therein). However, there has also been a backlash. For example, Eatwell (1996) argues that there is precious little evidence to support the benefits of KAC, in terms of either growth or inflation.

The currency crisis in East Asia has sharpened the criticism of KAC. The experience generated the argument that East Asian currencies suffered from a financial meltdown because they had KAC; countries like India, Chile, and China avoided a crisis precisely because they have limited or no KAC. This 'dual' proof, i.e. with KAC there seem to be a host of problems, and without KAC there are seemingly no problems, seems too strong to ignore. To complete the retrenchment, the IMF itself softpedals the desirability of KAC in its latest *World Economic Outlook* (IMF, 1997).

These developments have special reference to India. A committee was appointed by the Government of India to outline a road-map for the move towards KAC. This committee (henceforth the Tarapore Committee after its head) submitted its report (to the Reserve Bank of India [RBI]) on 31 May 1997, only slightly more than a month before speculative pressure led to a collapse of the Thai baht. Needless to say,

*I am thankful for the excellent research assistance of Arindom Mookerjee and Suraj Saigal.
[1]Hereafter referred to as KAC to distinguish it from current account convertibility or CAC.

India's move towards KAC is now being questioned by many Indian 'experts'.

This chapter examines the issues surrounding KAC at three levels: definition, theory, and empirical evidence on KAC's benefits and India's readiness for it. Perhaps the most important argument of this chapter is that with KAC one must consider the exchange regime as well as rules for convertibility. Without a floating exchange rate (or perhaps a currency board, which ties monetary policy to external objectives), countries with KAC sooner or later become vulnerable to the manipulations of the speculators. Moreover, the chapter argues that the benefits of floating are great in terms of economic freedom, which various studies suggest supports development. Two implications of KAC are examined: does KAC lead to lower real interest rates? And does KAC lead to a loosening of the correlation between domestic savings and domestic investment? The results suggest an answer in the affirmative to both questions (Section 3). Finally, the Indian macroeconomy seems more than ready for KAC, according to several indicators (Section 4).

What about the link between KAC and the Asian crisis. As argued elsewhere, the initial cause for the East Asia crisis lies in its own backyard—in particular, in China appropriating for itself, and being allowed to do so, the Japanese model of mercantilist development, i.e. maintenance of a highly undervalued exchange rate (Bhalla, 1998). The primary causes of the crisis are outside the purview of this chapter; it examines rather whether shocks to the system were magnified by KAC. It concludes that it is erroneous to attribute the East Asian crisis to KAC—the exchange regime played a major role in it.

Finally, the chapter suggests the emergence of a new world order, reflecting increased flows of international capital and increase in KAC, *de facto* or *de jure*. The implications of this new financial reality are understood by most players in the markets, except (until perhaps recently) the central bankers of the world. Simply put, assets markets are integrated across countries. And this is where the laws of flotation apply: if one market is not allowed to adjust, displacement occurs elsewhere. For example, the contagion devaluations are part of a systemic response of a KAC world to a non-KAC major player and non-adjustment of their exchange rates.

2. DEFINITION OF CAPITAL ACCOUNT CONVERTIBILITY AND THE IMPORTANCE OF THE EXCHANGE REGIME

Although several studies on KAC have been published, and descriptions and very useful analyses abound in various IMF documents, a 'core' definition of KAC is missing. Nor is such a definition to be found in the documents of the central banks that have undertaken KAC reforms. Given this situation, the Tarapore Committee offered its own formal definition (RBI, 1997, p. 4): '[KAC] refers to the freedom to convert local financial assets into foreign financial assets and vice-versa at market determined rates of exchange.' This definition is unique in that it explicitly considers the nature of the exchange rate regime in place—the importance of which is discussed in the analysis below.

The Tarapore Committee definition of KAC is straightforward: it is the right, and the ability, to transform domestic assets into foreign assets and *vice-versa*. The complication arises because the definition deliberately does not state an important consideration—at what exchange rate should this translation take place? In inter-country trade, the exchange rate, or more generally the exchange rate regime—the way the exchange rate is determined—is of major concern.

One common practice has been to let the government define the exchange rate. However, recent country experiences suggest that this form of KAC sooner or later has led to crises (e.g. England and France in 1993, Mexico in late 1994, Thailand in mid-1997). Such a policy gives a new free option to traders, investors, and speculators around the world to put pressure on the country, making a loss of reserves, and a crisis, inevitable.

There are other problems with the exchange rate not being market determined. First, there is always the fear of exchange controls being instituted to try to achieve some domestic macroeconomic goal. This reduces the integration of domestic and international capital markets by creating a risk premium—the so-called 'peso problem'. Second, there is the issue of economic rights—on what basis do government authorities have the right to set the value of a variable as important as the exchange rate, when citizens are chary of even granting the government the right to set the price of potatoes? Third, time and again history has shown the costly failures of a central bank's 'line in the sand', which allows low cost bets against the central bank. Some recent failed attempts at drawing the line are the Thai baht at 25, the Indian rupee at 37.5, and the Korean won at 1000. These 'lines' may last for a time, but they have all failed. That failure may even reflect that such 'lines' create the seeds of their own destruction by encouraging excessive inflows, then allowing low cost attacks.

While offering the definition of a market-determined exchange rate, the Tarapore report also expands on it by stating that it [KAC] is associated with changes of ownership in foreign/domestic financial assets and liabilities and embodies the creation and liquidation of claims on, or by, the rest of the world. KAC can be, and is, coexistent with restrictions other than on external payments. It also does not preclude the imposition of monetary/fiscal measures relating to foreign exchange transactions which are of a prudential nature.

This expansion of the definition is consistent with analogous descriptions of KAC contained in IMF and central bank documents; however, the use or relevance of such expansion is debatable. In particular, who is to decide whether the 'imposed measures' are 'prudential' in nature?

The problem with the expanded definition is that it provides government the authority to restrict, albeit 'prudentially', what would seem to be a basic economic right of citizens. The view that the market cannot possibly be expected to determine the 'correct' exchange rate perhaps has some relevance in a fixed exchange rate world and, not coincidentally, a relatively closed world. But today it is less relevant.

Moreover, there is the economic freedom issue mentioned above. The last few decades have shown that countries which provided economic freedom to their citizens have consistently outperformed those that did not (see Bhalla, 1992a and 1992b; Scully and Slottie, 1991; and World Bank, 1991). The explanation is the familiar one: markets allocate resources more efficiently than government bureaucrats.

Controlling the exchange rate is a major restraint in a globally integrated world and perhaps more potent, and dangerous, than any other economic control a bureaucrat can exercise. This was first raised by Hayek (1944). It is notable that these prescient comments were made more than fifty years ago.

The extent of control over all life that economic control confers is nowhere better illustrated than in the field of foreign exchanges. Nothing would at first seem to affect private life less than a state control of the dealings in foreign exchange, and most people will regard its introduction with complete indifference. Yet the experience of most Continental countries has taught thoughtful people to regard this step as the decisive advance on the path to totalitarianism and the suppression of individual liberty. . . . Once the individual is no longer free to travel, no longer free to buy foreign books or journals, once all the means of foreign contact can be restricted to those of whom official opinion approves or for whom it is regarded as necessary, the effective control of opinion is much greater than that ever exercised by any of the absolutist governments of the seventeenth and eighteenth centuries [p. 92, emphasis mine].

The market will also 'make errors', but economic man would much rather cope with these, just as political man is forced to cope with the politicians he himself elects. Allowing the government to set the exchange rate is akin to granting it the right to impose a 'political' emergency. Certain rights are inalienable, and KAC or a floating rate is in essence no more than a long overdue economic right.

3. BENEFITS OF CAPITAL ACCOUNT CONVERTIBILITY

While developing countries may not have reached full KAC, capital accounts have certainly been vastly liberalized in the 1990s. Net private capital flows to developing countries have increased markedly in the 1990s and have averaged above $ 150 million in each of the last five years with more than $ 240 billion in both 1996 and 1997. This compares with levels of around $ 50 billion less than a decade ago. An equal proportion of such flows has been allocated to both foreign direct investment (FDI) and portfolio investment (equity and bonds). The cause of such flows is easy to document—integration of world financial markets and associated large declines in cross-border transaction costs, and a movement towards KAC.

The presumed benefits of such capital flows are a more efficient utilization of capital worldwide. This is, in turn, expected to lead to lower real interest rates, a decrease in the variance of real rates across economies, and a separation of the close relationship between savings and investment that is observed for closed economies.

However, two important articles, Feldstein and Horioka (1980) and Feldstein and Bacchetta (1991) estimated an empirical relationship between savings and investment rates that is suggestive of an absence of capital market integration. The relationship estimated is as follows:

$$S/Y = a + b^*(I/Y) + e, \tag{1}$$

where S/Y and I/Y are saving and investment rates, respectively. The logic of estimating such a relationship to examine capital mobility is straightforward: if economies are closely linked via capital flows, then there should be a close to zero relationship between the two ratios. Phrased differently, investment rates will have little to do with *domestic* savings rates, especially when international capital flows are 'free', as in the 1990s. Thus this model has the following implication for a cross-section analysis of saving and investment rates: the relationship should be close to unity for the 1970s and 1990s, and close to zero for the capital mobile 1990s.

The above two articles find that the elasticity *b* is close to unity for the 1960s, 1970s, 1980s and 1990s. Eatwell (1996) reports that 'a very large number of subsequent examinations have found the Feldstein-Horioka result (that b is not significantly different from 1) to be remarkably robust'.

There is, however, a problem with the estimations of equation (1), the Feldstein and Horioka model: it should be estimated in first differences (to control for problems of cointegration) rather than in levels. Investment rates and savings rates have exhibited an upward trend for most developing economies—this common trend is likely to yield *an upwardly* biased estimate for the elasticity, b.

Table 10.1 reports the elasticity for selected years since 1975. Two sets of models are estimated—equation (1) and equation (2) as first differences for a large sample of developing and developed economies:

$$d(S/Y) = a + b^*d(I/Y) + e, \qquad (2)$$

The second column in Table 10.1 confirms the Feldstein, Horioka, and Bacchetta finding of an absence of capital market integration, i.e. the coefficient b is not much different from 1 for most of the years. The correctly specified model (equation 2) suggests the *opposite* result and one also forecast by the data on capital flows: domestic savings and domestic investment rates are no longer related with each other. The coefficient is insignificantly different from zero for the mid-1990s.

There are other advantages, and implications, of a world with KAC and corresponding free flow of capital. Real interest rates should be lower, and growth rates should be higher, *ceteris paribus*, as capital is allocated more efficiently. Table 10.2 documents some data on interest rates and growth rates. Comparable data on the former are difficult to obtain, especially for the developing economies with underdeveloped financial markets.

The method used to generate the short-term real rate is as follows: overnight money rate is used, failing which the three-month t-bill rate is used. For the long-term rate, the prime lending rate is used, failing which ten-year government bond yields are employed.[2] The mixture of rates suggests that measurement error bias is likely at a point in time, and less so for trends in interest rates. The real rate is derived by subtracting the year-to-year inflation rate (as measured by the CPI and not the WPI) from interest rate levels.

[2]All data from IMF (1997a).

TABLE 10.1
ARE CAPITAL MARKETS INTEGRATED: RELATIONSHIP BETWEEN
SAVINGS AND INVESTMENT RATES

Year	(I/Y)	Coeff. of Adjusted R^2	d(I/Y)	Coeff. of Adjusted R2
1970	0.85 (5.71)	0.52		
1971	0.83 (6.27)	0.56	0.74 (4.89)	0.44
1972	0.96 (8.62)	0.71	0.63 (2.73)	0.18
1973	0.92 (7.02)	0.62	0.66 (2.77)	0.18
1974	0.83 (4.99)	0.44	0.37 (2.09)	0.10
1975	0.92 (6.07)	0.54	0.39 (2.63)	0.16
1976	1.04 (6.65)	0.59	0.12 (0.44)	-0.03
1977	0.93 (7.27)	0.63	0.03 (0.16)	-0.03
1978	0.89 (7.12)	0.62	0.45 (3.09)	0.22
1979	1.03 (6.98)	0.61	0.23 (1.64)	0.05
1980	0.89 (5.09)	0.43	0.22 (1.92)	0.08
1981	1.06 (8.17)	0.67	0.17 (1.07)	0.004
1982	1.00 (7.33)	0.62	0.64 (5.02)	0.43
1983	0.91 (6.55)	0.57	0.3 (3.28)	0.23
1984	1.06 (7.92)	0.66	0.18 (1.14)	0.01
1985	0.98 (5.69)	0.49	0.60 (4.14)	0.33
1986	1.12 (6.96)	0.59	1.00 (0.37)	-0.02
1987	1.29 (7.31)	0.61	0.51 (2.84)	0.18
1988	1.33 (8.04)	0.66	-0.07 (-0.37)	-0.03
1989	1.19 (7.41)	0.62	-0.05 (-0.45)	-0.02
1990	0.99 (6.47)	0.56	0.53 (5.71)	0.49
1991	1.05 (8.70)	0.69	0.38 (1.77)	0.06
1992	1.16 (10.21)	0.76	0.29 (1.42)	0.03
1993	1.03 (8.94)	0.71	0.54 (5.22)	0.45
1994	0.99 (8.77)	0.71	-0.12 (-1.08)	0.01
1995	0.94 (8.72)	0.69	-0.003 (-0.02)	-0.03

The results contained in Table 10.2 are suggestive of the following:

1. Both short- and long-term real interest rates in developed countries have declined, and now approximate 3.5 per cent and 6.0 per cent, respectively.
2. The rates for less-developed economies are higher by only about 0.5 per cent in 1996. This is a sharp decline from the gap of about 300 basis points (or 3 per cent) that was observed earlier.
3. This decline in the gap between short and long rates between developing and developed countries is the surest sign of the effects of capital market integration.

Table 10.2 also indicates that output growth in developing countries has increased while that in developed countries has almost caught up with earlier levels. The combined evidence documented above is indicative of the benefits to be gained from movements towards KAC.

TABLE 10.2 : REAL INTEREST RATES AND OUTPUT 1981–96.

	1981–90	1991–95
World trade growth	4.1	6.3
World output growth	2.9	2.0
Output growth for DCs	2.5	1.4
Output growth for LDCs	3.9	4.7
Avg. s-t real interest rate for DCs	3.9	4.8
Avg. s-t real interest rate for LDCs	1.6	1.8
Avg. l-t real interest rate for DCs	5.9	7.5
Avg. l-t real interest rate for LDCs	4.7	5.3
Std dev. of s-t real interest rate for DCs	3.2	2.4
Std dev. of s-t real interest rate for LDCs	9.9	8.8
Std dev. of l-t real interest rate for DCs	2.9	2.9
Std dev. of l-t real interest rate for LDCs	10.9	9.0

Note: The short-term rate is either the rate of overnight money or three-month treasury-bill rate depending on availability of data. The long-term rate is either the prime lending rate or the ten-year bond rate.

Source: IMF. (1997a and 1997b).

4. IS INDIA READY FOR CAPITAL ACCOUNT CONVERTIBILITY?

Several developing countries have moved rather rapidly to KAC over the last few years. Is India ready to follow these countries? It is unclear what is meant by this question. Today, India has KAC for several agents in the system. Broadly speaking, on both inflows and outflows, there are five agents: individuals, corporates, banks, non-banking financial institutions, and the government. On the inflow side, there is close to full KAC. On the outflow side, there are controls for all agents, though exporters (part of all agents in *the* system) and corporates face *relatively* fewer restrictions. The recent ECB ruling has further relaxed restrictions for corporates, especially those involved in infrastructure.

The existing prejudice against outflows reflects a legitimate worry on the part of policy makers. Indeed, it is *the* worry with regard to KAC, i.e. what are the prospects of 'large-scale' capital flight? However, the conclusion that capital flight can be aided or abetted by the presence of KAC may be inappropriate. For it to be a legitimate conclusion, one would also need to observe that foreign exchange controls are effective. A vast amount of literature exists which negates this conclusion (e.g. Hanson, 1994; Mathieson and Rojas-Suarez, 1993; Obstfeld, 1995; and Quirk-Evans, 1995) that foreign exchange controls are effective in either controlling the flight of capital or the inflow of capital. Further, the effectiveness of controls (to the extent that it exists), is limited to non-crisis situations and most emphatically not applicable to the 'fear of crisis flight' alluded to above. In other words, controls cannot prevent capital flight from occurring and KAC cannot decrease the probability of capital flight. But what KAC in the presence of a non-fixed exchange rate regime can do is limit the extent of capital loss. In such an instance, the first set of movers will gain the advantage of flight at an undiscounted price; the followers will be faced with exit at highly unprofitable rates as the exchange rate would have devalued enough to make further outflows undesirable.

While the above conclusion suggests that it is inappropriate to look for indicators for KAC (much as the analogy is appealing, the economy and markets do not allow maturing to follow the gradual aging pattern of humans), Table 10.3 nevertheless presents data for more than twenty economic indicators. The Table compares the Indian economy with a set of economies (including industrialized economies like New Zealand), whose macroeconomic indicators reflect stability. Further, data were excluded from consideration if the inflation rate in any country in any one of the preceding three years was greater than 30 per cent, or devaluation in any year was greater than 75 per cent. In other words, crisis economies and crisis years were excluded from analysis.

Since the Indian indicators are being compared to twenty-six countries in a non-crisis or relatively stable macroeconomic situation, the data are *biased* against the Indian indicators. Table 10.3 presents only the comparison of Indian indicators with the average of other countries.

4.1 GROWTH, INFLATION, AND INTEREST RATES

The results reported in Table 10.3 suggest, in a heuristic manner, that except for one indicator, the Indian economy appears to be in a relatively healthy situation. Growth is considerably above average, inflation is no worse than average (PPI better, CPI worse; though for 1997 this indicator is considerably better than average), real interest rates are below average for overnight funds, and equal to average for ten-year government paper. Comparative data on corporate rates are not available but analysis of limited data suggests that the Indian rates are among the highest in the developing world (upwards of 10 per cent) and the spread between government and corporate paper—at approximately 700 basis points or 7 per cent—is the highest in the world.

4.2 TRADE

Eight debt and four trade indicators are also examined in Table 10.3. Here again the comparative data is encouraging. For the three years ending in 1995, India's average annual export growth (in $) was 19.8 per cent and import growth averaged 21.6 per cent. Trade deficit averaged –1.7 per cent of GDP and current account deficit was –0.7 per cent. The two deficits were less than half those of the comparators, and both export and import growth was higher. Clearly there is not much cause for concern except that given India's infrastructure needs, current account deficit is more than a bit on the low side.

4.3 DEBT

Ten debt indicators, as reported in the World Bank Debt Tables 1996 were examined. While the ratio of India's debt to exports is high, the ratio of debt to GNP is on the 'low' side. On the composition of debt, India's position is extremely favourable—almost half the entire debt is on a concessional basis, compared to only 25 per cent for the other countries. The status of reserves is also in a relatively comfortable state—the reserves/import ratio at seven months is somewhat higher than the average of 5 per cent.

4.4 SAVINGS, INVESTMENT, AND FISCAL DEFICIT

Both savings and investment rates are above average, and both government revenue and government expenditure below average. But there is one indicator on which the Indian performance is worse than most well-managed comparator countries—fiscal deficit. It is a moot point whether a fiscal deficit at 5 per cent of GDP is that much worse than the average of 3 per cent.[3] It is also intriguing to note that a bad fiscal deficit does not show up in most performance indicators (growth, inflation, etc.) It is obvious that if bad government expenditure were to be curtailed, then the performance of the economy will improve. It is beyond the scope of this chapter to examine whether reduction in fiscal deficit has exactly parallel effects as a reduction in government expenditure. (Recall that in developing countries the tax base is constantly increasing and therefore a reduction in deficits can hide the perpetuation of bad government expenditure.)

4.5 A QUESTION OF RESERVES

Discussions of managed exchange rate regimes often begin and end with the level of reserves. For the record, the level of Indian reserves today, and for the last few years, has been comfortably above the mean, and indeed close to the 90th percentile of developing countries (Table 10.3), appropriate reserves being defined as the ratio of reserves to imports.

However, the question of 'optimal' level of reserves for a developing country is expected to soon join the select dinosaur club of economic indicators—central planning, money supply growth, fixed exchange rates, and a yet to be extinct 'concern' for fiscal deficits. The problem is the new world order—an integrated world capital market that is fast diminishing the need for government control, or direction.

Two points need to be emphasized: first, reserves classified as excessive earlier (in the context of Korea) were later described by Mr Stanley Fischer, IMF, to be at 'abysmally low levels'. The second, and related, point is that a regime of KAC, i.e. a floating exchange rate, does not require any reserves. The calculation of a 'desired' level of reserves is identical to the calculation of the price and quantity of shoes in a centrally planned economy. Reserves are only needed to defend a misguided and misaligned exchange rate, by definition. No fixing, no loss of reserves—a lesson which several Asian and East European central bankers learnt before losing any sleep, or reserves, in 1997.

4.6 IS INDIA READY FOR CAPITAL ACCOUNT CONVERTIBILITY?

Over twenty-five indicators were examined. India's comparative economic performance appears to be in the top quintile. Further, given that

---

[3] All data are for fiscal deficits at the central level (IMF, 1997a).

TABLE 10.3
ECONOMIC INDICATORS: INDIA AND COMPARATOR COUNTRIES

Variable Description	India Last 3 Years Ending in	Most Recent Estimate or 1995	Comparator Countries Low	High	Mean	Std. Dev.	Percentile 10	50	90
Debt									
Debt stock/Exports	1995	247.0	43.8	291.1	166.5	83.5	47.6	175.6	261.2
Total debt/GNP	1995	34.2	14.4	104.8	48.6	23.1	21.4	49.0	65.9
Debt service paid/Exports	1995	26.3	7.9	32.7	20.8	9.4	9.2	23.4	32.6
Interest payments/Exports	1995	11.3	2.4	15.0	7.9	4.1	2.9	8.9	11.3
Interest payments/GNP	1995	1.6	0.9	3.6	2.3	0.9	0.9	2.1	3.4
Reserves/Debt stock	1995	24.5	7.7	120.8	38.4	29.9	13.9	32.6	59.9
Reserves/Imports	1995	6.7	1.7	10.2	4.8	2.5	2.6	3.9	8.4
ST debt/Total debt	1995	5.1	3.6	43.1	19.7	11.1	4.0	20.0	29.8
Concessional debt/Total debt	1995	48.2	1.2	78.2	25.3	23.1	1.5	16.1	51.4
Multilateral debt/Total debt	1995	32.0	6.6	38.0	17.8	10.9	6.8	13.6	34.8
Inflation									
CPI Inflation	1996	11.0	0.3	52.0	8.4	7.7	1.8	7.2	15.6
PPI Inflation	1996	7.2	-0.4	39.1	8.3	7.6	1.1	7.7	17.6
Exchange rate: % change	1995	-12.1	-71.4	18.0	-4.2	14.0	-19.8	-0.6	8.1
Overvaluation: %	1996	5.7	-51.2	57.6	7.2	14.4	-2.6	6.8	22.4
Change in overvaluation	1996	3.3	-59.2	50.0	2.9	11.7	-5.3	2.6	9.9
Black market premium	1996	0.0	0.0	4.0	0.4	0.9	0.0	0.0	1.0

Interest Rates									
Overnight money: real	1996	2.0	5.1	6.9	-6.4	30.4	-1.5	5.2	9.4
10 year paper: real	1995	4.0	5.4	2.2	-1.7	9.1	2.9	5.9	6.9
Real ex-post: returns on OM	1995	5.6	9.3	17.4	-14.3	80.9	-5.3	5.3	27.3
Real M1: % change	1995	7.0	5.7	10.3	-48.4	31.9	-3.0	7.0	14.8
Real monetary base: % change	1995		5.7	18.4	-62.8	82.0	-9.3	5.8	21.4
GDP growth rate	1995	7	5.1	-3.5	-6.9	11.9	0.7	-4.8	9.2
Government Related									
Fiscal deficit/GDP	1995	5.0	-2.5	5.6	-21.3	15.5	-8.5	-0.7	1.9
Govt. Revenue/GDP	1995	13.5	23.0	7.4	11.9	40.0	16.9	20.0	35.2
Govt. Expenditure/GDP	1995	16.8	25.9	9.5	13.2	47.3	16.6	24.3	36.5
Investment/GDP	1995	27.6	26.4	8.5	14.3	48.4	18.4	23.7	38.5
Savings/GDP	1995	25.6	23.2	10.4	8.0	50.8	11.3	19.5	35.9
Trade Related									
Current AIC Deficit/GDP	1995	-1.7	-1.5	4.6	-8.1	17.7	-5.9	-1.8	2.9
Trade Balance Deficit/GDP	1995	-2.7	-3.2	5.9	-13.6	10.0	-11.4	-3.2	4.5
Exports in $: % change	1995	20.9	16.8	14.9	-15.9	68.2	-1.9	15.7	34.6
Imports in $: % change	1995	30.0	14.2	15.3	-24.3	69.6	-5.4	17.1	28.9

even a bad economy would suggest reforms, and that KAC, with an appropriate exchange regime, yields large benefits, it is difficult to argue today that India is not ready for capital account convertibility.

REFERENCES

Bhalla, Surjit S. (1992a). 'Free Societies, Free Markets and Social Welfare'. Mimeo, World Bank, August 1992. Final Revision, February 1994.

————. (1992b). 'Freedom and Economic Growth: A Virtuous Cycle?'. In Axel Hadenius (ed.), *Democracy's Victory and Crisis: Nobel Symposium 1994*. Cambridge University Press.

————. (1997). 'Economic Freedom and Growth Miracles: India is Next'. Paper presented at the World Bank–IMF Meetings, Hong Kong, 18 September.

————. (1998). 'Exchange Rates and Chinese Competitiveness: Implications for Emerging Economies'. Mimeo.

Eatwell, John. (1996). 'International Capital and Liberalization: An Evaluation'. Mimeo, Trinity College, Cambridge, August.

Feldstein, M. and C. Horioka. (1980). 'Domestic Saving and International Capital Flows'. *Economic Journal*.

Feldstein, M. and P. Bacchetta. (1991). 'National Saving and International Investment'. In J. Shoven and D. Bernheim (eds), *The Economics of Saving*. Chicago: University of Chicago Press.

Hayek, Freidrich. (1944). *The Road to Serfdom*. Chicago: University of Chicago Press.

Hanson, J.A. (1994). 'An Open Capital Account: A Brief Survey of the Issues and the Results'. In G. Caprio, I. Atiyas, and J.A. Hanson (eds), *Financial Reform: Theory and Experience*. New York: Cambridge University Press.

International Monetary Fund (IMF). (1997a). *International Financial Statistics*. CD-ROM, September.

————. (1997b). *World Economic Outlook*, September.

Mathieson, D.J. and L. Rojas-Suarez. (1993). 'Liberalisation of the Capital Account: Experiences and Issues'. IMF Occasional Paper No. 103.

Obstfeld, M. (1995). 'International Currency Experience: New Lessons and Lessons Learned'. Brookings Papers on Economic Activity No. 1, pp. 119-211.

Quirk-Evans. (1995). 'Capital Account Convertability: Review of Experience and Implications for IMF policies'. IMF Occasional Paper No. 131.

Reserve Bank of India. (1997). *Report of the Committee on Capital Account Convertibility*. (Chairman: S.S. Tarapore). Mumbai.

Scully, Gerald W. and Daniel J. Slottie. (1991). 'Ranking Economic Liberty across Countries'. *Public Choice*, vol. 69.

World Bank. (1991). *World Development Report 1991: The Challenge of Development*. Washington, D.C.: World Bank.

Banking Crises: Epidemic Response and Policy Approaches

GERARD CAPRIO, JR.*

1. INTRODUCTION

Systemic bank insolvency has occurred in many countries in the last fifteen years and is quite costly. The typical banking crisis in an OECD country has been financed readily, albeit with some pain. In many developing countries the scope of the crisis and the cost have been much greater and the crises in East Asia promise to be near record setting. Economists and policy advisers have been responding with concerted efforts at the IMF, the World Bank, and other multilateral development banks, and now through G-10 deputies and the BIS, to put banking sector work in developing countries at the forefront of their efforts.

This chapter briefly reviews some of the salient facts related to banking busts in developing or emerging market economies, drawing on Caprio and Klingebiel (1996a; 1996b); Goldstein and Turner (1996); Honohan (1996); and Lindgren, Garcia, and Saal (1996). After briefly looking at information on the scope and cost of banking crises in developing countries, Section 2 will focus on the policy responses by authorities in some of the 'early' crisis countries—those which experienced insolvency episodes in the 1980s. Not surprisingly some of these responses have been more effective than others.

Lastly, Section 3 reviews a wider menu of responses, and discusses in particular the suggestion that the promulgation of an International

*This chapter draws on Gerard Caprio, 'Safe and Sound Banking in Developing Countries: We're not in Kansas Anymore' and Gerard Caprio and Daniela Klingebiel, 'Bank Insolvency: Cross Country Experience', World Bank Policy Research Paper #11. The views and interpretations expressed in this paper are those of the author, and do not necessarily represent the views and policies of the World Bank, or its Executive Directors, or the countries they represent.

Banking Standard (IBS) or the Basle Committee's Core Principles would significantly improve the safety and soundness of developing country banking systems. Although this approach has a great deal of appeal, and should have some pay off, particularly in some of the higher middle income countries, other approaches are likely necessary in developing countries where the risks are usually greater, economic activity more concentrated, financial institutions less diversified, markets less transparent, supervision relatively weak, and other critical ingredients for successful implementation of a supervisory-based 'cure' for unsafe banking absent. Given these differences, the chapter concludes by arguing that better incentives—bigger carrots and bigger sticks—will also be necessary in emerging markets if bank insolvency is to be successfully contained. Although improving bank supervision is a worthy goal, by itself exporting banking standards from industrial to developing countries will likely have relatively little impact on the safety and soundness of banking there in the next decade. It calls for a multi-pillar approach to safe and sound banking, strengthening the incentives and capacity of owners and managers, the market, and supervisors to contribute to prudent corporate governance of banks, as well as for greater attention to factors restricting banks' ability and willingness to diversify risk. Only if each of these four pillars is strengthened will the resulting system perform the important intermediation functions prudently.

2. THE EPIDEMIC AND THE RESPONSE

Banking crises have become an epidemic, affecting most developing and transitional economies at some point during the last fifteen years. For example, one study estimates that 69 countries have been hit by banking crises in the last decade and a half; including the economies in transition from communism to capitalism, the total might reach 90.[1] Often these crises have wiped out the net worth of the banking system, required transfers of 10–20 per cent of GDP, and contributed to macroeconomic instability and currency crises.

What factors led to these crises? Caprio and Klingebiel (1996b) examine twenty-nine crises in twenty-six countries for which substantial

[1]See Caprio and Klingebiel (1996b). Lindgren, Garcia, and Saal (1996) use a slightly different methodology, but the number of countries affected is roughly the same.

information is available. They find that macroeconomic factors were at least a contributing factor in all the crises. Partly this reflected problems in trade, in particular negative terms of trade effects in economies with exports that were concentrated in only a few products (see Caprio and Klingebiel 1996b). But weak incentive and regulatory systems were perhaps an even more important factor in most crises. Thus macroeconomic problems were often a 'proximate' cause, which led to bank runs and exposed the underlying weaknesses of the banking system. Also, delay in loss recognition appears to be a common characteristic in most experiences, leading to a larger ultimate cost.

The regulatory and incentive weaknesses included limited attention to whether loans were performing, 'evergreening' of bad loans through rollovers of interest and principal into new loans. Bank capital was often low and/or had been wiped out before the crisis became overt. Bank lending was often highly concentrated in a few borrowers and/or non-arms length transactions, and/or politically motivated loans (Benin, Chile, Philippines, Ghana, Indonesia, Turkey, Brazil). Better supervision might have brought out into the open some of these problems, if politics had permitted such disclosures. Finally, poor lending management and limited managerial skills were important in almost all countries with fraud an additional factor.

These financial crises have entailed high fiscal and quasi-fiscal costs, often 10–20 per cent of GDP, rising in some cases to 40–55 per cent (Argentina, Chile). The crises affected as much as 70–90 per cent of banks assets in a few cases (Benin,1988–90; Guinea, 1985; Ivory Coast, 1988–91; Poland, 1991). In many other cases it affected 20–60 per cent of assets (Argentina 1989–90, Chile, Colombia, Estonia, Philippines, Senegal, Spain, Uruguay).[2]

Governments in theory could have financed the costs of banking crises over a 10–20-year period and eased the macroeconomic burden, but in practice few had access to long-term finance. Thus those hit with large negative net worth in their banking systems had to consider a variety of unattractive choices. The low cost choice, at least in its immediate impact on the budget, would have been to let depositors bear the burden. However, few governments in the post-War period have been willing to make this choice, especially when losses were large; in all likelihood because such a choice was perceived as dangerous to the

---

[2]See Caprio and Klingebiel (1996b) and Lindgren, Garcia, and Saal (1996) for more details.

administration's survival or perhaps as dangerous to the economy and leading to long-term disintermediation of the formal financial system. Baer and Klingebiel (1995) show that the latter effect did not follow in selected cases.[3] Nonetheless, either because prevalent opinion among policy makers assumes extensive fallout from the imposition of losses on depositors, or due to political concerns, most governments try to hide the cost of bank failures.

A popular choice is to bury the losses in the central bank's balance sheet. However, this solution is risky: although the losses may remain hidden for some time, they eventually put pressure on the central bank to find revenue sources. Unless the economy is hit by positive shocks, the danger is that the central bank will resort to money creation as net income declines. The sharp rise in inflation in Argentina (from 165 per cent in 1982 to over 600 per cent in 1984–5), the Philippines (from 10 per cent in 1983 to 50 per cent and 23 per cent in 1984 and 1985, respectively), and to a lesser extent in Chile (in the early 1980s) derived in large part from this method of covering the cost of bank insolvency. Lastly, if domestic capital markets lack sufficient depth, foreign borrowing has tended to be favoured, with all the usual debt servicing problems.

Not surprisingly, macroeconomic stability was usually derailed by these high costs and their finance, despite the fact that the costs, other than external debt payments, were largely transfer payments. Governments were successful in dealing with the macroeconomic imbalances, that is they lowered their budget deficits, reduced inflation, and reduced external imbalances, in only six of the countries studied. In another four countries, a stable macro situation was in place and was maintained. But in the sixteen other countries, macroeconomic stability deteriorated.

Systemic bank insolvency also should be a source of concern because it demonstrates that capital has been—and often continues to be—misallocated. Occasionally countries charge out of a banking crisis with rapid growth, or at least begin to see more robust growth after a period of several years as reforms take root. Far more prevalent is not just a drop in growth but a recovery that is sluggish relative to the pre-crisis

---

[3]Interestingly, Baer and Klingebiel (1996) find, based on a study of five countries (Estonia, 1992; Argentina, 1989; Malaysia, 1986; Japan, 1946; and the United States, 1933), that imposing losses on depositors had minimal negative impact on economic performance when 'policy makers took a comprehensive approach to resolving financial system distress and sought to ensure that only well capitalized institutions will remain in operation' (p. 196).

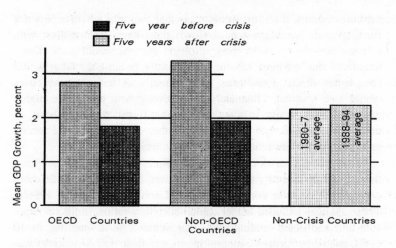

Figure 11.1 Percentage Change in GDP Five Years Before and After the
Initiation of Bank Insolvency 1975–94

period. Figure 11.1 shows this latter effect, as well as the impact of increased macroeconomic instability, showing the average growth rates five years prior to and five years following each of the insolvency episodes in the C-K sample, and the slowdown is statistically significant and slightly larger in developing than in industrialized countries. To be sure, this holds nothing constant, and many factors undoubtedly determine growth, but a more rigorous econometric examination will have to wait, as many crises were in the early 1990s still too recent to yield statistically meaningful results.[4] Nonetheless, the fact that the non-crisis countries did not experience a similar decline is consistent with the potential growth-reducing effects of a bank crisis. Also, although many argue that poor growth causes banking crises, on average countries experiencing banking crises saw sustained *weaker* growth following episodes of bank insolvency, compared with the pre-crisis period.

Widespread bank insolvency means that incentives for taking prudent risks are overwhelmed by other calculations, as low or negative net worth will encourage excessive risk taking (Kane and Yu, 1994) or looting (Akerlof and Romer, 1993). Banks that excel in allocating one part of their portfolio imprudently seldom also excel in allocating the rest of their portfolio brilliantly, and it is likely that the same is true of

---

[4]Thus only those countries with five years of post-crisis data were included.

banking systems. If so, this would mean that countries which experience banking crises would grow more slowly than others, or that those with a larger banking crisis (or more insolvent system) would grow slower than those that are more solvent, both directly, because the latter would have better allocated resources, and indirectly, as fewer/smaller crises would lead to greater financial sector development and hence higher growth. Unfortunately, it is not yet possible to test this hypothesis, as most of the episodes of insolvency in either data set are quite recent, and thus insufficient time has passed for a proper test.

Finally, in almost all countries some efforts were made to strengthen the underlying incentive framework; however, in only 16 of the 26 cases can these changes be considered major (Caprio and Kligebiel, 1996b). These changes included higher capital adequacy ratios, limits on exposure and connected lending, and improvements in accounting. In 10 cases, annual performance monitoring by reputable outside auditors was put in place. Limits on new lending to borrowers in default were also put in place in some. However, this was by no means the case in all of the countries. Indeed, in some cases bank managers suffered no loss of position or status, providing a negative signal to performance. Finally, it is also noteworthy that problems with the legislative framework for collection hindered the growth of the lending market after the crises in many countries, and drove up risk premia.

Although a similar analysis of the East Asian crises is premature, like those episodes reviewed above, both micro and macro factors are believed to have played a role. In particular, the combination of a sudden retreat by foreign investors, coupled with poor regulation and a low degree of transparency produced among the more significant crises of the twentieth century. Estimated fiscal costs in Thailand, Indonesia, and Korea are widely expected to exceed 20 per cent of GDP, though it will be a few years before the full costs—including the slowdown in growth—are known. It remains to be seen if the governments in these countries will add to 'best practice' in how they deal with the crisis.

2.1 Some Specific Countries' Responses

Chile and Malaysia stand out, for the crises experienced there in the 1980s, as having superior post-crisis performance, and also in terms of the response by authorities to the crisis. To be sure, in Chile there was considerable delay in the early 1980s in dealing with bank insolvency, as regulators applied easier rules to postpone loss recognition. In both cases, ultimately, managers were sacked, shareholders bore losses, and fraud was prosecuted. More recently, increased attention was devoted to improving the information available to banks and other market participants.

Chilean banks are now required to be rated by private rating agencies twice a year, and there are also mandatory restrictions on banks' portfolios as leverage increases.[5] In Malaysia, a credit bureau was established on borrowers, so banks could better determine how borrowers might perform. Another performer with mostly favourable post-crisis indicators, New Zealand, has moved to a market rating system in which the authorities do not collect or maintain information that is not in the public domain, and have otherwise moved strongly to improve incentives in banking. Most of the changes, such as increased liability for bank directors (when disclosed information is false or misleading), in this case have only been effected in 1996; however, so it is too early to say how they have been functioning.

It is interesting to speculate why Malaysia went from being a good performer to being severely affected in the 1997–9 crisis. One possibility is that the longer a sustained boom progresses, the more difficult it is to remind bankers and market participants that prices can move up and down, and that loans may be performing only because of exceptional macro circumstances, and not due to wise investment selection. Openness to capital flows, as in Malaysia and Indonesia, can exert some disciplining effect on government policy when the capital inflow itself is disciplined; when capital flows come indiscriminately, they feed the boom mentality and make effective supervision impossible (Caprio, Atiyas, and Hanson, 1994, Ch. 13). Chile had neither the sustained domestic boom nor the torrid pace of capital inflows that the East Asian countries experienced, and its banking system has proved resilient thus far. Econometric estimates of the impact of capital inflow tax, however, show that the tax had no impact on the volume of capital inflows, though perhaps some effect, if one can trust the data, on the maturity of the inflows. In other words, the lack of overwhelming capital inflows

---

[5] In the restructuring of bad debts, Chilean banks had their bad loans taken over by the central bank, with the stipulation that the originating banks had to buy them back over a period of time (which eventually was extended). The resignation this year by former central bank governor Roberto Zahler was associated with an attempt to put some of the cost onto that institution, rather than on the commercial banks or the Treasury, and indicates that there may still be some incentive problems in the banking system.

reflects other factors, rather than explicit policies to discourage inflows, and in this respect the Chilean authorities were fortunate.

The Argentine case is also instructive. Argentina experienced banking crises in the early 1980s, the late 1980s, and 1995 (the latter as a fallout from the Mexican crisis). Although financial depth has not recovered to the levels seen prior to the first crisis, it was rising in the 1990s and appears to have recovered quickly from the early 1995 episode. So although Argentina compared less favourably in post-crisis response, this may be misleading. After all, the Tequila crisis featured a run on smaller, provincial banks, plus a run on the currency for a few months when the commitment to the 1 : 1 convertibility of the peso into the dollar was in doubt. But the system recovered reasonably well, and the money centre banks, whose health did not appear to be in question, benefited from the consolidation, as the number of banks declined from 200 in 1994 to 124 in early 1996 (Caprio et al., 1996b). Also, the Argentine authorities instituted a number of policies—such as raising minimum capital requirements to a risk-weighted 11.5 per cent, one of the higher levels in the world, and varying the minimum as a function of credit and market risk. They also significantly strengthened supervision in 1994, and in 1996, instituted a subordinated debt plan, requiring the periodic issuance of large lumps of subordinated debt to create a class of uninsured creditors with a strong incentive to monitor the banks. Clearly, it is too soon to tell how effective these measures will be, but the system has held up well in the wake of the Tequila crisis and thus far in the East Asian contagion no system is immune to financial crisis, but the Argentine authorities have progressed significantly.

The Philippines, another relatively good post-crisis performer in the 1980s–early 1990s, saw marked improvement in the supervisory and regulatory framework: an independent central bank was established, with losses from the 1980s crisis carved out of its balance sheet, the deposit insurance fund was recapitalized, government interventions in banking were reduced, and supervision clearly upgraded. Still, the intervention by the judiciary in the bank closure process (by requiring a mandatory ninety-day minimum notification of banks after insolvency has been determined, so that shareholders have the opportunity to turnaround their bank before the authorities step in), would appear to be excessively generous to shareholders and managers. Moreover, the pace of real credit growth to the private sector in recent years has been quite rapid, as much as 5 times real GDP; such rapid expansion has proven difficult to manage safely in a variety of countries. And transparency is low.

The above list accounts for most of the relatively limited success stories. In many other countries, efforts to effect change in the regulatory/incentive environment were distinctly muted or entirely absent. For example, in one African country only a small fraction (5 per cent) of written off loans was collected, less than that spent on the collection effort. And in Guinea, after virtually the entire banking system was closed in the mid-1980s, there was little attempt to change the accounting, regulatory, or supervisory approach, nor was disclosure improved; another crisis ensued in the early 1990s. Moreover, few of the many small countries with bank insolvency problems have moved to improve diversification of bank portfolios by encouraging more foreign banks or greater foreign holdings by local banks. And fewer still have acted to close banks or to reduce state ownership in finance. Although merely relying on private ownership without improving the incentive environment is dangerous—witness Mexico in the early–mid-1990s—continued state ownership has not yet been able to produce efficient, well-managed banking.

Lastly, in several countries there has been an attempt to upgrade supervision, though there is no clear evidence that this has been successful. Many developing countries are experiencing improved macroeconomic environments, thanks both to improved domestic policies and low interest rates in industrial economies. Still, even where a favourable macro draw has restored banks to solvency, the underlying risks appear to be little changed except in very few countries.

3. STANDARDS, RULES, AND INCENTIVES

In searching for cures to any problem, a popular approach is to look for best practice and argue that it should be universally applied. One problem with this strategy with respect to dealing with bank insolvency is that there has not been a long enough time period to draw conclusions about how robust different remedies or regulatory structures are in practice. Moreover, as Kane (1993) suggests, regulators and regulatees are locked in a dynamic game, and it is always dangerous to assume that the game is over, not least when favourable macroclimates are bolstering bottom lines.

Another difficulty with applying best practice is that it is difficult to find. In arguing for an IBS, Goldstein (1996) implicitly takes the industrial countries as the standard, even though crises are almost as common in industrial as in developing countries. True, the data do suggest that bank insolvency is a less costly problem, relative to GDP or total bank credit, in the OECD area than in developing countries, but the smaller size of the latter countries, their larger shocks, and more concentrated economies alone would lead one to predict that their bank crises would be more costly. In other words, if industrial economies were characterized by the same quality of bank supervision as in developing countries, then one would expect to see a markedly lower incidence of banking problems among richer countries because of their other advantages, if, that is, the quality of bank supervision matters in determining the scope of banking problems. Thus one could conclude that it is not clear that richer countries have 'gotten supervision right', much less that effective supervision is a feasible, near term goal for developing countries.

Third, applying best practice in banking or bank regulation should be undertaken with care, and with the realization that institutions—the rules, procedures, and norms that frame decisions of economic and political actors—are crucial determinants of how well any reforms can be transplanted to a new setting. Merely well-intentioned efforts are not sufficient. In trying to lessen the incidence and cost of bank insolvency, one is attempting to get a group of powerful and usually wealthy bankers, in many cases with close ties to the current authorities, to behave in a socially more prudent fashion in the face of conflicting private incentives, such as to refrain from big bets when their downside risks are covered, or to ignore officials' guidance on lending decisions, even when to do so will strengthen or allow them to retain their monopoly power. Not surprising, then, such reforms often are implemented in half measure and enforced at best with some irregularity.

One key institution that differs dramatically in many developing countries from their industrial counterparts is the government revenue system: not just the weak revenue base associated with low incomes, but the efficiency of the system and the attitudes towards paying taxes. Indeed, a key reason why many governments in developing countries relied on financial repression was that they needed to make up for the inadequacies of the formal tax system. Revenue problems make it likely that the government will be providing an underfunded guarantee for bank depositors, and several observers such as Brock (1996) argue persuasively that it is this underfunding of .the guarantee scheme that accounts for systemic insolvency problems. Regardless of how sincere a government may be in upgrading its supervision or in, say, instituting prompt corrective action and structured early intervention, these attempts will likely founder to the extent that the supervisory authorities (or deposit insurer) fail to move against insolvent institutions due to a lack of funding as well as political will.

With these caveats in mind, what should developing countries do? As noted above, one reform being discussed at present is an IBS, defined as an attempt to bring 'more developing countries more quickly up to a minimum level of sound banking practice and strong banking-supervision' (Goldstein, 1996, p. 15), which is to include common disclosure requirements, an accounting and legal framework, transparency of government involvement, limits on connected lending, Bank of International Settlements (BIS) or higher risk-weighted capital ratios, consolidated supervision among host and home-country supervisors, and perhaps more importantly, some form of structured early intervention and prompt corrective action as embodied in the Federal Deposit Insurance Corporation Insurance Act (FDICIA).

To be sure, guidelines in many of these areas, along with an education programme to teach officials (where needed) and electorates about their importance are useful. The World Bank developed a set of supervisory guidelines in the early 1990s and since then has been promulgating and improving them. But it is one thing to propose best practice guidelines and distinctly different to say that a single set of rules should be imposed on all countries as the cure for what ails their banks. To see the issues and difficulties, consider limits on connected lending and bank ownership. First, are limits a good idea? Certainly the Chilean crisis in the early 1980s is a convincing example of the dangers of such lending, at least until one reads Lamoreaux (1994), who argues that connected lending was part of the reason for the growth of the New England economy and the success of early nineteenth-century banking there.

But even accepting that connected lending is to be avoided, or at least controlled,[6] can it be accomplished merely by promulgating limits? In fact an increasing number of countries have such limits, but it is rather easy to circumvent them. Although Goldstein (1996) argues that prac-

---

[6]In fact it is likely that the 'insider lending' Lamoreaux cites was controlled, in that, even though depositors evaluated banks on the basis of the underlying businesses in which bank directors were involved, they also would have disciplined banks from lending too much to one connected business. Also, this form of connected lending functioned well at least in part due to the importance of reputation. Failed bankers could not so easily decamp to other locales. Thus it may not be happenstance that this form of banking diminished as migration became more popular.

tices making it difficult or impossible for supervisors to verify the accuracy of reports pertaining to connected lending should be outlawed, this is likely to be a Herculean task. Many developing countries feature highly concentrated wealth and income, and several large families dominate a few.[7] Indicative of this concentration, in data for a cross-section of forty-nine industrial and developing countries (LaPorta et al., 1996), ownership of non-financial firms (the only ones for which they obtained data) was more concentrated in developing than in industrial countries, and the authors do not make any attempt to correct for the possibility that large shareholders might be affiliated with one another. Also, the stock market concentration ratios for industrial and developing countries show that concentration, measured by the capitalization of the largest ten listed firms to total market capitalization, was .44 in developing countries, compared with .31 in industrial economies (.28 if the lower income industrialized countries, Greece and Portugal, are omitted or included with the developing countries). In addition to greater concentration, institutions in many countries are often less oriented to a democratic system of checks and balances than, say, in the United States. These two characteristics together make the evasion of limits on connected lending 'child's play'. For the same reasons, limits on the ownership of banks can be and are easily rendered inoperative.

A second aspect of an IBS, the improvement of the accounting and legal framework, is also desirable but will be difficult to effect, and certainly cannot be accomplished soon in many countries. Progress has been seen in upper middle income countries, such as Argentina and Chile, but would appear to be unrealistic in the many developing countries, certainly in the ninety economies with per capita GDP below the upper middle income level.[8] To argue otherwise is tantamount to suggesting that legal reform could be achieved by mailing the US legal code to a low income country. Many countries in fact have quite serviceable laws or codes, but the judicial system shortcircuits implementation. Judges, lawyers, and citizens need to be educated if legal reform is to take root. For accounting, trained accountants are needed—more likely in middle income than in low income countries—and it takes

---

[7] Gini coefficients for the 1986–93 period are as follows: Sub-Saharan Africa, 44.7; East Asia, 36.2; South Asia, 34.1; Middle East and North Africa, 40.8; Latin America, 50.2; OECD, 33.2. See Deininger and Squire (1996).

[8] A per capita GDP of approximately $ 3000 was the cut off point for the upper middle income range.

time, effort, and incentives to get a chart of accounts accepted.[9] How would collateral be valued where markets are thin? Can a loan classification system be applied with few trained bankers or verified with few skilled supervisors? And even if supervisors had statutory authority to carry out their functions, how would supervision operate if supervisors were closely connected to the industry, such as through family or political ties, or if supervisors could be easily sued for their actions? And if institutions are linked through family ownership, how valid are any set of accounts as a guide to understanding the viability and prospects of an individual firm?

A third aspect of an IBS, the idea of mandating prompt corrective action and structured early intervention, also appears to be a laudable goal, namely lessening the extent to which supervisory forbearance can occur. Such an approach was taken in the reform of US deposit insurance, the FDICIA. Again, however, empirical evidence that such a system will limit bank insolvency is not yet apparent. Accepting that it will be forthcoming, Berger (1993) argues that a good accounting (and loan classification!) system is a requirement for the FDICIA to operate well, as decisions are to be made on capital levels. Moreover, even if the US legal system tolerates a government closing private businesses while they still have positive net worth, in many other countries it is so difficult to close those with negative net worth that it is hard to believe that significant progress will soon be made. As noted above, supervisors may well have close links with the regulated, and where governmental checks and balances are weaker, it will be difficult for anyone to oversee supervisory compliance.

Even in the United States, proponents of prompt corrective action and structured early intervention acknowledge that there may still be a 'too big to fail' problem. In developing countries, banking systems are often more highly concentrated, meaning that it may be more difficult still to believe that any prescribed 'automatic' intervention or closure steps will be taken. Where concentration in banking is linked to concentration of wealth and political power, it is even less likely that such changes will be readily introduced or honoured even if enacted. This is not to discourage attempts to make banking more safe and sound, but rather to suggest that pre-programmed changes cannot be quickly implanted, if

---

[9]I am indebted to Fernando Montes-Negret for pointing out that the Chinese Federation of Accountants estimates that they need to train 100,000 accountants by the year 2000 and 300,000 by 2010!

ever, in a variety of diverse institutional settings, and may create a false sense of security.

Lastly, Goldstein suggests that higher capital should be part of an IBS to the extent that risks are higher there, and this too would be set as part of the standard. Although encouraging some way to better align bankers' incentives with those of society is prudent, and higher minimum capital ratios have been argued by several, including this author, as a way to do so, it is by no means clear that they are adequate. First, higher capital may be useful but it is far harder to mandate the quality of capital. Owners often put up resources of differing degrees of quality, including borrowing funds from their own institution, and this can be difficult to detect, especially in countries dominated by relatively few groups or families. Second, the effect of higher capital on risk taking is theoretically ambiguous: it is quite possible that a higher requirement could lead owners to select a point further out on the risk–return frontier, and empirical investigations find relatively little difference in the probability of failure from different capital levels (Berger, Herring, and Szego, 1995). Third, it is not clear what role more capital would play in public banks. Governments clearly have difficulty in enforcing minimum returns on public enterprises. If this is so, more capital may simply mean more below market lending. Privatization is important especially since some of the largest losses have been in public banks (in Brazil and France); it can help bring owners' and managers' incentives in line with those of society, especially when privatization takes place in an effective regulatory environment. But in most countries, public sector banks were set up to reduce financial–industrial concentration. Privatization thus means concentration on foreign banks. So if authorities in a country, after understanding the alternative approaches, argue that raising capital may be the only feasible way, given their country's institutions, to bring about more prudent banking, it would be wise to support this attempt. Such support, however, is a far cry from mandating this approach.

What else can be done, besides more capital and an IBS? There are three distinct groups that can monitor banks: bank owners (and managers), the market (including uninsured debtholders and other possible 'co-owners'), and supervisors. These three groups could be regarded as three of the four pillars supporting a safe and sound banking system. Emphasizing the need to build the capacity and incentives for each of these groups to perform its function effectively would appear sensible, given both the uncertainty about which group is more effective and because ideally these three monitors would complement one another.

In official circles, the pendulum has swung excessively in favour of supervision; given the arguments above, greater emphasis on owners and the market is warranted. Moreover, it would seem indispensable to rely on local authorities and their assessment of their own institutions in deciding on the balance of emphasis among the different monitors. Local officials have to be relied on to decide how to balance these different monitors and how any changes would work in their own institutional setting.

Greater reliance on owners and the market, through an incentive-based approach is attractive for several reasons:

- it resembles closely the path followed by various industrialized nations when they were industrializing;
- it allows poor countries to employ scarce human capital in more directly productive pursuits, rather than in bank supervision; and
- improving incentives and information for owners and the market to monitor banks is likely to pay off by itself and would complement the development of supervision.

Improving incentives for owners, while minimizing the need for supervisory oversight, can be accomplished either by greater liability limits, increasing the franchise value of bank licences (see Caprio, 1997b), or by higher capital. Unfortunately there has not been sufficient experimentation, at least in recent times, with these different approaches, so statements about 'best practice' are on empirically shaky ground. Nor is it clear that one approach need work best in all economies. In particular, solutions such as relying more on franchise value or higher liability limits are attractive in economies in which capital is scarce and the capacity and institutional structure conducive for effective supervision (in particular, independence of the supervisory agency) are weak. Of course, it is not clear how incentives for 'owners' and 'managers' can work w! en banks are public and 'civil service' banking prevails.

The market's ability to oversee banks might be fostered not only by greater disclosure but also by using mutual liability, subordinated debt, or other ways to create large, uninsured debtholders. Mutual liability appeared to work well in the US clearinghouse associations in the nineteenth century, and in Canada, but more recent evidence is hard to uncover.

Importantly, convincing governments that substantially beefing up supervision (or any of the three above pillars) alone will produce safe and sound banking may well be unwise in small developing countries.

Broad diversification is the fourth pillar supporting a sound financial system. Where risks are both high and concentrated, it is difficult to believe that governments will raise capital (or liability limits) sufficiently high or allow immensely profitable banking to offset the disadvantages of large shocks and high covariance. In such cases, governments should only allow well-diversified banks, whether foreign or domestic. If a greater role were accorded the incentive system in ensuring safety and soundness, this would become more apparent, for example with better diversified banks being able to hold less capital.

Each of these various approaches has its strengths and weaknesses, just as with the IBS. Indeed, that is the point: there is no empirical evidence, or at least not a large sample, which would allow a disinterested observer to decide on the superiority of one path. Until such evidence is assembled, it would seem appropriate for industrial country authorities and multinational organizations to encourage developing counterparts to strengthen all four pillars and to advise them on the pros and cons of the various alternatives. The IBS approach relies excessively on supervision and discounts the importance of owners, the market, and diversification as ways to enhance safety and soundness.

In sum, this chapter argues that cures for bank insolvency have to be attuned to the institutional settings of developing countries. Poor countries do not differ from richer ones only in their GDP per capita, but also in an array of institutions that bear on how effective financial intermediation will be and on how effective attempts to fix the regulatory or incentive environment will be. Also, industrial economies put in place a safety net for the banking system when they had reached a high level of development—not just a higher income level but more effective legal institutions and greater reliance on democratic processes and arms-length transactions. In short, just as in the 1950s economists learned that 'merely' increasing capital would not convert poor countries into rich ones, it is unlikely that we will find that standardizing some regulations and improving supervision will cure the bank insolvency epidemic. Thus a more appropriate role for multilateral institutions and OECD governments is to encourage a multi-pillar approach to achieving an incentive-compatible banking system as well as to foster more research into what is still a remarkably under-researched field: how insolvency comes about, how authorities deal with it, and how different approaches compare and affect the development of the financial system and growth.

REFERENCES

Akerlof, George A. and Paul Romer. (1993). 'Looting: The Economic Underworld of Bankruptcy for Profit'. *Brookings Papers on Economic Activity*, no. 2, pp. 1–73.

Baer, Herbert and Daniela Klingebiel (1995). 'Systemic Risk when Depositors Bear Losses: Five Case Studies'. In George G. Kaufman (ed.), *Banking, Financial Markets, and Systemic Risk*. Greenwich, Conn.: JAI Press.

Bencivenga, Valerie and Bruce Smith. (1992). 'Deficits, Inflation, and the Banking System in Developing Countries: The Optimal Degree of Financial Repression'. *Oxford Economic Papers*, vol. 44 (October), pp. 767–90.

Berger, Alan. (1993). 'The Importance of Accurate Bank Accounting under FDICIA'. In *FDICIA: An Appraisal*. Proceedings of the 29th Annual Conference on Bank Structure and Competition. Chicago: Federal Reserve Bank of Chicago.

Berger, Alan, Richard J. Herring, and Giorgio P. Szego. (1995). 'The Role of Capital in Financial Institutions'. *Journal of Banking and Finance*, vol. 19, pp. 393–430.

Brock, Philip (ed.). (1992). *If Chile Were Texas: A Primer on Banking Reform*. San Francisco: Institute of Contemporary Studies Press.

———. (1996). 'High Real Interest Rates and Banking Crises in an Open Economy: A Case Study of Chile, 1975–83'. Mimeo, University of Washington, Seattle.

Caprio, Gerard. (1997a), 'Safe and Sound Banking in Developing Countries: We are not in Kansas Anymore'. World Bank Policy Research Working Paper 1739, March.

———. (1997b), 'Bank Regulation: The Case of the Missing Model'. In Bruce Smith and Allison Harwood (eds), *Sequencing Financial Reform: Strategy for Developing Countries*. The Brookings Institution, and Policy Research Discussion Paper 1574, January 1996.

Caprio, G., I. Atiyas and J.A. Hanson (eds). (1994). Financial Reforms: Theory and Experience. New York: Cambridge University Press.

Caprio, Gerard, Michael Dooley, Danny Leipziger, and Carl Walsh. (1996). 'The Lender of Last Resort Function under a Currency Board: The Case of Argentina'. *Open Economies Review*, vol. 7 (July), pp. 617–42.

Caprio, Gerard and Daniela Klingebiel. (1996a). 'Bank Insolvency: Bad Luck, Bad Policy, or Bad Banking'. Paper presented at the Annual Bank Conference on Development Economics, 25–6 April 1996, World Bank, and forthcoming in Michael Bruno and Boris Pleskovic (eds), *Annual World Bank Conference on Development Economics, 1996*.

———. (1996b). 'Bank Insolvency: Cross-Country Experience'. World Bank Policy Research Working Paper 1620, July.

de Capitani, Alberto and Douglass C. North. (1994). 'Institutional Development in Third World Countries: The Role of the World Bank'. Mimeo, HRO Working Paper 42, World Bank, Washington, D.C., October.

Deininger, Klaus and Lyn Squire. (1996). 'A New Data Set Measuring Income Inequality'. *World Bank Economic Review*, vol. 10 (September) no. 3.

Fetter, Frank W. (1931). *Monetary Inflation in Chile*. International Finance Section of the Department of Economics and Social Institutions in Princeton University. Princeton, NJ: Princeton University Press.

Goldstein, Morris. (1996). 'The Case for an International Banking Standard'. Mimeo, Institute for International Economics, Washington, D.C.

Goldstein, M. and P. Turner. (1996). 'Banking Crises in Emerging Economies: Origins and Policy Options'. BIS Economic Papers, no. 46, Basle.

Honohan, Patrick. (1996). 'Financial System Failures in Developing Countries: Diagnosis and Prediction'. Mimeo, International Monetary Fund, Washington, D.C.

Kane, Edward J. (1993). 'Reflexive Adaptation of Business to Regulation and Regulation to Business'. *Law and Policy*, vol. 15, no. 3 (July), pp. 179–89.

Kane, Edward J. and Min-Teh Yu. (1994). 'How Much Did Capital Forbearance Add to the Tab for the FSLIC Mess'. NBER Working Paper 4701, April.

La Porta, Rafael, Florencio Lopez de-Silanes, Andrei Shleifer, and Robert Vishny. (1996). 'Law and Finance'. Discussion Paper Number 1768, Harvard Institute of Economic Research, Cambridge, MA, June.

Lamoreaux, Naomi. (1994). *Insider Lending: Banks, Personal Connections, and Economic Development in Industrial New England, 1784–1912*. Cambridge: Cambridge University Press.

Lindgren, Carl-Johan, Gillian Garcia, and Matthew I. Saal. (1996). *Bank Soundness and Macroeconomic Policy*. Washington, D.C.: International Monetary Fund.

Nicholl, Peter. (1996). 'Market-Based Regulation'. Mimeo, World Bank, Washington, D.C.

Roubini, Nouriel and Xavier Sala-i-Martin. (1995). 'A Growth Model of Inflation, Tax Evasion, and Financial Repression'. *Journal of Monetary Economics*, vol. 35 (April), pp. 275–301.

Internationalization of Financial Services in Asia

STIJN CLAESSENS and TOM GLAESSNER*

1. OVERVIEW

The internationalization of financial services involves eliminating discrimination in treatment between foreign and domestic financial service providers (FSPs). Internationalization relates to, but is not the same as capital account liberalization, but capital account liberalization is an important factor in the potential gains and benefits from access to foreign financial services provided domestically, relative to access provided and obtained offshore. Internationalization also relates to domestic financial deregulation as the degree of deregulation influences the quality and competitiveness of domestic financial services providers.

Many developing countries are assessing whether domestic financial service sectors should be opened to foreign competition and, if so, how. Governments are interested in the questions of how fast to open up, in

*Paper presented at the conference: 'Investment Liberalisation and Financial Reform in the Asia-Pacific Region', 29–31 August , Sydney, Australia, and at the conference: 'India: A Financial System for the 21st Century', 6–8 December, Goa, India. The chapter was written while Glaessner was on the staff of the World Bank. We would like to thank a large number of people, too numerous to mention individually, in various agencies and private market institutions throughout Asia for their cooperation and information sharing; Jim Hanson, Leonardo Hernandez, Bernard Hoekman, Daniela Klingebiel, Chad Leechor, Philip Molyneux, Guy Pfeffermann, Edwin Truman, Zhen Kun Wang and Alan Winters for useful comments; Marinela Dado for her detailed analysis of the barriers and costs measures in Sections 7 and 8, and Catherine Downard for research assistance. The chapter also draws on Claessens and Hindley (1997). The chapter was written during the summer of 1997, before the East Asian financial crisis and before the conclusion of the WTO-negotiations in December 1997. The opinions expressed here are ours and do not necessarily represent those of the World Bank.

the design of policies to minimize transition costs and potential risks and maximize the benefits to their economies of increased openness, and in the required complementary policy measures. Introducing foreign competition in financial services also has come up as part of overall financial sector reform programmes or in the context of regional trade agreements. The negotiations on financial services in the General Agreement on Trade in Services (GATS), with a deadline of December 1997, have created another impetus to consider this issue. And as countries continue to review their policies towards foreign competition in their financial sector, internationalization will remain an important issue for the foreseeable future.

This chapter suggests that internationalization can help in the process of building more robust and efficient financial systems by introducing international practices and standards, by improving the quality, efficiency, and breadth of financial services, and by allowing more stable sources of funds, that are almost independent of the state of development of the domestic financial system and the openness of capital account. In Asia, these benefits could be substantial. The review of experiences also finds very little support for the notion that foreign entry leads to more volatile capital flows.

Cross-country empirical evidence for Asia specifically suggests that the limited openness to date has been costly in terms of higher expenses of financial services, slower institutional development, and more fragile financial systems. For eight Asian countries, the costs of financial services and the fragility of financial systems are negatively related to the degree of openness of the domestic market to foreign financial firms. The efficiency of financial services provision and institutional development of the financial sector are positively related to openness.

This chapter's conclusions thus suggest that the Asian countries could substantially benefit from accelerating the opening up of their financial systems, in conjunction with further capital account liberalization, domestic financial deregulation, and a strengthening of the supervisory and regulatory framework and the role of the market in monitoring financial institutions. The financial service negotiations at the WTO provides countries with the opportunity to commit to this opening up, with built-in safeguards and the possibility of phasing in to minimize the possible adjustment costs. This commitment can be an important part of a country's overall financial sector development strategy, on which, given the regional financial turbulence, there may be a large premium today.

This chapter analyses the issue of financial internationalization in eight Asian countries. Section 2 provides some context for the internationalization of financial services in Asia. Section 3 reviews the relationship among various financial reforms, while Sections 4 and 5 review the conceptual issues and the experiences with internationalization to date. Sections 6, 7, and 8 respectively provide measures of the costs of financial services, the structure of financial systems, the institutional development and the degree of internationalization in eight Asian countries. Section 9 relates measures of financial sector efficiency, costs of financial sector provision, institutional development, and fragility with the degree of openness for different financial services. The concluding section discusses the economic and financial policy implications of a process of further internationalization for Asia.

2. THE CONTEXT OF INTERNATIONALIZATION OF FINANCIAL SERVICES IN ASIA

Global trends in recent years include a process of more rapid financial integration and increased cross-border capital flows. Most Asian countries have actively participated in these trends and the bulk of private capital flows to developing countries has gone to Asia (World Bank, 1997a and 1997b). In recent years, Asian countries have also been in the process of deregulating their financial systems and allowing greater access of foreign investors and financial service providers (FSPs) to their domestic markets, albeit at different speeds. Table 12.1 suggests that these Asian countries are financially integrated in some areas and have experienced significant amounts of private capital inflows, much of it in recent years. While the share of domestic financial assets held by foreign-owned banks is relatively small, the share of foreign investors in stock market trading is quite large, in Indonesia being the highest. In general these countries are not important exporters of financial services (as also reflected in the relatively small number of foreign branches of banks from these countries and the fact that many foreign firms established in these countries continue to use services from foreign banks). Other global developments also affect Asian financial systems. Negotiation of a WTO agreement on international trade and investment in financial services was a post-Uruguay Round supplement to GATS. Most WTO members, but not the US, accepted the result.[1] Asian

[1]The stumbling block for the US was the obligation of signatories to the financial

TABLE 12.1

INDICATORS OF THE INTEGRATION OF FINANCIAL SYSTEMS OF ASIA
(1995, EXCEPT WHERE NOTED)

	Degree of Financial Integration[a]		Private External Debt as per cent of GDP	Foreign Bank Share[b]	Foreign Share of Capital Market Activity (%)	Cross-border Financial Services in Insurance as per cent of GDP[c]
	1985–7	1992–4				
Indonesia	Medium	High	22.9	0.35	75	0.22[d]
South Korea	High	High	N/A	0.23	6	0.30
Malaysia	High	High	24.0	0.09	50	0.009[e]
Philippines	Medium–	High	10.5	0.46	50	0.23
Singapore	N/A	N/A	N/A	0.29	N/A	1.63
Thailand	Medium+	High	26.5	0.08	34	0.63
India	Medium	Medium+	3.4	0.00	25	N/A

Notes: [a]The index of financial integration is based on a country's access to international financial markets, its ability to attract private external financing, and the level of diversification of its financing (World Bank, 1997b).
[b]Ratio of number of reporting foreign banks to total number of reporting banks averaged over the period 1988 to 1995 (Claessens, Demirguc-Kunt, and Huizinga, 1997).
[c]Defined as the sum of exports and imports of insurance services as a percentage of GDP (World Bank, 1997c).
[d]Imports only.
[e]Exports only, 1994.

Sources: Claessens, Demirguc–Kunt, and Huizinga (1997), World Bank (1997abc).

countries and other developing countries must therefore consider their interests in opening their financial services markets to international competition, in the context of their overall financial sector development strategies.

3. INTERNATIONALIZATION AND OTHER FINANCIAL REFORMS

There are important linkages between *internationalization of financial services* and two other financial reforms: *domestic financial deregulation*, and *capital account liberalization*. A definition of these three types of financial reform is as follows. *Domestic financial deregulation* allows market forces to work by eliminating controls on lending and deposit rates and on credit allocation, by reducing demarcation lines between different types of financial service firms (such as banks, insurance companies, stockbrokers), and more generally by reducing the role of the state in the domestic financial system. *Capital account liberalization* involves a process of removal of capital controls and restrictions on the convertibility of the currency. *Internationalization of financial services* eliminates discrimination in treatment between foreign and domestic financial services providers and removes barriers to the cross-border provision of financial services. In addition, there are important relationships between internationalization and the conduct of monetary policy[2] and cross-border taxation, but space precludes their discussion.

Internationalization and Domestic Financial Deregulation

In the last decade, many countries in Asia have gradually deregulated their financial markets. The relationships between financial market liberalization and economic development have been extensively explored;

---

services agreement (FSA) to provide most-favoured-nation (MFN) treatment to other signatories—which implies that services and service providers from countries with closed markets for financial services must be treated in the same way as services and service providers from members with open markets. The US was unwilling to accept this obligation when, in its view, the market access commitments of a number of developing country participants were such that their markets for financial services in effect remained closed. The US, though, is not the only source of such pressure. Other developed countries, particularly the EU, want the US membership of the WTO financial services agreement.

[2] See Glaessner and Oks (1994) that highlight these links in the context of discussing the impact of internationalization under NAFTA.

the results, including for Asia, indicate that liberalization of financial systems is a major factor in economic development, but needs to be carefully sequenced and managed (Caprio, Aityas, and Hanson, 1994; and Levine, 1997). In particular, experience shows that it is vital to strengthen the supporting institutional framework, i.e. the regulatory and supervisory functions of the state (including the screening of the entry of new financial firms) and the use of the market in disciplining financial institutions (especially through better information and greater disclosure, and improved standards for the governance of financial institutions).

Internationalization and domestic deregulation are related, but not in any easy or straightforward way. Neither, for example, implies the other. A country might deregulate its financial system but still keep its financial markets closed to foreign competition. Japan, for example, has been deregulating its domestic financial system, but is still often singled out by other developed countries as being relatively closed to foreign FSPs. Or a country might over-regulate its domestic markets for financial services, but freely allow foreign financial firms to open local establishments and to compete with domestic FSPs within that system of regulation. Banking in the US, for example, is often criticized as over-regulated, yet US financial service markets are very open to foreign FSPs.[3]

The costs and benefits of internationalization of financial services will, to a significant degree, depend on the efficiency and competitiveness of the domestic financial system, which in turn will importantly be influenced by the nature of domestic regulation. Countries with a highly regulated domestic financial system may well suffer from inefficiencies and poor quality and breadth of financial services. Opening up to FSPs may then—in the short run—negatively affect domestic FSPs, not necessarily because foreign FSPs have unfair advantages (see below), but because FSPs have been hindered in their development through regulations, have faced little competition, and have faced perverse incentives. At the same time, countries with poorly developed financial systems may benefit the most in the long run from opening up as it can accelerate financial sector development.

[3]Even when countries deregulate, important differences in regulatory systems are likely to remain and influence the degree of competition in financial services when countries open up. Japan and the US, for example, maintain significant legal separation between commercial and investment banking. Banks and insurance companies are also kept separate for most purposes in these two countries. See below.

Internationalization and Capital Account Liberalization

Many countries, including in Asia, have relaxed controls on international capital movements in recent years, and have experienced significant capital inflows, and more recently net capital outflows.[4] Research has generally found that reducing controls on international capital movements can lead to lower costs of capital and greater risk diversification (see Dooley, 1995 for a review of the literature on capital controls). The quality of the financial system, however, is a central factor. Countries with weak financial systems, particularly in terms of supervision, have sometimes experienced financial distress following a period of rapid inflow of foreign capital associated with the earlier removal of controls on international capital movements (Goldstein and Turner, 1996; Honohan, 1997a; Mathieson and Rojas-Suarez, 1993; World Bank, 1997a).

Internationalization and capital account liberalization are related, but not in an obvious way. With an open capital account, equities issued in a developing country market, for example, might be largely traded in New York in the form of an American Depository Receipt—but perhaps still owned by co-nationals of the original issuer. Or domestic firms may avail themselves of offshore financial services: many Asian firms, for example, borrow abroad and then repatriate funds in domestic currency for local use. Such cases involve both the movement of capital across borders and the use of foreign financial services, without the entry of foreign financial firms.

The degree of capital account liberalization can affect the costs and benefits of internationalization. First, capital account liberalization affects the incentives of foreign FSPs to establish a presence in the country, as opposed to servicing clients from offshore (which can include seeking business to be done offshore through representative offices onshore). Second, capital account liberalization determines the extent to which classes of domestic firms and individuals can already avail themselves of foreign financial services. Typically, as is the case for many Asian countries, with (largely) free capital mobility the largest and best credit firms and individuals will have access to foreign markets

[4]Capital account liberalization is a process and individual countries can be in different phases of this process ranging from fully controlled capital account to fully open. Asian countries span this range with China and India being quite controlled to Hong Kong being fully open. Even though being closed on the capital account, China has received large amounts of capital flows, mainly in the form of foreign direct investment.

and internationally provided financial services, while smaller and less creditworthy firms and individuals will be confined to the domestic market. Third, it can imply varying costs across different users of financial services in the event of a financial crisis. If some of the costs, of a financial crisis are passed on to the rest of the domestic economy (either through direct bailouts of corporates or support to financial institutions),[5] then segmentation will (further) hurt other firms and consumers. Fourth, segmentation can affect the political economy of internationalization. Internationalization allows benefits for a wide class of firms and individuals, but firms and individuals which currently already have access to foreign financial services (provided offshore) may be indifferent to internationalization. If those who do not have access to foreign financial service are politically less well-represented, then the political economy outcome could be a continuation of barriers to foreign FSPs.

Some degree of free capital movement will be necessary for effective and efficient internationalization. Some types of foreign (and domestic) FSPs need to be able to move capital across borders relatively freely to conduct their business efficiently. With limits on some forms of capital movements, distortions can easily be introduced. But, again, neither liberalization of the capital account nor internationalization is a precondition for the other. Capital might move relatively freely in and out of a country that maintains barriers against foreign firms providing financial services domestically. Many financial markets in Asia are still quite closed to international competition in financial services, even though these same economies have substantially relaxed their controls on capital movements in recent years. Chile, on the other hand, is quite open to foreign FSPs but maintains some controls on cross-border movements of capital. The key factor determining the optimal speed of capital account liberalization, however, appears to be the quality of the overall financial system, with the degree of internationalization more important indirectly—in terms of influencing the quality of the financial system—than in terms of directly affecting the optimal degree of capital account liberalization.

The relationships between internationalization, domestic deregula-

---

[5]In particular, much of access to international financial services will be denominated in foreign currency. This may create large currency mismatches, which in the event of a devaluation, can lead to large foreign exchange losses which can be passed on to other segments of the economy.

tion, and capital account liberalization are thus complex and empirical evidence on them is only starting to become available.[6] It is thus too difficult to discuss issues such as the optimal speed and other relationships between the three types of reform. It appears, however, that there is not a unique optimal sequence to these reforms: experiences as diverse as Indonesia (rapid capital account liberalization followed by gradual internationalization), Chile (slower capital account liberalization but more rapid internationalization), and the US (slower deregulation in the provision of financial services by different types of financial firms, but free entry) show very different approaches but no clear differences in impact (in terms of, for example, efficiency and enhancing competitiveness of banking system, speed of financial reform, or more generally, economic welfare).[7]

The relationships between the various reform processes may also differ by type of financial services. Non-life insurance services (e.g. motor insurance) and many other consumer financial services, for example, have mostly non-financial services' characteristics: they involve, for example, few investable funds. They thus have fewer linkages with capital account liberalization and monetary policy, and internationalization of these services might proceed more independently of other financial reform processes. The high degree of substitutability between the various financial services (for example, life-insurance contracts can have features equivalent to bank deposits), however, make a refined differentiation for other services difficult in practice and possibly unproductive.

4. CONCEPTUAL FRAMEWORK AND COSTS AND BENEFITS

A starting point for the study of internationalization of financial services is whether the theory of comparative advantage and the empirical evi-

---

[6]See for example, Glaessner and Oks (1994) and WTO (1997).

[7]It will be difficult to explain separately the effects of these financial reform processes for a specific country. Even in stable, developed countries it has been difficult or impossible to assess the impact of various financial systems (in current use or even in recent history) on the economies. In this respect, it is useful to recall that in the past many developing and now developed countries' financial systems were dominated by foreign FSPs without apparent adverse affects on financial flows. Under the gold-standard and further back in time, financial services were transacted through a limited number of internationally operating FSPs or individuals (e.g. the Rothschilds of the world).

dence on the benefits of openness developed for trade in goods applies to trade in services. Speaking generally, the broad conclusions of comparative-advantage theory hold also for services—but some modification in the detail of the analysis is needed to take account of the differences between goods and services (see Hindley, 1996a for a review). This suggests that internationalization of services has large potential benefits for developing countries.

Internationalization of financial services, however, is a much more recent field of study and has been studied much less systematically.[8] Most of the papers in this area are also based on first principles often derived from the analogy with liberalization of trade in goods (and only to a very limited degree on empirical evidence).[9] International transactions in goods and international transactions in services—especially in financial services—differ, however, in two important ways from other forms of trade which need to be taken into account. First, provision of services often requires the provider of the services to have a local presence. Efficient provision of financial products often requires information that is difficult to obtain from a foreign location—detailed information to tailor loans or other financial services to client characteristics, for instance, or the ability to offer advice that requires knowledge of local conditions. If financial services must be 'imported' through the locally-established branch or subsidiary of a foreign FSP, then local firms can be protected against competition by entry barriers. Other forms of barriers (e.g. higher taxes on foreign financial services) will then not be a equivalent measure, as tariffs can be in the case of trade. Because trade in services is more difficult to observe and monitor,

---

[8]Sagari, 1988, 1989, discusses internationalization of financial services specifically and derives the result that skilled labour can be the source of comparative advantage in the production of financial services. Gelb and Sagari (1990), discuss the case of multilateral negotiations in financial services specifically. They argue that developing countries should open their borders to foreign competition, but at a moderate pace. Several other papers have made the general conceptual case for internationalization of financial services (Levine, 1996, UNCTAD, 1994, Walter, 1987 and 1993, Walter and Gray, 1983). Glaessner and Oks (1994) and Musalem et al. (1994) present a case in the context of NAFTA; WTO (1997) reviews the literature and issues as well.

[9]One exception is Moshirian (1994), who shows empirically for 13 OECD countries that the supply of international financial services depends on national R&D, banks' international assets and physical and human capital, thus suggesting that comparative advantages are important in the delivery of financial services.

regulators may actually *require* domestic presence to ensure that they maintain control (many countries do so, for example, for the solicitation of insurance services).[10]

Second, the provision of financial services is typically highly regulated, both for prudential and for monetary policy purposes. The case for such regulation is universally accepted and is not at issue when it comes to the internationalization (for example, under the WTO any prudential measure is explicitly excluded). Regulation, however, affects the cost of providing a service. Hence, when FSPs subject to one set of regulations compete with FSPs subject to another, one element in the outcome of the competition is the relative cost of complying with the different regulatory systems. Differences in regulations between countries may thus affect— fairly or unfairly—competition in trade of services across borders as well as the local provision of financial services by foreign (regulated) firms.[11] And undue regulations risk distortions and may limit the efficiency gains derived from entry of foreign financial firms.

Benefits

The main conclusion of the conceptual papers is that, just as the removal of barriers to trade in goods leads to specialization according to comparative advantage and to formerly-protected producers improving their efficiency, so can foreign involvement in markets for financial services lead to an improvement in the overall functioning of domestic financial systems. Levine, 1996, who surveys these issues and the existing literature on internationalization, identifies three specific potential benefits: (a) better access to foreign capital; (b) better domestic financial services; and (c) better domestic financial infrastructure (including improved regulation and supervision), with the last two the most important benefits of internationalization for developing countries (Glaessner and Oks, 1994, provide a similar account in the context of NAFTA).

---

[10]The advent of electronic provision of financial services (e.g. through the Internet) has brought this to the forefront not only in the cross-border provision of financial services, but also within countries (e.g. see the discussion in the US on the use of electronic money).

[11]On this basis, it is sometimes said that national markets for financial services cannot be internationalized until national regulatory systems have been harmonized. An alternative view is that international competition will put pressures on regulators to deregulate, and possibly harmonize, and that internationalization should not be held hostage to attempts to harmonize. This latter view can be found in Glaessner and Oks (1994), and William White (1996a).

The specific benefits that countries might expect in these last two areas include: a more efficient financial sector; a broader range and improved quality of (consumer) services; better human skills; pressures for improved regulation and supervision, better disclosure rules and general improvements in the legal and regulatory framework for the provision of financial services; improved credibility of rules (as the country enters into international agreements and intensifies linkages with foreign regulators, thereby lowering the risk of policy reversals); and a reduction in (systemic) risks and improvements in (stock market) liquidity. These benefits of internationalization can follow both through top-down actions on the part of government and through bottom-up pressures from the markets as best international practices and experiences are introduced and competitive pressure increases.

As in other sectors, openness to foreign competition allows consumers to obtain better and more appropriate services more cheaply and puts pressure on domestic financial firms to improve their productivity and services. It also allows financial firms access to technologies and ideas to help them raise efficiency. Opening up could thus even help countries build up an export sector in financial services, an expressed desire of some Asian countries. Internationalization will also put pressures on improved supervision by authorities of domestic financial institutions. The presence of foreign FSPs can further help improve the screening of projects and monitoring of firms, thus leading to a better financial system. The most important benefits of an open financial system will likely stem from the positive spill-over effects on savings and investments and on the allocation of productive resources, which would translate into positive effects on economic growth. The general relevance of a good financial system for growth[12] and the mechanisms through which this occurs are well established (see Levine, 1997 for a review).

Costs

Specific evidence on the costs of internationalization is needed once one considers the relationship between internationalization and deregulation. Deregulation suggests a desire to improve the efficiency of the system;

---

[12]In a seminal piece of work, King and Levine (1993), use a cross-country sample of eighty cases over the period 1960–89 to show clear and convincing links between growth and finance and also to provide strong evidence that better developed finance *precedes* faster growth, after controlling for a variety of other factors (including income, education, political stability, and monetary, fiscal, trade and exchange rate policies).

but, if that is the objective, why exclude international competition? In other type of industries, international competition is regarded as the best guarantee that domestic producers are, and remain, efficient. The answer to this asymmetry between domestic deregulation and internationalization mainly relates to the desirable relative *speed* of internationalization and lies in both economic and political economy arguments.

Economic Arguments

Economic arguments against rapid internationalization are based upon adjustment costs. Costs often mentioned are the following. First, the ability of domestic institutions to monitor a more complex financial system may be limited (as a consequence of, for example, a poor legal framework, a lack of the skills needed for supervision, and poor market discipline). In the light of such problems, too rapid internationalization may lead to larger (systemic) risks as foreign FSPs cannot be supervised and monitored properly. Also significant participation of foreign banks in a country's payment system has been argued to possibly lead to adverse effects. Another issue is the possible lack of government credibility in enforcing prudential regulations and withdrawing an (implicit) insurance scheme, and as a consequence the government may be reluctant to reduce controls on the financial system and open up to foreign entry as it expects that liberalization will lead to excessive risk-taking at the final expense of the government.

Second, in cases where the financial system is currently undercapitalized, rapid entry could lead to (more) financial distress among domestic FSPs as profits decline. In particular, the presence in the banking system of large non-performing loans may require policies to maintain higher profits (higher franchise value) for existing banks, and therefore call for restrictions on the entry of new banks (both domestic and foreign).[13] Third, regulatory advantages possessed by foreign banks, which could make competition between domestic and foreign banks unfair, especially as emerging markets have special features. It might, for example, be useful to impose more stringent regulatory requirements in emerging markets than those imposed in more advance economies

---

[13]Similar arguments are used for other type of financial services, for example, insurance. The issue is not the relevance of franchise value for financial sector stability, reviewed by Caprio and Summers (1993), but rather the aim to shore up a financial sector through restricting entry excessively instead of encouraging exit and restructuring.

(due, for example, to the higher risks faced). Admitting financial firms chartered and supervised in other countries would then create and tilt playing field unfavourably, from the standpoint of domestic financial institutions. And fourth, the infant industry argument for protection, and relatedly possible adverse effects on domestic labour in the financial sector, have been mentioned.

Many of the arguments mentioned, even if valid, do not necessarily require limiting entry to foreign FSPs (or limiting the cross-border provision of financial services), or at least do not require considering domestic deregulation and internationalization separately. The presence of large, non-performing loans, for example, can in principle be dealt with through restructuring of individual financial institutions or through specific taxes on financial services, rather than through limiting entry. The infant industry argument against international competition has been tested and found wanting when liberalization of trade in goods is at issue. Even where its premises can be shown to provide a valid basis for intervention, it is easy to show that other forms of intervention are economically superior to barriers to imports. The playing filed can be leveled by requiring foreign financial firms to observe the same regulations as domestic financial firms, i.e. national treatment. The integrity of the payments systems can be assured by adopting clear rules on the quality and integrity of financial institutions which can participate. Some small countries have effectively turned over supervision and regulation and deposit insurance to foreign banks, recognizing that major international banks would be willing to sustain their local branches, rather than suffer a loss of reputation. And the effect of internationalization on domestic labour is likely to be limited as relatively little labour is employed by the financial sector, especially in Asian developing countries, as foreign FSPs will tend to employ nationals when they establish local presence and as, in any case, the effect is no more so than for labour from other sectors experiencing efficiency gains.

These economic arguments do not apply similarly to all financial services. While there may be a case for gradual internationalization of some bank-based financial services, this is not necessarily the case for some of the other non-bank-based financial services. There are few economic reasons why for example, non-life insurance services (e.g. car insurance) would have negative effects on financial sector stability and thus can not be internationalized rapidly. These services have few linkages to monetary policy and rules to assure consumer protection, rather than prudential regulation, will be important. Furthermore, since these services tend to be less developed in most developing countries, opening up will have little negative effects on domestic FSPs.

Political Economy Arguments

International competition, it is said, will eliminate local FSPs, and thus leave the domestic financial system at the mercy of foreigners. Furthermore, it is claimed, foreign banks will operate only in very profitable market segments; will have no commitment to the local market, and may contribute to capital flight. International competition must therefore be regulated, impeded and limited. These arguments are mainly put forward by interested parties standing to lose from opening up. As in the case of trade reform, e.g. tariff reductions, there will be fierce opposition by interested parties to opening up (which sometimes may include foreign financial firms already established). In part, the political economy arguments also arise from the notion that foreign domination of the domestic financial system must be avoided. National security and cultural integrity demand barriers to foreign competition.

The validity of these arguments is subject to debate. Most importantly, it should be clear that openness to foreign competition puts pressure on domestic financial firms to improve their productivity and services which is beneficial. Furthermore, the goal of authorities cannot be to maintain all financial institutions at all times: system stability rather than individual stability is what matters, and the exit of insolvent financial institutions is a necessary discipline.

Nevertheless, if there is to be intervention to ensure the survival of local FSPs—for economic or political reasons, the question needs to be answered whether alternative means of ensuring the survival of local FSPs exist and which of these is preferable? The analysis of trade has come up with some means which are more efficient than simply restricting trade, e.g. subsidies to local firms or taxes on foreign firms, or, if there are to be entry barriers, the auctioning of licenses. In principle, more efficient instruments could also be used temporarily in the case of financial services, with a view of eventually eliminating them.[14] But temporary measures can have disadvantages which, similarly

[14]Under the GATS-rules, laws and regulations may be applied differently to foreign FSPs, provided that their effect is equivalent in granting de facto national treatment and does not place foreign FSPs at a competitive disadvantage in the host country market. And GATS allows of course countries to schedule derogations from market access/national treatment. If a country has quantitative restrictions and has made an exception for them, it can therefore maintain differences in

384 / *India: A Financial Sector for the Twenty-first Century*

to the case of trade, largely stem from moral hazard and political economy reasons. Temporary subsidies to local FSPs may in principle allow them to prepare themselves to face international competition, but they can become a too powerful additive which can no longer be taken away. These risks appear to be larger with financial firms than with manufacturing firms and providers of other type of services as there often will be a greater (explicit or implicit) safety net already provided by the government for FSPs, making withdrawal of support in the future even less credible. Auctions may not attract the best qualified bidders in case of financial services as there is more room for adverse selection.[15]

5. REVIEW OF EXPERIENCES WITH INTERNATIONALIZATION

Benefits

Until recently, there were only a few studies on the costs and benefits of internationalization of financial services. Bhattacharya (1993), surveys experiences in Pakistan, Turkey and South Korea and finds that foreign banks helped to make foreign capital accessible to fund domestic projects. Pigott (1986), reviews the experiences of nine Pacific Basin countries specifically and provides some aggregate statistics on the size and scope of foreign banks activities. He finds that while foreign banks rely more than domestic banks on foreign borrowing, foreign banks still fund more than 3/4 of their domestic loans from domestic sources. McFadden (1994) provides a study of the effect of removal of restrictions on foreign FSPs in Australia and finds that this has led to improved domestic bank operations. Using aggregate accounting data for Fourteen developed countries, Terell (1986), finds that countries which allowed foreign bank entry had lower gross interest margins, lower before-tax profits and lower operating costs (all scale by the volume of business). There have also been some studies on the *potential* impact of regional trade agreements (which comprise major internationalization of financial services), most notably for the EU (EU/Price Waterhouse, 1988).[16]

---

treatment between foreign and domestic FSPs (see further Hoekman and Sauve, [1994]).

[15]Guash and Glaessner (1995) analyse the issue of bidding for credit lines, which has some analogous features.

[16]Other ex-ante studies include for the Canada–US FTA, Swedlove and Evanoff, (1992), Sauve and Gonzalez-Hermosillo (1993); and for NAFTA, Musalem et al.

Now, specific empirical evidence of the benefits of internationalization is starting to accumulate, particularly on the *ex-post* impact of opening up in the context of regional agreements (Arriazu, 1997 on Argentina; EU, 1997; Gardener, Molyneux and Moore, 1997, and other related papers on the effects in the EU; Honohan, 1995, on the effects in Ireland, Portugal, and Greece; Honohan, 1997b, on Portugal, and Greece; Nicholl, 1997, on New Zealand; Pastor, Perez, and Quesala, 1997, on Spain; and Vasala, 1995). White, 1996b, reviews financial sector issues for fifteen small open economies. It considers the impediments to liberalization; strategic issues of reform; some practical issues (related to monetary policy, money and capital market developments) and the benefits of foreign financial firm presence. These studies generally find that opening up has led to improvements in local institutions and standards, that open financial systems are more contestable and more efficient and have better services (Box 1).

These beneficial effects appear to occur with small increases in the presence of foreign FSPs. In Argentina, for example, the ratio of operational costs to assets declined from 1.3 per cent in 1990 to 0.5 per cent in April 1997, while during the same period the share of total assets held by foreign banks only rose from 15 per cent to 22 per cent (Arriazu, 1997).[17] The banking system in Colombia has low levels of foreign ownership, about 4 per cent, yet the marginal costs of providing banking services has declined substantially as financial reform, including allowing more entry, progressed (Barajas, 1996). And for the EU, while the announcement and implementation of the Single Market Programme (SMP) led to a dramatic shift in the strategic focus of banks in all countries towards competition and an increase in cross-border mergers and entry through new establishment, the expected widespread increase in foreign bank ownership of domestic banking firms has not materialized (Gardener, Molyneux and Moore, 1997a and 1997b).

There is much anecdotal evidence that foreign FSPs introduced new financial products and enhanced the quality of existing services, and spurred improvements in the quality of the institutional framework. In

---

(1993), and Glaessner and Oks (1994). Wang (1995), and Borish et al. (1996) review and assess the progress of central European countries in preparing their financial sectors for integration with the EU.

[17]This is corroborated by Dick (1996) who finds that X-efficiency levels for Argentine banks increased significantly over the 1991–4 period, due to increases in competition as a result of deregulation and growth.

BOX 1
RECENT EXPERIENCES WITH INTERNATIONALIZATION
OF FINANCIAL SERVICES

The effects of the 1992 Single Market Programme (SMP) have been recently reviewed in a number of studies (EU, 1997), with three studies on the financial services sectors in the EU. The major finding of the study on banking markets and credit sector (*Credit Institutions and Banking*) was that the SMP has made a substantial contribution to the restructuring of European banking markets and has contributed to the increased influence of external market forces on banking strategies throughout the EU. Particularly large effects were observed in those markets which had experienced less financial sector reform, such as Greece, Italy, Portugal and Spain. While a number of barriers still remain which restrain the exploitation of the full benefits of the EU, changes to date have facilitated more competitive banking systems. Especially retail loan and mortgage pricing in Greece, Italy, Portugal and Spain improved. Consumers are benefiting from a wider range of financial services and new channels of delivery have opened up. The SMP has also led to the further realization of economies of scale and greater opportunities for exploiting economies of scope. There has been no strong evidence that, in response to the SMP, banks have changed strategies in ways that threaten the stability of banking systems in the EU.

Reviews of the specific experiences of Greece, Ireland and Portugal (Honohan, 1995 and 1997b) show that domestic deregulation was probably more important than internationalization in reforming their financial sectors and leading to a large expansion in financial services. In all countries, however, EU entry triggered and accelerated this domestic deregulation and reform. Initially banking margins increased, as banks were freed from interest controls and regulated lending. As competition increased, however, margins subsequently fell and services, particularly for consumers, improved in quality and breadth. While the number of foreign FSPs which entered was substantial, their actual market penetration remained remarkably limited. In the short-run, domestic FSPs lost some market shares, but, the increased competition also spurred greater efficiency with downward trends in staff costs.

An experience particularly interesting is that of Spain. The Spanish banking system was traditionally a highly regulated one, characterized by a lack of foreign competition, significant investment and reserve requirements, and the domination of large banks (Vives, 1990). The onset of the liberalization process in Spain occurred in the early 1970s with the relaxation of limits on entry and branching and the freeing of interest rates, but suffered in its progress early on. During the period of 1978 to 1985, a banking crisis erupted that was in part the result of large banks having strong interests in industries which suffered heavily from the oil shock and general bad management and poor monitoring. Following the crisis, the process of financial sector reform in fact accelerated with the entry into the EU. Increased competition, lower margins and operating expenses, an increase in financial intermediation, and improved management within the banking sector resulted by the mid-1990s. Concentration increased, but market power declined, and quality of services improved. While there was much merger and acquisitions activity, actual entry by foreign financial firms remained small (see further Pastor, Perez, and Quesala, 1997).

For Mexico, NAFTA triggered internationalization of financial services, with a further acceleration following the December 1994 crisis. This has involved more foreign investment in the financial sector since 1995, with 16 newly chartered foreign banks and two large banks now majority foreign controlled, and about 18 per cent of the banking system is now in foreign hands, compared to about 1 per cent prior to 1994. This also has had a stabilizing influence on capital flows. The agreement also had a significant impact on reducing the tendency for policy reversal during the financial crisis.

For many countries, the effects of allowing greater foreign entry appears to be foremost in terms of increasing the number, rather than in greatly expanding the share of the market of foreign FSPs. The beneficial effects on the contestability of the domestic market also appear to be a function of the relative number of banks, rather than their size of the market. Claessens, Demirguc-Kunt, and Huizinga, 1997, for example, using data on individual bank balance sheets and profit statements of eighty countries (of which more than fifty developing countries and transition economies) over the period 1988–95—leading to about 7900 individual bank operations, find that it is the number of foreign banks, rather than their share of the domestic market, which is negatively correlated with domestic banks' profitability and overhead expenses.

many countries, for example, foreign FSPs have started new consumer financial products, initiated the development of local bond markets and initiated asset-backed securities programs. In the Philippines, foreign companies have led to improvements in insurance services. Throughout the developing world, one can find bankers who have formerly worked in foreign financial firms as indicators of beneficial spillovers.

The experience in the US with financial deregulation is also relevant. Banks in the US have been subject to extremely severe entry barriers in the form of branching restrictions. Traditionally, banks were regulated across state lines and until the 1980s were unable to cross county lines in many states as well. As a result, the US banking industry has been extremely segmented with thousand of banks and bank holding companies. Jayaratne and Strahan (1996) study the effects of the lifting of some of the inter-state and inter-county restrictions on bank expansion, a policy very similar to liberalizing the establishment of FSPs across borders. They find that banks' profits increase and loan quality improves after states permit statewide branching and interstate branching. They also find evidence that more competitive banking markets—following deregulation—better discipline bank managers, thereby further improving bank performance.

The effects of internationalization and capital account liberalization and monetary policy has also been considered. In some countries, for example, New Zealand, the financial system is largely in the hands of foreigners, without any adverse affects on monetary policy or more volatile capital outflows (Nicholl, 1997). There is also little evidence that foreign firms do not have the commitment to the local market. In New Zealand, so far as is evident at present, there have been no adverse affects on the access to financial services by various agents. Provided there exists a level playing field, there are little reasons to expect that foreign financial firms would not be willing to provide financial services across a broad section of the economy and instead would operate only in the most profitable segments. If gaps in service are a problem, nevertheless, foreign firms, like domestic firms, can be encouraged to provide financial services in less profitable market segments through explicit subsidies or regulations. There is also evidence for the US that foreign FSPs do not just follow firms from their home countries, but do allocate a significant share of their business to non-home, i.e. host-country borrowers (Nolle and Seth, 1997), thus generating beneficial spillovers.[18] Wengel (1995) studies the trade flows in banking services among 141 countries using information on more than 3600 banks which operate internationally. He finds, among others, that the relaxation of exchange and capital controls by potential host countries diminishes the incentives of banks to seek direct representation, thus confirming the substitution links between capital account liberalization and internationalization.

The argument that internationalization will lead to large capital outflows appears questionable. The experiences of capital flight from many developing countries in the 1970s and early 1980s under circumstances with significant capital controls and very limited presence of foreign banks suggests that foreign banks are not the main cause and that capital controls cannot limit capital flight. Rather the causes underlying capital flight are typically poor and inconsistent policies, political uncertainty, and high and variable taxes that make the domestic market an unattractive and risky place to invest in (see Claessens, 1997 and Schineller, 1997, for recent work). More generally, disintermediation and dollarization is mostly a function of the degree of domestic financial repression than of the degree of capital account liberalization.

---

[18]On the other hand, it has been found for the US that binding capital adequacy requirements associated with the decline in the Japanese stock markets resulted in a decline in commercial lending by Japanese banks in the US (Peek and Rosengren, 1997). The effects on US borrowers and financial flows more broadly are not known, however, and borrowers may have been able to off-set decline in financing.

Presence of foreign financial firms is more likely to reduce capital flight, as was observed in several recent episodes (e.g. in Argentina and Thailand foreign banks received large amounts of deposits from domestic banks when concerns arose about the quality of domestic banks).

Costs and Risks

Some questions on costs and potential risks of foreign entry have been addressed in the literature on experiences with internationalization. It is clear from the experiences of the EU and NAFTA that regulation that is justifiable in terms of fiduciary or monetary-policy concerns can be distinguished from regulation that is primarily motivated to protect domestic FSPs. And specific monetary policy concerns can be dealt with through traditional monetary policy instruments or capital controls (Nicholl, 1997). Most developed and some developing countries allow for free entry of foreign FSPs without any adverse effects on the conduct of monetary policy or soundness of the financial system (of course, foreign entrants are screened for 'fitness and properness'). At the opposite, in many countries, especially developing countries, foreign banks have proven to be a source of stable funding in the face of adverse shocks.[19] In Argentina especially (where 22 per cent of all bank assets are held by foreign banks) but also in Mexico in late 1994 and early 1995 the (then few) foreign banks were able to maintain access to offshore funding while domestic banks experienced strains.

Foreign banks have also played an important role in allowing banking systems to recover from crises. In Mexico and Venezuela foreign banks are emerging as key players in efforts to recapitalize and restructure banks (two troubled banks have been bought up by Spanish banks, a Canadian bank now controls a third bank, and foreign financial institutions are reportedly considering the purchase of several other troubled or intervened banks). In Poland and Hungary foreign banks have brought in very useful know-how and capital, and in New Zealand much new capital. Finally, in several small economies (e.g. Panama) foreign banks play a predominant role in the provision of domestic banking services.

Even though internationalization in the presence of a poorer functioning regulatory and supervisory domestic system may not allow the country to reap all the benefits and could lead to some risks, this needs

[19]The G–10 (1997, Annex 1) report has then also included the share of foreign participation in total assets in its illustrative list of indicators of robust financial systems.

to be balanced by the fact that foreign FSPs are likely better capitalized and also subject to more stringent supervisory systems (see further Gavin and Hausmann, 1996). This suggests that internationalization need not be limited by the quality of the domestic regulatory and supervisory system, rather the opposite may be the case. In fact, some least developed, lower-income countries have committed themselves under the Financial Services Agreement (FSA) to (almost) fully open their financial systems to foreign FSPs, suggesting that a poorly-developed financial system and a weak institutional framework need not be constraints to opening up.

It is of course correct that countries stand to benefit more from domestic deregulation (and internationalization) when their financial system satisfies certain minimum regulatory and supervisory requirements. Many of these requirements had already been identified in the literature on domestic deregulation and have been recently further refined (e.g. IMF, 1997; BIS, 1997; and G–10, 1997). These minimum standards cover prudential regulations, and a certain level of institutional development, independence and level of human skills of the regulators. It is also clear that, while national treatment of FSPs does not necessarily guarantee fair international competition, countries should not wait for harmonization to open up,[20] also since full harmonization can take considerable time.[21] The EU Single Market Programme (SMP), for

[20]Four reasons are typically mentioned (see also William White, 1996a, and Dermine, 1996): first, significant progress in harmonization has already been achieved, particularly through the BIS (for example, Basle capital adequacy requirements), but also through the work of IOSCO and others (see William White 1996a for a review). Second, the net differences in regulatory burden are not that large between many, albeit mostly developed, countries. Furthermore, with open capital accounts, market participants already engage in actions across regulatory jurisdictions which reduce unnecessary regulatory burdens. Thirdly, competition among regulatory systems can lead to an overall reduction in unnecessary regulatory burdens while fears of a race to the bottom are tempered because there are some automatic checks and balances. A race to the top is more likely, as on one hand there will be competition between regulatory agencies to attract financial services business while on the other hand the FSPs will have incentives to do business in strong regulatory jurisdictions (with no *undue* regulatory burden). Fourth, trying to achieve a harmonized set of standards may increase the chances of regulatory capture and poor regulations.

[21]Skipper (1996) describes the OECD harmonization experience for trade in insurance, which started in 1961 and which have essentially been abandoned as no agreement could be reached.

example, has proceeded in a beneficial way without full harmonization among EU-members.

While full harmonization may not be necessary, increased harmonization, including through regional agreements, can of course be beneficial. Many efforts are indeed underway (under the auspices of BIS, G–10, IOSCO, etc.) and these efforts have accelerated recently (William White, 1996a). Complementary cooperation between various regulatory agencies on the supervision of FSPs and more sharing of information on their cross-border transactions has also increased, and many bilateral and multilateral efforts are underway. Furthermore, the process of internationalization accelerates pressures for improving regulatory systems in many countries. Host countries, for example, may only allow access to their markets if they are sufficiently assured that the regulatory authorities in home countries appropriately supervise their domestic FSPs (for example, the establishment of branches of banks from some emerging markets in the US is being delayed by concerns of US regulators over the quality of supervision of banks in their respective host countries, thus creating additional pressures for further upgrading of host country supervision).[22]

Experiences in a number of countries which have been opened up suggest that local FSPs have not been eliminated—and the quality of the financial system and financial services has improved. Nevertheless, internationalization can put pressure on local FSPs (including foreign FSPs already established). This can lead to constituencies opposing further opening up. Experience and empirical analysis suggests a number of particular circumstances which influence how well domestic FSPs fare after exposure to international competition. As expected, the degree of (prior) domestic regulation has a negative impact on how domestic FSPs fare.[23] The existing asset-quality of banks and other financial institutions has also been a factor. Better capitalized domestic banks have been able to maintain profitability more easily (Claessens, Demirguc–Kunt, and Huizinga, 1997), suggesting that the existing

[22]An example is the requirement under NAFTA and the legislation in the US that required Mexican authorities to be capable of undertaking consolidated supervision before Mexican banks could gain greater access to the US market.
[23]At the same time, remaining macroeconomic domestic distortions, including inflation and high real interest rates, while clearly not beneficial from an overall economic point of view, has allowed domestic FSPs to maintain margins (see Claessens, Demirguc–Kunt and Huizinga, 1997).

incentive framework for banks is an important determinant of the adjustment process when opening up.[24] The scope for new business opportunities (through both old and new services), which in turn is a function of the overall economic growth, has allowed domestic FSPs in countries which opened up to maintain profitability (Claessens, Demir-guc–Kunt, and Huizinga, 1997). Possible adverse effects on domestic labour in the financial sector are sometimes mentioned. But the demand for trained labour typically increases as foreign financial firms establish a domestic presence. And in any case, the effects are no different from other sectors experiencing efficiency gains.

Furthermore, some countries which have suffered from severe financial crises—triggered in part by macro and micro distortions have opened up to foreign FSPs and greatly benefited, thus suggesting that initial conditions can truly be 'sunk' costs and need not restrain the opening up. Finally, market concentration, of both foreign banks as well as domestic banks, has a significant positive effect on domestic bank profitability, indicating that market structure and the contestability of the financial sector more generally needs to be taken into account when evaluating the impact of internationalization.

6. INITIAL CONDITIONS AND COST OF FINANCIAL SERVICES IN ASIA

Strengths

Countries in Asia are in a good position for internationalization as many of them have strong fundamentals, also in the financial sector. Most Asian countries have kept real deposit interest rates positive and have deep financial systems, with the ratio of credit to GDP above 50 per cent and for Hong Kong even up to 285 per cent. They also have gradually liberalized their capital account and have had ample access to foreign financing in recent years. Countries have also announced plans aimed at further deregulating their financial systems, e.g. India, South Korea and Japan. Some Asian countries have already created special, offshore centres with certain regulatory and tax advantages, which already suggests a desire to allow more internationalization. Several Asian countries have also stated their aim to make their country a regional financial centre, which must be based on a belief that their financial institutions can compete on a regional (or global) basis.

---

[24]Banks in lower-income countries appear to have fared worse when foreign banks entered, further indicating that initial institutional development matters.

High economic growth in Asia creates many new business and financial opportunities which can cushion any negative impact of opening up on existing FSPs. It is, for example, generally projected that financial services will grow at rates much exceeding overall economic growth, with consumer financial services in particular expected to expand at growth rates two to three times GDP growth rates. It also appears that most of Asia, with the possible exception of the transition economies, satisfies the minimum standards in financial system supervision to the same degree as or better than other developing countries do.[25]

Weaknesses

At the same time, it is clear, however, that Asian countries have financial systems which are, relative to income levels, *institutionally* not that well developed (Claessens and Glaessner, 1997, who focus on East Asia, but many of the arguments apply to India too). Many countries in the region, for example, need improvements in their payments systems and the development of money markets and central bank open market operations has lagged in many countries. Recent global advances in credit analysis and risk management techniques in banks have not been incorporated in banking practices in many Asian countries (many banks, for example, do not appear to measure and manage their currency and interest rates risks very carefully). There is a general scarcity in the region of people with qualified financial skills. And the region's financial system is burdened with relatively large amounts of non-performing loans, resulting in part from poor credit analysis skills.

This slower institutional progress reflects to some extent that institutional development typically lags real sector development and change, with the latter very rapid in East Asia in particular. It also, however, has been due to large state-ownership and poor incentives in many countries, and the heavy role of the government in the financial sector. To date, for example, almost always bank depositors, and often bank owners and managers as well, have not been asked to bear the burden of past mistakes leading to bank insolvencies and failures. In general, countries in the region need to work more on designing and implementing regulatory and supervisory frameworks aimed at creating more robust

---

[25]While regulators in most Asian countries would posses the capacity to regulate their financial systems adequately, not all may have the legal and political backing to exercise their judgments.

financial systems. But, these weaknesses need not present barriers to the (further) internationalization of financial services in Asia. At the opposite, foreign FSPs are likely to help in the inevitable transition process. In Thailand, for example, foreign investors and foreign banks may play an important role in the restructuring of weak banks and finance companies, including through the infusion of new capital.

COST OF FINANCIAL SERVICES IN ASIA

An analysis of the impact of internationalization will have to start with a comparison of the existing costs of and efficiency in providing financial services. In principle, cost estimates for a standardized set of financial services, across all Asian countries could be collected. This approach could follow that of the study of the EU–1992-programme (EU Price Waterhouse, 1988), or that for the recent ex-post 1992, EU study (1997).[26] The costs and performance measures could then be linked to the degree of de-facto openness.

The problem with a cross-country comparison of cost estimates is that there are a number of regulatory, tax and macro- and micro-economic factors that affect the costs of financial intermediation. In particular, simple comparisons of nominal and real interest rates across countries can be seriously flawed as a means to establish the competitiveness of banking systems. Box 2 provides an example for Argentina of some of the corrections which need to be made to allow for better estimates of the cost of financial intermediation using aggregate financial data. The decomposition shows that most of the level of the nominal

---

[26]In the first study, cost measures for a number of financial services (all standardized in some fashion, e.g. using share of GDP per capita as a way to standardize loan amounts) were obtained. The exact financial services covered were: banking (7 measures: spreads for: consumer loan, credit card, mortgage, and commercial loan to a small- and medium-sized enterprise; and costs of: LC, FX-draft and traveller cheque); insurance (5 measures: life, home, motor, fire/theft and public liability cover); and securities (4 measures: commission costs for: a private equity transaction, private bond transaction, institutional equity transaction and institutional bond transaction). In the 1997 banking sector study, data on bank performance, costs and economies of scale, interest rates on lending and deposits, mergers and acquisitions activities, cross-border joint-ventures, intra-EU trade in banking services, and banking concentration as well as qualitative responses from questionnaires and individual cases studies (on strategic issues) were used to study the effect of the Single Market Programme across countries and institutions.

BOX 2
DECOMPOSING THE LEVEL OF NOMINAL INTEREST RATES

Box Table 1 below provides a decomposition of the domestic lending interest rates to non-prime borrowers for Argentina. The domestic interest rate is decomposed into the international rates (US dollar or other relevant currency); country risk premium; expected nominal exchange rate depreciation (or appreciation) (or separately, real exchange rate depreciation (or appreciation) and expected inflation differential); exchange rate risk premium; direct and indirect taxes on financial services; credit risks of domestic banks; bank profit margins; and credit spreads.

BOX TABLE 1
DECOMPOSITION OF LENDING RATE: ARGENTINA

	April 1996	April 1997
Macroeconomic risks		
Base rate—US treasury bills (3 months)	4.96	5.10
Country risk	0.76	0.35
Argentina's treasury bills in dollars (3 months)	5.72	5.45
Exchange rate risk on government debt	1.20	0.15
Argentina's treasury bills in pesos (3 months)	6.92	5.60
Micro-economic risks		
CD in dollars (3 months)	7.83	5.79
Exchange rate risk on bank's deposits	2.87	0.98
Risk of banks	1.20	0.15
CD in pesos (3 months)	11.90	6.92
Average (peso + dollar) deposit rate	9.46	6.31
Operational costs	7.10	5.33
Pure costs	3.91	3.20
Greater rotation of deposits (-E-)	3.20	2.13
Reserves for non-performing loans	2.43	1.48
Taxes	1.80	0.97
(−) Income on services	− 2.70	− 2.91
Profits	2.35	2.79
Average lending rate (pesos + dollars)	20.40	13.98

Note: Argentina runs a currency board with the peso to the US dollar rate set at one.

Source: Arriazu (1997).

interest rate can be explained by factors other than the efficiency of financial intermediation.

Measuring directly financial intermediation costs on a comparable basis across countries can thus be difficult as there are many factors which affect the costs in providing financial services in a particular country. Banking margins, for example, are affected by reserve requirements (which raise the intermediation costs), inflation (which influence the degree of profitability necessary to maintain real capital), various aspects of taxation of financial services, (large) credit differentials between (firms in) countries, the effects of non-performing loans, and the presence of a deposit insurance scheme.[27]

To illustrate this complexity, we decomposed the raw, aggregate banking spread for seven East Asian countries using an accounting model (Montes-Negret and Papi, 1996) to get at a cost of financial intermediation which corrected aggregate margins for reserve requirements, inflation (to maintain real bank capital), some aspects of taxation, the required rate of return on bank capital and the effects of non-performing loans. Table 12.2 provides the figures (with substantial methodological and data problems remaining, for example, the (net) regulatory burden on the financial sector is very hard to compute).[28] The large differences between the actual reported margins and the derived intermediation costs (net of corrections) make clear that the corrections are large. But, the table makes the point that raw banking spreads can be a very misleading measure of intermediation costs.

The approach taken here is to document several measures of costs of financial intermediation, including average costs as reported from individual bank balance sheets and profits and loss statements, estimates of the efficiency of doing an equity transaction by an institutional investor in the respective markets (from institutional investors surveys), and operational costs and pay-back measures for insurance (Tables 12.3 through 12.5). We then try to relate these to measures of openness.

---

[27]Many other factors are important (See Vittas, 1991). The EU study (1997) found margins were affected by the stage of the business cycle.
[28]The importance of taxation on costs of financial services, for example, depends on the ability of the financial institutions to pass this tax on to their consumers (Demirguc–Kunt and Huizinga, 1997, find that banks are able to pass-through income taxes to consumers).

TABLE 12.2

DERIVED ACTUAL OPERATING COSTS TO ASSETS

(PERCENTAGES, END 1995)

	Derived from Aggregate Margins	Actual Reported[a]
Hong Kong	1.734	1.40
Indonesia	–0.746	2.67
South Korea	2.013	2.24
Malaysia	0.568	1.37
Philippines[b]	2.664	3.26
Singapore	N/A	1.26
Thailand[c]	2.998	1.79

Notes: [a] 'Actual Reported' operating costs to assets ratio here is an average of those ratios reported by both foreign and domestic banks (*Source*: Demirguc–Kunt and Huizinga, 1997).
[b] Applies to domestic Philippine banks only.
[c] Applies to domestic Thai banks only.

Source: Various other data sources. The derived operating cost are calculated by adjusting the difference between aggregate lending and deposit rates (as reported by the respective central banks) for the required rate of return on equity capital (set at 15 per cent), the effects of inflation (actually reported for 1995), the effect of non-performing loans (as reported by the authorities for the banking system for 1995), and reserve requirements (proxied by the actual amount of reserves held by the banking system at the central bank as a fraction of deposits). The residual would then represent the intermediation costs if the banking system behaved according to the model as capital constrained, optimizing firms. For further detail on the model, see Montes-Negret and Papi (1996).

TABLE 12.3

PERFORMANCE INDICATORS OF BANKING SECTOR[a]

	Years over which Averaged	Net Interest Margin/Total Assets	Overhead/Total Assets	Net Profit/Total Assets
Hong Kong	1990-5	1.9	1.5	1.7
Indonesia	1988-95	3.5	2.9	0.9
South Korea	1991-5	1.7	2.1	0.4
Malaysia	1988-95	2.4	1.6	0.9
Philippines	1988-95	4.2	4.4	2.0
Singapore	1991-5	1.9	1.3	1.1
Thailand	1988-95	3.1	2.0	1.1
India	1992-5	3.3	1.4	2.3
Comparators				
Germany	1992-5	1.9	2.1	0.4
Japan	1989-95	1.4	1.1	0.2
US	1988-95	3.1	3.2	0.5

Note: [a] Data presented are weighted averages of figures from all reporting banks, domestic and foreign.

Source: Demirguc–Kunt and Huizinga (1997).

TABLE 12.4
PERFORMANCE INDICATORS OF SECURITIES MARKETS[a]
(1995, UNLESS OTHERWISE NOTED)

	Settlement Benchmark	Safekeeping Benchmark	Operational Benchmark	GSCS Index[b]	Cumulative Transaction cost (bps)	Impact of Cumulative Cost on Net Return (%)
Hong Kong	90.2	90.1	89.1	241.07	234.27	1.63
Indonesia	73.3	88.4	88.5	246.01	395.97	2.64
South Korea	82.7	91.0	94.1	90.32	322.80	50.05
Malaysia	80.8	90.8	92.4	185.22	337.63	3.81
Philippines	51.7	73.5	72.7	96.68	225.38	192.63
Singapore	83.3	87.4	91.1	177.72	269.24	3.35
Thailand	82.2	91.5	89.5	63.74	283.01	8.47
India	16.8	75.0	28.0[c]	145.95	783.17	14.56

Notes: [a]Benchmarks are average for 1995; GSCS and cumulative cost data as of June 1997.
[b]Alternative dates used as index base for India and Philippines (31/3/93 and 28/2/95, respectively).
[c]Figure applies to 1994.

Source: Global Securities Consulting Services.

TABLE 12.5
PERFORMANCE INDICATORS OF LIFE INSURANCE (1993)

	Pay-back Ratio	Operating Expense/ Premium Income
Hong Kong	N/A	N/A
Indonesia	133.7	29.7
South Korea	101.8	15.0
Malaysia	93.9	43.5
Philippines	69.6	24.3
Singapore	88.5	32.9
Thailand	71.4	41.6
India	N/A	N/A

Source: Eguchi (1995).

7. STRUCTURE AND INSTITUTIONAL QUALITY OF FINANCIAL SERVICES PROVISION IN ASIA

The structure of the financial sector and its various subsectors matters in a number of respects for the costs and efficiency of financial services. First, as for any economic activity, the degree of competition can be influenced by the number and type of participants, both on the user and provider side of financial services. Demirguc–Kunt and Huizinga (1997) find, for example, that market concentration has a positive effect on bank profitability. Second, the way financial intermediaries are allowed to organize (and organize themselves in practice) can importantly influence whether possible economies of scope and scale in the joint production of various financial services can be realized (see for example, Saunders and Walter, 1994, which promote the case for universal banking in part on economics of scale and scope; see further Barth, Nolle and Rice, 1997, and Berger and Humphrey 1996). Third, there are broader links between the various parts of the financial sector as well as the real sector which can influence the costs of financial intermediation. Demirguc–Kunt and Huizinga (1997) find, for example, that the development of the stock market affects net interest margins positively, suggesting a complementarity between bank and equity financing. Fourth, the quality of the institutional framework will greatly influence the efficiency with which financial institutions are willing or able to operate.

In principle, detailed empirical work may allow one to separate the effects of (lack of) internationalization from other structural characteristics (which may or may not be related to policies) affecting costs end efficiency. We acknowledge this but at the same time realize that this is a new research area even for developed countries (see Berger and Humphrey, 1996 and Berger et al, 1993 for an overview). We rather present a simple overview of the structure of the financial system in each country, all as of the end of 1996 (Table 12.6), where the information is collected from World Bank and IMF, central banks and private markets reports in and outside the Asian countries.

TABLE 12.6
STRUCTURE AND SCOPE OF PROVISION OF FINANCIAL SERVICES

Hong Kong	Merchant banks with restricted licenses are the only ones allowed to engage in securities underwriting and trade.
India	Licensed banks are allowed to participate in issues of securities, including underwriting and placement.
Indonesia	Commercial banks are allowed to engage only in trust and foreign exchange activities in addition to deposit and lending business (not clear about securities business for banks).
South Korea	Only securities businesses are allowed to be active in dealing, brokering, underwriting, securities savings, credit granting. (Only representative offices, branches or joint ventures of foreign securities companies who meet the minimum paid-in capital requirement and have been in the securities business for more than 5 years.)
Malaysia	Commercial banks can participate through subsidiaries in merchant banking, stock brokering, fund management, etc. (without need for separate dealers license). Only banks in Tier-1 status (well managed and capitalized) can undertake securities borrowing and lending. Merchant banks engage in underwriting and portfolio management and can also take time deposits above a minimum amount and extend loans.
Philippines	Universal banking authority granted to new and existing foreign bank branches (called expanded commercial banking authority).
Singapore	Participation in issues of securities through commercial banks and merchant banks is allowed. With regard to trading for own account or for account of customers, commercial banks and merchant banks are required to set up separate subsidiaries.
Thailand	Participation in issues of securities, underwriting, asset management by banks are allowed.

Source: Various publications.

About half of the Asian countries (India, Malaysia, the Philippines, Singapore and Thailand) allow (with some restrictions) underwriting, stock brokering, and fund management by commercial banks. In Hong Kong only merchant banks are allowed to engage in securities underwriting and trading; in Indonesia and South Korea only securities firms are allowed to engage in these businesses. In all countries except Indonesia and South Korea, banks are allowed to have equity stakes in non-financial and financial institutions, up to certain percentages (varying from 15 per cent to 40 per cent) of banks' equity. Indonesia does allow investments by banks in securities companies, up to 15 per cent of the banks or the securities company's equity.

Table 12.7 provides the number of banks and branches, market concentration (share of top banks) and the number of domestic and foreign insurance companies. Indonesia has the largest absolute number of banks (domestic and foreign combined), more than 200. The least number of banks are in Thailand. India has the largest number of branches and Singapore the least. But, relative to population, Indonesia has the least number of bank branches (about 20 per million people) and Hong Kong the most (more than 200 per million people). Hong Kong has the largest number of foreign banks, more than 150 (which is actually more than the US), with Malaysia, the Philippines and Thailand about 15, and South Korea the least, 9. Singapore has the most concentrated banking system in the region, with the top three banks having about a 3/4 share of the total loan market. In Hong Kong, Malaysia, and Thailand, the top three banks have about half of the loan market, while in the other markets the top three banks have 1/3 or less of the market. State banks are most important in India, followed by Indonesia and least important in Thailand, Malaysia and Hong Kong. For insurance, the numbers of domestic companies are substantial for all countries except India, but foreign insurance firms are few—except for Singapore, and in India and Indonesia there are actually no foreign insurers present.

Table 12.8 provides the financial depth (ratio of credit provided by the banking system to GDP); stock and bond market capitalization (as a ratio to GDP), and liquidity of these markets (turnover as a share of market capitalization). Hong Kong and Singapore stand out as having very deep and broad financial systems. South Korea, Malaysia and Thailand have reasonable deep financial systems, while those of the Philippines and Indonesia are less deep, and that of India is the least deep.

TABLE 12.7

MARKET STRUCTURE IN BANKING AND INSURANCE SECTORS

as of	Banking							Insurance	
	No. of Banks		No. of Branches		Market Concentration		Share of State-owned Bank Assets[a] (1994)	No. of Companies (1993 data)	
	Foreign/Joint	Total	Foreign/Joint	Total	No. of Banks	Share of CB Assets (per cent)		Foreign Insurer	Total
Hong Kong 1995	154	185	N/A	N/A	N/A	N/A	0	N/A	N/A
Indonesia 1996	41	239	86	5919	7[b]	>50	48	0	140
South Korea 1995	9	40	N/A	N/A	6	65.7[c]	13	5	50
Malaysia 1995	16	37	144	1433	6	59.4[d]	8	10	61
Philippines 1995	14	47	4	~3000	6	51.5	N/A	12	126
Singapore 1993	22	35	347	90	N/A	N/A	0	52	141
Thailand 1996	14	29	14	3039	6	68.5[e]	7	5	75
India 1996	23	65	N/A	62849	9	58.7[f]	79	0	2

Notes: [a]Percentage share of assets. For India, 1993.

[b]These are the 7 state banks (five state-owned commercial banks, a former development bank, and a former savings bank); as of March 1994 they held 44 per cent deposits of banking system and 52 per cent total credits, 50 per cent of total banking system assets

[c]'Big 6' account for 65.7 per cent of total South Korean commercial banking assets (mkt. concentration data as of 8/95)

[d]Six largest banks account for 59.4 per cent of total commercial banking system assets; 80 per cent of domestic bank assets

[e]Six largest banks account for 68.5 per cent of total commercial banking system assets; 74.8 per cent of domestic bank assets

[f]These nine are all state-owned banks.

Source: various publications

TABLE 12.8

INDICATORS OF FINANCIAL SYSTEM DEVELOPMENT

	Credit of Banking System as a per cent of GDP (1995)	Stock Market Capitalization as a per cent of GDP (1996)	Stock Market Trading Value as a per cent of Market Capitalization (1996)	Bond Market Capitalization as a per cent of GDP (1994)	Bond Trading Volume as a per cent of Market Capitalization (1994)
Hong Kong	284.5	280.8	N/A	8.7	N/A
Indonesia	49.8	41.2	35.3	5.8	10.0
South Korea	69.9	25.4	127.7	24.1	43.0
Malaysia	131.9	315.5	56.5	56.0	32.6
Philippines	62.9	97.5	31.6	39.3	N/A
Singapore	76.2	169.0	42.8[a]	72.4	N/A
Thailand	136.5	54.0	44.4	13.7	4.0
India	23.9	35.1	21.7	33.9	9.0

Note: [a]1995 figure.

Sources: World Bank (1995b, 1997c), IFC.

Table 12.9 provides information on the institutional environment for banking and quality of loan portfolios. An indicator of quality of the operating and regulatory environment for banks (deposit insurance, regulatory integrity, quality of supervisory agencies, and legal framework) for Asian countries has been provided by Ramos (1997a). He ranks bank supervision quality from very good and improving for Hong Kong to weak for Thailand. He also classifies the degree of transparency and the quality of disclosure. Here the rating is from very good for Hong Kong to poor for Singapore. Ramos (1997b) provides an indicator of the overall fragility of Asian systems, FRAGILITY. Here he ranks as Hong Kong and Singapore as most solid, and Thailand as the most fragile. His CAMELOT indicator (Capital, Assets, Management, Earnings, Liquidity, Operating environment, and Transparency) for domestic banks' quality varies similarly, from Hong Kong as the best, India as the worst, and Thailand as the next to worst (South Korea is not reported). Table 12.9 also reports data on non-performing loans, both from official sources and as estimated recently by Ramos (1997b). The accuracy of the data from official sources in reporting the true degree of non-performing assets (NPAs) can be limited—as recent events in Thailand have made clear and as the much higher figure estimated by Ramos (1997b) for both Thailand and Indonesia compared to the officially reported figures suggest. Nevertheless, the banking systems of India, Indonesia and Thailand stand out as having a high degree of reported non-performing loans as of end-1996, 19.5 per cent, 10.4 per cent and 7.7 per cent respectively.

8. BARRIERS TO FREE FLOW OF FINANCIAL SERVICES IN ASIA

An analysis of barriers to the free flows of financial services will have to start with the current formal and practical barriers in place by type of financial services. These barriers can be further separated into entry (or market access) and lack of national treatment barriers, and limits on the cross-border provision of financial services.[29] Table 12.10 summarizes the degree of entry barriers as of the end of 1996, where we use an

---

[29]In the format followed under the GATS-negotiations, four modes of opening up are distinguished: commercial presence (i.e. entry of foreign FSP, through new establishment, joint ventures, or acquisition of existing firms, including through privatizations); cross-border supply; movement of consumers; or movement of suppliers. For internationalization of financial services, commercial presence and cross-border supply are in practice the most important.

TABLE 12.9

INDICATORS OF INSTITUTIONAL FRAMEWORK

(MID-1997, UNLESS OTHERWISE INDICATED)

	Bank Regulatory Framework	Bank Supervision Quality	Transparency	GS Fragility Score (0 = best, 24 = worst)	CAMELOT Scores[a] (1 = best, 10 = worst)	Non-performing Loans as a per cent of Total Loans	
						BIS Reported (1996)	GS Estimated
Hong Kong	Very Good, Improving	Good, Improving	Very Good	8	3.5	2.9	< 2
Indonesia	Satisfactory, Improving	Weak, Improving	Satisfactory	15	4.6	10.4	17, state 5, private
South Korea	Weak, Improving	Fair	Fair, Improving	18	N/A	0.9	6
Malaysia	Satisfactory, Improving	Weak, Improving	Satisfactory	15	4.5	6.1	4
Philippines	Good	Fair	Satisfactory	13	3.7	N/A	< 3
Singapore	Very Good	Very Good	Poor	7	4.0	N/A	< 1 est.
Thailand	Weak, Improving	Weak	Improving	22	5.2	7.7	> 15
India	Satisfactory, Improving	Fair, Improving	Fair, Improving	11	5.8	19.5	> 13

Note: [a]Goldman Sachs CAMELOT score for domestic banks only. Weightings for calculation of overall score: 25 per cent for asset quality; 20 per cent for management; 15 per cent for capital adequacy; 15 per cent for earnings; 5 per cent for liquidity; 15 per cent for operating environment; 5 per cent for transparency.

Sources: BIS (1997), Ramos, Roy (1997a and 1997b).

TABLE 12.10
DEGREE OF OPENNESS INDICES
(1 MOST CLOSED, 5 MOST OPEN)

	Banking		Securities		Insurance		Capital Controls
	Commitment	Practice	Commitment	Practice	Commitment	Practice	Practice
Hong Kong	4.20	4.75	4.00	4.40	4.40	4.00	4.80
Indonesia	3.15	3.20	3.50	3.00	3.10	2.60	3.60
South Korea	1.10	1.70	1.70	2.10	1.20	2.60	2.65
Malaysia	2.40	2.40	2.50	2.50	2.10	2.10	2.80
Philippines	2.80	3.35	2.40	2.40	2.90	2.80	2.45
Singapore	2.25	2.50	2.70	2.70	4.10	4.10	4.40
Thailand	2.95	2.85	2.00	2.00	2.80	2.80	4.20
India	2.70	2.25	2.50	2.10	1.00	1.00	1.50
Average	2.69	2.88	2.66	2.65	2.70	2.75	3.30

indicator of 1 through 5, with 1 being most closed and 5 most open. The indicator weighs the various type of barriers (right of establishment and ownership, limits on business activity (ability to establishes branch offices and ATMs, restrictions on lending, universal banking authority), and residency requirements).[30] The Table is based on a number of sources and has as much as possible been cross-checked with country officials and other sources (including private markets in and outside country). The table provides both current barriers as well as the degree to which countries have already committed themselves to opening up. Annexure Table 1 provides the criteria used to create the ratings (details on barriers for individual countries are available from the authors).

There is a large diversity in current entry barriers across the countries and sectors within the countries, varying from almost completely open (Hong Kong, for all financial services) to virtually closed (South Korea, particularly for banking services and India for insurance services). In some cases, restrictions apply equally to domestic and foreign FSPs. Malaysia, for example, while it has more barriers for foreigners, has not licensed any new domestic or foreign securities brokers or insurance companies in the last few years. And South Korea imposes very high capital requirements on all investment management firms. But, there are quite a number of restrictions which apply to foreign FSPs only. In many Asian countries, the ability of foreign banks to establish branches is much more limited than that of domestic banks and in all countries foreign banks face limits and tighter regulations in opening up ATMs.

Across the countries, entry into banking services tends to be slightly more liberal than for insurance or securities markets, although there are significant differences across countries in the treatment of the three type of financial services. For securities markets, the index shows Hong Kong as the most open and Thailand as the least open, with South Korea and India also very closed. For insurance markets, the practice index shows that Hong Kong and Singapore are the least restrictive, followed by Thailand, Philippines, Indonesia and South Korea, and then Malaysia, with India as essentially closed. Restrictions on cross-border trade are somewhat less than entry restrictions, with several countries allowing in

---

[30]All countries make entry dependent on the foreign FSP satisfying certain prudential guidelines. In some countries, entry is in addition explicitly limited to the world's top 200 (or some other number) of FSPs. We do not consider these conditions in principle to constitute barriers to entry, although if their implementation is, we would have tried to capture it.

principle free access to offshore banking services. India is an exception as it has significant capital controls. Nevertheless, barriers against free trade in financial services are highly correlated with entry barriers; most of Asia, for example, does not allow cross-border trade in insurance services.

Countries have already made commitments regarding the degree of financial services liberalization under the FSA of the GATS, 1995 (details on these countries' commitments[31] (or 'schedules') as per the end of the negotiations in mid-1995 are available from the authors). Table 12.10 summarizes these in the indicator 'commitments' which again ranges from 1 (most closed) to 5 (most open). Based on 1995 commitments, the most open banking market would be Hong Kong, followed by Indonesia, Thailand, the Philippines, India, Malaysia, Singapore and South Korea. Committed to the most open securities market is Hong Kong, followed by Indonesia, Singapore, India, Malaysia, the Philippines, Thailand and South Korea. The country committed to opening up its insurance sector the most is Hong Kong, followed by Singapore, Indonesia, Philippines, Thailand, Malaysia, South Korea and India.

Comparing the commitment and practice indicator (and more detailed analysis available from the authors) shows that commitments can fall short of current practices as well as go beyond them. Hong Kong, for example, is committed to more liberal entry in insurance services than current practices. Many Asian countries, however, have made commitments which fall short of current practices, particularly in banking services, but also in other financial services. The Philippines, for example, has committed to allowing ownership in banking only up to 49 per cent while current practice limits it to up to 60 per cent for existing banks and 100 per cent for new banks. And Indonesia did not bind to its current practice of allowing up to 80 per cent ownership in joint ventures in brokerage services, but, as most other Asian countries, only committed to allowing ownership in financial services up to 49 per cent. Compared to other countries, commitments also fall short of the actual state of openness. While the share of assets held by foreign banks in Asia is below that of many other countries, for example, the level of commitment in the 1995 agreement was relatively even lower that of many other countries (see Sorsa, 1997).

---

[31]Since this was an interim agreement, countries reserved the right to change them during the currently ongoing negotiations. We do not analyse already submitted offers for the current negotiations as not all Asian countries have made offers.

In addition to current barriers and commitments under the FSA, the analysis will also have to take into account the history and likely progression in these barriers. Several Asian governments have recently announced unilateral measures which go beyond the current schedules. Singapore (in part motivated by a desire to further expand itself as a regional financial centre), Japan (as part of the Big Bang), and South Korea (in the context of the accession to the OECD), for example, have announced liberalization of their financial systems, including greater access by foreign FSPs recently. Offers submitted under the current round also tend to go beyond the previous offers. In addition, countries have made some commitments under regional agreements (ASEAN and APEC). It is possible that some of this future opening up has been anticipated and led to changes in the current domestic financial industry and could thus be captured under current practice.[32]

Table 12.10 also provides an indicator for the severity of capital controls and exchange rate restrictions, both inward and outward.[33] The indicator shows that there is quite a variety among Asian countries in the severity of their capital controls: Hong Kong is almost completely open (except for some restrictions on inward investment), Indonesia has been very open—since 1970, South Korea still had significant controls until recently, and India is the most closed. Most of the capital controls, such as remittance restrictions, apply to all type of firms and investors, but many can be expected to affect FSPs more severely. In addition, there exist limits on foreign portfolio and direct investment—varying substantially among Asian countries[34]—that can affect the attractiveness to foreign FSPs of entering certain markets.

[32]There is evidence for the US and the EU that deregulation has had anticipatory effects (see EU 1997 and Berger and Humphrey, 1996). The removal of interstate branching requirements in the US has been anticipated and led to a consolidation of the banking industry.

[33]It is derived as the weighted average of six restrictions (inward remittances, foreign borrowing, lending to non-residents, investment abroad, investment into the country, and foreign exchange allowance) as reported in the latest IMF's Annual Yearbook on Exchange Rate Arrangements and Restrictions. The index is again from 1 (most closed) to 5 (most open).

[34]For equity investments, for example, individual approval is required in case of Malaysia (for amounts over M$ 5 million), ownership limits up to 25 per cent exist for South Korea, and up to 49 percent for Indonesia (the restriction in Indonesia has been recently been lifted). No restrictions exist in case of Hong Kong and for many sectors in the Philippines. See further Securities Industry Association, 1997.

In addition to these barriers, there are other, legal barriers, some of which are financial sector-specific and others which apply more generally (the latter would include, for example, general labour restrictions limiting the hiring of foreign professionals, etc.). Financial market and regulatory practices can also constitute barriers against foreign service providers (e.g. preferential access to central bank financing) and foreign FSPs may face some 'nuisance' barriers. Furthermore, financial intermediation depends on a host of auxiliary services (accounting, legal, consulting), many of which are not fully liberalized in Asian countries (accounting services in Indonesia, for example, have nationality limits) and which can make it more difficult for foreign FSPs to provide financial services in an efficient manner.

It is impossible to quantify all these factors, let alone to assert whether or not they constitute effective (binding) barriers to the establishment of foreign firms. Even low formal or other barriers may not be binding as some markets may not be attractive to foreign FSPs. It could also be the case that some of these barriers constitute one of the reasons for foreign FSPs to establish themselves in these markets as they have a comparative advantage in overcoming these hurdles or benefiting from resulting 'inefficiencies' (and, relatedly, the current costs of providing financial services may have a *positive* relationship with foreign FSP-presence as it increases the attractiveness of the entering). Analysing the exact importance of all these effects is beyond the scope of this study. But, it appears that in most countries barriers are binding. For the eight Asian countries, for example, the correlations between the openness indicator here and the number of foreign banks (relative to the total number of banks in the particular country) and the share of total bank assets held by majority-owned banks at the end of 1995 (as reported by Claessens, Demirguc–Kunt and Huizinga, 1997) are 0.86 and 0.54 respectively. And for insurance, the correlation between the openness indicator for insurance and the share of life-insurance premium volume collected by foreign-owned institutions is 0.86. In any case, these barriers are at least a cost, as they presumably would otherwise not so often be mentioned by foreign financial firms.

9. MAPPING MEASURES OF OPENNESS TO MEASURES OF COSTS OF FINANCIAL SERVICES

As will be clear by now, any attempt to link the costs of financial services with barriers to foreign FSPs, even by detailed types of financial service or sub-sector, will have to be very tentative given the many other factors involved. One approach is to use data on individual FSPs (with of course data adjusted to international comparable measures) to investigate margins (by type of activity), operating and other costs, and profits. This is done by Claessens, Demirguc–Kunt, and Huizinga (1997) for a large number (eighty) of countries. Separating domestically-owned from foreign-owned banks, they find that an increase in the share of foreign banks leads to lower profitability and overhead expenses for domestic banks.[35] We use the same measures here for our set of Asian countries.

Alternatively, individual firm (borrowers and issuers) data can be used to relate the effects of internationalization on the access firms have and costs they pay for various financial services, as well as improvements in the allocation of resources as a result of a better financial system and better corporate governance. These types of studies have been done in the context of domestic financial deregulation. Harris, Schianterelli, and Siregar (1994), for example, study the effect that deregulation in Indonesia has had on the access of firms to bank financing. They find that deregulation broadened the class of firms which had access to bank financing and lowered their costs. Similar studies could be done regarding the effect of foreign entry.

In addition, one can study the effects of (lack of) internationalization on the breadth and quality of financial services. While it is conceptually clear that one can expect better financial services from internationaliza-

---

[35]They also find that foreign banks achieve higher profits in developing countries than domestic banks and lower profit in developed countries than domestic banks. The first finding suggests that foreign banks have comparative advantage in these markets. One interpretation of the second finding is that the foreign banks are too eager to establish market share in developed countries and may therefore have lower profits. There is supporting empirical evidence for the US which shows that foreign banks are actually less efficient than domestic banks (Deyoung and Nolle, 1996). These tests can be expanded to include tests regarding the contestability of the industry, which would require developing measures of efficiency which adjust for relevant economies of scope and scale (using methodologies typically used in studies of the developed countries' financial systems, see Berger et al. 1993 and Berger and Humphrey, 1996 for reviews; Shaffer 1990 provides for an application of a non-structural test to Canada and Molyneux, Lloyd-Williams and Thornton, 1994, to European banking). Furthermore, state-owned banks could be distinguished from private banks to see whether there are significant differences in efficiency.

tion, so far this has, at best, only been documented anecdotally and a systematic review would be useful. In addition, it would be useful to document improvements in the institutional development of the financial sector, including supervision, and regulation. So far, lack of cross-country institutional development indicators on supervision and regulation makes this difficult (for work on Asia, see Ramos 1997a, and for Latin America, see Pearly, 1997). There is some indirect evidence, however, that the presence of foreign investors leads to an improvement in the overall institutional development of capital markets (see World Bank, 1997b, chapter 6).

Given the absence of this type of detailed information and ability to perform these tests and comparisons for a large number of Asia countries, we employ a number of simpler tests and comparisons. Specifically, we use our indicators reported in Section 5, Tables 12.3–5. We plot these measures against our quantitative measure of the barriers to foreign FSPs. Since we distinguish between the three services (banking, insurance and securities), we discuss the various costs and efficiency measures and barrier indexes separately.

Banking Services Provision

We use 1995 net margins, operating costs (overhead, including personnel costs) and before tax profitability (the figures are averages of individual domestic banks' reported balance sheets and profit and loss statements). Figure 12.1 indicates that there exists a negative relationship between net margins and the share of foreign banks (in numbers).[36] The Philippines has the highest net margin and little foreign bank presence (in terms of number of banks). Hong Kong and Singapore are countries in the lower-right hand quadrant, i.e. they score high on foreign bank presence and low on net margins and overhead. Net margins and overhead also have a negative correlation with the openness indicator for banking services. Interestingly, profit figures show a positive relationship with foreign bank presence, consistent with the findings of Claessens, Demirguc–Kunt and Huizinga (1997). This may reflect that foreign banks are attracted to markets with high profitability. It may also be the congruence of countries pursuing domestic deregulation which, in the short-run at least, is often associated with an increased emphasis on profitability due to more emphasis on profitability by owners and on

---

[36]Foreign banks are those banks in which foreigners have at least a 50 per cent ownership share. It includes subsidiaries as well as joint-ventures.

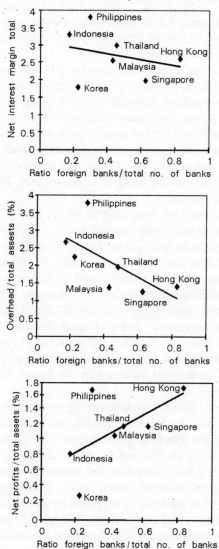

Figure 12.1   Foreign Participation in the Banking Sector and
Efficiency Measures (1995)*

Source: Demirguc–Kunt and Huizinga (1997) for net margins and overhead figures; various sources for number of banks.

Note: *Exceptions are Singapore (1993) and Indonesia (1996), as noted in Table 12.7.

increased capital adequacy by supervisors. Finally, it may reflect the positive influence of foreign banks in terms of encouraging domestic banks to pursue greater share-holder value.

The fact that more foreign bank presence goes together with greater profitability *and* lower net margins could be that where there are more foreign banks competition increases in deposit taking and lending, thus reducing margins, but forcing domestic (as well as foreign banks) to develop their fee-based (e.g. non-margin) business. Thus where there are more foreign banks, the incentives to diversify and provide a wider range of non-interest related products and services increase. In addition, as greater presence of foreign banks is associated with lower overhead costs, profits are boosted.

Figure 12.2 repeats the same analysis, except here we use the share of assets held by foreign banks in total assets. Note that these are the shares of foreign banks among those banks which report balance sheet and profit and loss statements. As a result, the shares very likely overstate the importance of foreign banks as foreign banks are more likely to provide complete statements.[37] For example, in Singapore, the share of reported foreign banks assets is almost 80 per cent, a significant overstatement in terms of local financial intermediation activity.[38] Nevertheless, the figures confirm the earlier result: a negative relationship between net margins and overhead and foreign banks' presence and a positive relationship between foreign banks' presence and profitability.

As noted, other country experiences suggest that there is likely a relationship between the degree of openness and the institutional quality and fragility of the financial sector. Figure 12.3 plots therefore the CAMELOT-score for the banking systems of Table 12.9 (with higher scores indicating a less transparent and institutionally less developed system) against the share of foreign banks (in numbers) as well as against the degree of openness (as measured by the practice indicator of Table 12.10). The CAMELOT-indicator is negatively associated with both the relative presence of foreign banks and the degree of openness, i.e. the institutional quality improves as countries become more open to foreign competition.[39] Figure 12.3 also plots the FRAGILITY score of

---

[37]A systematic overestimation of the presence of foreign banks would of course imply that the regression lines would be steeper.

[38]In Singapore, foreign banks are mainly involved in offshore business, rather than domestic intermediation.

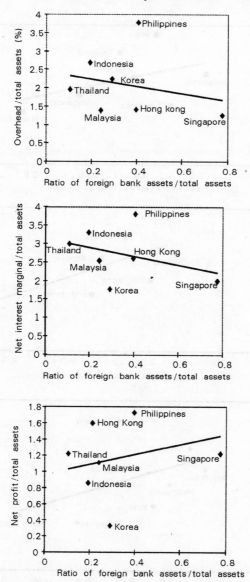

Figure 12. 2   Foreign Participation in the Banking Sector
and Efficiency Measures (1995)

Source: Demirguc–Kunt and Huizinga (1997) for net margins, overhead and asset figures of foreign and domestic banks.

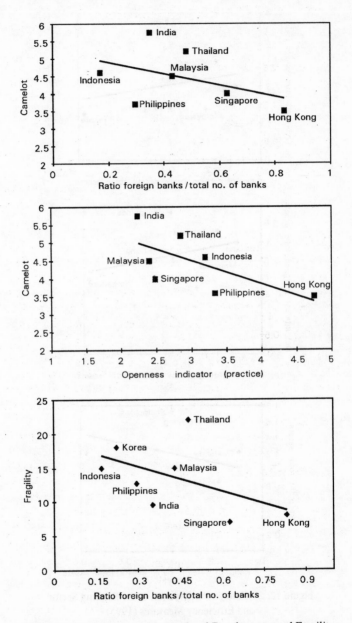

Figure 12.3   Openness and Institutional Development and Fragility
Measures for the Banking Sector (*contd.*)

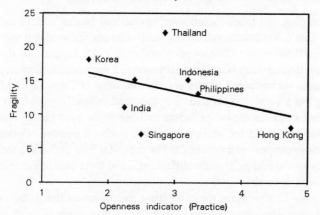

Figure 12.3   Openness and Institutional Development and Fragility
Measures for the Banking Sector

Source: Table 12.7 for share of foreign banks and Table 12.9 for institutional development measures.

Table 12.9 against the same two openness indicators. There also appears
to be a negative relationship between FRAGILITY and the openness:
the more open financial systems have a lower FRAGILITY score.[40]
Openness appears thus to be associated with improved institutional
development and greater robustness of banking systems in Asia.

Securities Markets

We first plot efficiency measures for the securities industry to the openness indexes. The efficiency measures for the comparisons were taken
from data from Global Securities Consulting Services (GSCS) and refer
to 1995. We took two efficiency measures: settlement and operational
benchmarks. The former measures the efficiency of the securities markets in fulfilling confirmed obligations; the indicator takes into account
the average trade size, local market interest rates, the share of failed
trades and the length of time for which trades failed. The latter measure
is an indicator of the securities industry's efficiency in settlement and

[39]The correlation coefficients between the CAMELOT-indicator and the ratio of
the number of foreign to domestic banks and the openness indicator are –0.67 and
–0.44 respectively.
[40]The correlation coefficients between the FRAGILITY-indicator and the ratio of
the number of foreign to domestic banks and the openness indicator are –0.53 and
–0.38 respectively

safekeeping; the index incorporates operational factors such as compliance with G30 recommendations, effectiveness of the legal and regulator majeure frameworks, counter-party and force risks. Figure 12.4 shows a positive relationship between settlement and operational efficiency and openness (as measured by the practice indicator of Table 12.10). Hong Kong has a very efficient trading system and relatively most open market, and India has the least efficient and one of the most closed markets. For Indonesia and the Philippines, there is also a positive relationship between openness and efficiency. For the other four countries, the efficiency of the trading systems differs little and there is no clear relationship with openness.

Figure 12.5 provides the cumulative rate of return index, the cumulative transaction cost measures, and the relative effect of costs on net rate of return (all from Table 12.4), plotted against the index of openness of the securities industries. There is clear positive relationship between the rate of return index and openness. And there are negative relationship between the level of transactions and relative transactions costs for these emerging markets. India appears to be an outlier in terms of cumulative absolute costs, while the Philippines is an outlier in terms of relative costs (mainly as the rate of return index showed a poor performance for the Philippines over this period). But, overall these figures suggest that more open securities markets are associated with higher rates of return and lower transaction costs.

Life-insurance Services Provision

We take two cost measures—the pay-back ratio and operating expense ratio for life insurance. The former relates earnings from a life insurance company's investments to income from premiums adjusted for the mismatching periods for revenue and outlay. A low pay-back ratio indicates relative inefficiency while an excessively high figure could suggest a low premium rate undermining the financial viability of insurers. The operating expense ratio shows the percentage of premiums spent for operating expenses. The cost measures for the insurance industry are obtained from the national supervisory authorities and the insurance associations in each country. These measures are standardized for definitions and classification of data as well as calculation methods across countries. Data for Hong Kong are not available.

We plot the insurance markets' openness index (current practice) and both cost measures for the six countries for which we have data (Figure 12.6). We find negative relationships between pay-back and operating

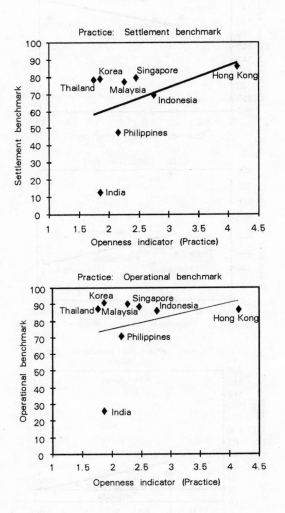

Figure 12.4 Openness and Efficiency Measures of Securities Markets (1995)

Source: See Table 12.4.

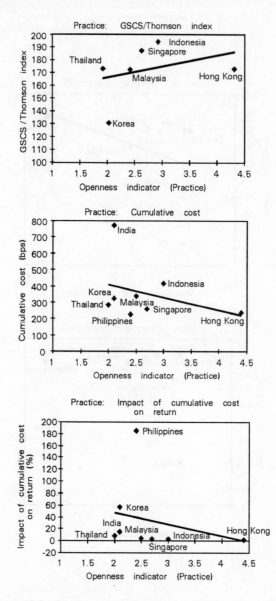

Figure 12.5   Openness and Rate of Return and Cost Measures for
Securities Markets (1995)

Source: See Table 12.4.

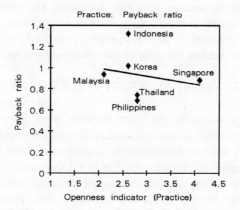

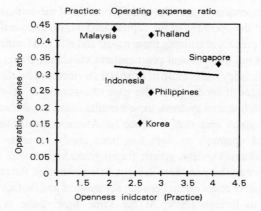

Figure 12.6   Life-Insurance: Openness and Efficiency Measures (1993)

Source: See Table 12.5.

costs and openness. In terms of operating costs, South Korea appears as an outlier, in the sense that South Korea's insurance sector is relatively closed, but has low costs efficiency. Life-insurance firms from Malaysia and Thailand appear to have relative high operating costs. The data we have on performance of insurance companies are weak, however. In South Korea, for example, many insurance companies are reportedly technically insolvent, so the low operating costs for firms in Korea could be a very misleading indicator of their true performance.

9. CONCLUSIONS AND POLICY IMPLICATIONS

The chapter discusses the links between three important reforms: internationalization of financial services, domestic financial deregulation, and capital account liberalization. Internationalization relates to the degree of capital account liberalization as it determines the potential gains and benefits from access to foreign financial services provided domestically relative to access provided and obtained offshore. Internationalization also relates to domestic financial deregulation as it influences the quality and competitiveness of domestic financial services providers. A review of experiences with internationalization suggests that almost independent of the state of development of the domestic financial system and the openness of the capital account, internationalization can help in the process of building more robust and efficient financial systems by introducing international practices and standards, by improving the quality, efficiency and breadth of financial services, and by allowing more stable sources of funds. Given the state of institutional development of many Asian financial systems, these benefits could be substantial.

Cross-country empirical evidence for Asia specifically suggests that the limited openness to date has been costly in terms of slower institutional development, greater fragility and higher costs of financial services. For banking services in eight Asian countries, the chapter finds a clear negative relationship between net margins and de-facto or de-jure openness to foreign FSPs. At the same time, there is a positive relationship between profitability and openness, suggesting that openness encourages banks to reduce costs and diversify their income (by greater reliance on fee-income). The more closed Asian banking systems also appear less developed institutionally and more fragile. For securities markets, there is a positive relationship between the degree of openness and measures of functional efficiency. For life-insurance markets, we find negative relationships between pay-back and operating costs and openness. Hong Kong stands out as having both open as well as efficient and robust financial markets for all three type of financial services.

What do these economic and political arguments, lessons from experiences and Asia-specific evidence imply for further internationalization, financial reform, and capital account liberalization? Asian countries will not benefit to the degree possible from financial services liberalization if their domestic financial system remains heavily restricted by regulations that inhibit foreign entry, and limit domestic competition and the efficient provision of financial services liberalization. This would put the domestic industry at a competitive disadvantage, create distortions, and risks inefficient resource allocation. Extensive capital controls will not allow the various FSPs to explore their comparative advantage and may introduce distortions and risks as domestic and foreign FSPs will try to circumvent them. In general, capital controls are unlikely to reduce outflows and have been found at best to change the composition of inflows, but not the level permanently. In case, controls are deemed necessary, internationalization does not limit the ability of authorities to impose controls or limits on financial institutions for prudential reasons, as long as they are applied even-handed to domestic and foreign financial firms. While in principle internationalization in the presence of a poorly regulated and supervised financial domestic system could create increased risks, this needs to balanced by the fact that foreign FSPs are likely better capitalized and also subject to more stringent supervisory systems in their home countries. This suggests that internationalization in Asia need not be limited by the quality of the domestic regulatory and supervisory system. This is confirmed by the fact that several institutionally very poorly developed countries have committed themselves under FSA to fully opening up.

What lessons are there for these countries for the current negotiations on financial services under GATS? Given the significant benefits of internationalization, Asian countries would appear to stand to gain from opening up, either unilateral or multilateral. Countries may, however, face adjustment cost in internationalizing their financial systems, including effects on labour. They might consider committing through the FSA to a phased programme of opening up over some agreed time frame (possibly complemented with measures which could smooth the transition to a more open environment). Mexico committed in the context of NAFTA to a phased programme of opening up over an agreed time frame, which included progressive market capitalization arrangements which could modulate the growth of foreign participation in the sector in the event of overly rapid foreign penetration. In the NAFTA safe-guards were also included in case 'adverse' effects were to arise when the share of all commercial bank assets held by foreign-owned banks exceeded certain threshold levels.[41] A commitment would provide greater security for foreign financial firms of the environment under which they will operate and thus could lead to a greater level of foreign participation in the financial sector. It could also reduce the risk premium charged by those foreign institutions which will enter the country, which in turn would lead to costs savings for consumers. And, it would lend credibility to countries' reform approaches, something which is at a premium today. By themselves, these factors would help in overcoming the adjustment costs.

The FSA does not cover activities by central banks and governments in pursuit of monetary policy or exchange rate policy and allows members to take any prudential measures, including for example, the imposition of limits on the access of domestic financial institutions to international financial markets, as long as they are not used as a means to avoiding commitments under the GATS. Furthermore, the WTO-process explicitly includes mechanisms which allow temporary suspension of commitments in the event of pronounced economic imbalances (so called prudential carve-out and balance of payments safeguard provisions). These provisions should already provide the flexibility needed for governments to deal with any adverse consequences and no further safeguards appear necessary.

Countries should try to avoid the use of quantitative restrictions, a well-known inefficient form of regulation, but rather give consideration to converting them into price-based measures (provided that their effect is equivalent in granting de facto national treatment and does not place foreign FSPs at a competitive disadvantage in the host country market). Where relevant, countries should also try to harness the interests of

---

[41]Specifically, Mexico could request consultations to limit entry and reduce adverse effects. Adverse effects could be associated with threat of control of domestic payments or effects on the independence of Mexican monetary and exchange rate policy. In the end, these safeguards were not used and the foreign banks' share exceeded the original threshold levels in 1996. In general, the merit of including safeguards which are triggered by adverse economic events and conditioned on market shares may have limited value as it will be exactly in time of adverse economic events that foreign banks can be a stabilizing influence and when the country may want to open up its financial sector more.

foreign FSPs in entering the country. This can done as part of the process of the restructuring of the domestic financial system. In many countries, foreign banks are assisting in the restructuring and recapitalization of existing institutions. In several transition economies, for example, twinning and other technical assistance arrangements with banks from developed countries is helping improve the level of institutional development of individual financial institutions.

In sum, in the current environment especially, there is a large premium on a credible, consistent financial sector development strategy. The FSA can help countries achieve this credibility, with built-in adequate safeguards.

Annex Table 1

CRITERIA: The rankings refer to relative degree of openness only among the eight countries included in the study as of the end of the Financial Services negotiations (mid-1995) or in practice as of end-1996. The rating may comprise one or a combination of features listed below.

A. ESTABLISHMENT AND OWNERSHIP

5   No limits on establishment or equity acquisition/participation in domestic banks/companies; current practice of granting new licenses.

4   Foreign branch establishment(s) permitted to establish within specific limits; allowed foreign equity participation in domestic banks/companies: 51 per cent and up but less than 100 per cent.

3   No new licenses granted in practice; entry limited to joint ventures only; allowed foreign equity participation in domestic banks/companies of 35–50 per cent.

2   Allowed foreign equity participation in domestic banks/ companies of 15–34 per cent. Economic needs test for foreign broker licenses.

1   Non-prudential government approval required for establishment (minimum limits on amount of DFI, 'certain criteria eligibility'); allowed foreign equity participation in domestic banks/companies: above zero–14 per cent.

B. OFFICES/ATMs

5   No branch offices nor ATM restrictions.

4   Restrictions on branches of foreign company but none on joint ventures; partial removal of restrictions on additional branches.

3   Restrictions on branches of foreign company; more than 5 ATMs allowed.

2   Extremely tight restrictions on sub-branching; up to 5 offices/ATMs permitted subject to Branches Act; ban on foreign branches from establishing own ATM network; permission from national ATM pool prior to setting-up ATM operations.

1   Non-prudential government approval required for all offices.

C. LENDING/BUSINESS ACTIVITY

5   No limits on lending/business activity; in insurance, market share of 75 per cent and up.

4   Foreign banks/companies not subjected to directed lending or mandated principal business activity as domestic firms; in insurance, foreign share in domestic market of 61–75 per cent.

3   Restrictions on computation of capital/lending limits or on issuance of securities; requirements on paid-up capital (e.g. higher for FSPs); in insurance, foreign share in domestic market of 31–60 per cent; limits for issues of/trading to selected securities only, or for transactions through established dealers.

2   Specified limits on offshore lending or lending of foreign branches; strict (non-capital) limits on foreign companies *vis-à-vis* domestic firms; in insurance, foreign share in domestic market of 11–30 per cent; limits on membership to the stock exchange.

1   Restrictions on management and operations such as mandatory lending, transactions only in local currency, ownership of real estate; in insurance, foreign share in domestic market of 1–10 per cent; restrictions on broking; securities trading limited to selected firms; limits on investment trust services to selected establishments; tight regulatory control.

D. UNIVERSAL BANKING

5   No limits on financial services.

4   Some limits on financial activities or approval required.

3   Limits on activities of offices of foreign branches to deposit-taking. Approval required for new products.

2   Limits on foreign branch activities in foreign exchange, credit cards, trust services.

1   Restrictions on all activities normally undertaken by international banks with universal banking rights.

E. RESIDENCY REQUIREMENT

5   No restrictions on composition of board membership; no residency requirement for membership to stock exchange.

4   Restrictions on composition of board membership to at least one national.

3   Restrictions on board membership by foreigners according to proportion of ownership; residency requirement for membership in the stock exchange; locally-based CEO; limits on temporary stay of executives.

2   Restrictions on board membership by foreigners to less than one half.

1   Restrictions on board membership by foreigners to one half or more.

F. CROSS-BORDER TRADE

5   Free access to offshore financial instruments; no capital controls.

4   Free access allowed but solicitation or advertising by foreign institutions not permitted.

3   Access to instruments subject to annual limits or access to certain specified products in insurance; registration for borrowing; permission required for participation in issues.

2   Limits on deposit acceptance, offshore borrowing/convertibility; minimum retention requirement for domestic insurers; dealing/trading limited to certain foreign stock exchanges or IPOs limited to residents; overseas investment for institutional investors allowed but subject to restrictions.

1   Controls on cross-border supply of all financial services.

REFERENCES

Arriazu, Ricardo. (1997). 'Open Financial Systems Argentina'. Paper presented at workshop organized by EDI on 'Internationalization of Financial Services', Singapore, August 8.

Barajas, Adolfo. (1996). 'Interest Rates, Market Power, and Financial Taxation: An Application to Colombian Banks 1974–88'. Mimeo, IMF.

Barfield, Claude E. (ed.). (1996). *International Financial Markets: Harmonization versus Competition.* Washington, D.C.: American Enterprise Institute.

Barth, James R., Daniel E. Nolle, and Tara N. Rice. (1997). 'Commercial Banking Structure, Regulation, and Performance, an International Comparison'. Comptroller of the Currency Economics Working Paper 97-6.

Bhattacharya, Joydeep. (1993). 'The Role of Foreign Banks in Developing Countries: A Survey of the Evidence'. Mimeo, Cornell University.

Berger, Allen, and David Humphrey. (1996). 'Efficiency of Financial Institutions: International Survey and Directions for Future Research'. Mimeo, Board of Governors of the Federal Reserve System, May.

BIS. (1997). 'Core Principles for Effective Banking Supervision'. Consultative Paper issued by the Basle Committee on Banking Supervision, Basle, April.

Borish, Michael S., Wei Ding, and Michel Nokl. (1996). 'On the Road to EU. Accession: Financial Sector Development in Central Europe'. World Bank Discussion Paper, no. 345.

Caprio, Gerard and Daniela Klingebiel. (1997). 'Bank Insolvency: Bad Luck, Bad Policy or Bad Banking?'. In Michael Bruno and Boris Pleskovic (eds), *Annual Bank Conference on Development Economics, 1996.* Washington, D.C.: World Bank.

Caprio, Gerard and Lawrence H. Summers. (1996). 'Financial Reform: Beyond Laissez Faire'. In Dimitri Papadimitriou (ed.), *The Stability of the Financial System: Reflections on the 60th Anniversary of the 1933 Banking Crisis.* London: MacMillan Press.

Caprio, Gerard, Itzak Atiyas, and James A. Hanson (eds). (1994). *Financial Reform: Theory and Experience.* New York: Cambridge University Press, pp. 323–56.

Claessens, Stijn. (1997). 'Estimates of Capital Flight and Its Behavior'. *Revista de Analisis Ecsnomico,* vol. 12, no. 1, pp. 3–34.

Claessens, Stijn, and Thomas Glaessner. (1997). 'Are Financial Sector Weaknesses Undermining the Asian Miracle?', In *Directions in Development,* World Bank Series, September. Washington D.C.: World Bank.

Claessens, Stijn, and Brian Hindley. (1997). 'Internationalization of Financial Services: Issues for Developing Countries', Mimeo, World Bank, March.

Claessens, Stijn, Asli Demirguc–Kunt, and Harry Huizinga. (1997). 'How does

Foreign Entry Affect the Domestic Banking Market?'. Mimeo, World Bank, July.

Demirguc–Kunt, Asli and Harry Huizinga. (1997). 'Determinants of Commercial Bank Interest Margins and Profitability: International Evidence'. Mimeo, World Bank, July.

Deyoung, Robert and Nolle, Daniel. E. (1996). 'Foreign-owned Banks in the United States: Earning Market Share or Buying It?'. *Journal of Money Credit and Banking*, vol. 28, no. 4 (November) Part 1, pp. 622–36.

Dick, Astrid. (1996). 'X-Inefficiency in the Private Banking Sector of Argentina: Its Importance with Respect to Economics of Scale and Economies of Joint-Production'. Mimeo, Banco Central de La Republica Argentina, October.

Dooley, Michael. (1995). 'Capital Controls: A Survey of the Literature'. NBER Working Paper, no. 5352.

Eguchi, Takehisa. (1995). 'Insurance Industry in East Asian Markets'. Mimeo, Financial Sector Development Department, June.

EU/Price Waterhouse. (1988). 'Research on the Costs of Non-Europe: Basic Findings'. *European Economy*, vol. 9.

EU. (1997). 'Credit Institutions and Banking'. *The Single Market Review*, vol. 11, no. 3. Published for the European Commission by Kogan Page, London, UK. (In mimeo form: 'A Study of the Effectiveness and Impact on Internal Market Integration on the Banking and Credit Sector: A Summary Report'. by Economic Research Europe Ltd., in collaboration with Public and Corporate Consultants (PACEC) and The Institute of European Finance).

G–10. (1997). 'Financial Stability in Emerging Market Economies: A Strategy for the Formulation, Adoption and Implementation of Sound Principles and Practices to Strengthen Financial Systems'. Report of the Working Party on Financial Stability in Emerging Market Economies, Basle, April.

Gardener, E.P.M. and P. Molyneux. (1996). *Efficiency in European Banking*. Chichester. UK: John Wiley & Sons Publishers.

Gardener, Edward, Philip Molyneux and B. Moore. (1996). 'Impact of the Single Market Programme on the EU Banking and Credit Sectors'. Study for ECDGXV, prepared by Institute of European Finance.

———. (1997a). 'The Impact of the Single Market Programme on EU Banking'. Paper presented at workshop organized by EDI on 'Internationalization of Financial Services', Singapore, August 8.

———. (1997b). 'The Impact of the Single Market Programme on EU Banking: Select Policy Experiences for Developing Countries'. Mimeo, Institute of European Finance.

Gardener, Edward and J. Tepett. (1993). 'The impact of 1992 on the Norwegian Financial Services Sector: A Select Duplication Exercise Using the Price Waterhouse/Cecchini Methodology'. Mimeo, Institute of European Finance.

Gavin, Michael and Ricardo Hausmann. (1996). 'Make Or Buy? A Case for Deep Financial Integration'. Mimeo, Inter-American Development Bank, Washington, D.C., September.

Gelb, Alan and Silvia Sagari. (1990). 'Trade in Banking Services: Issues for Multilateral Negotiations'. World Bank Policy Research and External Affairs Working Papers, no. 381.

Glaessner, Thomas and Daniel Oks. (1994). 'North American Free Trade Agreement, Capital Mobility, and Mexico Financial System'. World Bank, processed, April.

Goldstein, Morris and Philip Turner. (1996). 'Banking Crises in Emerging Economies: Origins and Policy Options'. *BIS Economic Papers*, no. 46, October).

Guash, J. Luis and Thomas Glaessner. (1993). 'Using Auctions to Allocate and Price Long-Term Credit'. *World Bank Research Observer*, vol. 8, no. 2, pp. 169–94.

Harris, John R., Fabio Schianterelli, and Miranda G. Siregar. (1994). 'How Financial Liberalization in Indonesia Affected Firms' Capital Structure and Investment Decisions', In Caprio, Atiyas and Hanson (1994). (Also Country Economics Department. World Bank (1992), Policy Research Working Papers, no. 997)

Hoekman, Bernard, and Pierre Sauvi. (1994). 'Liberalizing Trade in Services', World Bank Discussion Paper, no. 243.

Hoekman, Bernard, and Carlos A. Primo Braga. (1997). 'Protection and Trade in Services: A Survey' World Bank Policy and Research Working Paper, no. 1747.

Honohan, Patrick. (1995). 'Measuring European Financial Integration: Flows and Intermediation in Greece, Ireland and Portugal'. ESRI Working Paper, no. 60, Dublin, Ireland.

———. (1997a). 'Banking Systems Failures in Developing and Transition Countries: Diagnosis and Prediction'. BIS Working Paper, no. 39, January.

———. (1997b). 'Consequences for Greece and Portugal of the Opening-Up of the European Banking Market'. Draft, The Economic and Social Research Institute, Dublin, Ireland.

International Finance Corporation (IFC). (1997). Emerging Markets Factbook. Washington, D.C.: IFC.

IMF. (1997). 'Towards a Framework for Sound Banking'. Main paper and supplement, Washington, D.C.: April.

Jayaratne, Jith and Philip E. Strahan. (1996). 'Entry Restrictions, Industry Evolution and Dynamic Efficiency: Evidence from Commercial Banking'. Mimeo, Federal Reserve Bank of New York.

Levine, Ross. (1996). 'Foreign Banks, Financial Development, and Economic Growth' in Barfield (ed.).

———. (1997). 'Financial Development and Economic Growth'. *Journal of Economic Literature* vol. 35 (June), pp. 688–726.

Mathieson, Donald and Liliana Rojas-Suarez. (1993). 'Liberalization of the Capital Account: Experiences and Issues'. IMF Occasional Paper, no. 102.

McFadden, Catherine. (1994). 'Foreign Banks in Australia'. Mimeo, World Bank, processed.

Molyneux, Philip, D.M. Lloyd-Williams and John Thornton. (1994). 'Competitive Conditions in European Banking'. *Journal of Banking and Finance*, vol. 18, no. 3, pp. 445–59.

Montes-Negret, Fernando and Luca Papi. (1996). 'Are Bank Interest Rate Spreads Too High: A Simple Model for Decomposing Spreads'. Public Policy Note for the Private Sector, World Bank.

Moshirian, Fariborz. (1994). 'What Determines the Supply of International Financial Services?' *Journal of Banking and Finance*, vol. 18, pp. 495–504.

Musalem, Alberto, Dimitri Vittas and Asli Demirguc–Kunt. (1993). 'North American Free Trade Agreement, Issues on Trade in Financial Services for Mexico'. World Bank Policy and Research Working Paper, no. 1153.

Neven, Darrien J. (1989). 'Structural Adjustment in European Retail Banking'. Discussion Paper no. 311, Centre for European Policy Research, April.

Nicholl, Peter. (1997). 'New Zealand's Experience with Foreign Ownership in its Financial System'. Mimeo, IMF, paper presented at workshop organized by EDI on 'Internationalization of Financial Services', Singapore, August 8.

Nolle, Daniel, E. and Rama Seth (1996). 'Do Banks Follow Their Customers Abroad?'. Federal Reserve Bank of New York, Research Paper 96-20.

OECD (1996). 'Regulatory Reform in the Financial Services Industry: Where Have We Been? Where Are We Going?'. DAFFE/ECO, Paris, October.

Pastor, Jose M., Francisso Perez, and Javier Quesada. (1997). 'The Opening of the Spanish Banking System: 1985–96'. Mimeo, Universitat de Valencia, September.

Pearly, Brian (1997). 'Latin American Banks: How Conservative Regulations Help Create Profits'. Mimeo, Equity Research, JP Morgan, New York.

Peek, Joe, and Eric S. Rosengren. (1997). 'The International Transmission of Financial Shocks: The Case of Japan'. *American Economic Review*, vol. 87, no. 4 (September).

Pigott, C.A. (1986). 'Financial Reform and the Role of Foreign Banks in Pacific-Basin Nations'. In H. Cheng (ed.). *Financial Policy and Reform in Pacific-Basin Countries*. Lexington: Lexington Books.

Ramos, Roy (1997a). 'Prudential Norms and CAMELOT: How Real are

Reported Earnings and Book Values'. Banking Research Mimeo, Goldman Sachs, Hong Kong, January 8.

Ramos, Roy. (1997b). 'Asian Banks at Risk: Solidity, Fragility'. Banking Research Mimeo, Goldman Sachs, Hong Kong, September 4.

————. (1997b) '1998 Issues and Outlook: Cyclical Slowdowns, Structural Ills and the Odds for Recovery'. Mimeo, Goldman Sachs, Banking Research, Hong Kong, December.

Reisen, Helmut and Bernard Fischer. (1993). *Financial Opening: Policy Issues and Experiences in Developing Countries*. Paris: OECD Development Center.

Sagari, Silvia. (1986). 'The Financial Service Industry: An International Perspective'. Ph.D. dissertation, New York University.

————. (1989). 'International Trade in Financial Services'. World Bank, Policy, Planning, and Research Working Papers, no. 134.

Sapir, Andre. (1993). 'The Structure of Services in Europe: A Conceptual Framework'. *European Economy*, vol. 3, pp. 83–99.

Saunders, Anthony and Ingo Water. (1994). *Universal Banking in the United States: What Could We Gain? What Could We Lose?* New York: Oxford University Press.

Sauve, Pierre and Brenda Gonzalez-Hermisollio. (1993). 'Financial Services and the North American Free Trade Agreement, Implications for Canadian Financial Institutions'. In *The NAFTA Papers: C.D. Howe Commentary*. Toronto: C.D. Howe Institute.

Schineller, Lisa. (1997). 'An Econometric Model of Capital Flight from Developing Countries'. International Finance Discussion Paper, 579, Board of Governors of the Federal Reserve Board, March.

Securities Industry Association. (1997). *Asian Capital Markets: Market Access Restrictions and Regulatory Environment Facing U.S. Securities Firms in Selected Asian Markets*. Washington, D.C.: Securities Industry Association.

Skipper, Harold D. (1996). 'International Trade in Insurance'. In C. Barfield (ed.), pp. 125–46.

Sorsa, Piritta. (1997). 'The GATS Agreement on Financial Services—A Modest Start to Multilateral Liberalization'. IMF Working Paper, 97/55, May.

Stiglitz, Joseph and Marilou Uy. (1996). 'Financial Markets, Public Policy and the Asian Miracle'. *The World Bank Research Observer*, vol. 11, no. 2 (August), pp. 249–76.

Swedlove, Frank and Patricia Evanoff. (1992). 'Financial Services in the NAFTA Free Trade Agreement: A Canadian Perspective'. *Canadian Financial Services Alert*, vol. 2, no. 7, pp. 49–58.

Terrell, H.S. (1986). 'The Role of Foreign Bank in Domestic Banking Markets', in H. Cheng, (ed.) *Financial Policy and Reform in Pacific-Basin Countries.* Lexington: Lexington Books.

Vittas, Dimitri. (1991). 'Measuring Commercial Bank Efficiency, Use and Misuse of Bank Operating Ratios'. World Bank Policy Research Working Paper.

Vives, Xavier. (1990). 'Deregulation and Competition in Spanish Banking'. *European Economic Review*, vol. 34, pp. 403–11.

Walter, Ingo (1985). *Barriers to Trade in Banking and Financial Services.* Thames, no. 41.

———. (1987). *Global Competition in Financial Services.* Washington, D.C.: American Enterprise Institute.

———. (1993). *High Performance Financial Systems: Blueprint for Development.* ASEAN/ISEAS Current Economic Affairs Series. Singapore: ASEAN.

Wang, Zhen Kun. (1995). 'Financial Sector Integration of the Visegrad Countries with the European Union'. Mimeo, World Bank.

Wengel, Jan ter (1995). 'International Trade in Banking Services'. *Journal of International Money and Finance*, vol. 14, no. 1, pp. 47–64.

White, Lawrence J. (1996). 'Competition versus Harmonization: An Overview of International Regulation of Financial Services'. In C. Barfield (ed.), pp. 198–211.

White, William R. (1996a). 'International Agreements in the Area of Banking and Finance: Accomplishments and Outstanding Issues'. BIS Working Paper, no. 38, Basle, October.

———. (1996b). 'Changing Financial Systems in Small Open Economies'. BIS Working Paper, Basle, December.

World Bank. (1995a). *The Emerging Asian Bond Market*, Washington, D.C.: World Bank, Asia and Pacific Region.

———. (1995b). *World Development Indicators.* Washington, D.C.: World Bank.

———. (1997a). *Global Development Finance.* Washington, D.C.: World Bank.

———. (1997b). *Private Capital Flows to Developing Countries: The Path to Financial Integration.* OUP/WB.

———. (1997c). *World Development Indicators.* Washington, D.C.: World Bank.

World Trade Organization (WTO). (1997). *Opening Markets in Financial Services and the Role of GATS.* Geneva.

Index

157, 337, 338
Eatwell, John 337, 342
economic arguments, against inter-
    nalization of financial services
    381–3
efficiency, in banking sector 83, 96–7,
    104
Electronic Clearing System 130
Electronic Funds Transfer 130, 257
Employees' Deposit Linked Insurance
    Scheme 1976 307, 311
Employees' Family Pension Scheme
    1971 307, 310
Employees Fund Miscellaneous
    Provisions Act 1952 (EPFMF
    Act) 306
Employees' Pension Scheme (EPS)
    1995 310–11
Employees, Provident Fund Organiza-
    tion (EPFO) 307, 310, 311,
    313, 316n, 317, 327, 329
Employees' Provident Fund Scheme
    306, 307–10, 327
Employees' Retirement Income
    Security Act 1974 (ERISA),
    USA 332
entry barriers, to financial services
    378, 382, 383, 387, 404, 407–
    10
equity 50, 173, 176, 187, 318, 331,
    401
  'cult' 170
  derivates 232–3, 243, 244
  financing 174, 175, 190, 195
  markets 17, 19, 105, 186, 189, 190,
    207, 208, 216–19, 270–7
  problems facing 223–4
  secondary 222–38, 277–8
European Union 384, 385, 386, 387,
    390, 394
  SMP of 390, 394n
Evanoff, Patricia 384n
Evidence Act of 1872 256

Exchange rate,
  policies in East Asian crisis 24
  regime, KAC and 338–41
  –traded derivatives 244, 246
  versus OTC 239–42
external capital workets, links with
    22–7

Fama, E.F. 279n
Faruquee, R. 246
FCNR (B) Scheme 79
FDICIA, USA 361, 363
Feldstone, M. 341, 342
financial institutions, changing roles of
    67–8
financial intermediaries 90–4, 176,
    396, 399, 410
financial markets 30–2, 171
financial reforms 9
  internalization and 373–7
financial sector, reforming India's 29ff
financial services 21–2, 300
  in Asia, internalization of 369, 378–
    81
  competition from foreign 380–3
  openness of 410–22
  structure and institutional quality of,
    in Asia 399–404
Financial Services Agreement (FSA),
  of GATS 408, 423–5
financial service providers (FSPs),
  domestic 371, 374, 383, 384, 391,
    407, 423
  foreign 369–70, 375, 379–81, 383–
    5, 387, 389, 390, 394, 407,
    409, 410, 422–3, 425
financial system,
  development in Asia 401, 403
  India's 3
  in pre-reform era 7–9
  liberalization of 409
financing of Indian firms 164ff, 178–
    81